PROLEGOMENA TO ETHICS

PROLEGOMENA TO ETHICS

THOMAS HILL GREEN

EDITED BY A. C. BRADLEY

THOMAS Y. CROWELL COMPANY

New York

Established 1834

INTRODUCTION

1. *Green's Life, Work, and Influence.* Thomas Hill Green was born April 7, 1836, at Birkin, a village in Yorkshire, and died from blood poisoning March 26, 1882, in Oxford. He was the youngest of four children, two sons and two daughters. His mother died when he was only a year old, and the children were brought up by their father, who was rector at Birkin. In 1850 Green went to school at Rugby, and in 1855 entered Balliol College in Oxford, where his undergraduate tutor was Benjamin Jowett. The remainder of his life was spent at Oxford, with the exception of a period of about a year in 1865–66, which he spent travelling about inspecting schools as a member of a schools' inquiry commission. In 1860 he began lecturing at Balliol, in the same year was elected a fellow of the college, and in 1878 was appointed Whyte's Professor of Moral Philosophy in the University of Oxford. He married in 1871, but never had any children.

From the early 1870's until his death Green was the dominant philosophical figure at Oxford. He was convinced that the true result of Hume's philosophy was the demonstration of the bankruptcy implicit in the empiricistic principles of Locke and Berkeley, that Kant and Hegel had pointed the way to an acceptable alternative account of experience and knowledge, and that nineteenth-century British philosophy—in particular that of the two leading philosophers of that century, John Stuart Mill and Herbert Spencer—was consequently anachronistic, since it sought to continue along the bankrupt lines laid down by Hume, ignoring the work of Kant and Hegel. Much of his philosophical labor was devoted to exhibiting in detail the untenability of empiricism, the anachronistic character of British philosophy of the nineteenth century, and the need for a return to Kant and Hegel. This labor led to a change in the climate of British philosophy that persisted for almost fifty years, for Green is as responsible as any other thinker for the shift away from traditional British empiricism and toward Kantian and Hegelian idealism that dominated British philosophy for the last quarter of the nineteenth century and the first quarter of the twentieth. He is the first in the line of British idealists that includes R. L. Nettleship (1846–92), F. H. Bradley (1846–1924), Bernard Bosanquet (1848–1923), and H. H. Joachim (1868–1938) at Oxford, and J. M. E. McTaggart (1866–1925) at Cambridge. Green's work, however, was not merely philosophical, nor did it influence only philosophers. It was instead religious, social, and political as well as philosophical, and influenced non-philosophers as well as philosophers. This work, like his writings in moral and political philosophy, was throughout informed or pervaded by the spirit of liberalism.

But although Green was essentially liberal in religion—so much so that he regarded himself as at best a "questionable churchman"—he was, nevertheless, also sufficiently orthodox in religion to remain within the Church of England. And although he regarded the moral and social teaching of the Christian religion as immeasurably more important than an allegiance to creeds, dogmas, and institutions, the eternal consciousness for which he argues in certain of his writings, particularly in the *Prolegomena to Ethics,* is quite akin to a kind of God; and on his deathbed he expressed a belief in God and immortality, and requested that the eighth chapter of St. Paul's Epistle to the Romans be read to him. Yet study of his religious writings in the third volume of his *Works* reveals his essential liberalism in religion and his conviction that what is of fundamental importance in the Christian message is its moral and social teaching.

His interest in social and political questions was practical as well as theoretical; it was manifested in practical, even prosaic, activity as well as in his philosophical conversation, lecturing, and writing. Prior to Green's active participation in local social and political affairs, Oxford dons had lived in something of an ivory tower, isolated from any practical involvement in the day-to-day social and political problems of the Oxford townspeople. Green did not consider it condescension, but his simple duty as a citizen, to mix with and work with the relatively uneducated Oxford "man in the street" in an attempt to contribute what he could toward the

solution of the problems of the people of Oxford. This led to
his election to the Oxford town council in 1876. He had been
elected previously, in 1874, to the Oxford school board. One
of his primary concerns was the improvement of the English
educational system, especially the extension of educational
opportunity, so that no English child need be deprived of the
chance to develop his capacities fully through lack of education. This interest in education is evidenced not only by
Green's work on the schools' inquiry commission and on the
Oxford school board, but also by his lectures on education, such
as those included in the third volume of his *Works*. He was
also involved in the temperance movement of his day, believing that excessive drinking was sapping the energies of
many among the working class. This belief he expressed not
merely by speaking publicly for temperance, but also by holding office in temperance societies and by setting up a coffee
tavern in 1875.

In addition to these activities, Green also made speeches
both in Oxford and in other cities in support of liberal policies
and legislation. His lecture on ''Liberal Legislation and Freedom of Contract,'' delivered at Leicester in 1881 in support of
two liberal measures of the preceding year, applies to these two
acts the principles of the liberalism elaborated at considerably
greater length in his *Lectures on the Principles of Political
Obligation*. This work constitutes a turning point in the
history of the philosophy of liberalism, and remains even to-
day the classic statement of the philosophical foundations of
contemporary liberalism, as distinguished from the liberalism
of the nineteenth century prior to its publication. Until its
publication nineteenth-century liberalism, as exemplified philosophically in the writings of John Stuart Mill (at least in
those written before he began to change his views toward the
end of his life) and Herbert Spencer, had been more or less
laissez-faire, contending that the function of the state is
limited primarily to the protection of individual liberty. What
Green does is to argue that the state has a more positive role
to play—as well as this rather negative role—that it has not
only the task of protecting the negative freedom of individuals, i.e., of protecting them from unjustifiable coercive restrictions upon their freedom of speech and action, but also

the task of promoting the positive freedom of every person within the state, i.e., of establishing and maintaining those conditions the presence of which is necessary if each person is to have the opportunity, and therefore the freedom, to develop fully his highest potentialities. He was convinced that if the activity of the state were limited merely to the protection of negative freedom, the positive freedom of many persons within the state would be nonexistent and their negative freedom insignificant, if not in many cases also nonexistent.

2. *Green's Writings.* For Green the task of the philosopher is negative or critical as well as positive or constructive: his task is not only to present a positive or constructive account of experience, knowledge, man, and the world, but also to criticize mistaken and inadequate accounts. Accordingly, as much of Green's philosophical writing is directed to the criticism of the positions of other philosophers as to the development of his own positive position. The philosophical positions to which he devotes his major criticism are sensationalistic empiricism in epistemology, naturalism and materialism in metaphysics, hedonistic utilitarianism in moral philosophy, and atomic individualism, as represented in laissez-faire liberalism and social-contract theories of political obligation, in political philosophy. As opposed to these, he argues for rationalism in epistemology, idealism in metaphysics, self-realization in moral philosophy, and what may be referred to as "positive liberalism" in political philosophy.

Green's critique of empiricism is presented primarily in his Introductions to Hume's *Treatise of Human Nature*, but also in his "Lectures on Logic," delivered at Oxford in 1874–75, and devoted mainly to a criticism of Mill's logic. His Introductions to Hume's *Treatise* were published in 1874, in volumes one and two of the four-volume edition of Hume's philosophical works edited by Green and T. H. Grose. In these Introductions Green presents what is probably the most detailed, meticulous, unrelenting, and damaging criticism of the empiricism of Locke and Hume ever published. They are almost entirely critical. The "Lectures on Logic," on the other hand, although devoted primarily to a criticism of the empiricism of Mill's logic, also contain elements of Green's positive epistemological position. Green's critique of naturalism is presented primarily in a series of five essays entitled "Mr. Herbert Spencer and Mr. G. H. Lewes: Their Application of the Doctrine of Evolution to Thought" and in Book One of the *Prolegomena to Ethics.* The first three and the fifth of these essays on Spencer and Lewes were published in the *Contemporary Review* in 1877–78, but the fourth was withheld from publication because of Lewes' death. The essays on Spencer and Lewes, like the Introductions to Hume and the "Lectures on Logic," are mainly critical, although traces of Green's idealism are clearly present in them. But it is not until the *Prolegomena to Ethics* that Green develops systematically his idealist alternative to naturalism. Green's critique of hedonistic utilitarianism is presented in the *Prolegomena to Ethics,* and his critique of atomic individualism in politics is presented primarily in his *Lectures on the Principles of Political Obligation,* delivered at Oxford in 1879–80.

The various aspects of Green's positive or constructive philosophy are primarily set forth in the following places. His argument for rationalism is to be found mainly in his "Lectures on the Philosophy of Kant," delivered at Oxford in the 1870's, and also to some extent in the "Lectures on Logic" and the *Prolegomena to Ethics.* His argument for idealism, as mentioned above, is not presented systematically until the *Prolegomena to Ethics,* although traces of his idealism are clearly present in his essays on Spencer and Lewes and in his "Lectures on Logic" and especially in his "Lectures on the Philosophy of Kant." His argument for an ethics of self-realization is, of course, presented systematically in the *Prolegomena to Ethics,* and his argument for what I have referred to as "positive liberalism" in his *Lectures on the Principles of Political Obligation* and in his lecture on "Liberal Legislation and Freedom of Contract." Also important for understanding the Kantian element in Green's moral philosophy is the second of the two parts of his "Lectures on the Philosophy of Kant," which deals with Kant's moral philosophy.

There are various unpublished essays, lectures, and letters among Green's papers in the Balliol College Library, but an examination of them has convinced me that all his important philosophical writing is included in his *Prolegomena to Ethics* and in his *Works*, edited by R. L. Nettleship and published in three volumes between 1885 and 1888. The first volume of his *Works*, published in 1885, contains Green's Introductions to Hume's *Treatise* and the five essays on Spencer and Lewes. The second, published in 1886, consists of the three series of lectures mentioned above which Green delivered between 1874 and 1880 in his capacity as a lecturer at Oxford—the "Lectures on the Philosophy of Kant," the "Lectures on Logic," and the *Lectures on the Principles of Political Obligation*. The third volume, published in 1888, contains a long memoir of Green by the editor, Nettleship; various philosophical essays and reviews; extracts from lectures on St. Paul's Epistles to the Galatians and to the Romans and on the Fourth Gospel; addresses or lay sermons on texts from St. Paul's Epistles to the Romans and to the Corinthians; four lectures on the English Revolution; four lectures on elementary and secondary schools; and the important lecture on "Liberal Legislation and Freedom of Contract." The only important philosophical work of Green's not included in Nettleship's edition of his *Works*, the *Prolegomena to Ethics*, was edited by A. C. Bradley, the brother of F. H. Bradley, and published in 1883. Green, according to a letter written shortly before his death, still had some twenty or thirty pages to add to this work when he died. What he had written was edited and divided into books, chapters, and sections by Bradley, who also prefaced it with the excellent analytical table of contents.

Several printings were made of Green's *Works* within a few years of their initial publication, and the *Prolegomena to Ethics* went through five editions (without, however, any change in its content), the fifth and last edition appearing in 1906 with a brief preface by Edward Caird. The present edition of this work is therefore the first to appear in over sixty years. Green's Introductions to Hume's *Treatise* were republished separately in 1968 by Apollo Editions as a paperback volume entitled *Hume and Locke,* and his *Lectures on the Principles of Political Obligation* were published as a separate volume in 1895. The latter work has been continually reprinted since then, most recently in 1967 by the University of Michigan Press as an Ann Arbor paperback: it is the only one of Green's works that has been almost constantly in print since its initial publication.

The fact that Green's *Lectures on the Principles of Political Obligation* is the only one of his works that has been continually reprinted over the last sixty years has been due, at least in part, to the fact that political philosophers and scientists have continued to hold it in higher esteem than philosophers have continued to hold his *Prolegomena to Ethics* and his epistemological and metaphysical writings. On the other hand, the continued reprinting of his work in political philosophy has in turn contributed to the persistence of the high regard for this work that political philosophers and scientists continue to have.

Had his *Prolegomena to Ethics* and his epistemological and metaphysical writings received the same continued reprinting it is possible that Green would be remembered not only as a political philosopher of some distinction, but also as an epistemologist, metaphysician, and moral philosopher of some merit. It is at least probable that his epistemological, metaphysical, and moral writings would be more widely read today. The only one of his works still widely read today is his work in political philosophy, which has become recognized as a classic and therefore as required reading for the serious student of political philosophy.

The fact that the last edition of the *Prolegomena to Ethics* was published over sixty years ago means that it has become almost inaccessible to the serious student of Green's philosophy, of the development of British idealism, or of the history of British moral philosophy who is interested in owning his own copy. It, taken in conjunction with the *Lectures on the Principles of Political Obligation,* constitutes the only systematic presentation of the positive or constructive side of Green's philosophy—epistemological, metaphysical, moral, and political—that he ever committed to writing. As has been said, his Introductions to Hume, his essays on Spencer and Lewes, and his lectures on Kant and on logic deal critically—though sympathetically in the case of Kant—with the thought of other philosophers, so that it is to the *Prolegomena to Ethics* and the *Lectures on the Principles of Political Obligation* that we must turn for a systematic presentation of the constructive aspect of his philosophy.

These two works form a kind of organic whole, since the work in political philosophy presupposes at various points certain of the claims and arguments of the *Prolegomena to Ethics*, whereas the major implications for political philosophy of the latter work are developed by Green only in the work in political philosophy. The work in political philosophy therefore presupposes, and is a development of, the work in ethics. This means that each work can be adequately understood only by taking it in the context of the other. The work in political philosophy, however, probably ranks higher in the history of political philosophy than the work in ethics does in the history of moral philosophy. Indeed, I think it no exaggeration to claim that it ranks as one of the ten or twelve greatest works in the entire history of political philosophy. But while the work in ethics cannot legitimately be given a comparable ranking in the history of moral philosophy, it can nevertheless, I believe, be justifiably ranked as one of the ten or twelve greatest classics in the history of British moral philosophy, along with the work of Hobbes, Butler, Hume, Bentham, Mill, Sidgwick, and F. H. Bradley.

3. *Green's Prolegomena to Ethics.* As has been indicated, the *Prolegomena to Ethics* is not merely a work in ethics. On the contrary, it not only contains the most systematic statement of Green's moral philosophy he ever presented, but it is also prefaced by the most systematic presentation of his constructive epistemological and metaphysical position he ever wrote. It was divided by the editor, A. C. Bradley, into four books. The first deals with what Green refers to as "the metaphysics of experience or knowledge"; the second, entitled by Bradley "The Will," deals with moral psychology or what Green designates as "the metaphysics of moral action"; the third, to use Bradley's expression, deals with the moral ideal and moral progress; and the fourth, again to use Bradley's expression, deals with the application of moral philosophy to the guidance of conduct. I shall discuss briefly each of these books in order.

i. *The Metaphysics of Knowledge.* Green's concern throughout the first book of the *Prolegomena to Ethics* is twofold. On the one hand, he is concerned to argue against metaphysical naturalism by arguing that neither (a) the existence of nature as an intelligible world of objects standing in various relations to one another nor (b) the possibility of human knowledge of this world can be accounted for in naturalistic terms. Instead, he argues, both the existence of nature and the possibility of human knowledge of it presuppose the operation of a spiritual principle in both nature and knowledge. Although Green never mentions Darwin, this concern to repudiate naturalism and to vindicate spiritualism or idealism was at least partly occasioned by the growth of evolutionary naturalism as a consequence of the publication of Darwin's *Origin of Species* in 1859, some twenty years before Green wrote the *Prolegomena to Ethics*. His argument may be interpreted as contending that even though one be compelled by the accumulation of scientific data to acknowledge some form of Darwinism to account satisfactorily for the development of later forms of life out of earlier forms, the fact still remains that neither the existence of nature nor the existence of human knowledge can be accounted for in naturalistic terms, but, instead, can be rendered intelligible only through supposing the operation of a spiritual principle both in nature and in knowledge.

Green's argument in support of his contention that an intelligible world of objects standing in various relations to one another presupposes the operation of a spiritual principle in nature may be summarized briefly as follows. *First*, the world, or nature, is a single unalterable system of relations between terms of various sorts. Everything that is real in any sense at all, with the exception of that which makes the entire system possible, has its place within this system. To say that this system of relations is unalterable is to say that it is eternal or timeless. Although natural objects and events, as part of nature, exist or occur in time, the fact of the existence or occurrence of any object or event at any point in time is an unalterable or eternal fact, in the sense that an assertion of its existence or occurrence, regardless of whether it be made prior to, contemporaneously with, or subsequently to its existence or occurrence, is unalterably or timelessly true. *Secondly*, relations cannot exist independently of consciousness. This is not to say merely that they must exist for some consciousness; instead, it is also to say that they are the product of consciousness. If two objects or events stand in some relation to one another, it is because some consciousness has related them to one another. To use Kantian language, it is the understanding that makes nature, through relating the data of experience to one another. But, *thirdly*, although relations cannot exist independently of consciousness, they can and do exist independently of the finite human consciousness. The human consciousness apprehends at best only some of the relations constituting the system of relations which is nature, not all of them; this system in its totality transcends the apprehension of the human consciousness, and therefore exists independently of the human consciousness. But since reality is an unalterable or eternal system of relations, and since relations cannot exist independently of the consciousness of and the relating activity of some intelligence, there must exist an eternal consciousness for which the eternal system of relations is an eternal object, and which is also the ground or source of this system through its relating activity. And, *finally*, since no object, sensation, or feeling has any nature or reality taken in isolation from the rest of the system of which it is a part, but, on the contrary, derives its reality from its membership within this system, the eternal consciousness that is the source of this system of relations is at the same time the ultimate source or ground of these objects, sensations, and feelings. There is thus no need to postulate the existence of an unknowable and hence unintelligible realm of Kantian things-in-themselves in order to account for their existence. Instead, reality is a single intelligible system of relations with a single source or ground, and is not divisible into two compartments, one intelligible or knowable and the other unintelligible or unknowable.

We turn now to summarizing briefly Green's argument that human knowledge cannot be accounted for naturalistically, but, instead, can only be explained by supposing the operation in man of a spiritual principle. The argument essentially rests upon the contention that to attempt to account for human knowledge in naturalistic or materialistic terms is to be guilty of a *hysteron proteron*; it is to suppose that nature makes understanding possible, when in fact it is the understanding that makes nature. This is to say that the acquisition of knowledge of nature presupposes the operation in man of the conception

of nature as an unalterable system of relations, although a reflective or explicit consciousness of the operation of this conception is not arrived at until it has already operated for some
time to make both knowledge of nature and knowledge of its
own operation possible. We assume, that is, that nature is
such a system of relations, and such an assumption is necessary
if we are to acquire knowledge of nature, even though we do
not become explicitly or reflectively conscious of this assumption until long after we have operated in terms of it in attempting to acquire knowledge. Yet the existence or operation of
such a conception or assumption cannot be accounted for naturalistically, since it is only through having it or making it
that we have any conception at all of nature as a system, and
only through operating in terms of it that we acquire knowledge of the details of nature. But if its existence or operation
cannot be accounted for naturalistically, then it can be explained only through supposing that it is the operation in man
of the same eternal consciousness that is the ultimate source or
ground of nature. Thus the same consciousness that makes nature also reproduces itself in man in human knowledge. Its
reproduction of itself in human knowledge, however, is conditioned by the stage of development of the human animal
organism, both individually and as a species. But although
Green admits that both the development of the human animal
organism and its conditioning of the acquisition of knowledge
can, at least to some extent, be explained naturalistically, he
denies that the full significance of its development and functioning can be accounted for in naturalistic terms, but, instead,
maintains that it can be adequately apprehended only by taking into account the human knowledge to which the development and functioning of the animal organism are organic.
His point here is that the processes within living organisms,
and particularly within the human animal organism, can be
adequately understood only by looking at them from two complementary points of view: from the standpoint of the order
of efficient causes and from the standpoint of the order of final
causes.

Some readers, at least, will undoubtedly find that Green's
argument against naturalism fails on both counts: that he fails
both to establish that there is a spiritual principle in nature

and to establish that there is a spiritual principle in knowledge. The crucial step in the argument designed to establish the first contention is the second step—the contention that relations cannot exist independently of consciousness, but must exist as objects for some consciousness and be produced through the action of some act of consciousness. Green nowhere presents any argument in support of this contention, but rather seems to assume it as self-evident. But not only does it seem not to be self-evident, it also appears to be questionable and even false, since some relations, at least, seem to be discovered rather than made by acts of consciousness, and therefore exist independently of consciousness, or at least may do so. But if so, then Green's entire argument for the existence of a spiritual principle in nature fails, since it rests upon this second step of the argument.

His argument for a spiritual principle in knowledge also seems to me to fail. Its crucial defect is that Green seems to be confusing an epistemological with a metaphysical question. In the *Prolegomena to Ethics,* as in his essays on Spencer and Lewes, he argues—rightly I am convinced—that the philosophical or epistemological question of the conditions that must be satisfied if knowledge is to be possible cannot be answered by means of natural science—that the sorts of question which Kant raised in the *Critique of Pure Reason* as to the *a priori* conditions of the possibility of knowledge cannot be answered naturalistically by making empirical observations of nature or man or by performing experiments. But the fact that epistemological questions, and philosophical questions in general, cannot be answered by using the methods of the natural sciences—the fact that philosophy cannot be replaced by the natural sciences—does not in itself constitute a refutation of metaphysical naturalism, much less establish spiritualism or idealism. Thus, even though it be true that a philosophical analysis of the conditions that must be satisfied if knowledge is to be possible cannot be supplanted by a naturalistic or empirical account of the empirical or naturalistic conditions present whenever anyone knows anything, it may nevertheless be the case that there are certain empirical or naturalistic conditions the satisfaction of which is both a necessary and a sufficient condition of the satisfaction of the epistemological or philosophical conditions which must be satisfied if knowledge is to be possible. If so, an appeal to some nonnaturalistic metaphysical principle in order to account for knowledge becomes otiose, and the existence and operation of such a principle, if it is to be established at all, must be argued for on other grounds.

But, of course, the fact—if, indeed, it be a fact—that Green's arguments against naturalism and for idealism or spiritualism fail to refute the former and to establish the latter does not mean that naturalism is a satisfactory position, since there may be arguments other than those that Green presents which do establish the inadequacy of naturalism and the need for accepting some form of idealism or spiritualism if nature and man's knowledge of nature are satisfactorily to be accounted for. Certainly arguments—some idealistic and some non-idealistic—other than the one Green presents have been offered in support of the position that there is a spiritual principle in nature, in the sense that the existence of nature can be adequately accounted for only by supposing the operation of such a principle; and arguments—nonidealistic as well as idealistic —other than the one Green presents have been constructed to show that human knowledge cannot be adequately explained in naturalistic terms. And although Green seems to have thought that idealism is the only acceptable alternative to naturalism, this is by no means so obvious as he seems to have believed.

Nor is it as obvious as Green thought that the content of his moral philosophy, as distinguished from his metaphysics of knowledge and of moral action, requires an idealistic epistemology and metaphysic as an epistemological and metaphysical foundation. Indeed, one could well argue that it does not even presuppose a nonnaturalistic epistemology and metaphysic, on the ground that a naturalist in epistemology and metaphysics could consistently accept the essential contentions of Green's moral philosophy proper. Whether he could or not would depend ultimately upon whether a satisfactory naturalistic account can be given of the kind of knowledge and moral action that is presupposed by the content of the moral philosophy. Should such an account prove impossible, then, of course, the naturalist would be inconsistent in accepting both a naturalis-

tic explanation of knowledge and moral action on the one hand
and the content of Green's moral philosophy on the other, and
would therefore be compelled either to abandon his naturalistic
interpretation of knowledge and moral action or to reject the
content of Green's moral philosophy. But, again, it is quite
questionable that Green does in fact succeed in showing that an
acceptance of his moral philosophy requires an abandonment
of naturalism. Yet although it may be doubted that Green does
succeed in showing this, he nevertheless does have the unquestionable merit of seeing that a thorough treatment of
moral philosophy requires that a system of moral philosophy
be prefaced by epistemological and metaphysical prolegomena
sufficient to establish the possibility of the kind of knowledge
and moral action presupposed or required by the content of
the system. It is in this sense that any system of moral philosophy presupposes or rests upon certain epistemological and
metaphysical foundations.

ii. *The Metaphysics of Moral Action.* In Book One, on
the metaphysics of knowledge, Green presents an analysis of
speculative or theoretical thought; in Book Two, on the metaphysics of moral action, he presents an analysis of practical
thought. Just as a man gradually attains a speculative or theoretical apprehension of a world of objects through distinguishing himself from his impressions, so also he gradually
attains a conception of a world of practice through distinguishing himself from his wants and his impulses to satisfy them.
Wants and impulses are to be distinguished from desires, for
the former are purely natural and do not presuppose a distinction between oneself and an object desired, whereas desire does
presuppose this distinction. Only self-conscious beings are
therefore capable of desire, since only a being that is conscious
of itself can distinguish itself from its desires and the objects
it desires. Thus intellect is essentially involved in desire, since
desire involves not only the thought of oneself, of the object
desired, and of the distinction between the two, but may also
involve thought of the conditions that must be satisfied if the
desire is to be satisfied. This, however, does not mean that a
man attempts to satisfy every desire he has. Instead, his desires may conflict, so that it is impossible that all should be
satisfied. In this event, as also in the case in which there is no

conflict of desires, he may choose whether to satisfy any of his desires or not and, if so, which desire to satisfy. This choice is an act of will, in which he identifies himself with one of his desires. Moreover, since intellect is involved in desire in the ways already suggested, and since will presupposes desire, intellect is also involved in will.

Indeed, Green goes so far as to maintain that not only do desire and will involve intellect, but also that acts of intellect involve desire and will, since acts of intellect are not performed unless one desires and wills to attain some end, even though this be merely the discovery of the solution to some speculative or theoretical problem. Thus intellect on the one hand and desire and will on the other are distinguishable only in thought; they are not separable in reality. No act of intellect occurs independently of desire and will, and every desire and act of will involves the operation of intellect. Each of the three— intellect, desire, and will—considered separately from both of the others, is therefore an abstraction, not a concrete reality. Each is simply a distinct kind of operation of a single self, or rather a distinct aspect of the operation of a single self, which both desires and performs acts of intellect and will. But just as each considered as standing alone is an abstraction, so also is the self considered in isolation from its desires and acts of will and intellect. Just as neither desire nor will nor intellect has any concrete reality taken in isolation from both of the others and from the self, so also the self has no concrete reality taken in abstraction from its desires and acts of will and intellect; that is, a self could no more exist which has no desires and performs no acts of intellect or of will than a desire or act of will or intellect could exist or occur without being the desire or act of a self.

Both the acts of intellect and the acts of will of the self are free. Acts of intellect are free in the sense that they are not determined by antecedent natural conditions. As we have seen, Green maintains in his discussion of the metaphysics of knowledge that it is the understanding that makes nature rather than nature that makes the understanding. Since nature is constituted or determined through acts of intellect or understanding, the latter cannot be determined by nature, and therefore cannot be accounted for in naturalistic terms. Acts of will are also free in the sense that they are not determined by antecedent natural conditions. In particular, they are not determined by desires. An act of will is not the result of the strongest desire cancelling competing but weaker desires, nor is it a kind of vector or combined result of the confluence or conjunction of competing desires. Instead, an act of will is a man's decision or choice to satisfy a desire and the action he takes to carry out this decision. Of two desires soliciting him in different directions, he may well choose to satisfy the weaker of the two at the expense of the stronger. This means that the strength of a desire is determined by how strongly it is felt, and not by whether the agent chooses to satisfy it. If his choice is determined at all, it is determined only by his motive, which in turn depends upon his character.

The agent's motive in acting is always some idea of personal good, which he seeks to realize by means of the action. This, however, does not mean that Green is espousing psychological egoism, for the idea of personal good one seeks to realize may be impersonal—in the sense that it may comprehend the good of others as well as one's own good. What the determinate character of the agent's idea of personal good is depends upon his character, so that the determinate character of both the agent's motive and his action is an expression of his character. The agent is nevertheless responsible for his motive and his action, for he is responsible for his character, which develops as a consequence of or function of the choices he makes and the acts he performs.

iii. *The Moral Ideal and Moral Progress.* The content of Green's moral philosophy proper is presented primarily in Book Three. There he argues not only for an ethics of self-realization, but also against both psychological and ethical hedonism. We have already seen that Green maintains that in all action the agent wills the satisfaction of some desire and that the motive of the action is an idea of personal good which the agent seeks to realize. This means that in all action the agent seeks self-satisfaction and that all successful action, i.e., action in which the desire the agent seeks to satisfy is in fact satisfied, results in pleasure, since the satisfaction of desire is pleasurable. This misleads the psychological hedonist into supposing that all desire is desire for pleasure and that every act aims at either the acquisition of pleasure or the avoidance of pain. This, however, is a mistake, for although the desire one seeks to satisfy in acting may be a desire for pleasure, it need not be, and usually is not, but is, instead, usually a desire for the attainment of specific objects of various sorts.

And not only is the psychological hedonist misled through a faulty analysis or understanding of desire, will, and action, the ethical hedonist is also. Although "the common characteristic of the good is that it satisfies some desire" (sec. 171), and although in all satisfaction of desire there is pleasure, this does not mean that the good is pleasure. Instead, desires are usually desires for specific objects of different kinds, and not simply desires for pleasure, the occurrence of which may therefore be merely incidental to the satisfaction of the desire and not intended by the agent. Accordingly, the good can be identified, not with pleasure, but, instead, only with the attainment of the various specific objects the attainment of which the agent seeks in acting and which is a necessary condition of the satisfaction of his desire.

But although "the common characteristic of the good is that it satisfies some desire," this does not mean that any and every satisfaction of desire is good. As we have seen, Green maintains that the motive of every act is the realization of some idea of personal good. This means that a distinction must be drawn between the satisfaction of some particular desire on the one hand and the realization of the idea of personal good on the other. The idea of personal good is an idea of a good at least as permanent as a person, and the realization of this idea is the permanent or constant motive of action. But a particular desire for the attainment of some specific object may well be temporary, and so may the particular object the attainment of which one desires. It is true that the idea of personal good, taken in abstraction from the ideas of various particular goods, is an empty abstraction, and that the realization of the idea of personal good involves the satisfaction of particular desires for specific objects of various kinds. But whether the satisfaction of some particular desire is good or not depends upon whether its satisfaction is compatible or not with the realization of the idea of personal good. The recognition of this leads to a rejection of the satisfaction of some particular desires as

bad, as incompatible with the realization of the idea of personal
good.

But not only are particular desires criticized, and approved
or rejected in terms of the standard of the idea of personal
good, in addition the content of the idea of personal good is
itself subject to revision as the individual and the race grows
in experience and wisdom. In this way the content of earlier
ideas of personal good is approved or rejected as inadequate in
terms of the standard of a later idea or ideal of personal good.
This is an unending process, so that it is impossible to spell
out definitively once and for all the detailed content of the
ideal of personal good in such a way that we can rest assured
that the ideal as we grasp it will never stand in need of further revision. On the contrary, our grasp of this detailed content is always conditioned by, and relative to, the stage of historical development reached by our own age and culture.

There are, however, certain personal, social, and formal
characteristics of the ideal that can be grasped once and for
all, regardless of however inadequate and subject to revision
our grasp of its detailed content may be. First, the ideal is
and must forever remain an ideal of personal goodness, real-
izable only in and for persons. This is recognized in Kant's
second formulation of the moral law, which commands us
categorically to treat persons as ends in themselves, never
merely as means. Secondly, the ideal is and must forever remain a social ideal. This is so because the individual—at least
the developed individual—taken in abstraction from society
is as much an abstraction as is society taken in abstraction
from the individuals who constitute it, so that the ideal of
personal good can be realized only through the realization of
this ideal by individuals in society. The conjunction of the
personal and social characteristics of the moral ideal yields
the conception of an ideal society structured by customs, institutions, laws, and recognized rights and duties in such a
way that each individual is treated as an end in himself and
is enabled to realize those of his potentialities the realization of
which is compatible with the treatment of each person as an
end in himself. Thirdly, the moral ideal is and must forever
remain such that the effort to realize it has an absolute or
intrinsic worth, regardless of however successful one's effort

may be, and regardless of however inadequate one's conception of the detailed content of the ideal may be. This is to say that virtue and good will, regarded as the conscientious effort to contribute toward the realization of the moral ideal, are in themselves constituents of this ideal, and as such always have an intrinsic worth, regardless of however inadequate the conception of the detailed content of the moral ideal animating the conscientious or virtuous man of good will may be, and regardless of whether his conscientious act succeeds or fails in achieving its goal.

iv. *The Application of Moral Philosophy to the Guidance of Conduct.* In Book Four Green devotes his attention to two principal questions: (1) Of what practical value is moral philosophy in the guidance of conduct, and, in particular, to the resolution of moral perplexity? (2) Of what practical value is the theory he presents as compared with hedonistic utilitarianism?

(1) Green admits that it is not the function of moral philosophy to attempt to specify the ordinary duties which constitute the content of recognized or established morality. Nor is it its function to attempt to remove those perplexities that arise either from ignorance concerning the precise circumstances or effects of action or from the operation of concealed egoistic motives. The specification of the ordinary duties of conventional morality, if it is necessary at all, is an empirical matter, not the task of moral philosophy. Similarly, perplexities arising from ignorance concerning the circumstances or effects of action or from the operation of concealed egoistic motives are not genuine moral perplexities, but, instead, empirical difficulties that can be resolved only by attending to specific empirical situations, and not by appealing to moral philosophy.

But if the function of moral philosophy is not the resolution of empirical difficulties of these sorts, then of what practical value is it in the guidance of conduct? Green's answer is that it is of practical value in two respects. The first is the resolution of genuine moral perplexities. These arise when rules and institutions believed by the conscientious moral agent to have absolute authority conflict, so that he is confused as to what his duty really is. Moral philosophy seeks to remove such perplexity by attempting to show that the rules and institutions in question do not have the absolute authority they are supposed to have, but, instead, derive whatever authority they may have from their contribution to the realization of the moral ideal. Accordingly, should obedience to them become incompatible with action in accordance with the moral ideal, they are to be superseded by rules or institutions obedience to which is more compatible with the realization of this ideal. The second respect in which moral philosophy is of practical value consists in the criticism of inadequate moral theories that may vitiate practice in various ways.

(2) An example of such a theory is hedonistic utilitarianism, as developed by Bentham, Mill, and Sidgwick. Green concedes that utilitarianism has been of more public service in modern Europe than any other moral theory. This, however, has been due to three factors, none of which logically requires an acceptance of utilitarianism, and two of which are in fact incompatible with utilitarianism. The first factor has been the public spirit and action of utilitarians such as Bentham and Mill. The second has been the espousal by utilitarians of the democratic principle that each man is to count as one and no man as more than one (a principle that is incompatible with utilitarianism if accepted as an absolute principle, since more total pleasure might well accrue by acting incompatibly with it). The third factor has been an acceptance by others of various of the social reforms suggested by the utilitarians, not on utilitarian grounds, but on grounds such as those Green has presented in his own theory.

But despite the public service that the utilitarians have rendered, their theory is inadequate in various respects. First, the utilitarianism of Bentham and Mill, if not also that of Sidgwick, rests upon an inadequate moral psychology. Secondly, although Green admits that his own theory of the moral ideal as human perfection is somewhat vague, since we cannot in the present specify in detail the determinate character which advances in human perfection will assume in the future, the idea of human perfection which we have succeeded in attaining is nevertheless more precise in content than the idea of as much pleasure as possible for as many people as possible, and therefore affords a more precise guide for conduct than the utilitarian ideal. Finally, the utilitarian, in supposing that pleasure alone is intrinsically good, can assign no intrinsic worth to the conscientious effort of the man who seeks to advance human good, with the result that the man who doubts the success of his efforts in increasing human pleasure may well hesitate in sacrificing his own pleasure for the sake of achieving a doubtful goal if, on utilitarian grounds, he believes that the sacrifice has no intrinsic worth.

The reader of the *Prolegomena to Ethics* will doubtlessly see that in large measure the positive side of Green's moral philosophy, as distinguished from his criticism of utilitarianism, is a development of the moral philosophy of Plato, Aristotle, and Kant. There is also a fair amount of Butler in Green, particularly in his discussion of moral psychology, and the influence of Hegel is evident in Green's historical approach, even though Green never mentions Hegel. The reader will also find, particularly in the last three books, a position expounded that in certain respects is anticipatory of the moral philosophy of John Dewey. As a young man Dewey was quite profoundly influenced, not only by Green's moral philosophy, but also by his political philosophy, and this influence left its traces on Dewey's moral, social, and political philosophy throughout his long life.

The reader of the *Prolegomena to Ethics* will perhaps also be inclined to compare it with the major works in ethics of two of Green's contemporaries: Sidgwick's *Methods of Ethics*, first published in 1874, and F. H. Bradley's *Ethical Studies*, initially published in 1876. It must be admitted that Green's work does not have quite the analytic rigor one finds in the *Methods of Ethics*, and that it has by no means the fire and brilliance of expression one finds in Bradley's work, and is in fact somewhat diffuse and repetitive. Some of its diffusiveness and repetitiveness would perhaps have been eliminated had Green lived to subject it to a final revision. But despite its shortcomings in these respects in comparison with the works of Sidgwick and Bradley, the morally sensitive reader cannot fail to be impressed, I believe, with the moral earnestness that pervades it, an earnestness that also characterizes Green's *Lectures on the Principles of Political Obligation*. Just as the sensitive reader of the latter work is left with the impression that it is the work not only of a philosopher but also of a good and conscientious citizen, so also the sensitive reader of the *Prolegomena to Ethics* will find it to be, not only an expression of the mind of a philosopher, but also a revelation of the heart of a conscientious and good, perhaps even saintly, man. Judging from the reports of his contemporaries who knew him well, Green seems to have been one of those rare individuals (but fortunately not so rare as never to be met with) whose mere presence acts upon those within its radius as a source of moral inspiration and resolution. Something of this character shines forth on almost every page of the work before us.

RAMON M. LEMOS

DEPARTMENT OF PHILOSOPHY
UNIVERSITY OF MIAMI
CORAL GABLES, FLORIDA

PREFACE.

THE works by which Professor Green has hitherto been chiefly known to the general public are his *Introduction* to Messrs. Longmans' edition of Hume's Philosophical Works, and his articles in the *Contemporary Review* on some doctrines of Mr. Spencer and Mr. Lewes.

When in the year 1877 Mr. Green became Whyte's Professor of Moral Philosophy, his main desire was, both in his teaching and writing, to develope more fully and in a more constructive way the ideas which underlay his previous critical writings and appeared in them. The present treatise is the first outcome of that desire; and doubtless it would have been only the first but for the premature and unexpected death of the author in March, 1882.

Even the *Prolegomena to Ethics* (the title is the author's own) was left unfinished. The greater part of the book had been used, some of it twice over, in the Professorial lectures; and about a quarter of it (the first 103 pages) was printed in the numbers of *Mind* for January, April, and July, 1882. But, according to a letter of the author written not long before his death, some twenty or thirty pages remained to be added, and, though with this exception the whole was written out nearly ready for printing, no part of it can be considered to have undergone the final revision.

At his death Mr. Green left the charge of the manuscript to me; and I have now only to explain the course I have followed in preparing it for publication.

The manuscript was written in paragraphs, but otherwise was continuous; and I may add that it was composed without regard to arrangement in Books and Chapters. For

that arrangement I am responsible, and also for the num-
bering and occasional re-division of the sections, and for the
frequent division of a section into two or more paragraphs.
I have also made the few corrections in expression which
seemed to be necessary, and in one case I have ventured,
for the sake of clearness, to transfer a passage from one
place to another. References have been verified and supplied;
translations of Greek quotations have been given, where
their meaning was not obvious from the text; and a few
notes have been added by way of explanation or qualification, for the most part only where a mark in the author's
manuscript showed that he intended to reconsider the
passage. The Editor's notes, except where they give merely
a reference or translation, are enclosed in square brackets.

My desire throughout has been to make no changes except
in passages which I felt sure Mr. Green would have altered
had his attention been called to them. With the further
object of rendering the work as intelligible as possible to
the general reader I have ventured to print an analysis.
Mr. Green would probably have followed the plan he adopted
in the *Introduction* to Hume, and have placed a short
abstract on the margins of the pages. I have thought it
better to print my analysis as a Table of Contents, as that
arrangement clearly separates my work from the author's,
and will also probably be the most useful to those who care
to read an analysis at all. Perhaps I may further suggest
to any reader who is unaccustomed to metaphysical and
psychological discussions that much of the author's ethical
views, though not their scientific basis, may be gathered from
the Third and Fourth Books alone.

It has been already explained that the book was left unfinished. But on the whole I thought it best to make no
attempt to add anything, especially as the comparison which
occupies the last chapter seems to have reached a natural
conclusion. The reader will also find in the text indications
of subjects which were to have been discussed. In particular

the author—at any rate at one time—intended to introduce a criticism of Kant's ethical views (see page 163). But I think this intention must have been abandoned during the composition of the book, and, as it is hoped that before long Mr. Green's published writings will be collected and edited, together with a short biography and selections from his unpublished manuscripts, it seemed best that the materials on this subject furnished by the author's notes for lectures should be reserved for a future occasion.

I have received material assistance in preparing the present work for the press. Mrs. Green has compared the whole of the book in proof with the original manuscript. Professor Edward Caird, of Glasgow University, and Mr. R. L. Nettleship, Fellow of Balliol, read through the proofs and the analysis and sent me many suggestions. I feel, in particular, that but for Professor Caird's very full and valuable notes the analysis must have been far more imperfect than it remains. But it would seem to me, and to those who have helped me, out of place to express any gratitude for work given to a book which, more than any writing of Mr. Green's yet published, may enable the public outside Oxford to understand not only the philosophical enthusiasm which his teaching inspired, but the reverence and love which are felt for him by all who knew him well.

A. C. BRADLEY.

UNIVERSITY COLLEGE, LIVERPOOL,
April, 1883.

There is no change in the SECOND or THIRD EDITION beyond the correction of a few verbal mistakes and errors of the press.

ANALYTICAL TABLE OF CONTENTS.

INTRODUCTION.

THE IDEA OF A NATURAL SCIENCE OF MORALS.

BOOK I.

Metaphysics of Knowledge.

CHAPTER I.

THE SPIRITUAL PRINCIPLE IN KNOWLEDGE AND IN NATURE.

The Spiritual Principle in Knowledge.

CHAPTER II.

THE RELATION OF MAN, AS INTELLIGENCE, TO THE SPIRITUAL PRINCIPLE IN NATURE.

CHAPTER III.

THE FREEDOM OF MAN AS INTELLIGENCE.

BOOK II.

The Will.

CHAPTER I.

THE FREEDOM OF THE WILL.

PAGE

CHAPTER II.

DESIRE, INTELLECT, AND WILL.

Desire.

BOOK III.

The Moral Ideal and Moral Progress.

CHAPTER I.

GOOD AND MORAL GOOD.

Pleasure and Desire.

The Intrinsic Nature of Moral Good.

CHAPTER II.

CHARACTERISTICS OF THE MORAL IDEAL.

A. The Personal Character of the Moral Ideal.

B. The Formal Character of the Moral Ideal or Law.

192. Thus the idea which the good will seeks to realise is identical in form with the idea of the end as realised in the eternal mind. We have now

CHAPTER III.

THE ORIGIN AND DEVELOPMENT OF THE MORAL IDEAL.

A. Reason as Source of the Idea of a Common Good.

B. The Extension of the Area of Common Good.

CHAPTER IV.

THE DEVELOPMENT OF THE MORAL IDEAL—CONTINUED.

C. The Determination of the Idea of Common Good.

Pleasure and Common Good.

CHAPTER V.

THE DEVELOPMENT OF THE MORAL IDEAL—CONTINUED.

D. *The Greek and the Modern Conceptions of Virtue.*

BOOK IV.

The Application of Moral Philosophy to the Guidance of Conduct.

CHAPTER I.

THE PRACTICAL VALUE OF THE MORAL IDEAL.

CHAPTER II.

THE PRACTICAL VALUE OF A THEORY OF THE MORAL IDEAL.

CHAPTER III.

THE PRACTICAL VALUE OF A HEDONISTIC MORAL PHILOSOPHY.

CHAPTER IV.

THE PRACTICAL VALUE OF UTILITARIANISM COMPARED WITH THAT OF THE THEORY OF THE GOOD AS HUMAN PERFECTION.

382. Our conclusion, then, is that in the two cases which claim...
or time to apply to philosophy for guidance elsewhere...
as an end in itself is more available and I say...
versa in Hedonism.

PROLEGOMENA TO ETHICS.

INTRODUCTION.

1. A WRITER who seeks to gain general confidence scarcely goes the right way to work when he begins with asking whether there really is such a subject as that of which he proposes to treat; whether it is one to which enquiry can be directed with any prospect of a valuable result. Yet to a writer on Moral Philosophy such a mode of procedure is prescribed, not only by the logical impulse to begin at the beginning, but by observation of the prevalent opinions around him. He can scarcely but be aware that Moral Philosophy is a name of somewhat equivocal repute; that it commands less respect among us than was probably the case a century ago; and that any one who professes to teach or write upon a subject to which this name is in any proper or distinctive sense applicable, is looked upon with some suspicion.

There is, indeed, no lack of utterance in regard to the great problems of life or the rights and wrongs of human conduct. Nor does it by any means confine itself to what are commonly counted secular or 'positive' considerations. Guesses as to some

> 'sweet strange mystery,
> Of what beyond these things may lie,
> And yet remain unseen,'

are announced with little reserve and meet with ready acceptance. These, we may say, are for the multitude of the educated, who have wearied of the formulas of a stereotyped theology, but still demand free indulgence for the appetite which that theology supplied with a regulation-diet. But the highest poetry of our time—that in which the most serious and select spirits find their food—depends chiefly for its interest on what has been well called 'the application of ideas to life;' and the ideas so applied are by no means sensibly verifiable. They belong as little to the domain of natural science, strictly so-called, as to that of dogmatic theology. A moral philosopher may be excused for finding much excellent philosophy, in his special sense of the word, in such poems as the 'In Memoriam' of Lord Tennyson and Mr. Browning's 'Rabbi ben Ezra,' to say nothing of the more explicitly ethical poetry of Wordsworth. Presented in the rapt unreasoned form of poetic utterance, not professing to do more than represent a mood of the individual poet, it is welcomed by reflecting men as expressing deep convictions of their own. Such men seem little disturbed by the admission to a joint lodgement in their minds of inferences from popularised science, which do not admit of being reconciled with these deeper convictions in any logical system of beliefs.

But if any one, alarmed at this dangerous juxtaposition, and unwilling that what seem to him the deepest and truest views of life should be retained merely on scientific sufferance, seeks to find for them some independent justification, in the shape of a philosophy which does not profess to be a branch either of dogmatic theology or of natural science, he must look for little thanks for his trouble. The most intelligent critics had rather, it would seem, that the ideas which poetry applies to life, together with those which form the basis of practical religion, should be left to take their chance alongside of seemingly incompatible scientific beliefs, than that anything calling itself philosophy should seek to systematise them and to ascertain the regions to which they on the one side, and the truths of science on the other, are respectively applicable. 'Poetry we feel, science we understand;'—such will be the reflection, spoken or unspoken, of most cultivated men;—'theology professes to found itself on divine revelation, and has at all events a sphere of its own in the interpretation of sacred writings which entitles it at least to respectful recognition; but this philosophy, which is neither poetry nor science nor theology, what is it but a confusion of all of these in which each of them is spoilt? Poetry has a truth of its own, and so has religion—a truth which we feel, though from the scientific point of view we may admit it to be an illusion. Philosophy is from the scientific point of view equally an illusion, and has no truth that we can feel. Better trust poetry and religion to the hold which, however illusive, they will always have on the human heart, than seek to explain and vindicate them, as against science, by help of a philosophy which is itself not only an illusion but a dull and pretentious one, with no interest for the imagination and no power over the heart.'

2. With such opinion in the air all around him, it must be with much misgiving that one who has no prophetic utterance to offer in regard to conduct, but who still believes in the necessity of a philosophy of morals which no adaptation of natural science can supply, undertakes to make good his position. He will gain nothing, however, by trying to sail under false colours, or by disguising his recognition of an antithesis between the natural and the moral, which can alone justify his claim to have something to say that lies beyond the limits of the man of science. It is better that he should make it clear at the outset why and in what sense he holds that there is a subject-matter of enquiry which does not consist of matters of fact, ascertainable by experiment and observation, and what place he assigns to morals in this subject-matter. In other words, at the risk of repelling readers by presenting them first with the most difficult and least plausible part of his doctrine, he should begin with explaining why he holds a 'metaphysic of morals' to be possible and necessary; the proper foundation, though not the whole, of every system of Ethics.

This has not been the method commonly pursued by English writers on the subject, and, in the face of present tendencies, is likely to seem something of an anachronism. To any one who by idiosyncrasy, or by the accident of his position, is led to occupy himself with Moral Philosophy, the temptation to treat his subject as a part of natural science is certainly a strong one. In so doing he can plead the authority of eminent names and is sure of intelligent acceptance ; nor can he fail by patient enquiry to arrive at a theory of some phenomena of human life, which, though it may leave certain primary problems untouched, shall be not only plausible but true so far as it goes. He can reckon securely on having more to show for his life's work, when it comes to an end, than if he spent himself on questions which he may recognise as of real interest, but to which he will also be aware that experiment and observation, strictly so called, cannot afford an answer. It thus would not be wonderful that, with most enquirers and teachers, the interest once taken in Moral Philosophy should be mainly transferred to the physical science conveniently called Anthropology, even if the insufficiency of the latter to deal with the most important questions of Moral Philosophy were admitted.

This admission, however, has of late been fast coming to be thought unnecessary. That a physical science of Ethics is not intrinsically impossible, however difficult it may be rendered by the complexity, and inaccessibility to direct experiment, of its subject-matter; that there are no intelligible questions—no questions worth asking—as to human life which would be beyond the reach of such a science; this would seem to be the general opinion of modern English 'culture,' so far as it is independent of theological prepossessions. And it is natural that it should be so. The questions raised for us by the Moral Philosophy which in England we have inherited, are just such as to invite a physical treatment. If it is the chief business of the moralist to distinguish the nature and origin of the pleasures and pains which are supposed to be the sole objects of human desire and aversion, to trace the effect upon conduct of the impulses so constituted, and to ascertain the several degrees in which different courses of action, determined by anticipation of pleasure and pain, are actually productive of the desired result; then the sooner the methods of scientific experiment and observation are substituted for vague guessing and an arbitrary interpretation by each man of his own consciousness, the better it will be. Ethics, so understood, becomes to all intents and purposes a science of health, and the true moralist will be the physiologist who, making the human physique his specialty, takes a sufficiently wide view of his subject; who traces the influence of historical and political factors, or of what it is now the fashion to call the 'social medium,' in giving a specific character to those susceptibilities of pleasure and pain on which, according to the theory supposed, the phenomena of human action depend.

3. There were two elements, indeed, in the system of popular ethics inherited from the last century, which were long thought

incompatible with its complete reduction to the form of a physical science. These were the doctrines of free-will and of a moral sense. Each, however, was understood in a way which suggested to the naturalist a ready explanation of its supposed claim to lie beyond his sphere. The moral sense, according to the accepted view, was a specific susceptibility to pleasure or pain in the contemplation of certain acts. What was the quality in the acts which excited this pleasure or pain in the contemplation of them? If it were something in the conception of which any originative function of the reason was implied, then the existence of the moral sense would have meant that there was a determining agent in the inner life of man, of which no natural history could be given. But those writers who had made most of the moral sense had been very indefinite in their account of the quality in action to which it was relative. The most consistent theory on the subject was Hume's. According to him the pleasure of moral sense is pleasure felt in the 'mere survey' of an act, independently of any consequences of the act to the person contemplating it; and that which occasions this pleasure is the tendency of the act to bring pleasure to the agent himself or to others [1]. Moral sense, in short, is a social sentiment either of satisfaction in the view of such conduct as has been generally found to increase the pleasure or diminish the pain of others, or of uneasiness in the reverse, quite apart from any expectation of personal advantage or loss. It is thus properly not by the action of the person feeling it, but by that of others, that it is excited. An act of a man's own, necessarily proceeding, according to Hume, from some desire for pleasure which it satisfies or fails to satisfy, must have personal consequences for him, incompatible with that disinterested survey which alone yields the pleasure or pain of moral sense, properly so called. Sympathy, however, with the effect which he knows that his act produces on the moral sense of others, may modify the feeling which it causes to the doer of it. An act, in gratification of some passion, which he would otherwise look forward to as pleasant, may become so painful in anticipation from sympathy with the general uneasiness which he knows would arise upon the contemplation of it that, without any fear of punishment, he abstains from doing it.

[1] Treatise on Human Nature, Book III, Pt. i. §§ 1, 2, and Pt. iii. § 1.

4. Thus moral sense and sympathy jointly, as understood by Hume, serve plausibly to explain the office ordinarily ascribed to conscience, as the judge and possible controller in each man of his own acts. At the same time the lines are indicated along which a physical theory of ' conscience ' might be logically attempted. The problem which Hume bequeathed to a successor who adopted his principles was mainly to account for the two-fold fact, that the mere survey of actions as tending to produce pleasures in which the contemplator will have no share, is yet a source of pleasure to him; and that, among the pleasures taken into account in that estimate of the tendency of an action which determines the moral sentiment, are such as have no direct connexion with the satisfaction of animal wants. A theory which will account for this will also account for the affection of the agent by sympathy with the sentiment which the contem-plation of his action excites in others. Can we find any scientific warrant for believing in a process by which, out of susceptibility to pleasures incidental to the merely animal life, there have grown those capacities for enjoyment which we consider essential to general well-being, and those social interests which not only make the contemplation of general well-being an independent source of pleasure, but also make the pleasure of exciting this pleasure—the pleasure of satisfying the moral sentiment of others—an object of desire so strong as in many cases to deter-mine action ? If we can, it would seem that we have given to our national system of ethics—the ethics of moral sentiment— the solid foundation of a natural science.

5. It is no wonder, therefore, that the evolutionists of our day should claim to have given a wholly new character to ethical enquiries. In Hume's time a philosopher who denied the in-nateness of the moral sentiments, and held that they must have a natural history, had only the limits of the individual life within which to trace this history. These limits did not give room enough for even a plausible derivation of moral interests from animal wants. It is otherwise when the history may be supposed to range over an indefinite number of generations. The doctrine of hereditary transmission, it is held, explains to us how susceptibilities of pleasure and pain, of desire and aver-sion, of hope and fear, may be handed down with gradually

accumulated modifications which in time attain the full measure
of the difference between the moral man and the greater ape.
Through long ages of interaction between the human organism
and the social medium in which it lives, there has been developed that 'sensibility of principle which feels a stain like
a wound;' that faculty of moral intuition which not only pronounces unerringly on the social tendencies of the commoner
forms of human action, but enables us in some measure to see
ourselves as others see us; that civil spirit through which the
promptings of personal passion are controlled even in the individual by the larger vision and calmer interest of society.

Thus it would seem that for the barren speculation of the old
metaphysical ethics we should seek a substitute in a scientific
' Cultur-geschichte;' in a natural history of man conducted on
the same method as an enquiry into any other form of life
which cannot be reduced to the operation of strictly mechanical
laws. For the later stages of this history we have, of course,
abundant materials in the actual monuments of human culture
—linguistic, literary, and legal—and these, the physiologist may
say, have yet to be considered in connexion with the data which
his own science furnishes. It is true that, however far they
carry us back, however great the variations of moral sentiment
to which they testify, they do not bring us to a state of things
in which the essential conditions of that sentiment were absent.
The most primitive man they exhibit to us is already conscious
of his own good as conditioned by that of others, already capable
of recognising an obligation. But the theory of descent and
evolution opens up a vista of possibilities beyond the facts, so
far ascertained, of human history, and suggests an enquiry into
the antecedents of the moralised man based on other data than
the records which he has left of himself. Such enquiry, it is
thought, will in time give us the means of reducing the moral
susceptibilities of man to the rank of ordinary physical facts,
parts of one system, and intelligible by the same methods, with
all the natural phenomena which we are learning to know. Man
will then have his ascertained place in nature, as perhaps the
noblest of the animals but an animal still.

6. When the moral sentiment has been explained on the principles of natural science, free-will is not likely to be regarded as

presenting any serious obstacle to the same mode of treatment. By those of our national philosophers who have asserted its existence, it has generally been understood as a faculty of determining action apart from determination by motives; as a power, distinct alike from reason and from desire, which chooses between motives without being itself dependent on any motive. So crude a notion must long ago have given way before the questions of science, if there had not been a practical conviction behind it which it failed fairly to interpret. What after all, it is asked, is any faculty but an hypostatised abstraction? A faculty is no more than a possibility. Whatever happens implies no doubt a possibility of its happening. Voluntary action implies a possibility of voluntary action, just as the motion of a billiard-ball implies a possibility of that motion; but the possibility in each is determined by definite conditions. In the case of the billiard-ball these conditions, or some of them, are so obvious that we do not think of treating the possibility of the ball's moving as a faculty inherent in the ball, and of ascribing the ball's motion to this faculty as its cause; although, as we know, when the causes of a motion are less apparent, the uninstructed are quite ready to ascribe it to a faculty or power in the moving body. In ascribing any voluntary action to a faculty in man we are doing, it is said, just the same as in ascribing any particular motion to a faculty in the moving body. The fact is the particular voluntary action, which must be possible, no doubt, or it would not be done, but of which the real possibility consists in the assemblage of conditions which make up its cause. To include any faculty of action among these is merely to express our ignorance of what they are or our unwillingness to examine them. Among them, it is true, is the wish which happens to be predominant in the agent at the moment of action; but this, too, has its definite conditions in the circumstances of the case and the motives operating on the agent. It may be owing to the character of the agent that one of these motives gets the upper hand; but his character again is only a name for an assemblage of conditions, of which it may be scarcely possible for us completely to trace the antecedents, but which we are not on that account justified in assigning to a cause that is no cause, but merely a verbal substantiation of the abstraction of our ignorance. Human freedom must be understood in some different sense from that with which our anthropologists are familiar, if it is to stand in the way of the scientific impulse to naturalise the moral man.

7. We will suppose then that a theory has been formed which professes to explain, on the method of a natural history conducted according to the principle of evolution, the process by which the human animal has come, according to the terminology in vogue, to exhibit the phenomena of a moral life—to have a conscience, to feel remorse, to pursue ideals, to be capable of education through appeals to the sense of honour and of shame, to be conscious of antagonism between the common and private good, and even sometimes to prefer the former. It has generally been expected of a moralist, however, that he should explain not only how men do act, but how they should act : and as a matter of fact we find that those who regard the process of man's natural development most strictly as a merely natural one are as forward as any to propound rules of living, to which they conceive that, according to their view of the influences which make him what he is, man *ought* to conform. The natural science of man is to them the basis of a practical art. They seek to discover what are the laws—the modes of operation of natural forces—under which we have come to be what we are, in order that they may counsel us how to seek our happiness by living according to those laws.

Now it is obvious that to a being who is simply a result of natural forces an injunction to conform to their laws is unmeaning. It implies that there is something in him independent of those forces, which may determine the relation in which he shall stand to them. A philosopher, then, who would reconstruct our ethical systems in conformity with the doctrines of evolution and descent, if he would be consistent, must deal less scrupulously with them than perhaps any one has yet been found to do. If he has the courage of his principles, having reduced the speculative part of them to a natural science, he must abolish the practical or preceptive part altogether. Instead, for instance, of telling men of a greatest sum of pleasures which they ought to seek, and which by acting in the light of a true insight into natural laws they may attain, he will content himself with ascer-

taining, so far as he can, whether such and such a temperament
under such and such circumstances yields more frequent, durable,
and intense pleasures than such another temperament under such
other circumstances. He will not mock the misery of him who
fails, nor flatter the self-complacency of him who prospers, by
speaking of a happiness that is to be obtained by conformity to
the laws of nature, when he knows that, according to his own
principles, it is a struggle for existence determined by those laws
which has brought the one to his wretchedness and the other to
his contentment. He will rather set himself to show how the
phraseology of 'ought' and 'ought not,' the belief in a good
attainable by all, the consciousness of something that should be
though it is not, may according to his philosophy be accounted
for. Nor, if he has persuaded himself that the human consciousness, as it is, can be physically accounted for, will he find
any further difficulty in thus explaining that language of moral
injunction which forms so large an element in its expression.
He will probably trace this language to the joint action of two
factors—to the habit of submission to the commands of a physical
or political superior, surviving the commands themselves and the
memory of them, combined with that constant though ineffectual wish for a condition of life other than his own, which is
natural to a being who looks before and after over perpetual
alternations of pleasure and pain.

8. The elimination of ethics, then, as a system of precepts, involves no intrinsic difficulties other than those involved in the
admission of a natural science that can account for the moralisation of man. The discovery, however, that our assertions of
moral obligation are merely the expression of an ineffectual wish
to be better off than we are, or are due to the survival of habits
originally enforced by physical fear, but of which the origin
is forgotten, is of a kind to give us pause. It logically carries
with it the conclusion, however the conclusion may be disguised,
that, in inciting ourselves or others to do anything because it
ought to be done, we are at best making use of a serviceable
illusion. And when this consequence is found to follow logically
from the conception of man as in his moral attributes a subject
of natural science, it may lead to a reconsideration of a doctrine
which would otherwise have been taken for granted as the most

important outcome of modern enlightenment. As the first charm of accounting for what has previously seemed the mystery of our moral nature passes away, and the spirit of criticism returns, we cannot but enquire whether a being that was merely a result of natural forces could form a theory of those forces as explaining himself. We have to return once more to that analysis of the conditions of knowledge, which forms the basis of all Critical Philosophy whether called by the name of Kant or no, and to ask whether the experience of connected matters of fact, which in its methodical expression we call science, does not presuppose a principle which is not itself any one or number of such matters of fact, or their result.

Can the knowledge of nature be itself a part or product of nature, in that sense of nature in which it is said to be an object of knowledge? This is our first question. If it is answered in the negative, we shall at least have satisfied ourselves that man, in respect of the function called knowledge, is not merely a child of nature. We shall have ascertained the presence in him of a principle not natural, and a specific function of this principle in rendering knowledge possible. The way will then be so far cleared for the further question which leads us, in the language of Kant, from the Critique of Speculative to that of Practical Reason: the question whether the same principle has not another expression than that which appears in the determination of experience and through it in our knowledge of a world— an expression which consists in the consciousness of a moral ideal and the determination of human action thereby.

BOOK I.

METAPHYSICS OF KNOWLEDGE.

CHAPTER I.

THE SPIRITUAL PRINCIPLE IN KNOWLEDGE AND IN NATURE.

9. THE question Can the knowledge of nature be itself a part or product of nature? must not be confused with that commonly supposed to be at issue between spiritualists and materialists. It is one which equally remains to be put, in whatever way we understand the relation between body and mind. We may have admitted most unreservedly that all the so-called functions of the soul are materially conditioned, but the question how there come to be for us those objects of consciousness, called matter and motion, on which we suppose the operations of sense and desire and thought to be dependent, will still remain to be answered. If it could be admitted that matter and motion had an existence *in themselves*, or otherwise than as related to a consciousness, it would still not be by *such* matter and motion, but by the matter and motion which we know, that the functions of the soul, or anything else, can for us be explained. Nothing can be known by help of reference to the unknown. But matter and motion, just so far as known, consist in, or are determined by, relations between the objects of that connected consciousness which we call experience. If we take any definition of matter, any account of its 'necessary qualities,' and abstract from it all that consists in a statement of relations between facts in the way of feeling, or between objects that we present to ourselves as sources of feeling, we shall find that there is nothing left. Motion, in like manner, has no meaning except such as is derived from a synthesis of the different

positions successively held by one and the same body; and we shall try in vain to render an account to ourselves of position or succession, of a body or its identity, except as expressing relations of what is contained in experience, through which alone that content possesses a definite character and becomes a connected whole.

What then is the source of these relations, as relations of the experienced, in other words, of that which exists for consciousness? What is the principle of union which renders them possible? Clearly it cannot itself be conditioned by any of the relations which result from its combining and unifying action. Being that which so organises experience that the relations expressed by our definitions of matter and motion arise therein, it cannot itself be determined by those relations. It cannot be a matter or motion. However rigidly, therefore, we may exclude from our explanations of phenomena all causes that are not reducible to matter and motion, however fully we may admit that the nature which we know or may know is knowable only under strictly physical laws, we are none the less in effect asserting the existence of something which, as the source of a connected experience, renders both the nature that we know and our knowledge of it possible, but is not itself physically conditioned. We may decide all the questions that have been debated between materialists and spiritualists as to the explanation of particular facts in favour of the former, but the possibility of explaining them at all will still remain to be explained. We shall still be logically bound to admit that in a man who can know a nature—for whom there is a 'cosmos of experience [1]'—there is a principle which is not natural and which cannot without a ὕστερον πρότερον be explained as we explain the facts of nature.

10. There are certain accepted doctrines of modern philosophy—*e.g.*, that knowledge is only of phenomena, not of anything unrelated to consciousness, and that object and subject are correlative—from which this conclusion seems to follow so inevitably, that any one who has adopted it must enquire anxiously why it is not more generally recognised. If nothing can enter into knowledge that is unrelated to consciousness; if

---

[1] I borrow the phrase from Mr. G. H. Lewes.

relation to a subject is necessary to make an object, so that an object which no consciousness presented to itself would not be an object at all; it is as difficult to see how the principle of unity, through which phenomena become the connected system called the world of experience, can be found elsewhere than in consciousness, as it is to see how the consciousness exercising such a function can be a part of the world which it thus at least co-operates in making; how it can be a phenomenon among the phenomena which it unites into a knowledge. Why then do our most enlightened interpreters of nature take it as a matter of course that the principle of unity in the world of our experience is something which, whatever else it is—and they can say nothing else of it—is at any rate the negation of consciousness, and that consciousness itself is a phenomenon or group of phenomena in which this ' nature' exhibits itself or results? And why is it that, when we have professedly discarded this doctrine, we still find it to a great extent controlling our ordinary thoughts? There must be reasons for this inconsistency, which should be duly considered if we would understand what we are about in maintaining that there is a sense in which man is related to nature as its author, as well as one in which he is related to it as its child.

11. The reader is probably acquainted with Kant's dictum that ' the understanding makes nature.' It gives no doubt a somewhat startling expression to the revolution in philosophy which Kant believed himself to have introduced, and which he compared to the change effected by the Copernican theory in men's conception of the relative positions of the earth and the sun. When we enquire, however, into the precise sense in which Kant used the expression, we find that its meaning is subject to a qualification which testifies to the difficulty experienced by Kant himself in carrying out the doctrine which the words seemed to convey. ' Macht zwar der Verstand die Natur, aber er schafft sie nicht.' The understanding ' makes' nature, but out of a material which it does not make. That material, according to Kant, consists in phenomena or 'data' of sensibility, given under the so-called forms of intuition, space and time. This apparent ascription of nature to a twofold origin—an origin in understanding in respect of its form as a nature, as a single

system of experience; an origin elsewhere in respect of the 'matter' which through the action of understanding becomes a nature—cannot but strike us as unsatisfactory. Perhaps it may not be a doctrine in which we can permanently acquiesce, but meanwhile it represents fairly enough on its two sides the considerations which on the one hand lead us to regard nature as existing only in relation to thought, and those on the other which seem obstinately opposed to such a view.

12. To say with Kant that the understanding is the principle of objectivity, that only through understanding is there for us an objective world, is sure to seem at first sight the extreme of perversity. We have come to think of the understanding as specially an agency of our own, and of the objective world as specially that which is presented to us independently of any such agency; as that which we find and do not make, and by which we have to correct the fictions of our own minds. When we ask, however, whether any impression is or represents anything 'real and objective,' what exactly does the question mean, and how do we set about answering it? It is not equivalent to a question whether a feeling is felt. Some feeling must be felt in order to the possibility of the question being raised at all. It is a question whether a given feeling is what it is taken to be; or, in other words, whether it is related as it seems to be related. It may be objected indeed that, though *some* feeling or other must be felt in order to give any meaning to the question as to the objectivity of the impression or its correspondence with reality, yet still this question may and often does mean merely whether a *particular* feeling is felt. This is true; but a particular feeling is a feeling related in a certain way, and the question whether a particular feeling is really felt is always translatable into the form given—Is a feeling, which is undoubtedly felt, really related as some one thinking about it takes it to be? If an engine-driver, under certain conditions, permanent with him or temporary, 'sees a signal wrong,' as we say, his disordered vision has its own reality just as much as if he saw right. There are relations between combinations of moving particles on the one side and his visual organs on the other, between the present state of the latter and

certain determining conditions, between the immediate sensible
effect and the secondary impressions which it in turn excites,
as full and definite—with sufficient enquiry and opportunity, as
ascertainable—as in any case of normal vision. There is as
much reality in the one case as in the other, but it is not the
same reality: *i.e.*, it does not consist in the same relations. The
engine-driver mistakes the effect of one set of relations for that
of another, one reality for another, and hence his error in action.
He may be quite innocent of a scientific theory of vision, but
he objectifies his sensations. He interprets them as related in
a certain way, and as always the same in the same relations; or,
to use an equivalent but more familiar expression, as signs of
objects from which he distinguishes his feelings and by which
he explains them. Were this not the case, his vision might be
normal or abnormal, but he would be incapable of mistaking
one kind of reality for another, since he would have no conception of reality at all.

13. The terms 'real' and 'objective,' then, have no meaning
except for a consciousness which presents its experiences to itself
as determined by relations, and at the same time conceives a
single and unalterable order of relations determining them, with
which its temporary presentation, as each experience occurs, of
the relations determining it may be contrasted. For such a
consciousness, perpetually altering its views of the relations
determining any experience under the necessity of combining
them in one system with other recognised relations, and for
such a consciousness only, there is significance in the judgment
that any experience seems to be so and so, *i.e.*, to be related in
a certain way, but really is otherwise related. We shall have
afterwards [§ 19 and foll.] to consider the question whether the
consciousness, for which alone this contrast of the real and the
apparent is possible, has anything to do with the establishment
of the relations in which it conceives reality to consist—whether
the conception of reality has any identity with the act by which
reality is constituted. But even if this latter question is waived
or answered in the negative, there will still be an important
sense in which understanding, or consciousness as acting in the
manner described, may be said to be the principle of objectivity.
It will be through it that there is *for us* an objective world;

through it that we *conceive* an order of nature, with the unity of which we must reconcile our interpretations of phenomena, if they are to be other than 'subjective' illusions.

14. Of course it may very well be that many a man would disclaim any such conception, who is yet constantly acting upon the distinction between what he believes to be mere appearance and what he believes to be reality. But want of familiarity with the abstract expression of a conception, want of ability to analyse it, is no evidence that the conception is inoperative upon the experience of the person who, from this want of familiarity or ability, would say, if he were asked, that he had it not or knew not what it meant. The proof of the necessity of certain ideas has never been supposed, by any one who knew what he was about, to rest upon the fact that every one was aware of having them. Such a proof, to say nothing of the well-worked appeal to savages or the uneducated, would be at the mercy of every lively gentleman who was pleased to say that he searched his breast for such ideas in vain. The necessity of a conception, as distinct from the logical (or rather rhetorical) necessity of a conclusion contained in premisses already conceded, means that it is necessary to the experience without which there would not for us be a world at all; and there can be neither proof nor disproof of such necessity as is claimed for any conception, but through analysis of the conditions which render this experience possible. Unless the accuracy or sufficiency of the analysis can be disputed, the necessary character of the ideas which it exhibits as operative in the formation of experience, is unaffected by the inability of any one to recognise them in that abstract form to which the analysis reduces them, but which, just because they are operative in a concrete experience, is not the form of their familiar use.

Thus a man who is quite at home with the distinction between facts and fancies may think it strange to be told that the distinction implies a conception of the world as a single system of relations; that this is the conception on the strength of which he constantly sets aside as fancy what he had taken to be fact, because he finds that the supposed relations, which for him formed the nature of the fact, are not such as can be combined with others that he recognises in one intelligible system. Such language may convey no meaning to him, but the question will still remain whether upon reflection the distinction can be otherwise accounted for. When we analyse our idea of matter of fact, can we express it except as an idea of a relation which is always the same between the same objects; or our idea of an object except as that which is always the same in the same relations? And does not each expression imply the idea of a world as a single and eternal system of related elements, which may be related with endless diversity but must *be* related still? If we may properly call the consciousness which yields this idea 'understanding,' are we not entitled to say that understanding is the source of there being for us an objective world, that it is the principle of objectivity?

15. So far we have only reached the conclusion that a conception, to which understanding is related as faculty to function, is the condition of our ability to distinguish a real from the unreal, matter of fact from illusion. It will be said perhaps that so much pains need not have been spent on establishing a proposition which in effect merely tells us that without a conception of an order of nature we could not conceive an order of nature. Is not this, it may be asked, either an identical proposition or untrue—an identical proposition, if understood strictly as thus put; untrue, if taken to mean that the conception of an order of nature does not admit of being generated out of materials other than itself? Now it is just the difficulties in the way of explaining the origin of the conception in question out of anything else than judgments which presuppose it, that we wish to exhibit. They are the difficulties which beset any theory that would treat the knowledge of nature as itself the result of natural processes. It is through *experience* that every such theory must suppose the resulting knowledge to be produced. But experience, as most students of philosophy must now be aware, is a term used in very different senses. In this case an experience which is to yield the required result must not be merely an experience in the sense in which, for instance, a plant might be said to experience a succession of atmospheric or chemical changes, or in which we ourselves pass through a definite physical experience during sleep or in respect of the

numberless events which affect us but of which we are not aware. Such an experience may no doubt gradually alter to any extent the mode in which the physical organism reacts upon stimulus. It may be the condition of its becoming organic to intellectual processes, but between it and experience of the kind which is to yield a knowledge of nature there is a chasm which no one, except by confusion of speech, has attempted to fill. Or to speak more precisely, between the two senses of experience there is all the difference that exists between change and consciousness of change.

16. Experience of the latter kind must be experience of matters of fact *recognised as such*. It is possible, no doubt, to imagine a psychological history of this experience, and to trace it back to a stage in which the distinction between fact and fancy is not yet formally recognised. But there is a limit to this process. An experience which distinguishes fact from fancy cannot be developed out of one which is not, in some form or other, a consciousness of events as related or as a series of changes. It has commonly, and with much probability, been held that the occurrence of the unexpected, by exciting distrust in previously established associations of ideas, has at any rate a large share in generating the distinction of what seems from what is. But the shock of surprise is one thing, the correction of a belief quite another. Unless there were already a consciousness alike of the events, of which the ideas have become associated, as a related series, and of the newly observed event as a member of the same, the unfamiliar event might cause a disturbance of the nerves or the 'psychoplasm,' but there would neither be an incorrect belief as to an order of events to be corrected by it, nor any such correlation of the newly observed event with what had been observed before as could suggest a correction. But a consciousness of events as a related series—experience in the most elementary form in which it can be the beginning of knowledge—has not any element of identity with, and therefore cannot properly be said to be developed out of, a mere series of related events, of successive modifications of body or soul, such as is experience in the former of the senses spoken of. No one and no number of a series of related events can be the consciousness of the series as related. Nor can any product

of the series be so either. Even if this product could be anything else than a further event, it could at any rate only be something that supervenes at a certain stage upon such of the events as have so far elapsed. But a consciousness of certain events cannot be anything that thus succeeds them. It must be equally present to all the events of which it is the consciousness. For this reason an intelligent experience, or experience as the source of knowledge, can neither be constituted by events of which it is the experience, nor be a product of them.

17. 'Perhaps not,' it may be replied, 'but may it not be a product of *previous* events?' If it is so, a series of events of which there is no conscious experience must be supposed to produce a consciousness of another series. On any other supposition the difficulty is only postponed. For if the series of events which produces a certain consciousness of other events is one of which there *is* a consciousness, this consciousness, not being explicable as the product of the events of which it is the consciousness, will have in turn to be referred to a prior series of events; and ultimately there will be no alternative between the admission of a consciousness which is not a product of events at all and the supposition stated—the supposition that the primary consciousness of events results from a series of events of which there is no consciousness. But this supposition, when we think of it, turns out to be a concatenation of words to which no possible connexion of ideas corresponds. It asserts a relation of cause and effect, in which the supposed cause lacks all the characteristics of a cause. It may be questioned whether we can admit anything as a cause which does not explain its supposed effect, or is not equivalent to the conditions into which the effect may be analysed. But granting that we may, a cause must at least be that to which experience testifies as the uniform antecedent of the effect. Now a series of events of which there is no consciousness is certainly not a set of conditions into which consciousness can be analysed. And as little can it be an antecedent uniformly associated with consciousness in experience, for events of which there is no consciousness cannot be within experience at all.

18. It seems necessary, then, to admit that experience, in the sense of a consciousness of events as a related series—and in

Knowledge not a natural event

no other sense can it help to account for the knowledge of an order of nature—cannot be explained by any natural history, properly so called. It is not a product of a series of events. It does not arise out of materials other than itself. It is not developed by a natural process out of other forms of natural existence. Given such a consciousness, the scientific conception of nature, no less than the everyday distinction between fact and fancy, between objective reality and subjective illusion, can be exhibited as a development of it, for there is an assignable element of identity between the two. But between the consciousness itself on the one hand, and on the other anything determined by the relations under which a nature is presented to consciousness, no process of development, because no community, can be really traced. Nature, with all that belongs to it, is a process of change: change on a uniform method, no doubt, but change still. All the relations under which we know it are relations in the way of change or by which change is determined. But neither can any process of change yield a consciousness of itself, which, in order to be a consciousness of the change, must be equally present to all stages of the change; nor can any consciousness of change, since the whole of it must be present at once, be itself a process of change. There may be a change into a state of consciousness of change, and a change out of it, on the part of this man or that; but within the consciousness itself there can be no change, because no relation of before and after, of here and there, between its constituent members—between the presentation, for instance, of point A and that of point B in the process which forms the object of the consciousness.

19. From the above considerations thus much at any rate would seem to follow: that a form of consciousness, which we cannot explain as of natural origin, is necessary to our conceiving an order of nature, an objective world of fact from which illusion may be distinguished. In other words, an understanding—for that term seems as fit as any other to denote the principle of consciousness in question—irreducible to anything else, 'makes nature' for us, in the sense of enabling us to conceive that there is such a thing. Now that which the understanding thus pre-

sents to itself consists, as we have seen, in certain relations regarded as forming a single system. The next question, then,
will be whether understanding can be held to 'make nature' in
the further sense that it is the source, or at any rate a condition,
of there being these relations. If it cannot, we are left in the
awkward position of having to suppose that, while the conception of an order of nature on the one side, and that order itself
on the other, are of different and independent origin, there is
yet some unaccountable pre-established harmony through which
there comes to be such an order corresponding to our conception
of it. This indeed might be urged as a reason for seeking some
way of escape from the conclusion at which we have just arrived.
But before we renew an attempt which has often been made and
failed, let us see whether the objections to the other alternative—to the view that the understanding which presents an
order of nature to us is in principle one with an understanding
which constitutes that order itself—have really the cogency
which common-sense seems to ascribe to them.

20. The traditional philosophy of common-sense, we shall find,
speaks upon the point with an ambiguity which affords a presumption of its involving more difficulty than might at first
sight appear. No one is more emphatic than Locke in opposing
what is real to what we 'make for ourselves,' the work of nature
to the work of the mind. Simple ideas or sensations we certainly do not 'make for ourselves.' They therefore and the
matter supposed to cause them are, according to Locke, real[1].
But relations are neither simple ideas nor their material arche-
types. They therefore, as Locke explicitly holds, fall under the
head of the work of the mind, which is opposed to the real[2].
But if we take him at his word and exclude from what we have
considered real all qualities constituted by relation, we find that
none are left. Without relation any simple idea would be un-
distinguished from other simple ideas, undetermined by its surroundings in the cosmos of experience. It would thus be unqualified itself, and consequently could afford no qualification of
the material archetype, which yet according to Locke we only
know through it or, if otherwise, as the subject of those 'primary

[1] Essay concerning Human Understanding, II. xii. 1.
[2] Ibid. II. xxv. 8.

qualities' which demonstrably consist in relations[1]. In short, the admission of the antithesis between the real and the work of the mind, and the admission that relation is the work of the mind, put together, involve the conclusion that nothing is real of which anything can be said.

Our ordinary way out of the difficulty consists in keeping the two admissions apart, without, however, surrendering either. We maintain the opposition between the real and the work of the mind exactly as it was asserted by Locke; and if we are less explicit in accounting relations to be the work of the mind, it is not because we have any theory of the real which more logically admits them than does Locke's. Yet we have no scruple in accepting duly verified knowledge as representing reality, though what is known consists in nothing else than relations. We neither ask ourselves how it can be that a knowledge of relations should be a knowledge of reality, if the real is genuinely simple sensation or that which copies itself in simple sensation, nor what other account we can give of the real without qualifying the antithesis between the work of the mind and it. It is in fact from our adoption of this antithesis that we come to accept that identification of the real with simple sensation or its archetype which, as Locke was aware, implies the unreality of relations. But when in our processes of knowledge we have virtually recognised relations as constituting the very essence of reality, we do not reconsider our definition of the real in the light of this recognition. We do not lay our procedure in what we regard as knowledge of the real alongside Locke's view of the real, which is also ours, so as to ask whether they are consistent with each other. And hence we are not led to call in question the antithesis on which that view depends.

21. As it is a serious matter, however, to accept a view of the real which such a thinker as Locke could not reconcile with the reality of relations, and which logically implies that knowledge is not of the real; and as on the other hand there is something in the opposition between the real and the work of the mind which seems to satisfy an imperative demand of common-sense; it becomes important to enquire whether we interpret that de-

[1] Essay concerning Human Understanding, II. viii. 15 and 23; xxx. 2.

mand aright. Is there not a conception of the real behind the opposition in question, which seems to require us to accept it, but which in truth we misinterpret in doing so?

We constantly find Locke falling back on the consideration that of simple ideas ' we cannot *make* one to ourselves.' They ' force themselves upon us whether we will or no.' It is this which entitles them in his eyes to be accounted real. ' The work of the mind,' on the other hand, he considers arbitrary. A man has but to think, and he can make ideas of relation for himself as he pleases. Locke thus indicates what we may call the operative conception—operative as governing the action of our intelligence—which underlies the opposition between the real and the work of the mind. This is the conception which we have described already as that of a single and unalterable system of relations. It is not the work of the mind, as such, that we instinctively oppose to the real, but the work of the mind as assumed to be arbitrary and irregularly changeable.

22. In truth, however, there is no such thing. The very question, What is the real?—which we seem to answer by help of this opposition—is a misleading one, so far as it implies that there is something else from which the real can be distinguished. We are apt to make merry over the crude logic of Plato in supposing that there are objects, described as μὴ ὄντα, which stand in the same relation to ignorance as τὰ ὄντα to knowledge, and other objects, described as τὰ μεταξύ, which stand in a corresponding relation to mere opinion. Of this fallacy, as of most others that are to be found in him, Plato himself supplies the correction, but much of our language about the real implies that we are ourselves its victims. If there is a valid opposition between the work of the mind and something else which is not the work of the mind, the one must still be just as real as the other. Of two alternatives, one. Either ' the work of the mind ' is a name for nothing, expressing a mere privation or indeterminateness, a mere absence of qualities,—in which case nothing is conveyed by the proposition which opposes the real or anything else to it: or, on the other hand, if it has qualities and relations of its own, then it is just as real as anything else. Through not understanding the relations which determine the one kind of object—that ascribed to the work of the mind—as distinct from

those which determine the other—that ascribed to some other agency—we may confuse the two kinds of object. We may take what is really of the one kind to be really of the other. But this is not a confusion of the real with the unreal. The very confusion itself, the mistake of supposing what is related in one way to be related in another, has its own reality. It has its history, its place in the development of a man's mind, its causes and effects; and, as so determined, it is as real as anything else.

23. It is thus in vain that we seek to define the real by finding, either in the work of the mind or elsewhere, an unreal to which it may be opposed. Is there, then, no meaning in an opposition which is constantly on our tongues? Undoubtedly that which any event seems to us to be may be—nay always is—more or less different from what it really is. The relations by which we judge it to be determined are not, or at any rate fall short of, those by which it is really determined. But this is a distinction between one particular reality and another; not between a real, as such or as a whole, and an unreal, as such or as a whole. The illusive appearance, as opposed to the reality, of any event is what *that* event really is not; but at the same time it really is something. It is real, not indeed with the particular reality which the subject of the illusion ascribes to it, but with a reality which a superior intelligence might understand. The relations by which, in a false belief as to a matter of fact, we suppose the event to be determined, are not non-existent. They are really objects of a conceiving consciousness. As arising out of the action of such a consciousness, as constituents of a world which it presents to itself, they are no less real than are the actual conditions of the event which is thought to be, but is not really, determined by them. It is when we reflect on the judgments in which we are perpetually deciding that what has previously been taken to be the reality of a particular event is a mere appearance, *i. e.*, not the reality of that particular event—or rather when we reflect on the language in which those judgments have been expressed—that we come to speak of the real, as an abstract universal, in contrast with another abstract universal, the unreal. Thus for a contrast which is in truth a contrast between two acts of judgment—the act of judging an event

to be determined by certain relations which, according to the order of the universe, do determine it, and that of judging it to be determined by relations other than these—we substitute another, which exists merely in words, but to which we fancy that we give a meaning by identifying the unreal with the work of the mind, as opposed to a real which has some other origin, we cannot say what.

24. What we have so far sought to show has been (1), generally, that an attempt to define the real by distinction from anything else is necessarily futile—the result of a false abstraction from the distinction between the real nature of one event or object and that of another—and (2), specially, that the antithesis between the real and the work of the mind is invalid, not because the real is the work of the mind—whether it is so or not we have yet to enquire—but because the work of the mind is real. The 'mere idea' of a hundred thalers, to use the familiar instance, is no doubt quite different from the possession of them, not because it is unreal, but because the relations which form the real nature of the idea are different from those which form the real nature of the possession.

So much it was necessary to show, in order that the enquiry, whether it is due to 'understanding' not merely that we are able to conceive a nature but that there is such a thing as nature at all, might not be prejudiced by a preconception which would make it seem equivalent to an enquiry whether the real could be the work of the unreal. If now from the futile question, What is the real? which we can only answer by saying that the real is everything, we pass to one more hopeful—How do we decide whether any particular event or object is really what it seems to be, or whether our belief about it is true?—the answer must be that we do so by testing the unalterableness of the qualities which we ascribe to it, or which form its apparent nature. A certain hill appears to-day to be near: yesterday under different conditions of atmosphere it appeared to be remote. But the real nature of the event which took place in yesterday's appearance cannot, we judge, thus change. What it was really, it was unalterably. There may have been a change from that appearance to another, but not a change of or in whatever was the reality of the appearance. The event of yesterday's appearance, then, must have been determined by conditions other than those which determine to-day's. But if both appearances depended solely on the position of the hill, they would be determined by the same conditions. Therefore we must have been wrong in believing the hill to be so remote as we believed it to be yesterday, or in believing it to be so near as we believed it to be to-day, or in both beliefs: wrong in respect of the relation which we supposed to exist between the several appearances and the distance of the hill.

25. With sufficient time and command of detail it would not be difficult to show how the conviction here illustrated, that whatever anything is really it is unalterably, regulates equally our most primitive and our most developed judgments of reality —the every-day supposition of there being a multitude of separate things which remain the same in themselves while their appearances to us alter, and the scientific quest for uniformity or unalterableness in a law of universal change. Through a slight confusion of thought and expression, this conviction may issue either in the sensational atomism of Locke or in the material atomism of popular science. A sensation is the unalterable effect of its conditions, whatever those conditions may be. It is unalterably related to other sensations. Our opinion about its conditions or relations may vary, but not the conditions or relations themselves, or the sensation determined by them. Hence when a man looks into his breast, as Locke bids him do, simple feelings—feelings apart from intellectual interpretations and combinations of them—seem alone unalterable in contrast with our judgments about them. In truth the unalterableness belongs not to any simple feeling, for our feelings change every moment upon us, but, as we have said, to the relation between it and its conditions or between it and other feelings; and such a relation is neither itself a feeling nor represented in our consciousness by a feeling. This distinction, however, is overlooked. The unalterableness of the fact that a certain feeling is felt under certain conditions, is ascribed to the simple feeling, or simple idea, as such: and unalterableness being the test by which we ascertain whether what we have believed to be the nature of any event is really so or not, the simple feeling, which by itself cannot properly be said to

be really anything, comes to be regarded either as alone real, according to the ideal form of sensationalism, or as alone representing an external reality, according to the materialistic form of the same doctrine.

On the other hand, reflection upon the 'perpetual flux' of sensation suggests the view that it is not real in the same sense as its material conditions. The old dictum ascribed to Democritus—νόμῳ γλυκὺ καὶ νόμῳ πικρὸν, νόμῳ θερμὸν, νόμῳ ψυχρόν, νόμῳ χροιή· ἐτεῇ δὲ ἄτομα καὶ κενόν [1]—expresses a way of thinking into which we often fall. The reality which in truth lies in the relations, according to one law or system of relation, between feelings and their material conditions—not in the material conditions abstracted from the feelings any more than in the feelings abstracted from their material conditions—we are apt to ascribe exclusively to the latter. We think obscurely of matter and motion as real in some way in which nothing else is. Nor do we stop here. The demand for unalterableness in what we believe to be real, when once we are off the right track of seeking it in a uniform law of change, leads us to suppose that the 'reality of things' is only reached when we have penetrated to atoms which in all changes of their motion and distribution remain intrinsically the same.

26. Let us consider now how we stand. We have rejected the question, What is or constitutes the real? as intrinsically unmeaning, because it could only be answered by a distinction which would imply that there was something unreal. The question arises, we have seen, out of an abstraction from our constant enquiry into the real nature of this or that particular appearance or event—an enquiry in which we always seek for an unchanging relation between the appearance and its conditions, or again for an unchanging relation between these and certain other conditions. The complete determination of an event it may be impossible for our intelligence to arrive at. There may always remain unascertained conditions which may render the relation between an appearance and such conditions of it as we know, liable to change. But that there *is* an un-

---

[1] Sweet, bitter, hot, cold, colour, are by convention; only atoms and void are real.

alterable order of relations, if we could only find it out, is the presupposition of all our enquiry into the real nature of appearances; and such unalterableness implies their inclusion in one system which leaves nothing outside itself. Are we then entitled to ask—and if so, are we able to answer—the further question, What is implied in there being such a single, all-inclusive, system of relations? or, What is the condition of its possibility? If this question can be answered, the condition ascertained will be the condition of there being a nature and of anything being real, in the only intelligible sense that we can attach to the words 'nature' and 'real.' It would no doubt still be open to the sceptic, should this result be attained, to suggest that the validity of our conclusion, upon our own showing, depends upon there really being such an order of nature as our quest of knowledge supposes there to be, which remains unproven. But as the sceptic, in order to give his language a meaning, must necessarily make the same supposition—as he can give no meaning to reality but the one explained—his suggestion that there really may not be such an order of nature is one that conveys nothing at all.

27. First, then, is there any meaning in the question just put? Having set aside as unmeaning the question, What is the real? can we be entitled to ask, What is implied in there being a nature of things? If the former question would have been only answerable on the self-contradictory supposition of there really being something other than the real from which it could be distinguished, will not the latter in like manner be only answerable on the equally impossible supposition of there being something outside the nature of things, outside the one all-inclusive system of relations, by reference to which this nature or system can be explained? To this we reply that the question stated is or is not one that can be fitly asked, according as the conception of nature, of a single all-inclusive system of relations, is or is not one that can stand alone, is or is not one that requires something else to render it intelligible. To suppose that this 'something else,' if nature were found unthinkable without it, is related to those conditions, of which the relation to each other forms the system of nature, in the same way in which these are related to each other, would no doubt be in contradiction with

our account of this system as one and all-inclusive. It could not therefore be held to be related to them as, for instance, an invariable antecedent to an invariable sequent, or as one body to another outside it. But there would be no contradiction in admitting a principle which renders all relations possible, and is itself determined by none of them, if, on consideration of what is needed to constitute a system of relations, we found such a principle to be requisite.

28. This, then, is the consideration which we have now to undertake. Relation is to us such a familiar fact that we are apt to forget that it involves all the mystery, if it be a mystery, of the existence of many in one. Whether we say that a related thing is one in itself, manifold in respect of its relations, or that there is one relation between manifold things, *e.g.*, the relation of mutual attraction between bodies—and one expression or the other we must employ in stating the simplest facts—we are equally affirming the unity of the manifold. Abstract the many relations from the one thing, and there is nothing. They, being many, determine or constitute its definite unity. It is not the case that it first exists in its unity, and then is brought into various relations. Without the relations it would not exist at all. In like manner the one relation is a unity of the many things. They, in their manifold being, make the one relation. If these relations really exist, there is a real unity of the manifold, a real multiplicity of that which is one. But a plurality of things cannot of themselves unite in one relation, nor can a single thing of itself bring itself into a multitude of relations. It is true, as we have said, that the single things are nothing except as determined by relations which are the negation of their singleness, but they do not therefore cease to be single things. Their common being is not something into which their several existences disappear. On the contrary, if they did not survive in their singleness, there could be no relation between them—nothing but a blank featureless identity. There must, then, be something other than the manifold things themselves, which combines them without effacing their severalty. consciousness

29. With such a combining agency we are familiar as our intelligence. It is through it that the sensation of the present moment takes a character from comparison with the sensation

of a moment ago, and that the occurrence, consisting in the transition from one to the other, is presented to us. It is essential to the comparison and to the character which the sensations acquire from the comparison, essential, too, to their forming an observable event or succession, that one should not be fused with the other, that the distinct being of each should be maintained. On the other hand, in the relation to which their distinctness is thus necessary they are at the same time united. But if it were not for the action of something which is not either of them or both together, there would be no alternative between their separateness and their fusion. One might give place to the other, or both together might be combined into a third; but a unity in which their distinctness is preserved could not be constituted without the relating act of an intelligence which does not blend with either.

The above is an instance of relation between sensations which, as brought into relation by intelligence, become sensible objects or events. But the same or an analogous action is necessary to account for any relation whatever—for a relation between material atoms as much as any other. Either then we must deny the reality of relations altogether and treat them as fictions of our combining intelligence; or we must hold that, being the product of our combining intelligence, they are yet 'empirically real' on the ground that our intelligence is a factor in the real of experience; or if we suppose them to be real otherwise than merely as for us, otherwise than in the 'cosmos of our experience,' we must recognise as the condition of this reality the action of some unifying principle analogous to that of our understanding.

30. As we have seen, the first of these alternative views, if consistently carried out, will not allow us to regard anything as real of which anything can be said, since all predication is founded on relation of some kind. It therefore naturally leads to the second. All that we in fact count real turns out to be determined by relations. Feeling may be the revelation or the test of the real, but it must be feeling in certain relations, or it neither reveals nor tests anything. Thus we are obliged to recognise a reality, at least of that kind which in our every-day knowledge and action we distinguish from illusion, in what is

yet the work of the mind, or at any rate must be held to be so until relations can be accounted for without a relating act or that act referred to something else than the mind. Hence with those who adhere to the opposition between the real and the work of the mind, and who at the same time cannot ignore the work of the mind in the constitution of relations, there arises a distinction between reality in some absolute sense—the reality of 'things-in-themselves,' which are supposed to be wholly exempt from any qualification through relating acts of the mind, but of which, for that reason, nothing can be known or said—and the 'empirical' reality of that which we distinguish from illusion, as standing in definite relations to the universe of our experience.

31. This distinction governs the theory of Kant. It is more easy to point out the embarrassments and inconsistencies into which it leads him, than to get rid of the distinction itself. Ordinary criticism of Kant, indeed, has not taken much heed of the distinction or of its perplexing results. It has been too busy in refuting his doctrine that 'laws of nature' are derived from understanding, to enquire closely into his view of the relation between nature, in his sense of the term, and 'things-in-themselves.' It has been gaining apparent triumphs, due to a misunderstanding of the question at issue, over the strongest part of his system, while it has left the weakest unassailed. There have been abundant proofs of what was not in dispute, that our knowledge of laws of nature is the result of experience; but the question whether phenomena could be so related as to constitute the nature which is the object of our experience without the unifying action of understanding is seldom even touched. Given an experience of phenomena related to each other in one system—so related that, whatever an object is really, or according to the fulness of its relations, it is unalterably—it is easy to show that our knowledge of laws of nature is derived from it. Such experience in its most elementary form is already implicitly a knowledge that there are laws of nature, and only needs to be reflected on in order to become so explicitly. When it has become so explicitly, the development of the experience—through cognisance of relations of which there has previously been no experience, or of which the experience

has not been reflected on—becomes a growing knowledge of
what the laws of nature in particular are.

But the derivation of knowledge from an experience of unalterably related phenomena is its derivation from objects unalterably related in consciousness. If the relation of the objects
were not a relation of them in consciousness, there would be no
experience of it. The question then arises how a succession
of feelings becomes such a relation of objects in consciousness. If a relation of objects existed or could be known to exist
otherwise than for consciousness, this would not help to account
for what has to be accounted for, which is wholly a process of
consciousness. The feelings which succeed each other are no
doubt due to certain related conditions, which are not feelings.
But granting for the moment that these conditions and their
relation exist independently of consciousness, in accounting for
a multitude of feelings they do not account for the experience
of related objects. Of two objects which form the terms of a
relation one cannot exist as so related without the other, and
therefore cannot exist before or after the other. For this reason
the objects between which a relation subsists, even a relation
of succession, are, just so far as related, not successive. In
other words, a succession always implies something else than
the terms of the succession, and that a 'something else' which
can simultaneously present to itself objects as existing not
simultaneously but one before the other.

32. Thus, in order that successive feelings may be related
objects of experience, even objects related in the way of succession, there must be in consciousness an agent which distinguishes
itself from the feelings, uniting them in their severalty, making
them equally present in their succession. And so far from this
agent being reducible to, or derivable from, a succession of
feelings, it is the condition of there being such a succession;
the condition of the existence of that relation between feelings,
as also of those other relations which are not indeed relations
between feelings, but which, if they are matter of experience,
must have their being in consciousness. If there is such a
thing as a connected experience of related objects, there must
be operative in consciousness a unifying principle, which not
only presents related objects to itself, but at once renders them

objects and unites them in relation to each other by this act of presentation; and which is single throughout the experience. The unity of this principle must be correlative to the unity of the experience. If all possible experience of related objects— the experience of a thousand years ago and the experience of to-day, the experience which I have here and that which I might have in any other region of space—forms a single system; if there can be no such thing as an experience of unrelated objects; then there must be a corresponding singleness in that principle of consciousness which forms the bond of relation between the objects.

33. It is such a principle that Kant speaks of sometimes as the 'synthetic unity of apperception,' sometimes simply as 'understanding.' For the reasons stated there seems no way of escape from the admission that it is, as he says, 'the basis of the necessary regularity of all phenomena in an experience[1]:' the basis, that is to say, not merely of our knowledge of uniform relations between phenomena, but of there being those uniform relations. The source of the relations, and the source of our knowledge of them, is one and the same. The question, how it is that the order of nature answers to our conception of it—or, as it is sometimes put, the question, whether nature really has, or, having, will continue to have, the uniformity which belongs to it in our conception—is answered by recognition of the fact that our conception of an order of nature, and the relations which form that order, have a common spiritual source. The uniformity of nature does not mean that its constituents are everywhere the same, but that they are everywhere related; not that 'the thing which has been is that which shall be,' but that whatever occurs is determined by relation to all that has occurred, and contributes to determine all that will occur. If nature means the system of objects of possible experience, such uniformity necessarily arises in it from the action of the same principle which is implied in there being any relation between the objects of experience at all. A relation not related to all other relations of which there can be experience, is an impossibility. It cannot exist except as constituted by the unifying

[1] Kant's Werke, ed. Rosenkranz, II. p. 114; ed. Hartenstein (1867), III. p. 585.

subject of all experienced relations, and this condition of its possibility implies its connexion with all other relations that are, or come to be, so constituted. Every real relation, therefore, that is also knowable, is a necessary or 'objective' or unalterable relation. It is a fact of which the existence is due to the action of that single subject of experience which is equally, and in the same way, the condition of all facts that can be experienced; a fact which thus, through that subject, stands in definite and unchangeable connexion with the universe of those facts, at once determining and determined by them.

34. The result of this view is to overcome the separation, which in our ordinary thinking we assume, between the faculty or capacity or subjective process of experience on the one side and the facts experienced on the other. In first reflecting on our knowledge of a world, we always regard the facts known as existing quite independently of the activity by means of which they are known. Since it is obvious that the facts of the world do not come into existence when this or that person becomes acquainted with them, so long as we conceive of no intellectual action but that which this or that person exercises, we necessarily regard the existence or occurrence of the facts as independent of intellectual action. Hence arises the antithesis between the known or knowable world and the subject capable of knowing it, as between two existences independent of each other, or of which the former is at any rate independent of the latter. The mind is supposed to derive its materials from, and to act only in response to, the action of the world upon it; but the relations which it establishes between the materials, so derived, in its processes of distinction and comparison, of conception, judgment, and discourse, are supposed to be quite different, and to have a different source, from the relations between things or matters of fact in the world known. Upon further reflection, however, the untenableness of this view becomes apparent. It renders knowledge, as of fact or reality, inexplicable. It leaves us without an answer to the question, how the order of relations, which the mind sets up, comes to reproduce those relations of the material world which are assumed to be of a wholly different origin and nature. Nor, as we pursue the analysis of the operations involved in the

simplest perception of fact, are we able to detect any residuary phenomenon amounting to a fact at all, that can be held to be given independently of a combining and relating activity, which, if the antithesis between the work of the mind and the work of things be accepted, must be ascribed to the former.

35. The necessity, therefore, of getting rid of the antithesis in question forces itself upon us : and it is natural that the way of doing so, which at first sight most commends itself to us, should consist in treating the mind and its work as a secondary result of what had previously been opposed to it as operations of nature. The weakness of such a method is twofold. In the first place there is the objection upon which we have already dwelt and which may be put summarily thus : that ' nature ' is a *process of change,* and that the derivation of a *consciousness* of change from such a process is impossible. Secondly, such an explanation of the work of the mind, if nothing is known of it otherwise, is an explanation of it by the inexplicable. It is taking nature for granted, and at the same time treating that as a result of nature which is necessary to explain the possibility of there being such a thing as nature. For nature, as a process of continuous change, implies something which is other than the changes and to which they are relative. As a system of related elements it implies a unity, through relation to which the elements are related to each other. But with the reduction of thought or spirit or self-consciousness to a result of nature, if such reduction were possible, we should be eliminating the only agent that we know as maintaining an identity with itself throughout a series of changes, or as a principle that can unite a manifold without cancelling its multiplicity. In so explaining spirit we should be rendering the basis of our explanation itself inexplicable.

36. From the Kantian point of view, the dualism of nature and knowledge is disposed of in a different way. They are not identified but treated as forming an indivisible whole, which results from the activity of a single principle. It is not that first there is nature, and that then there comes to be an experience and knowledge of it. Intelligence, experience, knowledge, are no more a result of nature than nature of them. If it is true that there would be no intelligence without nature, it

is equally true that there would be no nature without intelligence. Nature is the system of related appearances, and related appearances are impossible apart from the action of an intelligence. They are not indeed the same as intelligence; it is not reducible to them nor they to it, any more than one of us is reducible to the series of his actions or that series to him; but without it they would not be, nor except in the activity which constitutes them has it any real existence. Does this then imply the absurdity that nature comes into existence in the process by which this person or that begins to think? Not at all, unless it is necessary to suppose that intelligence first comes into existence when this person or that begins to understand—a supposition not only not necessary, but which, on examination, will be found to involve impossibilities analogous to those which prevent us from supposing that nature so comes into existence.

The difference between what may be called broadly the Kantian view and the ordinary view is this, that whereas, according to the latter, it is a world in which thought is no necessary factor that is prior to, and independent of, the process by which this or that individual becomes acquainted with it, according to the former it is a world already determined by thought, and existing only in relation to thought, that is thus prior to, and conditions, our individual acquaintance with it. The growth of knowledge on our part is regarded not as a process in which facts or objects, in themselves unrelated to thought, by some inexplicable means gradually produce intelligible counterparts of themselves in thought. The true account of it is held to be that the concrete whole, which may be described indifferently as an eternal intelligence realised in the related facts of the world, or as a system of related facts rendered possible by such an intelligence, partially and gradually reproduces itself in us, communicating piece-meal, but in inseparable correlation, understanding and the facts understood, experience and the experienced world.

37. There are difficulties enough, no doubt, in the way of accepting such a form of 'idealism,' but they need not be aggravated by misunderstanding. It is simply misunderstood if it is taken to imply either the reduction of facts to feelings—

impressions and ideas, in Hume's terminology—or the oblitera-
tion of the distinction between illusion and reality. The reduction of facts to relations is the very reverse of their reduction
to feelings. No feeling, as such or as felt, is a relation. We
can only suppose it to be so through confusion between it and
its conditions, or between it and that fact of its occurrence which
is no doubt related to other facts, but, as so related, is not felt.
Even a relation between feelings is not itself a feeling or felt.
A feeling can only be felt as successive to another feeling, but
the terms of a relation, as we have seen, even though the relation be one of succession, do not succeed one another. In order
to constitute the relation they must be present together; so
that, to constitute a relation between feelings, there must be
something other than the feelings for which they are equally
present. The relation between the feelings is not felt, because
it is only for something that distinguishes itself from the feelings that it can subsist. It is our cognisance of the successive-
ness or transitoriness of feelings that makes us object intuitively
to any idealism which is understood to imply an identification
of the realities of the world with the feelings of men. Facts,
we are sure, are in some way permanent. They are not 'like
the bubble on the fountain,' a moment here, then 'gone, and for
ever.' But if they were feelings as we feel them, they would be
so. They would not be 'stubborn things;' for as each was felt
it would be done with. They would not form a world to which
we have to adapt ourselves; for in order to make a world they
must coexist, which feelings, as we feel them, do not.

But the idealism which interprets facts as relations, and can
only understand relations as constituted by a single spiritual
principle, is chargeable with no such outrage on common-sense.
On the contrary, its very basis is the consciousness of objectivity.
Its whole aim is to articulate coherently the conviction of there
being a world of abiding realities other than, and determining,
the endless flow of our feelings. The source of its differences
from ordinary realism lies in its being less easily satisfied in its
analysis of what the existence of such a world implies. The
mere statement that facts are not feelings, that things are not
ideas, that we can neither feel nor think except contingently
upon certain functions of matter and motion being fulfilled, does

not help us to understand what facts and things, what matter and motion, are. It does not enable us, when we seek to understand these expressions, to give them any meaning except such as is derived from experience, and, if from experience, then from relations that have their being only for an intelligent consciousness.

38. So far we have been following the lead of Kant in en-quiring what is necessary to constitute, what is implied in there being, a world of experience—an objective world, if by that is meant a world of ascertainable laws, as distinguished from a world of unknowable 'things-in-themselves.' We have fol-lowed him also, as we believe every one must who has once faced the question, in maintaining that a single active self-conscious principle, by whatever name it be called, is necessary to constitute such a world, as the condition under which alone phenomena, *i.e.* appearances to consciousness, can be related to each other in a single universe. This is the irrefragable truth involved in the proposition that 'the understanding makes nature.' But so soon as we have been brought to the accept-ance of that proposition, Kant's leading fails us. We might be forward, from the work thus assigned to understanding in the constitution of nature, to infer something as to the spirituality of the real world. But from any such inference Kant would at once withhold us. He would not only remind us that the work assigned to understanding is a work merely among and upon phenomena; that the nature which it constitutes is merely a unity in the relations of phenomena; and that any conclusion we arrive at in regard to 'nature' in this sense has no applica-tion to 'things-in-themselves.' He insists, further, on a dis-tinction between the form and matter of 'nature' itself, and, having assigned to its 'form' an origin in understanding, ascribes the 'matter' to an unknown but alien source, in a way which seems to cancel the significance of his own declarations in regard to the intellectual principle necessary to constitute its form. We do not essentially misrepresent him in saying that by the 'form' of nature or, as he sometimes phrases it, 'natura formaliter spectata,' he means the relations by which phenomena are connected in the one world of experience; by its 'matter,'

or ' natura materialiter spectata,' the mere phenomena or sensations undetermined by those relations[1]. 'Natura formaliter
spectata' is the work of understanding : but ' natura materialiter spectata' is the work of unknown things-in-themselves,
acting in unknown ways upon us.

39. Now, if the distinction, thus drawn, between the form
and matter of the world of experience were necessary or even
admissible, the effect of tracing those relations between phenomena, which form the laws of nature as we know it, to the action
of a spiritual principle, would simply have been to bring us to a
dead-lock. The distinction implies that phenomena have a real
nature as effects of things-in-themselves other than that which
they have as related to each other in the universe of our experience : and not only so, it puts the two natures in a position
towards each other of mere negation and separation, of such a
kind that any correspondence between them, any dependence of
one upon the other, is impossible. As effects of things-in-themselves, phenomena are supposed to have a nature of their own,
but they cannot, according to Kant's doctrine, be supposed to
carry any of that nature with them into experience. All the
nature which they have in experience belongs to them in virtue
of relations to each other which the action of the intellectual
principle, expressly opposed to the action of things-in-themselves, brings about. The nature which a sensation is supposed
to possess ' materialiter spectata,' as the appearance of a thing-
in-itself, must not be confused with its nature as conditioned by
a particular mode of matter and motion—the nature which the
man of science investigates. It is probably from this confusion
that Kant's doctrine of the relation between phenomena and
things-in-themselves derives any plausibility which it may have
for most of his readers : but, after what has been said above, a
moment's consideration will show how unwarrantable according
to his principles it is. The nature of a sensation, as dependent
upon any motion or configuration of molecules, is still a nature
determined by its relation to other data of experience—a relation
which (like every other relation within, or capable of coming
within, experience) the single self-distinguishing principle, which

[1] Kant's Werke, ed. Rosenkranz, II. p. 755; ed. Hartenstein (1867), III.
p. 133.

Kant calls understanding, is needed to constitute. It is not such a nature, but one to which no experience or interrogation of experience brings us any the nearer, that we must suppose to belong to the phenomenon as an appearance of a thing-in-itself, if Kant's antithesis is to be maintained.

And if phenomena, as 'materialiter spectata,' have such another nature, it will follow—not indeed that all our knowledge is an illusion in the ordinary sense of the term, for that implies a possibility of correction by true knowledge—but that there is no ground for that conviction of there being some unity and totality in things, from which the quest for knowledge proceeds. The 'cosmos of our experience,' and the order of things-in-themselves, will be two wholly unrelated worlds, of which, however, each determines the same sensations. All that determination of a sensible occurrence which can be the object of possible experience or inferred as an explanation of experience—its simple position of antecedence or sequence in time to other occurrences, as well as its relation to conditions which regulate that position and determine its sensible nature —will belong to one world of which a unifying self-consciousness is the organising principle: while the very same occurrence, as an effect of things-in-themselves, will belong to another world, will be subject to a wholly different order of determinations, which may have—and indeed, in being so described, is assumed to have—some principle of unity of its own, but of which, because it is a world of things-in-themselves, the principle must be taken to be the pure negation of that which determines the world of experience. If this be so, the conception of a universe is a delusive one. Man weaves a web of his own and calls it a universe; but if the principle of this universe is neither one with, nor dependent on, that of things-in-themselves, there is in truth no universe at all, nor does there seem to be any reason why there should not be any number of such independent creations. We have asserted the unity of the world of our experience only to transfer that world to a larger chaos.

40. A tempting but misleading way out of the difficulty is to reduce the world of experience to dependence on that of things-in-themselves by taking the intellectual principle, which, in the

sense explained, 'makes' the world of experience, to be not, as Kant considered it, an independent thing-in-itself, but itself a product of things-in-themselves. Our readiness to confuse things-in-themselves, as just pointed out, with the material conditions of sensation, may easily bring us to put the case in this way to ourselves. Certain combinations of moving matter, we are ready to believe, issue, by processes yet to be ascertained, in those living organisms which again, in reaction upon certain modes of motion, yield sensation; and the sensitive subject, under a continuance of like physical influences, somehow grows into the intellectual subject of which the action is admitted to be necessary to constitute the 'cosmos of our experience.' But we have learnt Kant's lesson to very little purpose if we do not understand that the terms, which in such psychogenesis are taken to stand for independent agents, are in fact names for substantiated relations between phenomena; relations to which an existence on their own account is fictitiously ascribed, but which in truth only exist for, or through the action of, the unifying and self-distinguishing spiritual subject which they are taken to account for. If this subject is to be dependent on things-in-themselves, something else must be understood by these 'things' than any objects that we know or can know; for in the existence of such objects its action is already implied.

The question then arises whether, when we have excluded from things-in-themselves every kind of qualification arising from determination by, or relation to, an intelligent subject, any meaning is left in the assertion of a dependence of this subject upon them. Does not any significant assertion of that dependence, either as a fact or even as a mere possibility, imply a removal of the things-in-themselves from the region of the purely unknowable, and their qualification by an understood relation to the intelligent subject said to be dependent on them? But if this is so, and if it is impossible for such a relation, any more than any other, to exist except through the unifying action of spirit, what becomes of the independence of the things-in-themselves? Are they not being determined by a spiritual action exactly of that kind which is being alleged to depend on them, and their exclusion of which is the one point expressed by their designation as things-in-themselves?

41. These considerations seem to preclude us, when once we have recognised the ground of distinction between a world of experience and a world of things-in-themselves, from any attempt to overcome that absolute separation between the two worlds, which Kant's doctrine implies, by treating the organising subject of the world of experience as in any sense a product of things-in-themselves. Kant himself lends no countenance to any such attempt; but on further reflection we may begin to question whether the view, which Kant himself gives, of the relation between things-in-themselves and the 'matter' of experience, or 'natura materialiter spectata'—the view out of which the whole difficulty arises—is not itself open to the same charge of inconsistency as that method of escape from its consequences which we have examined. When we say that sensations, or phenomena in respect of their mere 'matter,' are effects of things-in-themselves, we may exclude as carefully as possible all confusion of the things-in-themselves with the ascertainable material conditions, or formal causes, of feeling, but we cannot assert such a relation of cause and effect between the things and sensation without making the former a member of a relation which, as Kant himself on occasion would be ready to remind us, we have no warrant for extending beyond the world of experience, or for considering as independent of the intellectual principle of unity which is the condition of there being such a world. Causation has no meaning except as an unalterable connexion between changes in the world of our experience—an unalterableness of which the basis is the relation of that world throughout, with all its changes, to a single subject. That sensations therefore, the matter of our experience, should be connected as effects with things-in-themselves, of which all that can be said is that they belong to a world other than the world of our experience and are not relative to the subject to which it is relative, is a statement self-contradictory or at best unmeaning.

That Kant should not have seen this merely goes to show that his own doctrine, being the gradual conquest of his later years, had not obtained full possession of his mind. The antithesis between the real and the work of thought had still such command over him that, after he had himself traced the agency of thought in all that gives the world of experience a definite character, he still could not help ascribing to this world, in terms of the knowable, a relation to an unknowable opposite; though that very relation, if it existed, would according to his own showing bring the unknowable opposite within that world (dependent on an intelligent subject) from which it is expressly excluded.

42. At this point we may probably anticipate a rejoinder to some such effect as the following. It appears to be impossible to take the matter of experience to be the effect of things-in-them-selves, since these things, if they are to be things-in-themselves, cannot be supposed to exist in a relation which only holds for the world of experience, as determined by an intelligent subject. But it must be equally impossible to consider it a product of the intelligent subject, to which, when we have allowed every function that can be claimed for it in the way of uniting in a related system the manifold material of sensation, we must still deny the function of generating that material. Yet we cannot ignore sensation. We cannot reduce the world of experience to a web of relations in which nothing is related, as it would be if everything were erased from it which we cannot refer to the action of a combining intelligence. After all our protests against Dualism, then, are we not at last left with an unac-countable residuum—an essential element of the real world of experience, which we cannot trace to what we regard as the organising principle of that world, but which is as necessary to make the world what it is as that principle itself? What do we gain by excluding other ways of accounting for it, if it is finally irreducible to the only agency by which we can explain the order of the world? Does it not remain a thing-in-itself, alien and opposite to anything that we can explain as the con-struction of intelligence, just as much as if it were admitted to be the product of an unknowable power?

43. The best hope of answering these questions lies in con-sidering further how they arise. They are due to the abstrac-tion of the 'matter' from the 'form' of experience. This ab-straction we inevitably make in reflecting on the process by which we obtain such knowledge as we have, but it deceives us when we make it a ground for supposing a like separation of

elements in the world of experience. It is true indeed, according to the doctrine previously stated, that the principle which enables us to know that there is a world, and to set about learning its nature, is identical with that which is the condition of there being a world; but it is not therefore to be imagined that all the distinctions and relations, which we present to ourselves—and necessarily present to ourselves—in the process of learning to know, have counterparts in the real world. Our presentation of them, as a part of our mental history, is a fact definitely related and conditioned in the reality of the world; but the distinctions presented may exist only for us, in whom the intellectual principle realises itself under special conditions, not in the world as it is in itself or for a perfect intelligence.

The distinction between the form and matter of experience is a distinction of this kind. In reflecting on the process by which we have come to know anything, we find that, at any stage we may recall, it consists in a further qualification of a given material by the consideration of the material under relations hitherto unconsidered. Thus as contrasted with, and abstracted from, the further formation which upon continued observation and attention it may acquire, any perception, any piece of knowledge, may be regarded as an unformed matter. On the other hand, when we look at what the given perception or piece of knowledge is in itself, we find that it is already formed, in more complex ways than we can disentangle, by the synthesis of less determinate data. But there is a point at which the individual's retrospective analysis of the knowledge which he finds himself to possess necessarily stops. Antecedently to any of the formative intellectual processes which he can trace, it would seem that something must have been given for those processes to begin upon. This something is taken to be feeling, pure and simple. When all accretions of form, due to the intellectual establishment of relations, have been stripped off, there seem to remain the mere sensations without which the intellectual activity would have had nothing to deal with or operate upon. These then must be in an absolute sense the matter—the matter excluding all form—of experience.

44. Now it is evident that the ground on which we make this statement, that mere sensations form the matter of experience, warrants us in making it, if at all, only as a statement in regard to the mental history of the individual. Even in this reference it can scarcely be accepted. There is no positive basis for it but the fact that, so far as memory goes, we always find ourselves manipulating some data of consciousness, themselves independent of any intellectual manipulation which we can remember applying to them. But on the strength of this to assume that there are such data in the history of our experience, consisting in mere sensations, antecedently to any action of the intellect, is not really an intelligible inference from the fact stated. It is an abstraction which may be put into words, but to which no real meaning can be attached. For a sensation can only form an object of experience in being determined by an intelligent subject which distinguishes it from itself and contemplates it in relation to other sensations; so that to suppose a primary datum or matter of the individual's experience, wholly void of intellectual determination, is to suppose such experience to begin with what could not belong to or be an object of experience at all.

45. But the question we are here concerned with is not whether any such thing as mere sensation, a matter wholly unformed by intelligence, exists as a stage in the process by which the individual becomes acquainted with the world; it is the question whether there is any such element in the world of knowable facts. Has nature—the system of connected phenomena, or facts related to consciousness, which forms the object of experience—a reality of that kind which Kant describes as 'natura materialiter spectata;' a reality consisting of mere sensations, or sensations of which the qualities, whatever they may be, are independent of such determination as arises from the action of a unifying and self-distinguishing subject? Or has it in any other sense a 'matter' which does not depend on a combining intelligence for being what it is, as much as does the relation between my experience of to-day and that of my previous life?

Phenomena are facts related to consciousness. Thus, when we enquire whether there is such a thing in the world of phenomena as sensation undetermined by thought, the question may be considered in relation either to the facts, as such, or to the consciousness for which the facts exist. It may be put either thus—Among the facts that form the object of possible experience, are there sensations which do not depend on thought for being what they are? or thus—Is sensation, as unqualified by thought, an element in the consciousness which is necessary to there being such a thing as the world of phenomena?

46. After what has been already said, the answer to these questions need not detain us long. If it is admitted that we know of no other medium but a thinking or self-distinguishing consciousness, in and through which that unification of the manifold can take place which is necessary to constitute relation, it follows that a sensation apart from thought—not determined or acted on by thought—would be an unrelated sensation; and an unrelated sensation cannot amount to a fact. Mere sensation is in truth a phrase that represents no reality. It is the result of a process of abstraction; but having got the phrase we give a confused meaning to it, we fill up the shell which our abstraction has left, by reintroducing the qualification which we assumed ourselves to have got rid of. We present the *mere* sensations to ourselves as determined by relation in a way that would be impossible in the absence of that connecting action which we assume to be absent in designating them *mere* sensations. The minimum of qualification which we mentally ascribe to the sensation in thus speaking of it, is generally such as implies sequence and degree. A feeling not characterised either by its connexion with previous feeling or by its own intensity we must admit to be nothing at all, but at first sight we take it for granted that the character thus given to a feeling would belong to it just the same, though there were no such thing as thought in the world. It certainly does not depend on ourselves—on any power which we can suppose it rests with our will to exert or withhold—whether sensations shall occur to us in this or that order of succession, with this or that degree of intensity. But the question is whether the relation of time between one sensation and another, or that relation between a sensation and other possible modes of itself which is implied in its having a degree, could exist if there were not a subject

for which the several sensations, or modes of the same sensation, were equally present and equally distinguished from itself. If it is granted that these relations, which constitute the minimum determination of a sensible fact, only exist through the action of such a subject, it follows that thought is the necessary condition of the existence of sensible facts, and that *mere* sensation, in the sense supposed, is not a possible constituent in the realm of facts.

47. Or, if the consequence be disputed, the dispute can only turn on a secondary question as to the fitness of the term 'thought' to represent a function of which the essential nature is admitted. If by thought is necessarily understood a faculty which is born and dies with each man; which is exhausted by labour and refreshed by repose; which is exhibited in the construction of chains of reasoning, but not in the common ideas which make mankind and its experience one; on which the 'great thinker' may plume himself as the athlete on the strength of his muscles; then to say that the agency which makes sensible facts what they are can only be that of a thinking subject, is an absurd impropriety. But if it appears that a function in the way of self-consciousness is implied in the existence of relations, and therefore of determinate facts—a function identical in principle with that which enables the individual to look before and after, and which renders his experience a connected system—then it is more reasonable to modify some of our habitual notions of thought as exercised by ourselves than, on the strength of these notions, to refuse to recognise an essential identity between the subject which forms the unifying principle of the experienced world, and that which, as in us, qualifies us for an experience of it. It becomes time to consider whether the characteristics of thought, even as exercised by us, are not rather to be sought in the unity of its object as presented to all men, and in the continuity of all experience in regard to that object, than in the incidents of an individual life which is but for a day, or in abilities of which any man can boast that he has more than his neighbour.

48. Our question, then, in the first of the two forms suggested, must be answered in the negative. A fact consisting of *mere* feeling, in the sense supposed, is a contradiction, an

impossibility. This does not of course mean that no being can feel which does not also think. We are not called on here to enquire whether there are really animals which feel but have not the capacity of thinking. All that the present argument would lead us to maintain would be that, so far as they feel without thinking, their feelings are not facts for them—for their consciousness. Their feelings *are* facts; but they are facts only so far as determined by relations, which exist only for a thinking consciousness and otherwise could not exist. And, in like manner, that large part of our own sensitive life which goes on without being affected by conceptions, is a series of facts with the determination of which, indeed, thought, as ours or in us, has nothing to do, but which not the less depends for its existence as a series of facts on the action of the same subject which, in another mode of its action, enables us to know them. But in saying this, it may be objected, we have already admitted that there is such a thing as a merely feeling consciousness; and, in the presence of this admission, what becomes of the denial to feeling of any separate or independent reality? The answer is that the distinction of the merely feeling consciousness is just this, that what it is really it is not consciously—that the relations by which it is really determined do not exist for it, but for the thinking consciousness on which it and they alike depend for being what they are. Its very characteristics as a merely feeling consciousness depend on conditions, in the universe of things, by which it would not be conditioned if it were really no more than it feels itself to be; if it were not relative to, and had not its existence for, another form of consciousness which comprehends it and its conditions.

49. In the second of the forms in which the question before us admits of being presented—Can sensation exist as an independent element in a consciousness to which facts can appear? —it has been virtually answered in being answered in the first. To that thinking subject, whose action is the universal bond of relation that renders facts what they are, their existence and their appearance must be one and the same. Their appearance, their presence to it, is their existence. Feeling can no more be an independent element in that subject, as the subject to which they appear, than it can be an independent element in it, as the

subject through whose action they exist. It is true on the one hand, as has just been admitted, that in a great part of our lives we feel without thinking and without any qualification of our feelings by our thoughts; while yet, on the other hand, we are subjects to whom facts can appear, who are capable of conceiving a world of phenomena. But just so far as we feel without thinking, no world of phenomena exists for us. The suspension of thought in us means also the suspension of fact or reality for us. We do not cease to be facts, but facts cease to exist for our consciousness. However then we may explain the merely temporary and interrupted character of the action of thought upon feeling in us, that temporary character affords no reason why we should hesitate to deny that feeling unqualified by thought can be an element in the consciousness which is necessary to there being such a thing as a world of phenomena.

50. Mere feeling, then, as a matter unformed by thought, has no place in the world of facts, in the cosmos of possible experience. Any obstacle which it seemed to present to a monistic view of that world may be allowed to disappear. We may give up the assumption that it needs to be accounted for as a product of things-in-themselves; or that, if not accounted for in this way, it still remains an unaccountable opposite to thought and its work. Feeling and thought are inseparable and mutually dependent in the consciousness for which the world of experience exists, inseparable and mutually dependent in the constitution of the facts which form the object of that consciousness. Each in its full reality includes the other. It is one and the same living world of experience which, considered as the manifold object presented by a self-distinguishing subject to itself, may be called feeling, and, considered as the subject presenting such an object to itself, may be called thought. Neither is the product of the other. It is only when by a process of abstraction we have reduced either to something which is not itself, that we can treat either as the product of anything, or apply the category of cause and effect to it at all. For that category is itself their product. Or rather, it represents one form of the activity of the consciousness which in inseparable union they constitute. The connexion between a phenomenon

and its conditions is one that only obtains in and for that consciousness. No such connexion can obtain between that consciousness and anything else; which means that the con-sciousness itself, whether considered as feeling or considered as thought, being that by means of which everything is accounted for, does not in turn admit of being accounted for, in the sense that any 'whence' or 'why' can be assigned for it.

Any constituent of the world of possible experience we can account for by exhibiting its relation to other constituents of the same world; but this is not to account for the world itself. We may and do explore the conditions under which a sentient organism is formed, and the various forms of molecular action by which particular sensations on the part of such an organism are elicited. We may ascertain uniformities in the sequence of one feeling upon another. In the life of the individual and the race we may trace regular histories of the manner in which a particular way of thinking has been affected by an earlier, and has in turn affected a later way; of the determination of certain ideas by certain emotions, and of certain emotions by certain ideas. But in all this we are connecting phenomena with phe-nomena within a world, not connecting the world of phenomena with anything other than itself. We are doing nothing to account for the all-uniting consciousness which alone can render these sequences and connexions possible, for which alone they exist, and of which the action in us alone enables us to know them. We can indeed show the contradictions involved in sup-posing a world of phenomena to exist otherwise than in and for consciousness, and upon analysis can discern what must be the formal characteristic of a consciousness for which a system of related phenomena exists. So far we can give an account of what the world as a whole must be, and of what the spirit that constitutes it does. But just because all that we can experience is included in this one world, and all our inferences and expla-nations relate only to its details, neither it as a whole, nor the one consciousness which constitutes it, can be accounted for in the ordinary sense of the word. They cannot be accounted for by what they include, and being all-inclusive—at any rate so far as possible experience goes—there remains nothing else by which they can be accounted for. And this is equally true of consciousness as feeling and of consciousness as thought, for each in its reality involves the other.

51. We are now in a position to reconsider the restriction which Kant puts on the interpretation of his own dictum that 'understanding makes nature.' This with him means that understanding, as the unifying principle which is the source of relations, acts formatively upon feelings as upon a material given to it from an opposite source called 'things-in-themselves,' rendering them into one system of phenomena called 'nature,' which is the sole object of experience, and to which all judgments as to matters of fact relate. We demur to the independent reality, or reality as determined by something else than thought, which is thus ascribed to feeling. It is not that we would claim any larger function for thought than Kant claims for understanding as separate from feeling, supposing that separation to be once admitted. It is the separation itself that is in question. We do not dispute the validity of Locke's challenge to a man by any amount of thinking to produce a single 'simple idea' to himself. We admit that mere thought can no more produce the facts of feeling, than mere feeling can generate thought. But we deny that there is really such a thing as 'mere feeling' or 'mere thought.' We hold that these phrases represent abstractions to which no reality corresponds, either in the facts of the world or in the consciousness to which those facts are relative. We can attach no meaning to 'reality,' as applied to the world of phenomena, but that of existence under definite and unalterable relations; and we find that it is only for a thinking consciousness that such relations can subsist. Reality of feeling, abstracted from thought, is abstracted from the condition of its being a reality. That great part of our sensitive life is not determined by *our* thought, that the sensitive life of innumerable beings is wholly undetermined by any thought of theirs or in them, is not in dispute : but this proves nothing as to what that sensitive life really is in nature or in the cosmos of possible experience. It has no place in nature, except as determined by relations which can only exist for a thinking consciousness. For the consciousness which constitutes reality and makes the world one it exists, not in that separateness which belongs to it as an attribute of beings that think

only at times or not at all, but as conditioned by a whole which thought in turn conditions.

As to what that consciousness in itself or in its completeness is, we can only make negative statements. *That* there is such a consciousness is implied in the existence of the world; but *what* it is we only know through its so far acting in us as to enable us, however partially and interruptedly, to have knowledge of a world or an intelligent experience. In such knowledge or experience there is no mere thought or mere feeling. No feeling enters into it except as qualifying, and qualified by, an interrelated order of which a self-distinguishing subject forms the unifying bond. Thought has no function in it except as constantly co-ordinating ever new appearances in virtue of their presence to that one subject. And we are warranted in holding that, as a mutual independence of thought and feeling has no place in any consciousness on our part, which is capable of apprehending a world or for which a world exists, so it has none in the world-consciousness of which ours is a limited mode.

52. The purpose of this long discussion has been to arrive at some conclusion in regard to the relation between man and nature, a conclusion which must be arrived at before we can be sure that any theory of ethics, in the distinctive sense of the term, is other than wasted labour. If by nature we mean the object of possible experience, the connected order of knowable facts or phenomena—and this is what our men of science mean by it when they trace the natural genesis of human character—then nature implies something other than itself, as the condition of its being what it is. Of that something else we are entitled to say, positively, that it is a self-distinguishing consciousness; because the function which it must fulfil in order to render the relations of phenomena, and with them nature, possible, is one which, on however limited a scale, we ourselves exercise in the acquisition of experience, and exercise only by means of such a consciousness. We are further entitled to say of it, negatively, that the relations by which, through its action, phenomena are determined are not relations *of* it—not relations by which it is itself determined. They arise out of its presence to phenomena, or the presence of phenomena to it, but the very condition of

their thus arising is that the unifying consciousness which constitutes them should not itself be one of the objects so related. The relation of events to each other as in time implies their equal presence to a subject which is not in time. There could be no such thing as time if there were not a self-consciousness which is not in time. As little could there be a relation of objects as outside each other, or in space, if they were not equally related to a subject which they are not outside; a subject of which outsideness to anything is not a possible attribute; which by its synthetic action constitutes that relation, but is not itself determined by it. The same is true of those relations which we are apt to treat as independent entities under the names matter and motion. They are relations existing for a consciousness which they do not so condition as that it should itself either move or be material.

53. If objection is taken to the interpretation of matter as consisting in certain relations, if its character as substance is insisted on, it remains to ask what is meant by substance. It is not denied that there are material substances, but their qualification both as substances and as material will be found to depend on relations. By a substance we mean that which is persistent throughout certain appearances. It represents that identical element throughout the appearances, that permanent element throughout the times of their appearance, in virtue of which they are not merely so many different appearances, but connected changes. A material substance is that which remains the same with itself in respect of some of the qualities which we include in our definition of matter—qualities all consisting in some kind of relation—while in other respects it changes. Its character as a substance depends on that relation of appearances to each other in a single order which renders them changes. It is not that first there is a substance, and that then certain changes of it ensue. The substance is the implication of the changes, and has no existence otherwise. Apart from the changes no substance, any more than apart from effects a cause. If we choose to say then that matter exists as a substance, we merely substitute for the designation of it as consisting in relations, a designation of it as a certain correlatum of a certain kind of relation. Its existence as a substance depends on the

action of the same self-consciousness upon which the connexion of phenomena by means of that relation depends.

And the subject, of which the action is implied in the connexion of phenomena in one system of nature by means of this correlatum of change, is one that can itself be as little identified with that correlatum—with any kind of substance—as with the change to which substance is relative. It has already been pointed out that a consciousness, to which events are to appear as changes, cannot itself consist in those events. Its self-distinction from them all is necessary to its holding them all together as related to each other in the way of change. And, for the same reason, that connexion of all phenomena as changes of one world which is implied in the unity of intelligent experience, cannot be the work of anything which is the substance qualified by those changes. Its self-distinction from them, which is the condition of their appearance to it under this relation of change, is incompatible with its being so qualified. Even if we allow it to be possible that a subject, which connects certain appearances as changes, should itself be qualified by— should be the substance persistent in—certain other changes, it is plainly impossible that a subject which so connects all the appearances of nature should be related in the way of substance to any or all of them.

54. We may express the conclusion to which we are thus brought by saying that nature in its reality, or in order to be what it is, implies a principle which is not natural. By calling the principle not natural we mean that it is neither included among the phenomena which through its presence to them form a nature, nor consists in their series, nor is itself determined by any of the relations which it constitutes among them. In saying more than this of it we must be careful not to fall into confusion. We are most safe in calling it spiritual, because, for reasons given, we are warranted in thinking of it as a self-distinguishing consciousness. In calling it supernatural we run the risk of misleading and being misled, for we suggest a relation between it and nature of a kind which has really no place except *within* nature, as a relation of phenomenon to phenomenon. We convey the notion that it is above or beyond or before nature, that it is a cause of which nature is the effect,

a substance of which the changing modes constitute nature; while in truth all the relations so expressed are relations which, indeed, but for the non-natural self-conscious subject would not exist, but which are not predicable of it. If we employ language about it in which, strictly taken, they are implied, it must only be on a clear understanding of its metaphorical character.

On the other hand, there is no imperative reason why we should limit 'nature' to the restricted sense in which we have been supposing it to be used, if only the same sense can be covered by another term. If we like, we may employ the term 'nature' to represent the one whole which includes both the system of related phenomena and the principle, other than itself, which that system implies. But in that case, if we would avoid confusion, we must find some other term than nature to represent the system of phenomena as such, or as considered without inclusion of the spiritual principle which it implies, and some other term than 'natural' to represent that which this system contains. We are pretty sure, however, to fail in this, and 'nature' in consequence becomes a term that is played fast and loose with in philosophical writing. It is spoken of as an independent agent; a certain completeness and self-containedness are ascribed to it; and to this there is no objection so long as we understand it to include the spiritual principle, neither in time nor in space, immaterial and immovable, eternally one with itself, which is necessary to the possibility of a world of phenomena. But it is otherwise if 'nature' is at the same time thought of, as it almost inevitably is, under attributes only applicable to the world of phenomena, and thus as excluding the spiritual principle which that world indeed implies, but implies as other than itself. In that case, to ascribe independence or self-containedness to it—if for a moment the use of theological language may be allowed which it is generally desirable to avoid—is to deify nature while we cancel its title to deification. It is to speak of nature without God in a manner only appropriate to nature as it is in God. Or—to employ language less liable to misleading associations—it is to involve ourselves in perpetual confusion by seeking for a completeness in the world of phenomena, the world existing under conditions of space and time, which, just because it exists under those conditions, is not to be found there. The result of the confusion will generally be that, being unable to discover any perfection or totality or independent agency among the matters of fact which we know, and having ignored the implication by those facts of a spiritual principle other than themselves, we come to assume that no perfect or self-determined being exists at all, or at any rate in any relation to us.

CHAPTER II.

THE RELATION OF MAN, AS INTELLIGENCE, TO THE SPIRITUAL PRINCIPLE IN NATURE.

55. THE conclusion of the preceding chapter has brought us to the question which lies at the root of ethical enquiry. In what relation do we ourselves stand to the one self-distinguishing subject, other than nature, which we find to be implied in nature? To a certain extent an answer to this question has been involved in the considerations which have led to the conviction of there being such a subject. That if we were merely phenomena among phenomena we could not have knowledge of a world of phenomena, appears from analysis of the conditions of an intelligent experience. Our experience, we have seen, has two characteristics, of which neither admits of being reduced to or explained by the other. On the one hand it is an order of events in time, consisting in modifications of our sensibility. On the other hand it is a consciousness of those events—a consciousness of them as a related series, and as determined in their relations to each other by relation to something else, which is from the first conceived as other than the modifications of our sensibility, and which with growing knowledge comes to be conceived as involving relations between objects that are not events at all, and between events that preceded or lie beyond the range of sentient life. But, as has been further pointed out, a consciousness of related events, as related, cannot consist in those events. The modifications of our sensibility cannot, as successive events, make up our consciousness of them. *Within* the consciousness that they are related in the way of before and after there is no before and after. There is no such relation between components of the consciousness as there is between the events of which it is the consciousness. They

Something within man which keeps him from being a thing

form a process in time. If *it* were a process in time, it would not be a consciousness of them as forming such a process.

56. Thus that man is not merely a phenomenon or succession of phenomena, that he does not consist in a series of natural events, is implied in the fact that phenomena appear to him as they do, that for him or for his consciousness there is such a thing as nature. There are certain current phrases of modern psychology, which no doubt have their warrant in facts to be considered presently, but which, as commonly used, are apt to blind us to this essential characteristic of the position in which we stand towards the world we know. We use the term 'phenomena of consciousness' as if it covered the whole range of knowledge and morality—all our thought about the world, all our perceptions and conceptions of objects, all the ideas which we seek to realise in action. We speak of consciousness universally, without qualification or distinction, as a succession of states; and the figure of the stream is the accepted one for expressing the nature of our spiritual life. Now it would be idle to deny that there is an appropriateness in a way of speaking which none of us can avoid, but it is important to call attention to that kind of activity undoubtedly exercised by us, implied in all distinctively intelligent or moral experience, to which it is wholly inappropriate.

If we reflect on what is contained in our knowledge, or in any conception or perception contributory to it, we shall see that the relation in which its constituents stand to each other is essentially different from the relation between stages of the process by which the knowledge or perception is arrived at. The figure of the stream may be applicable to the latter, though the more we think of it the less we shall find it so, but it is quite inapplicable to the former. Successive states of consciousness may be represented as waves of which one is for ever taking the place of the other, but such successive states cannot make a knowledge even of the most elementary sort. Knowledge is of related facts, and it is essential to every act of knowledge that the related facts should be present together in consciousness. Between the apprehensions of those facts, so far as they make up a certain piece of knowledge, there is no succession. I may have apprehended some of them, no doubt, before I apprehend the rest; or, after having apprehended the latter, my consciousness may lose its hold on some apprehended before. In this sense different states of knowledge succeed each other in the individual, but not so the manifold constituents of that which in any act of knowledge is present to his mind as the object known; not so the determinations of consciousness in which those constituents are presented, and which make up the complex act of knowledge. For a known object, as known, is a related whole, of which, as of every such whole, the members are necessarily present together; and the acts of consciousness in which the several members are apprehended, as forming a knowledge, are a many in one. None is before or after another. This is equally the case whether the knowledge is of successive events or of the ' uniformities ' which are said to constitute a law of nature. For, as we have previously had occasion to point out, between the constituents of a knowledge of succession there can be no succession : so long as certain events are *contemplated* as successive, no one of them is an object to consciousness before or after another.

57. For this reason no knowledge, nor any mental act involved in knowledge, can properly be called a ' phenomenon of consciousness.' It may be *of* phenomena; if the knowledge is of events, it is so. The attainment of the knowledge, again, as an occurrence in the individual's history, a transition from one state of consciousness to another, may properly be called a phenomenon; but not so the consciousness itself of relations or related facts— not so the relations and related facts present to consciousness —in which the knowledge consists. For a phenomenon is a sensible event, related in the way of antecedence and consequence to other sensible events; but the consciousness which constitutes a knowledge, or (if we may be allowed the use of a word which, though unfamiliar in this connexion, avoids some ambiguity) the content of such consciousness, is not an event so related nor made up of such events. We cannot point to any other events, as we can in the case of a phenomenon proper, from antecedence or consequence to which it takes its character as an event.

As an instance, let us take a man's knowledge of a proposition in Euclid. This means a relation in his consciousness between certain parts of a figure, determined by the relation of those parts to other parts. The knowledge is made up of those relations as in consciousness. Now it is obvious that there is no lapse of time, however minute, no antecedence or consequence, between the constituent relations of the consciousness so composed, or between the complex formed by them and anything else. To call such knowing consciousness a phenomenon, in the ordinary meaning of a sensible event, is a confusion between it and the process of arriving at or losing it. That in the learning or forgetting a proposition of Euclid, as in the acquisition or loss of any other piece of knowledge, a series of events takes place, is plain enough; and such events may legitimately be called 'phenomena of consciousness.' But it must be noticed that when these events of the mental history come to be reviewed in intelligent memory or experience—when we know them as the connected facts of a history—their existence as in consciousness is no longer that of events. They do not succeed each other in time, but are present in the unity of relation, as much as are the parts of a geometrical figure which has been apprehended by, or taken into, an intelligent consciousness.

58. The discrepancy here pointed out, between the reality of consciousness as exhibited in knowledge and anything that can properly be called phenomena or successive states of consciousness, would be more generally acknowledged but for two reasons. One of these is the ambiguity attending all our terms expressive of mental activity—knowledge, conception, perception, &c.—which may denote events in our mental history, the passing into certain states of consciousness, as well as that of which in those states we are conscious, the content and object of consciousness. At the same time—and this is the second of the reasons referred to—this content or object is looked upon as existing quite otherwise than in or for consciousness; as independent of it, though from time to time affecting it in a certain way and producing a certain state of consciousness. Hence it is only the successive changes in our apprehensive attitude towards the objects of our knowledge and experience that are commonly put to the account of consciousness. Its nature is not taken to be exhibited in the structure of those objects, any more than it would be if, instead of being objects known and experienced, they were 'things-in-themselves.' By perception

is understood a modification of our sensibility in which some present external object is revealed to us. Conception we regard equally as an *occurrence* in consciousness; and, though we suppose it to take place in the absence of any object at the time affecting the senses, we practically separate in our thoughts the conceived content or object from the conception, and imagine it vaguely as residing elsewhere than in consciousness. We thus avoid the necessity of facing the question how an object determined by relations can have its being in a consciousness which consists of a series of occurrences. Even 'knowledge,' though we often mean by it a system of known facts or laws, is apt to lose this sense when we speak of it as a form of consciousness. It then becomes merely the mental event of arriving at an apprehension of related facts. It does not represent the relation of the facts in consciousness. That there must be such a relation of them in consciousness, and that a consciousness consisting of events cannot contain such a relation, is a conclusion which we avoid by eviscerating knowledge of its content, and transferring this content from consciousness to 'external things.'

59. Even those who recognise the difficulty of extruding the object conceived or known, an object constituted by relations, from the consciousness which conceives or knows, and in consequence of describing conception and knowledge as mental events or phenomena, will be apt to ignore the same difficulty in regard to *Perception.* The externality of the perceived object to consciousness seems to be taken for granted, even by those who would be quite ready to tell us that the 'things' which we talk of conceiving are but 'nominal essences.' This arises from the connexion of perception with sensation, and from the real explicability of sensation by external impact. It is admitted on all hands that there can be no perception without (in Locke's phraseology) 'actual present sensation.' The difference between a perception of the moon and any mere conception of it is that, when it is perceived, although it is only in virtue of some conception of relations that it is perceived as a qualified object, there is necessarily some present sensation which those relations are conceived as determining. From this necessary presence of sensation in the act of perception, there easily arises a confusion between the perceived object and the exciting cause of sensation;

which again leads to an extrusion of the perceived object from
the consciousness in which perception consists, and to the view
of it as an external something to which perception is related
as an occurrence to its cause.

60. A little reflection, however, will show us that the exciting
cause, the stimulant, of the sensation involved in a perception is
never the object perceived in a perception. It is necessary to
a perception of colour that there should be a sensation, arising
out of a stimulus of the optic nerve by a particular vibration
of ether. That vibration, however—the external exciting cause
of the sensation—is not the object perceived in the perception
of the colour. That object, indeed, will not be the same for
every percipient. It will vary according to the extent of his
knowledge and to the degree of attention aroused in him in the
particular case. The perception may be no more than consciousness of the fact that a particular colour is presented to
him—a fact to be aware of which is already to be aware of a
certain rudimentary relation—or it may be a consciousness of
various relations by which this fact is determined. And the
relations thus apprehended in the perception may vary, again,
from those by which the colour is connected with accompanying
appearances in superficial experience, to those less obvious ones
which science has ascertained. It may thus come to include a
knowledge that the sensation of light arises out of a certain
relation between vibrations of ether and the optic nerve. If
the perception is that of a man of science, observing light or
colour for scientific purposes, it probably does so. Such knowledge is present to his mind in the perception. But it is a mere
confusion to imagine that, in this or any other form of such
a perception, the vibration of ether enters into the object perceived—into the content of the perception—in the same sense
in which it acts as the exciting cause of the sensation; or
to suppose that this object or content is external to the percipient consciousness, as the stimulant matter is to the sentient
organism.

The sentient organism to which the vibratory ether may be
considered external is not consciousness, either as exercised in
perception or in any other way, any more than the vibratory
ether, as external, is the object perceived. Strictly speaking, it

is not a vibratory ether but the fact consisting in the relation
between this and the optic nerve—this fact as existing for consciousness—that enters into or determines the perceived object,
as the scientific man perceives it. This fact, as forming part of
the content of the perception, is wholly within consciousness;
or, to speak more accurately, the opposition of without and
within has no sort of application to it. A *within* implies a
without, and we are not entitled to say that anything is without
or outside consciousness; for externality, being a relation which,
like any other relation, exists only in the medium of consciousness, only between certain objects as they are for consciousness,
cannot be a relation between consciousness and anything else.
An affection of the sentient organism by matter external to it
is the condition of our experiencing the sort of consciousness
called perception; a relation of externality between objects is
often part of that which is perceived; but in no case is there
such a relation, any more than a relation of before and after,
between the object perceived and the consciousness of it, or
between constituents of that consciousness.

61. If, having got rid of the confusion between the stimulant
of sensation and the perceived object, we examine the constituents of any perceived object—not as a 'thing-in-itself,' or
as we may vainly try to imagine it to be apart from our perception, but as it actually is perceived—we shall find alike that
it is only for consciousness that they can exist, and that the
consciousness for which they thus exist cannot be merely a series
of phenomena or a succession of states. For a justification of
this statement we may appeal to the account given of perception
by the accepted representatives of empirical psychology. 'Our
perception of an animal or a flower,' says Mr. Lewes, 'is the
synthesis of all the sensations we have had of the object in
relation to our several senses[1].' This object itself, he tells us,
is a 'group of sensibles;' which corresponds with Mill's account
of it as a combination of 'permanent possibilities of sensation.'
Such language is no doubt susceptible of a double interpretation,
and it is only upon one of the two possible interpretations
that it justifies the conclusion we shall draw from it. It is
true also that this interpretation is not sanctioned by the

[1] Problems of Life and Mind, I. 191.

writers mentioned, who seem not to distinguish the two interpretations, and avail themselves sometimes of the one, sometimes
of the other. It is the only interpretation of the definition,
however, that is really suitable to it as a definition of
perception.

62. What exactly is it that is combined in the synthesis
spoken of ? Is it a synthesis of feelings as caused by the action
of external irritants on the nervous system, or is it a synthesis
of known and remembered facts that such feelings have occurred
under certain conditions and relations ? The two kinds of synthesis are perfectly distinct; and, though the former may be
presupposed in perception, it is the latter alone which constitutes it in the distinctive sense. It is true, no doubt, that
an excitement of sensation by some present irritant may revive,
in a fainter degree, feelings that have been previously associated
with this sensation. But such a revival does not constitute
a perception. It cannot result in a synthesis of the feelings as
feelings of an object, or in the apprehension of a sensible fact,
recognised as a symbol of many other related facts of which
there would be experience if certain conditions on the part of
a sentient subject were fulfilled—in other words, as a symbol
of possibilities of sensation. If past feelings were reinstated
merely as feelings, they could not properly be said to be combined in an object or in consciousness of an object at all, nor
would their reinstatement be in any sense an inference, such as
Mr. Lewes rightly holds to be involved in all perception[1].
They could only be combined, either in the way of producing
and giving place to a further feeling, as little a consciousness of
fact or object as any of them, or in the sense that their effects
are accumulated in the nervous organism so as to modify its
reactions upon stimulus. Anything more than this—any combination of the data of feeling as qualities of an object, or as
facts related to a certain sensation, which the recurrence of that
sensation may recall to us—implies the action of a subject which
thinks of its feelings, which distinguishes them from itself and
can thus present them to itself as facts.

Such action is as necessary to the original presentation of all
that is recalled in perception, as to the incorporation of what is

[1] Problems of Life and Mind, I. 257.

recalled in the total fact perceived. As we have seen, no feeling, as such or as merely felt, enters into the perceived object—not even the present sensation which is admitted to be a necessary condition of perception. It is not the sensation, but the fact, presented by the self-distinguishing subject to itself, that such a sensation is here and now occurring, occurring under certain relations to other experience—it is this that is the nucleus on which the recalled experience gathers, suggesting other possibilities of sensation, not themselves 'actual present sensations,' but no less present, as facts, than the fact that the given sensation is here and now being felt. The knowledge of such possibilities of sensation is doubtless in every case founded on actual sensation experienced in the past, but on this as on an observed fact, determined by relation to other like facts through the equal presence of all to a thinking subject. Except to an intelligence which has thus observed sensations as related facts, there can be no suggestion, upon the recurrence of one of them, that others are possible upon certain conditions being fulfilled.

The revival of the past sensations themselves, with whatever intensity, is no such suggestion. It may be that the excitement of sensation by an external stimulant, which is the occasion of perception, is always followed by a revival, with some less intensity, of the sensations known to be possible as accompaniments of the given sensation; but the knowledge of their possibility—the apprehension of the relation between their several possibilities, as facts, and the fact of the given sensation occurring—this, the essential thing in perception, is as different from the revival of the sensations themselves or their images as is the given sensation from the presentation of its occurrence as a fact. And on this difference depends the susceptibility of combination in a perceived object, of presentation as a many in one, which belongs to known possibilities of sensation, to known facts that certain feelings would occur under certain conditions, in distinction from feelings as felt. Manifold feelings may combine, as we have seen, in one result, but in that one result their multiplicity as feelings is lost. The constituents of a perceived object, on the contrary, whether we consider them qualities or related facts, survive in their multiplicity at the same time that they constitute a single object. The condition of their doing so is the self-distinction of the thinking subject from the data of sensation, which it at once presents to itself in their severalty as facts, and unites as *related* facts in virtue of its equal presence to them all.

63. It thus appears that the common objects of experience—not those 'things in general' which are sometimes supposed to be the object of conception, but the particular things we perceive, this flower, this apple, this dog—in the only sense in which they are objects to us or are perceived at all, have their being only for, and result from the action of, a self-distinguishing consciousness. As perceived, they consist in certain groups of facts, which again consist in possibilities of sensation, known to be related in certain ways to each other and to some given fact of sensation. The extent of the group in the case of each perception, and the particular mode in which the constituent facts are related, depend on the experience and training of the percipient, as well as on the direction of his mind at the time of the perception. In every case the relations by which the given sensation is determined in the apprehension of the percipient, are but a minute part of those by which it is really determined. The object which the most practised botanist perceives in his observation of a flower, is by no means adequate to the real nature of the flower. That real nature, indeed, if our previous conclusions have been true, must consist in relations of which consciousness is the medium or sustainer, though not consciousness as it is in the botanist. It is not, however, with the real nature of the flower, but with its nature as perceived—a fragment of the real nature—that we are here concerned; and it is relations of which the percipient consciousness is the sustainer, which exist only through its action, that make the object, as in each case the percipient perceives it, what it is to him. Facts related to those of which the percipient is aware in the object, but not yet known to him, can only be held to belong to the perceived object potentially or in some anticipatory sense [1], in so far as upon a certain development of intelligence, in a direction which it does not rest with the will of the individual to follow or no, they will become incorporated with it. But they become

[1] [See, however, § 69.]

so incorporated with it only through the same continued action of a combining self-consciousness upon data of sensation, through which this object, as the percipient already perceives it, has come to be there for him.

64. Common sense is apt to repel such statements as these, because they are taken to imply that we can perceive what we like; that the things we see are fictions of our own, not determined by any natural or necessary order. But in truth it implies nothing of the sort, unless it is supposed that our whole consciousness is a fiction of our own, of which it rests with ourselves to make what we please. Objects do not cease to be 'objective,' facts do not cease to be unalterable, because we find that a consciousness which we cannot alter or escape from, beyond which we cannot place ourselves, *for* which many things indeed are external to each other but *to* which nothing can be external, is the medium through which they exist for us, or because we can analyse in some elementary way what it must have done in order to their thus being there for us. It is not the conception of fact, but the conception of the consciousness for which facts exist, that is affected by such analysis.

So long as consciousness is thought to have nothing to do with the constitution of the facts of which we are conscious, it is possible to look upon it merely as a succession of events or phenomena 'of the inner sense.' The question how these inner events or successive phenomena come to perform a synthesis of themselves into objects is not raised, because no such work of synthesis is thought to be required of consciousness at all. The objects we perceive are supposed to be there for us independently of any action of our minds; we have but passively to let their appearances follow each other over the mental mirror. While this view is retained, the succession of such appearances and of the mental reactions upon them—reactions gradually modified through accumulated effects of the appearances—may fairly be taken to constitute our spiritual being. But it is otherwise when we have recognised the truth, that a sensation excited by an external irritant is not a perception of the irritant or (by itself) of anything at all; that every object we perceive is a congeries of related facts, of which the simplest component, no less than the composite whole, requires in order to its presentation the action of a principle of consciousness, not itself subject to conditions of time, upon successive appearances, such action as may hold the appearances together, without fusion, in an apprehended fact. It then becomes clear that there is a function of consciousness, as exercised in the most rudimentary experience, in the simplest perception of sensible things or of the appearances of objects, which is incompatible with the definition of consciousness as any sort of succession of any sort of phenomena. Something else than a succession of phenomena is seen to be as necessary in the consciousness that perceives facts, as it is necessary to the possibility of the world of facts itself.

65. We have dwelt at length on this implication in ordinary perception of a spiritual action irreducible to phenomena, because the question whether and how far man is a part of nature, is apt to be debated exclusively on what is considered higher ground and, in consequence, without an admitted issue being raised. The transcendence of man is maintained on the ground of his exercising powers, which it may plausibly be disputed whether he exercises at all. The notion that thought can originate, or that we can freely will, is at once set down as a transcendental illusion. There is more hope of result if the controversy is begun lower down, with the analysis of an act which it is not doubted that we perform.

Now, if the foregoing analysis be correct, the ordinary perception of sensible things or matters of fact involves the determination of a sensible process, which is in time, by an agency that is not in time,—in Kant's language, a combination of 'empirical and intelligible characters,'—as essentially as do any of those 'higher' mental operations, of which the performance may be disputed. The sensation, of which the presentation as a fact is the nucleus of every perception, is an event in time. Its conditions again have all of them a history in time. It is true, indeed, that the relation between it and its cause, if its cause is understood strictly as the sum of its conditions, is not one of time. The assemblage of conditions, 'external' and 'internal,' constitutes the sensation. There is no *sequence* in time of the sensation upon the assembled conditions. But the assemblage itself is an event that has had a determinate history; and each of the constituent conditions has come to be what it is through a process in time. So much for the sensation proper. The presentation of the sensation, again, as of a fact related to other experience, is in like manner an event. A moment ago I had not so presented it: after a brief interval the perception will have given place to another. Yet the content of the presentation, the perception of this or that object, depends on the presence of that which in occurrence is past, as a fact united in one consciousness with the fact of the sensation now occurring; or rather, if the perception is one of what we call a developed mind, on numberless connected acts of such uniting consciousness, to which limits can no more be set than they can to the range of experience, and which yield the conception of a world revealed in the sensation. The agent of this neutralisation of time can as little, it would seem, be itself subject to conditions in time as the constituents of the resulting whole, the facts united in consciousness into the nature of the perceived object, are before or after each other.

66. We are not, however, fully stating the seemingly paradoxical character of everyday perception, in merely saying that it is a determination of events in time by a principle that is not in time. That is a description equally applicable to fact and to the perception of fact. For fact always implies relation determined by other relations in a universe of facts; and such relations, again, though they be relations of events to each other in time, imply, as has been previously pointed out, something out of time, for which all the terms of the several relations are equally present, as the principle of the synthesis which unites them in a single universe. But, in thus explaining the ultimate conditions of the possibility of fact, we need not assign the events themselves, and the determination of them by that which is not an event—the process of becoming, and the regulation of it as an orderly process,—to one and the same subject; as if the events happened to and altered the subject that unites them, or as if the source of order in becoming itself became. We cannot indeed suppose any real separation between the determinant and the determined. The order of becoming is

only an order of becoming through the action of that which is not in becoming; nor can we think of this order as preceded by anything that was not an order of becoming. We contradict ourselves, if we say that there was first a chaos and then came to be an order; for the 'first' and 'then' imply already an order of time, which is only possible through an action not in time. As little, on the other hand, can we suppose that which we only know as a principle of unity in relation, to exist apart from a manifold through which it is related. But we may avoid considering this principle, or the subject of which the presence and action renders possible the relations of the world of becoming, as itself in becoming, or as the result of a process of becoming. It seems to be otherwise with our perceiving consciousness. The very consciousness, which holds together successive events as equally present, has itself apparently a history in time. It seems to vary from moment to moment. It apprehends processes of becoming in a manner which implies that past stages of the becoming are present to it as known facts; yet is it not itself coming to be what it has not been?

67. It will be found, we believe, that this apparent state of the case can only be explained by supposing that in the growth of our experience, in the process of our learning to know the world, an animal organism, which has its history in time, gradually becomes the vehicle of an eternally complete consciousness. What we call our mental history is not a history of this consciousness, which in itself can have no history, but a history of the process by which the animal organism becomes its vehicle. 'Our consciousness' may mean either of two things; either a function of the animal organism, which is being made, gradually and with interruptions, a vehicle of the eternal consciousness; or that eternal consciousness itself, as making the animal organism its vehicle and subject to certain limitations in so doing, but retaining its essential characteristic as independent of time, as the determinant of becoming, which has not and does not itself become. The consciousness which varies from moment to moment, which is in succession, and of which each successive state depends on a series of 'external and internal' events, is consciousness in the former sense. It consists in what may properly be called phenomena; in successive modi-

fications of the animal organism, which would not, it is true, be what they are if they were not media for the realisation of an eternal consciousness, but which are not this consciousness. On the other hand, it is this latter consciousness, as so far realised in or communicated to us through modification of the animal organism, that constitutes our knowledge, with the relations, characteristic of knowledge, into which time does not enter, which are not in becoming but are once for all what they are. It is this again that enables us, by incorporation of any sensation to which attention is given into a system of known facts, to extend that system, and by means of fresh perceptions to arrive at further knowledge.

68. For convenience sake, we state this doctrine, to begin with, in a bald dogmatic way, though well aware how unwarrantable or unmeaning, until explained and justified, it is likely to appear. Does it not, the reader may ask, involve the impossible supposition that there is a double consciousness in man? No, we reply, not that there is a double consciousness, but that the one indivisible reality of our consciousness cannot be comprehended in a single conception. In seeking to understand its reality we have to look at it from two different points of view; and the different conceptions that we form of it, as looked at from these different points, do not admit of being united, any more than do our impressions of opposite sides of the same shield; and as we apply the same term 'consciousness' to it, from whichever point of view we contemplate it, the ambiguity noticed necessarily attends that term.

In any case of an end gradually realising itself through a certain organism a like difficulty arises. If we would state the truth about a living and growing body, we can only do it by the help of two conceptions, which we shall try in vain to reduce to a third. One will be the conception of the end, the particular form of life realised in the body—an end real and present, because operative, throughout the development of the body, but which we cannot identify with any stage of that development. The other will be that of the particular body, or complex of material conditions, organic to this end, as on the one hand dependent on an inexhaustible series of other material conditions, on the other progressively modified by results of the action, the life, to which it is organic. The particular living being is not less one and indivisible because we cannot dispense with either of these conceptions, if we would understand it aright, or because it is sometimes one, sometimes the other, of them that is predominant in our usage of the term 'living being.' In like manner, so far as we can understand at all the reality of consciousness, one and indivisible as it is in each of us, it must be by conceiving both the end, in the shape of a completed knowledge that gradually realises itself in the organic process of sentient life, and that organic process itself with its history and conditions. We have not two minds, but one mind; but we can know that one mind in its reality only by taking account, on the one hand, of the process in time by which effects of sentient experience are accumulated in the organism, yielding new modes of reaction upon stimulus and fresh associations of feeling with feeling; on the other, of the system of thought and knowledge which realises or reproduces itself in the individual through that process, a system into the inner constitution of which no relations of time enter.

69. If we examine the notion of intellectual progress common to all educated men, we find that it virtually involves this twofold conception of the mind. We regard it as a progress towards the attainment of knowledge or true ideas. But we cannot suppose that those relations of facts or objects in consciousness, which constitute any piece of knowledge of which a man becomes master, first come into being when he attains that knowledge; that they pass through the process by which he laboriously learns, or gradually cease to be as he forgets or becomes confused. They must exist as part of an eternal universe—and that a spiritual universe or universe of consciousness—during all the changes of the individual's attitude towards them, whether he is asleep or awake, distracted or attentive, ignorant or informed. It is a common-place indeed to assert that the order of the universe remains the same, however our impressions may change in regard to it; but as the common-place is apt to be understood, the universe is conceived in abstraction from consciousness, while consciousness is identified simply with the changing impressions, of which the unchanging order is independent. But the unchanging order is an order of relations; and, even if

relations of any kind could be independent of consciousness, certainly those that form the content of knowledge are not so. As known they exist only for consciousness; and, if in themselves they were external to it, we shall try in vain to conceive any process by which they could find their way from without to within it. They are relations of facts, which require a consciousness alike to present them as facts and to unite them in relation. We must hold then that there is a consciousness for which the relations of fact, that form the object of our gradually attained knowledge, already and eternally exist; and that the growing knowledge of the individual is a progress towards this consciousness.

70. It is a consciousness, further, which is itself operative in the progress towards its attainment, just as elsewhere the end realised through a certain process itself determines that process; as a particular kind of life, for instance, informs the processes organic to it. Every effort fails to trace a genesis of knowledge out of anything which is not, in form and principle, knowledge itself. The most primitive germ from which knowledge can be developed is already a perception of fact, which implies the action upon successive sensations of a consciousness which holds them in relation, and which therefore cannot itself be before or after them, or exist as a succession at all. And every step forward in real intelligence, whether in the way of addition to what we call the stock of human knowledge, or of an appropriation by the individual of some part of that stock, is only explicable on supposition that successive reports of the senses, successive efforts of attention, successive processes of observation and experiment, are determined by the consciousness that all things form a related whole—a consciousness which is operative throughout their succession and which at the same time realises itself through them.

71. A familiar illustration may help to bring home that view of what is involved in the attainment of knowledge for which we are here contending. We often talk of reading the book of nature; and there is a real analogy between the process in which we apprehend the import of a sentence, and that by which we arrive at any piece of knowledge. In reading the sentence we see the words successively, we attend to them successively,

we recall their meaning successively. But throughout that succession there must be present continuously the consciousness that the sentence has a meaning as a whole; otherwise the successive vision, attention and recollection would not end in a comprehension of what the meaning is. This consciousness operates in them, rendering them what they are as organic to the intelligent reading of the sentence. And when the reading is over, the consciousness that the sentence has a meaning has become a consciousness of what in particular the meaning is,— a consciousness in which the successive results of the mental operations involved in the reading are held together, without succession, as a connected whole. The reader has then, so far as that sentence is concerned, made the mind of the writer his own. The thought which was the writer's when he composed the sentence, has so determined, has so used as *organs*, the successive operations of sense and soul on the part of the reader, as to reproduce itself in him through them; and the first stage in this reproduction, the condition under which alone the processes mentioned contribute to it, is the conviction on the reader's part that the sentence is a connected whole, that it has a meaning which may be understood. This conviction, it is true, is not wrought in him by the thought of the writer expressed in that particular sentence. He has learnt that sentences have a meaning before applying himself to that particular one. Before any one can read at all, he must have been accustomed to have the thought of another reproduced in him through signs of one kind or another. But the first germ of this reproduction, the first possibility or receptivity of it, must have consisted in so much communication of some one else's meaning as is implied in the apprehension that he has a meaning to convey. It is through this elementary apprehension that certain functions of one man's soul, the soul of a listener or reader, become so organic to the thought of another, as that this thought gradually realises itself anew in the soul of the listener.

May we not take it to be in a similar way that the system of related facts, which forms the objective world, reproduces itself, partially and gradually, in the soul of the individual who in part knows it? That this system implies a mind or consciousness for which it exists, as the condition of the union in relation of the related facts, is not an arbitrary guess. We have seen that it is the only answer which we have any ground for giving to the question, how such a union of the manifold is possible. On the other side, our knowledge of any part of the system implies a like union of the manifold in relation; such a presentation of feelings as facts, and such a determination of the facts by mutual relation, as is only possible through the action upon feelings of a subject distinguishing itself from them. This being so, it would seem that the attainment of the knowledge is only explicable as a reproduction of itself, in the human soul, by the consciousness for which the cosmos of related facts exists—a reproduction of itself, in which it uses the sentient life of the soul as its organ.

72. Because the reproduction has thus a process in time for its organ, it is at once progressive and incapable of completion. It is 'never ending, still beginning,' because of the constant succession of phenomena in the sentient life, which the eternal consciousness, acting on that life, has perpetually to gather anew into the timeless unity of knowledge. There never can be that actual wholeness of the world for us, which there must be for the mind that renders the world one. But though the conditions under which the eternal consciousness reproduces itself in our knowledge are thus incompatible with finality in that knowledge, there is that element of identity between the first stage of intelligent experience—between the simplest beginning of knowledge—and the eternal consciousness reproducing itself in it, which consists in the presentation of a many in one, in the apprehension of facts as related in a single system, in the conception of there being an order of things, whatever that order may turn out to be. Just as the conviction that a speaker or writer has a meaning is at once the first step in the communication of his thought to a listener or reader, and the condition determining all the organic processes of reading and listening which end in the reproduction of the thought, so the conception described is at once the primary form in which that mind to which the world is relative communicates itself to us, and the influence which renders the processes of sensuous experience into organs of its communication. It is only as governed by the forecast of there being a related whole that

these processes can yield a growing, though for ever incomplete, knowledge of what in detail the whole is.

73. There should by this time be no need of the reminder, that the evidence of the action of this fore-casting idea, in the several stages of our learning to know, does not depend on any account of it which the learner may be able to give. Whether he is able to give such an account or no, depends on the development of his powers of reflection; and the idea is at work before it is reflected on. The evidence of its action lies in results inexplicable without it. Nor must we imagine it, as the doctrine of innate ideas might lead us to do, antecedent in time to the processes of learning through which it realises itself, and which, in so doing, it makes what they are. This would be the same mistake as to suppose the life of a living body antecedent in time to the functions of the living body. It is inconsistent with the essential notion that the consciousness of a related whole, *so far as it is ours*, is an end realising itself in and determining the growth of intelligence. Thus when the question is raised, whether the conception of the uniformity of nature precedes or follows upon the inartificial or unmethodised exercise of induction, the answer must be either that it does both or that it does neither; or, better, that the question, being improperly put, does not admit of an answer. The conception of the uniformity of nature is one form of the consciousness on which we have been dwelling; and the processes of experience are related to it as respiration or the circulation of the blood is related to life. It is the end to which they are organic; but, at the same time, it is so operative in them that without it they would not be what they are. It is no more derivable from processes of sense, *as these would be without it*—from excitements and reactions of the nervous system—than life is derivable from mechanical and chemical functions of that which does not live. Under various expressions, it is the primary form of the intellectual life in which the eternal consciousness, the spirit for which the relations of the universe exist, reproduces itself in us. All particular knowledge of these relations is a filling up of this form, which the continued action of the eternal consciousness in and upon the sentient life renders possible.

CHAPTER III.

74. THROUGHOUT the foregoing discussion of the conditions of knowledge our object, it will be remembered, has been to arrive at some conclusion in regard to the position in which man himself stands to the system of related phenomena called nature—in other words, in regard to the freedom of man; a conclusion on which the question of the possibility of Ethics, as other than a branch of physics, depends. Arguing, first, from the characteristics of his knowledge, postponing for the present the consideration of his moral achievement, our conclusion is that, while on the one hand his consciousness is throughout empirically conditioned,—in the sense that it would not be what at any time it is but for a series of events, sensible or related to sensibility, some of them events in the past history of consciousness, others of them events affecting the animal system organic to consciousness,—on the other hand his consciousness would not be what it is, *as knowing*, or as a subject of intelligent experience, but for the self-realisation or reproduction in it, through processes thus empirically conditioned, of an eternal consciousness, not existing in time but the condition of there being an order in time, not an object of experience but the condition of there being an intelligent experience, and in this sense not 'empirical' but 'intelligible.' In virtue of his character as knowing, therefore, we are entitled to say that man is, according to a certain well-defined meaning of the term, a 'free cause.' Let us reconsider shortly what that meaning is.

75. By the relation of effect to cause, unless the 'cause' is qualified by some such distinguishing adjective as that just employed, we understand the relation of a given event, either to another event invariably antecedent to it and upon which it is invariably sequent, or to an assemblage of conditions which

together constitute the event—into which it may be analysed.
Such a cause is not a 'free' cause. The uniformly antecedent
event is in turn dependent on other events; any particular sum
of conditions is determined by a larger complex, which we at
least cannot exhaust. But the condition of the possibility of
this relation in either of its forms—the condition of events
being connected in one order of becoming, the condition of
facts being united in a single system of mutual determination—

is the action of a single principle, to which all events and facts
are equally present and relative, but which distinguishes itself
from them all and can thus unite them in their severalty. In
speaking of this principle we can only use the terms we have
got; and these, being all strictly appropriate to the relations, or
objects determined by the relations, which this principle renders
possible but under which it does not itself subsist, are strictly
inappropriate to it.

Such is the term 'cause.' So far indeed as it indicates the
action of something which makes something else what it is,
it might seem applicable to the unifying principle which makes
the world what it is. But we have no sooner so applied it than
we have to qualify our statement by the reminder, that to the
unifying principle the world, which it renders one, cannot be
something else than itself *in the same way* as, to ordinary
apprehension, a determined fact is something else than the conditions determining it, or an event caused something else than
the antecedent events causing it. That the unifying principle
should distinguish itself from the manifold which it unifies,
is indeed the condition of the unification; but it must not be
supposed that the manifold has a nature of its own apart from
the unifying principle, or this principle another nature of its
own apart from what it does in relation to the manifold world.
Apart from the unifying principle the manifold world would be

nothing at all, and in its self-distinction from that world the
unifying principle takes its character from it; or, rather, it is in
distinguishing itself from the world that it gives itself its character, which therefore but for the world it would not have.

76. It is true indeed of anything related as a cause to anything
else on which it produces effects, that its efficiency in the production of those effects is an essential part of its nature, just as

susceptibility to those effects is an essential part of the nature of that in which they take place. No group of conditions would be what they are but for the effect which it lies in them to produce, no events what they are but for the other events that arise out of them; any more than, conversely, the conditioned phenomenon, or necessarily sequent event, has a nature independent of its conditions or antecedents. Still every particular cause, whether agent or assemblage of conditions or antecedent event, has a nature, made for it by other agents, conditions, or antecedent events, which appears but partially in any particular effect; and again the patient or conditioned phenomenon or sequent event, in which that effect appears, has a nature other than that which it derives from the particular cause. Therefore in the determined world there is a sense in saying that a cause is something on which something *else* depends for being what it is, which no longer holds when the effect is the whole determined world itself, and the cause the unifying principle implied in its determinateness. There is nothing to qualify the determined world *as a whole* but that inner determination of all contained in it by mutual relation, which is due to the action of the unifying principle; nor anything to qualify the unifying principle but this very action, with the self-distinction necessary to it.

When we transfer the term 'cause,' then, from a relation between one thing and another within the determined world to the relation between that world and the agent implied in its existence, we must understand that there is no separate particularity in the agent, on the one side, and the determined world as a whole, on the other, such as characterises any agent and patient, any cause and effect, within the determined world. The agent must act absolutely from itself in the action through which that world is—not, as does everything within the world, under determination by something else. The world has no character but that given it by this action; the agent no character but that which it gives itself in this action.

77. This is what we mean by calling the agent a 'free cause.' But the question at once arises whether, when we have thus qualified the term 'cause' by an epithet which effectually distinguishes it from any cause cognisable within the world of

phenomena, it still has a meaning for us. The answer is that but for our own exercise of such causality it would have none. But, in fact, our action in knowledge—the action by which we connect successive phenomena in the unity of a related whole— is an action as absolutely from itself, as little to be accounted for by the phenomena which through it become an intelligent experience, or by anything alien to itself, as is that which we have found to be implied in the existence of the universal order. This action of our own 'mind' in knowledge—to say nothing of any other achievement of the human spirit—becomes to us, when reflected on, a *causa cognoscendi* in relation to the action of a self-originating 'mind' in the universe; which we then learn to regard as the *causa essendi* to the same action, exercised under whatever limiting conditions, by ourselves. We find that, quite apart from the sense in which all facts and events, including those of our natural life, are determined by that mind without which nature would not be, there is another sense in which we ourselves are not so much determined by it as identified by it with itself, or made the subjects of its self-communication. *All* things in nature are determined by it, in the sense that they are determined by each other in a manner that would be impossible but for its equal, self-dis- tinguishing presence to them all. It is thus that the events of our natural life are determined by it; not merely the mechanical and chemical processes presupposed by that life, but the life itself, including all that can properly be called the successive phenomena of our mental history. But to say that it is thus determined, though it is true of our natural life, is not the full account of it; for this life, with its constituent events or phenomena, is organic to a form of consciousness of which knowledge is the development, and which, if for no other reason than that it conceives time, cannot itself be in time. While the processes organic to this consciousness are deter- mined by the mind to which all things are relative, in the sense that they are part of a universe which it renders possible, this consciousness itself is a reproduction of that mind, in respect, at least, of its attributes of self-origination and unification of the manifold.

78. It may be asked here, what after all is the conclusion as to

the freedom of man himself to be drawn from these considerations in regard to knowledge. 'Granted,' it may be said, 'that the knowledge of nature is irreducible to a natural process, that it implies the action of a principle not in time, which you may call, if you please, an eternal mind; still you admit that man's attainment of knowledge is conditional on processes in time and on the fulfilment of strictly natural functions. These processes and functions are as essential to man, as much a part of his being, as his knowledge is. How then can it be said that the being itself, thus conditioned, is not a part of nature but is free? Or, if this statement is made and can be justified, must it not be left alongside of an exactly contrary statement? Do you not after all leave man still "in doubt to deem himself a God or beast;" still perplexed with the "partly this, partly that" conclusion, for which philosophy, if good for anything, should substitute one more satisfactory, but which, on the contrary, it seems merely to restate in a more prolix form?'

79. We answer that, if the foregoing considerations have any truth in them, we are not shut up in this ambiguity. To say that man in himself is *in part* an animal or product of nature, on the ground that the consciousness which distinguishes him is realised through natural processes, is not more true than to say that an animal is in part a machine, because the life which distinguishes it has mechanical structures for its organs. If that activity of knowledge on the part of man, to which functions provisionally called natural are organic, is as absolutely different from any process of change or becoming as we have endeavoured to show that it is, then even the functions organic to it are not described with full truth when they are said to be natural. For the constituent elements of an organism can only be truly and adequately conceived as rendered what they are by the end realised through the organism. The mechanical structure organic to life is not adequately conceived as a machine, though, for the purpose of more accurate examination of the structure in detail, it may be convenient to treat it as such. And, for a like reason, the state of the case in regard to a man is not fairly represented by saying that, though not merely an animal or natural, he is so in respect of the processes

of physical change through which an intelligent consciousness is realised in him. In strict truth the man who knows, so far from being an animal altogether, is not an animal at all or even in part. The functions, which would be those of a natural or animal life if they were not organic to the end consisting in knowledge, just because they are so organic, are not in their full reality natural functions, though the purposes of detailed investigation of them—perhaps the purpose of improving man's estate—may be best served by so treating them. For one who could comprehend the whole state of the case, even a digestion that served to nourish a brain, which was in turn organic to knowledge, would be essentially different from digestion in an animal incapable of knowledge, even if it were not the case that the digestive process is itself affected by the end to which it is mediately relative. And, if this is true of those processes which are directly or indirectly organic to knowledge but do not constitute or enter into it, much more is it true of the man capable of knowledge, that in himself he is not an animal, not a link in the chain of natural becoming, in part any more than at all.

80. The question whether a man himself, or in himself, is a natural or animal being, can only mean whether he is so in respect of that which renders him conscious of himself. There is no sense in asking what anything *in itself* is, if it has no self at all. That which is made what it is wholly by relations to other things, neither being anything but their joint result nor distinguishing itself from them, has no self to be enquired about. Such is the case with all things in inorganic nature. Of them at any rate the saying 'Natur hat weder Kern noch Schale' is true without qualification. The distinction between inner and outer, between what they are in themselves and what they are in relation to other things, has no application to them. In an organism, on the other hand, the distinction between its relations and itself does appear. The life of a living body is not, like the motion of a moving body, simply the joint result of its relations to other things. It modifies those relations, and modifies them through a nature not reducible to them, not constituted by their combination. Their bearing on it is different from what it would be if it did not live; and there is so

far a meaning in saying that the organism is something in itself other than what its relations make it—that, while it is related to other things according to mechanical and chemical laws, it has itself a nature which is not mechanical or chemical. There is a significance, accordingly, in the enquiry what this nature in itself is, which there is not in the same enquiry as applied to anything that does not live. But the living body does not, as such, present its nature to itself in consciousness. It does not consciously distinguish itself from its relations. Man, on the other hand, does so distinguish himself, and his doing so is his special distinction. The enquiry, therefore, what he in himself is, must refer not merely to a character which he has as more, and other, than a joint result of relations to other things—such a character he has as simply living,—but to the character which he has as consciously distinguishing himself from all that happens to him.

81. Now this distinction by man of himself from events is no less essentially different from any process in time or any natural becoming than is the activity of knowledge, which indeed depends upon it. It is through it that he is conscious of time, of becoming, of a personal history; and the active principle of this consciousness cannot itself be determined by these relations in the way of time or becoming, which arise for consciousness through its action. The 'punctum stans,' to which an order of time must be relative that it may be an order of time, cannot itself be a moment or a series of moments in that order; nor can the 'punctum stans' *in consciousness*, necessary to the *presentation* of time, be itself a succession in consciousness. And that which is true in regard to the mere presentation of time is true also of everything presented in time, of all becoming, of every history. To be conscious of it we must unite its several stages as related to each other in the way of succession; and to do that we must ourselves be, and distinguish ourselves as being, out of the succession. Ἀνάγκη ἄρα ἀμιγῆ εἶναι τὸν νοῦν, ὥσπερ φησὶν Ἀναξαγόρας, ἵνα κρατῇ, τοῦτο δ' ἐστὶν, ἵνα γνωρίζῃ[1]. It is only through our holding ourselves aloof, so to speak, from the

[1] Mind, then, must be unmixed with anything else, as Anaxagoras says, in order that it may master things; that is, in order that it may know them. Arist. de anim. III. iv. 4.

manifold affections of sense, as constant throughout their variety, that they can be presented to us as a connected series, and thus move us to seek the conditions of the connexion between them. And again, when the conception of such conditions has been arrived at, it is only through the same detachment of self from the succession of its experiences that we can conceive the conditions as united in their changes by an unchanging law, which, as determining the order of all events in time, is itself unaffected by time.

82. Thus, while still confining our view to man's achievement in knowledge, we are entitled to say that in himself, *i. e.* in respect of that principle through which he at once is a self and distinguishes himself as such, he exerts a free activity,—an activity which is not in time, not a link in the chain of natural becoming, which has no antecedents other than itself but is self-originated. There is no incompatibility between this doctrine and the admission that all the processes of brain and nerve and tissue, all the functions of life and sense, organic to this activity (though even they, as in the thinking man, cannot, for reasons given, properly be held to be merely natural), have a strictly natural history. There would only be such an incompatibility, if these processes and functions actually constituted or made up the self-distinguishing man, the man capable of knowledge. But this, as we have seen, is what they cannot do. Human action is only explicable by the action of an eternal consciousness, which uses them as its organs and reproduces itself through them.

The question why there should be this reproduction, is indeed as unanswerable as every form of the question why the world as a whole should be what it is. Why any detail of the world is what it is, we can explain by reference to other details which determine it; but why the whole should be what it is, why the mind which the world implies should exhibit itself in a world at all, why it should make certain processes of that world organic to a reproduction of itself under limitations which the use of such organs involves—these are questions which, owing perhaps to those very limitations, we are equally unable to avoid asking and to answer. We have to content ourselves with saying that, strange as it may seem, it is so. Taking all the facts of the case together, we cannot express them otherwise. The unification of the manifold in the world implies the presence of the manifold to a mind, for which, and through the action of which, it is a related whole. The unification of the manifold of sense *in our consciousness* of a world implies a certain self-realisation of this mind in us through certain processes of the world which, as explained, only exists through it—in particular through the processes of life and feeling. The wonder in which philosophy is said to begin will not cease when this conclusion is arrived at; but, till it can be shown to have left some essential part of the reality of the case out of sight, and another conclusion can be substituted for it which remedies the defect, this is no reason for rejecting it.

83. Before proceeding, it may be well to point out that it is a conclusion which can in no wise be affected by any discovery, or (legitimately) by any speculation, in regard either to the relation between the human organism and other forms of animal structure, or to the development of human intelligence and the connexion of its lower stages with the higher stages of the intelligence of brutes. Having admitted that certain processes in time are organic in man to that consciousness exercised in knowledge which we hold to be eternal, we have no interest in abridging those processes. If there are reasons for holding that man, in respect of his animal nature, is descended from 'mere' animals—animals in whom the functions of life and sense were not organic to the eternal or distinctively human consciousness,— this does not affect our conclusion in regard to the consciousness of which, as he now is, man is the subject; a conclusion founded on analysis of what he now is and does. This conclusion could only be shaken by showing either that a consciousness of the kind which, for reasons already set forth, we describe as eternal, is not involved in knowledge, or that such a consciousness can in some intelligible way be developed out of those successions of feeling which can properly be treated as functions of the animal system; and this must mean that it has some element of identity with them. That countless generations should have passed during which a transmitted organism was progressively modified by reaction on its surroundings, by struggle for existence, or otherwise, till its functions became such that an eternal consciousness could realise or reproduce itself through them—

this might add to the wonder with which the consideration of what we do and are must always fill us, but it could not alter the results of that consideration. If such be discovered to be the case, the discovery cannot affect the analysis of knowledge— of what is implied in there being a world to be known and in our knowing it,—on which we found our theory of the action of a free or self-conditioned and eternal mind in man.

84. The question, however, of the development of the human organism out of lower forms is quite different from that of the relation between the intelligence exercised in our knowledge and the mere succession of 'impressions and ideas,' *i. e.* of feelings in their primary, or more lively, and in their secondary, or less lively, stage. Till some flaw can be shown in the doctrine previously urged, we must hold that there is an absolute difference between change and the intelligent consciousness or knowledge of change, which precludes us from tracing any development of the one into the other, if development implies any identity of principle between the germ and the developed outcome. When we speak of a development of higher from lower forms of intelligence, there should be no mistake about what we mean, and what we do not mean. We mean the development of an intelligence which, in the lowest form from which the higher can properly be said to be developed, is already a consciousness of change, and therefore cannot be developed out of any succession of changes in the sensibility, contingent upon reactions of the 'psychoplasm' or nervous system, however that system may have been modified by accumulated effects of its reactions in the past.

To deny categorically on this account that the distinctive intelligence of man, his intelligence as knowing, can be developed from that of 'lower' animals would indeed be more than we should be warranted in doing. We have much surer ground for saying what, in respect of our knowledge, we are than for saying what the animals are not. The analysis of what we do and have done in knowledge, which entitles us to certain conclusions as to what we must be in order to do it, is inapplicable to beings with whom we cannot communicate. If the animals have a consciousness corresponding to that which we exercise in knowledge, at any rate we cannot enter into it. Their actions, as observed from outside, would seem to be explicable without it—explicable as resulting from the determination of action by feeling and that of feeling by feeling, in other words as resulting from successive changes of the sensibility,—without any need for ascribing to them any consciousness of change, any synthesis of the modifications they experience as belonging to an inter-related world. We are thus warranted in saying that we have no evidence of the presence in 'brutes' of such an intelligence as that which forms the basis of our knowledge; and that, *if it is absent*, there can, properly speaking, have been no development of our mind from such a mind as theirs. But this hypothetical negation is quite compatible with the admission that there may have been a progressive development, through hereditary transmission, of the animal system which has become organic to the distinctive intelligence of man; that the particular modes of successive feeling upon which a unifying intelligence supervenes in man, rendering them for him into a related world, may be the result of a past experience on the part of beings in whom such intelligence had not yet supervened, and who were in that sense not human; and that certain modifications of the sensibility, arising from this pre-human history, may have been the condition, according to some unascertained law, of that supervention of intelligence in man.

BOOK II.

THE WILL.

CHAPTER I.

THE FREEDOM OF THE WILL.

85. So far we have been dealing with what we may venture
to call the metaphysics of experience or knowledge, as distinct
from the metaphysics of moral action. We have been considering the action of the self-conditioning and self-distinguishing
mind, which the existence of a connected world implies, in
determining a particular product of that world, *viz.* the animal
system of man, with the receptive feelings to which that system
is organic,—in so determining it as to reproduce itself, under
limitations, in the capacity for knowledge which man possesses.
The characteristic of this particular mode of its reproduction in
the human self is the apprehension of a world which *is*, as distinct from one which *should be*. It constitutes a knowledge of
the conditions of the feelings that occur to us, and of uniform
relations between changes in those conditions. But the animal
system is not organic merely to feeling of the kind just spoken
of as receptive, to *impressions*, according to the natural meaning
of that term, conveyed by the nerves of the several senses. It
is organic also to *wants*, and to impulses for the satisfaction of
those wants, which may be in many cases occasioned by impressions of the kind mentioned, but which constitute quite a
different function of the animal system.

These wants, with the sequent impulses, must be distinguished
from the consciousness of wanted objects, and from the effort to
give reality to the objects thus present in consciousness as
wanted, no less than sensations of sight and hearing have to be
distinguished from the consciousness of objects to which those

sensations are conceived to be related. It has been sufficiently pointed out how the presentation of sensible things, on occasion of sensation, implies the action of a principle which is not, like sensation, in time, or an event or a series of events, but must equally be present to, and distinguish itself from, the several stages of a sensation to which attention is given, as well as the several sensations attended to and referred to a single object. In like manner the transition from mere want to consciousness of a wanted object, from the impulse to satisfy the want to an effort for realisation of the idea of the wanted object, implies the presence of the want to a subject which distinguishes itself from it and is constant throughout successive stages of the want.

So much is implied in the conversion of a want into the presentation of a wanted object, though the want be of strictly animal origin, and however slightly the object may be defined in consciousness. Every step in the definition of the wanted object implies a further action of the same subject, in the way of comparing various wants that arise in the process of life, along with the incidents of their satisfaction, as they only can be compared by a subject which is other than the process, not itself a stage or series of stages in the succession which it observes. At the same time as the reflecting subject traverses the series of wants, which it distinguishes from itself while it presents their filling as its object, there arises the idea of a satisfaction on the whole—an idea never realisable, but for ever striving to realise itself in the attainment of a greater command over means to the satisfaction of particular wants.

86. For the present we take no notice of any wanted objects but such as arise from the presentation by a reflecting subject to itself of wants that are of a purely animal origin. With the exception of the object consisting in a general satisfaction of such wants, we take no account as yet of wants that are of distinctively human origin, of wants that arise out of conceptions. The form of consciousness which we are considering does indeed differ absolutely from the mere succession of animal wants; but it so differs, not in respect of the presence of such wants as are not of animal origin, but in virtue of that distinction of self from the wants, through which there supervenes upon the

succession of wants a consciousness—not a succession—of wanted objects. It is this consciousness which yields, in the most elementary form, the conception of something that *should be* as distinct from that which *is*, of a world of practice as distinct from that world of experience of which the conception arises from the determination by the Ego of the receptive senses. Whereas in perceptive experience the sensible object carries its reality with it—in being presented at all, is presented as real, though the nature of its reality may remain to be discovered,—in practice the wanted object is one to which real existence has yet to be given. This latter point, it is true, is one which language is apt to disguise. The food which I am said to want, the treasure on which I have set my heart, are already in existence. But, strictly speaking, the objects which in these cases I present to myself as wanted, are the eating of the food, the acquisition of the treasure; and as long as I want them, these exist for me only as ideas which I am striving to realise, as something which I would might be but which is not.

Thus the world of practice depends on man in quite a different sense from that in which nature, or the world of experience, does so. We have seen indeed that independence is not to be ascribed to nature, in the sense either that there would be nature at all without the action of a spiritual self-distinguishing subject, or that there could be a nature for us, for our apprehension, but for a further action of this subject in or as our soul. It is independent of us, however, in the sense that it does not depend on any exercise of our powers whether the sensible objects, of which we are conscious, shall become real or no. They are already real. On the other hand, it is characteristic of the world of practice that its constituents are objects of which the existence in consciousness, as wanted, is prior to, and conditions, their existence in reality. It depends on a certain exercise of our powers, determined by ideas of the objects as wanted, whether those ideas shall become real or no.

87. The same thing may perhaps be otherwise stated by saying that the world of practice—the world composed of moral or distinctively human actions, with their results—is one in which the determining causes are *motives*; a *motive* again being

an idea of an end, which a self-conscious subject presents to itself, and which it strives and tends to realise. Now, *prima facie*, as will be admitted on all hands, this causality of motives effectually distinguishes the world which moral action has brought, and continues to bring, into being, from the series of natural events. In the latter the occurrence of an event does not depend on an idea of the event, as a desired object, being previously presented. If then moral action is to be brought within the series of natural phenomena, it must be on supposition that the motives which determine it, having natural antecedents, are themselves but links in the chain of natural phenomena; and that thus moral action, though distinguished from other kinds of natural event by its dependence on prior ideas, is not denaturalised, since the ideas on which it depends are themselves of natural origin.

The question whether this is so is the point really at issue in regard to the possibility and indispensableness of a Moral Philosophy which shall not be a branch of natural science; or, if we like to put it so, in regard to the freedom of moral agents. It is not the question commonly debated, with much ambiguity of terms, between 'determinists' and 'indeterminists'; not the question whether there is, or is not, a possibility of unmotived willing; but the question whether motives, of that kind by which it is the characteristic of moral or human action to be determined, are of properly natural origin or can be rightly regarded as natural phenomena.

88. If the foregoing analysis be correct, even those motives (defined above) which lie nearest, so to speak, to animal wants, are yet effectually distinguished from them and from any kind of natural phenomena. No one would pretend to find more than a strictly natural event either in any appetite or want incidental to the process of animal life, or in the effect of such a want in the way of an instinctive action directed to its satisfaction. But it is contended that such appetite or want does not constitute a motive proper, does not move to any distinctively human action, except as itself determined by a principle of other than natural origin. It only becomes a motive, so far as upon the want there supervenes the presentation of the want by a self-

conscious subject to himself, and with it the idea of a self-satisfaction to be attained in the filling of the want.

89. It is not indeed that the want is intrinsically altered, or ceases to be a want, through the supervention upon it of the moral motive, properly so called; but that, while it continues or ceases and begins again, there arises a new agency, other than it, from its presence to a self-conscious subject which takes from it an idea of an object in which self-satisfaction is to be sought. And the new agency, thus resulting, is no more a natural event or process, or the product of any such event or process, than is the self-consciousness to which it owes its distinguishing character. We may illustrate the state of the case from what takes place in physical life. A chemical process does not cease to be a chemical process because it goes on in a living organism, but it does become contributory to a result wholly different from any which, apart from a living organism, it could have yielded. On the other hand, life is not a chemical or mechanical process because chemical and mechanical processes are necessary to the living body, unless such processes can by themselves constitute life. No more is any moral action, or action from motives, a natural event because natural want is necessary to it, unless the self-consciousness, in and through which a motive arises out of the want, is itself a natural event or series of events or relation between events.

90. That it is not so is scarcely less plain of self-consciousness, in that relation to want which yields a motive, than it is of it in that relation to sensation which yields perception and, through it, knowledge. Can that be an event or phenomenon, whether in the way of want or otherwise, which throughout the successive stages, the abatements and revivals, of a want presents the single idea of the self-satisfaction to be attained in its filling; which unites successive wants in the idea of a general need for which provision is to be made, and holds together the successive wants and fillings as the connected but distinct incidents of an inner life, as an experience of happiness or the reverse? Can it, again, be a *series* of events, either the series of which the connexion in an inner life thus arises through its action, or any other series? Can it, finally, be the connexion or *relation* thus arising, or any other relation?

But when we have rejected all these alternatives, when we have said that the practical self-consciousness, which is the distinguishing factor in all motives, is not an event or series of events or relation between events, we have said that it is not *natural* in the ordinary sense of that term; not natural at any rate in any sense in which naturalness would imply its determination by antecedent events, or by conditions of which it is not itself the source.

91. If the reader is satisfied by these considerations that there is something more than natural in the motive to a moral or distinctively human action, he may be apt to assume—since there is no disputing the dependence on animal impulse at any rate of those elementary motives to which we have so far confined our view—that animal impulse is one component of the motive, while self-consciousness is another; that the moral agent is partly an animal, partly a rational or self-realising subject. But against such a view we should protest as much as previously [§ 68] against the notion that the presence of a double consciousness in man was implied in the distinction pointed out between the process of sensation in time and its determination by a subject not in time, as alike necessary to perception and knowledge. If it would be untrue to say of the functions of life that they are partly chemical, because without chemical processes they could not be exercised, it is even more untrue to say of a motive, in the proper sense, that it is partly animal, because, unless an animal want occurred, it would not arise. The motive is not made up of a want and self-consciousness, any more than life of chemical processes and vital ones. It is one and indivisible; but, indivisible as it is, it results, as perception results, from the determination of an animal nature by a self-conscious subject other than it; so results, however, as that the animal condition does not survive *in* the result.

The want, no doubt, may remain along with the new result—the motive, properly so called—which arises from its relation to self-consciousness, but it is not a part of it. Hunger, for instance, may survive along with the motive, involving some form of self-reference, which arises out of it in the self-conscious man—whether that motive be the desire to relieve himself from pain, or to give himself pleasure, or to qualify himself for work, or to provide himself the means of living,—but hunger neither is that motive nor a part of it. If it were, the resulting act would not be moral but instinctive. There would be no moral agency in it. It would not be the man that did it, but the hunger or some 'force of nature' in him. The motive in every imputable act for which the agent is conscious on reflection that he is answerable, is a desire for personal good in some form or other; and, however much the idea of what the personal good for the time is may be affected by the pressure of animal want, this want is no more a part or component of the desire than is the sensation of light or colour, which I receive in looking at this written line, a component part of my perception in reading it.

92. Whether our conclusion be accepted or no, it may be hoped that the point which it is sought to make good in regard to the distinctive character of motives has at least been made clear. What instinct is, whether there are in truth merely instinctive actions, is a question on which, though of late some men seem almost to have argued themselves into believing the contrary, there is much more room for doubt than there is as to the nature and reality of motives and the moral action determined by them. If we have to explain what we mean by instinct and instinctive action, we have to do it by excluding the essential characteristic of our own motives and motived action. By an instinctive action we mean one *not* determined by a conception, on the part of the agent, of any good to be gained or evil to be avoided by the action. It is superfluous to add, good *to himself*; for anything conceived as good in such a way that the agent acts for the sake of it, must be conceived as *his own* good, though he may conceive it as his own good only on account of his interest in others, and in spite of any amount of suffering on his own part incidental to its attainment. By a moral action, an action morally imputable or that can be called good or bad, we mean one that *is* so determined as the instinctive action is not. Clearly it is nothing but our knowledge of what moral or motived action is, that gives a meaning to the negation conveyed in the description of another sort of action as instinctive. Whether there in fact are actions, either done by ourselves under certain conditions or by other

agents, that correspond to this negative description can never be known with the same intimate certainty with which it is known that actions belonging to our conscious experience are related to motives in that manner of which the negative forms the meaning of the description of any action as instinctive.

93. It is true that it makes no difference to the outward form of an action whether it is so related to a motive or no; whether it has a moral quality or—as would be the case, if it were determined *directly* by animal want—is merely instinctive, in the sense of not proceeding from a conception of personal good. It may have the same effect on the senses of an on-looker, the same nervous and muscular motions may be involved in it, the same physical results may follow from it, in the one case as in the other. But it is not by the outward form, thus understood, that we know what moral action is. We know it, so to speak, on the inner side. We know what it is in relation to us, the agents; what it is as our expression. Only thus indeed do we know it at all. In knowledge so derived, where from the nature of the case our judgments are incapable of verification in the ordinary sense by reference to matters of fact—for the motive which an act expresses is not what we commonly mean by a matter of fact—there is, no doubt, much liability to arbitrariness in the interpretation of the self-consciousness to which alone we can appeal. Against such arbitrariness, it would seem, we can only protect ourselves by great circum-spection in the adoption of our formulæ, so that they may be as nearly adequate as possible to the inner experience which we mean them to convey, and by constant reference to the expres-sion of that experience which is embodied, so to speak, in the habitual phraseology of men, in literature, and in the institutions of family and political life.

94. However insufficient such safeguards may be, it remains the case that self-reflection is the only possible method of learning what is the inner man or mind that our action expresses; in other words, what that action really is. Judgments so arrived at must be the point of departure for all enquiry into processes by which our actual moral nature may have been reached, and into links of connection between it and that of animals other-

wise endowed. Whatever the result of such enquiries, it can only be through a confusion that we allow them to affect our conclusions in regard to the actuality of our conscious life. Our knowledge of what that life is may not seldom entitle us to reject speculations as to a process by which it has come about, on the ground that such a product as can be legitimately traced from the process is not the inner life which we know. But no inference from such supposed processes can entitle us to decide that this life is not that which a sufficiently comprehensive view of the evidence afforded by itself would authorise us in taking it to be; since the acceptance of this evidence as the given reality is the presupposition of any enquiry into a process by which the given reality has come to be.

95. It must be plainly admitted, then, that self-reflection is the basis of the view here given in regard to the distinctive character of the motives which moral actions represent. Any one making this admission will of course endeavour to conduct his self-reflection as circumspectly as possible, and to save it as far as may be from errors which personal idiosyncracy might occasion, by constant reference to the customary expressions of moral consciousness in use among men, and to the institutions in which men have embodied their ideas or ideals of permanent good. In the interpretation, however, of such expressions and institutions self-reflection must be our ultimate guide. Without it they would have nothing to tell; and it is to it, avowedly, that we make our appeal when we say that to every action morally imputable, or of which a man can recognise himself as the author, the motive is always some idea of the man's personal good—an idea absolutely different from animal want, even in cases where it is from anticipation of the satisfaction of some animal want that the idea of personal good is derived.

Now a motive so constituted, like the perception which answers to it in the sphere of speculative intelligence, clearly admits of being considered in seemingly opposite ways. Two seemingly incompatible, yet equally true, sets of statements may be made in regard to it; which, however, are not really incompatible, because one relates to the motive in its full reality, which is not a sensible event, the other to a sensible event which is implied

in it (as sensation is implied in perception) but is not it.   The
sensible event or phenomenon, implied in the motive, is, like
every other event, determined by antecedent events according to
natural laws.   The motive itself, though it too is in its own way
definitely determined, is not naturally determined.   It is constituted by an act of self-consciousness which is not a natural
event, an act in which the agent presents to himself a certain
idea of himself—of himself doing or himself enjoying—as an idea
of which the realisation forms for the time his good.   It is true
that the moral quality of this act, its virtue or its vice, depends
on the character of the agent.   It is this that determines what
the kind of personal good, which under any set of circumstances
he presents to himself, shall be.   This character, in turn, has had
its history, just as a man's developed intelligence, as it at any
time stands, has had a history.   But just as this latter history,
though to call it a history *of* an eternal consciousness would be a
contradiction, has yet taken its distinctive nature, as a history
of *intelligence*, from a certain action of an eternal self-distinguishing consciousness upon the processes of feeling; so the history of
human character has been one in which the same consciousness
has throughout been operative upon wants of animal origin,
giving rise through its action upon them to the specific quality
of that history.

96. The view which it is sought to convey may be made more
plain by an instance.   When Esau sells his birthright for a mess
of pottage, his motive, we might be apt hastily to say, is an
animal want.   On reflection, if by 'motive' is meant that which
an action represents or expresses, the inner side of that of
which the action is the outer, we shall find that it is not so.
The motive lies in the presentation of an idea of himself as
enjoying the pleasure of eating the pottage, or (which comes
practically to the same thing) as relieved from the pain of
hunger.   Plainly, but for his hunger Esau could have no such
motive.   But for it his presentation of himself as a subject of
pleasure could have taken no such form.   But the hunger is not
the presentation of himself as the subject of pleasure, still less
the presentation of that particular pleasure as under the circumstances his greatest good; and therefore it is not his motive.
If the action were determined directly by the hunger, it would

have no moral character, any more than have actions done in
sleep, or strictly under compulsion, or from accident, or (so far
as we know) the actions of animals. Since, however, it is not
the hunger as a natural force, but his own conception of himself,
as finding for the time his greatest good in the satisfaction of
hunger, that determines the act, Esau recognises himself as
the author of the act. He imputes it to himself, and it is
morally imputable to him—an act for which he is accountable,
to which praise or blame are appropriate. If evil follows from
it, whether in the shape of punishment inflicted by a superior,
or of calamity ensuing in the course of nature to himself or
those in whom he is interested, he is aware that he himself has
brought it on himself. Hence remorse, and with it the possibility of change of heart. He may 'find no place for repentance'
in the sense of cancelling or getting rid of the evil which his
act has caused; but in another sense the recognition of himself as the author of the evil is, in promise and potency, itself
repentance.

97. 'But how,' it will be asked, 'does this analysis of Esau's
motive affect the question of his moral freedom?' We admit at
once that, if he is not free or self-determined in his motive, he is
not free at all. To a will free in the sense of unmotived we can
attach no meaning whatever. Of the relation between will and
desire more shall be said in the sequel. For the present the
statement may suffice, that we know of no other expression
of will but a motive in the sense above explained, or, as it may
be called to avoid ambiguity, a strongest motive. Such a motive
is the will in act. The question as to the freedom of the will
we take to be a question as to the origin of such a strongest
motive.

98. The assertion that Esau's motive, and with it the action
which expresses his character, is the joint outcome of his circumstances and character, however true it may be, throws
little light on the matter, unless followed by some further
analysis of the circumstances and character. One 'circumstance' no doubt is his hunger, and this has a definite physical
history. The physiologist, with sufficient knowledge and opportunity of examination, could trace its determining antecedents

with the utmost precision. But even this hunger, *as it affects Esau's action*, is not really what it would be in relation to a merely natural agent, any more than the visual sensation, which this flower conveys to an intelligent person who attends to it, is really the same as that which it conveys to a merely sentient animal. The want in the one case, the sensation in the other, may rightly be abstracted from the self-consciousness by relation to which, in the cases supposed, it is really determined, for the purpose of investigating those natural conditions and antecedents which are unaffected by that relation; but it must not be forgotten that there *is* an abstraction in so treating it, and that, when the moral bearing of the want is in question, the abstraction may become misleading. The circumstances which in combination with character affect moral action, just because they are so combined, are no longer what they would be merely as circumstances. They are not like forces converging on an inert body which does not itself modify the direction of the resulting motion. Thus even a circumstance in itself and in its antecedents so strictly physical as hunger, if it is Esau's hunger, the hunger of an agent morally endowed, has in effect a quality not determined by natural antecedents.

Of the other circumstances bearing on Esau's action, or of the most important among them, it could not be admitted that they are merely physical at all, even in their origin or antecedents as distinct from their bearing on his act. We may perhaps classify them roughly under three heads—the state of his health, the outward manner of his life (including his family arrangements and the mode in which he maintains himself and his family), and the standard of social expectation on the part of those whom he recognises as his equals. All these have their weight in affecting the result which his character yields under the pressure of animal want, but they are all of them influences which have come to be what they are through processes in which human character or will has been an essential factor. Just as the result to which they contribute in his conduct only arises from the particular mode in which the self-presenting and self-seeking Ego in him reacts upon them, so it is only through previous conduct similarly determined, on his own part or that of others,

that such circumstances have taken their actual shape. Their
formation at every stage has indeed been affected by events
which, like the particular experience of hunger in Esau's case,
have each had their definite chain of physical antecedents; but
it has only been as determined by relation to the human self that
these events have yielded the given result in the shape of these
particular circumstances. In the last resort, then, we are thrown
back on the question of the character of the agency so exerted,
alike in the formation of those circumstances by which the
motive expressed in any moral action is affected, and in that
reaction of the man upon the circumstances which actually yields
that motive.

99. When we thus speak of the human self, or the man, re-
acting upon circumstances, giving shape to them, taking a
motive from them, what is it exactly that we mean by this self
or man? The answer must be the same as was given to a corresponding question in regard to the self-conscious principle
implied in our knowledge. We mean by it a certain reproduction of itself on the part of the eternal self-conscious subject of
the world—a reproduction of itself to which it makes the
processes of animal life organic, and which is qualified and
limited by the nature of those processes, but which is so far
essentially a reproduction of the one supreme subject, implied
in the existence of the world, that the product carries with it
under all its limitations and qualifications the characteristic of
being an object to itself. It is the particular human self or
person, we hold, thus constituted, that in every moral action,
virtuous or vicious, presents to itself some possible state or
achievement of its own as for the time its greatest good, and
acts for the sake of that good. The kind of good which at any
point in his life the person presents to himself as greatest
depends, we admit, on his past experience—his past passion
and action—and on circumstances. But throughout the past
experience he has been an object to himself, and thus the
author of his acts in the sense just stated. And as for the
circumstances, in the first place they only affect his action
through the medium of that idea of his own good upon which
he makes them converge; and, secondly, in respect of that
part of them which is most important in its bearing on conduct,

they themselves presuppose personal, self-seeking[1] agency of the kind described.

100. It will probably be objected that it makes no practical difference to the moral freedom of the individual, whether or no the circumstances by which he is influenced are of strictly natural or of specially human origin, so long as it is not to the individual's own action that they are due. That there is a sense of 'freedom,' indeed, in which it is very differently affected by such a 'circumstance' as hunger or imminent death, and by such another 'circumstance' as the customs and expectations of a society to which the individual belongs, will hardly be disputed. The freedom of an action must be taken to mean simply its imputability in the juristic sense, if it is alleged that it makes no difference to its freedom whether the agent is influenced in doing it by the circumstance of pressing physical need, or by the circumstance that his honour is appealed to by his family or his state. Before taking further notice, however, of the very various senses in which freedom is asserted of man, and of the relation in which our doctrine stands to them, it will be well to guard against further liability to misapprehension in respect of the doctrine itself[2].

'Do you mean,' it may be asked, 'to assert the existence of a mysterious abstract entity which you call the self of a man, apart from all his particular feelings, desires, and thoughts—all the experience of his inner life?' To such a question we should reply, to begin with, that of 'entities' we know nothing, except as a dyslogistic term denoting something in which certain English psychological writers seem to suppose that certain other writers believe, but in which, so far as known, no one has stated his own belief. That the self, as we conceive it, is in a certain sense 'mysterious' we admit. It is in a sense mysterious that there should be such a thing as a world at all. The old question, why God made the world, has never been answered, nor will be. We

---

[1] The distinction between that sort of self-seeking which is the characteristic of all action susceptible of moral attributes, and that which is specially characteristic of bad moral action, will be considered in the sequel.

[2] [The author must have determined, after this paragraph was written, to omit the fuller account of the different senses of 'freedom' which was sometimes given in his lectures and is promised here. It is now (1890) printed in the second volume of Green's *Works*, edited by R. L. Nettleship.

know not why the world should be; we only know that there it is. In like manner we know not why the eternal subject of that world should reproduce itself, through certain processes of the world, as the spirit of mankind, or as the particular self of this or that man in whom the spirit of mankind operates. We can only say that, upon the best analysis we can make of our experience, it seems that so it does. That in thus reproducing itself, however, it remains an 'abstract' self, apart from the desires, feelings, and thoughts of the individual man, is just the notion we seek to set aside. Just as we hold that our desires, feelings, and thoughts would not be what they are—would not be those of a man—if not related to a subject which distinguishes itself from each and all of them; so we hold that this subject would not be what it is, if it were not related to the particular feelings, desires, and thoughts, which it thus distinguishes from and presents to itself. If we are told that the Ego or self is an abstraction from the facts of our inner experience—something which we 'accustom ourselves to suppose' as a basis or substratum for these, but which exists only logically, not really, – it is a fair rejoinder, that these so-called facts, our particular feelings, desires, and thoughts, are abstractions, if considered otherwise than as united in the character of an agent who is an object to himself. The difficulty of saying what this all-uniting, self-seeking, self-realising subject is—the 'mystery' that belongs to it—arises from its being the only thing, or a form of the only thing, that is real (so to speak) in its own right; the only thing of which the reality is not relative and derived. For this reason it can neither be defined by contrast with any co-ordinate reality, as the several forms of inner experience which it determines may be defined by contrast with each other; nor as a modification or determination of anything else. We can only know it by a reflection on it which is its own action; by analysis of the expression it has given to itself in language, literature, and the institutions of human life; and by consideration of what that must be which has thus expressed itself.

101. Having said that the self, as here understood, is not something apart from feelings, desires and thoughts, but that which unites them, or which they become as united, in the

character of an agent who is an object to himself, we have implied that there is a sense in which the self has a history, though there is another in which it has none. As has already often enough been pointed out, the eternal subject, which is the condition of there being a succession in time, cannot itself exist as a succession. And its reproduction of itself in man carries with it the same characteristic, in so far as the man presents himself to himself as the subject to which the experiences of a life-time and, mediately through them, the events of the world's history are relative. Such presentation is a timeless act, through which alone man can become aware of an order of time or becoming, or can be capable of such development as can rightly be called moral; of which it is an essential condition that it be united by a single consciousness. On the other hand, just as there is a growth of knowledge in man, though knowledge is only possible through the action in him of the eternal subject, so is there a growth of character, though the possibility of there being a character in the moral sense is similarly conditioned. It grows with the ever-new adoption of desired objects by a self-presenting and, in that sense, eternal subject as its personal good. The act of adoption is the act of a subject which has not come to be; the act itself is not in time, in the sense of being an event determined by previous events; but its product is a further step in that order of becoming which we call the formation of a character, in the growth of some habit of will.

102. We can only express this state of the case by saying that the form in which the self or Ego at any time presents a highest good to itself—and it is on this presentation that conduct depends—is due to the past history of its inner life; but that, throughout, to make this history there has been necessary an action of the Ego, which has no history, has not come to be, but which is the condition of our being conscious of any history or becoming. The particular modes in which I now feel, desire and think, arise out of the modes in which I have previously done so; but the common characteristic of all these has been that in them a subject was conscious of itself as its own object, and thus self-determined. Whatever influences have determined it have done so through, or as taken into, its self-consciousness.

It is to the Ego thus constituted, conscious of its nature— of all that makes it what it is, temper, character, ability—as its own, that new feelings and desires occur from moment to moment, upon the suggestion (to use the most general term) of circumstances. Just as feelings may, and constantly do, come and go without being attended to, so desires constantly arise and pass without exciting any reaction on the part of the Ego, without its placing itself in an attitude of acceptance or rejection towards them. In that case no action, in the moral sense, takes place, and the character, in that sense in which it is the basis of moral goodness or badness, is not affected; though probably even from such 'unconscious'[1] experiences there remain consequences affecting the conditions with which the character afterwards has to deal. In other cases the Ego does react upon the experience of the moment. Through this reaction, in the region of knowledge as distinct from practice, an image recurring becomes an object to be thought about, a feeling becomes a fact to be known; other facts and objects are recalled from past experience, to be brought into relation with the given fact or given object, and there is thus constituted an act of speculative thought or knowledge, an act in which the man sets himself to understand something. Or, through another form of the same reaction, the Ego identifies itself with some desire, and sets itself to bring into real existence the ideal object, of which the consciousness is involved in the desire. This constitutes an act of will; which is thus always free, not in the sense of being undetermined by a motive, but in the sense that the motive lies in the man himself, that he makes it and is aware of doing so, and hence, however he may excuse himself, imputes to himself the act which is nothing else than the expression of the motive.

103. An ambiguity in the use of this term motive has caused much ambiguity in the controversy that has raged over 'free-will.' The champions of free-will commonly suppose that,

---

[1] I use the word 'unconscious' here advisedly, in order to call attention to an ambiguity in the use of the term; which is sometimes applied in a strict sense to a process which is not one of consciousness at all, but merely nervous or automatic, sometimes in a less strict sense to a process of consciousness not attended to or reflected upon.

before the act, a man is affected by various motives, none of which necessarily determines his act; and that between these he makes a choice which is not itself determined by any motive. Their opponents, on the other hand, argue that there is no such thing as this unmotived choice, but that the motive which, possibly after a period of conflict with other motives, ultimately proves the strongest, necessarily determines the act. They have to admit, indeed, that the prevalence of this or that motive depends on the man's character; but the character, they say, itself results from the previous operation of motives, by which they understand simply desires and aversions.

As against the former view it must be urged that, however we may try to give meaning to the assertion that an act of will is a choice without a motive, we cannot do so. Unless there is an object which a man seeks or avoids in doing an act, there is no act of will. Thus a motive is necessary to make such an act. It is involved in it, is part of it; or rather it *is* the act of will, in its relation to the agent as distinct from its relation to external consequences. On the other hand, the motive which is thus necessarily involved in the act of will, is not a motive in the same sense in which each of the parties to the controversy constantly uses the term. It is not one of the mere desires or aversions, between which the advocate of 'free-will' supposes a man to exercise an arbitrary choice, and of which the strongest, according to the opposite view, necessarily prevails. It is constituted by the reaction of the man's self upon these, and its identification of itself with one of them, as that of which the satisfaction forms for the time its object.

104. We may say, for instance, that there are various 'motives,' *i. e.* desires and aversions, which tend to make *A. B.* pay a debt, others which tend to prevent him from paying it. He wishes for the good opinion of others, for the approval of his conscience, for the sense of relief which he would obtain by paying it. On the other hand, he wishes for sundry pleasures which he would have to forego in paying it. Let us suppose that finally the debt is paid. The act of payment represents, expresses, is made what it is by a motive; by the consciousness of an object which the man seeks in doing the act. This object, however, as an object *of will*, is not merely one of the objects

of desire or aversion, of which the man was conscious before he willed. It is a particular self-satisfaction to be gained in attaining one of these objects or a combination of them. The 'motive' which the act of will expresses is the desire for this self-satisfaction. It is not one of the 'motives,' the desires or aversions, of which the man was conscious previously to the act, as disposing him to it; at any rate, not one of these or a combination of them, as they were before the determination of the will, before the man 'made up his mind.' It is only as they become through the reaction of the self-seeking self upon them, and through its formation to itself of an object out of them— only as they merge in an effort after a self-satisfaction to be found in this object,—that they yield the motive of the act of will, properly so called.

105. This motive does indeed necessarily determine the act; it *is* the act on its inner side. But it is misleading to call it the *strongest* motive; for this implies a certain parity between it and the impulses which have been previously soliciting the will. The distinction of greater or less strength properly applies only to 'motives' in that sense in which they do *not* determine the will—to desires and aversions, as they are without that reaction of the self upon them which yields the final motive expressed by the action. It may very well happen that the desire which *affects* a man most strongly is one which he decides on resisting. In spite of its strength, he cannot make its object *his* object, the object with which he seeks to satisfy himself. His character prevents this. In other words, it is incompatible with his steady direction of himself towards certain objects in which he habitually seeks satisfaction.

If we like, we may express the state of the case by saying that his strength of character overcomes the strength of the desire. There is no intrinsic objection to this metaphorical application of the term 'strength;' all our terms for what is spiritual being metaphors from what is physical. But, if we would save ourselves from being misled by our metaphor, we must bear two things in mind. In the first place the power by which the 'strong' desire or motive is overcome, is not that of a *co-ordinate* desire or motive—not that of a desire or motive in the same sense of the words—but the power of a desire with the satisfaction of which (as explained) the man has identified his good, as he had not identified it with the satisfaction of the desire overcome. In the second place, the term 'strength' is not applied in the same sense to the desire which *affects* a man, and to the character which *is* the man. A 'strong' desire means generally a desire which causes much disturbance in the tenour of a man's conscious life : a strong character means that habitual concentration of a man's faculties towards the fulfilment of certain purposes, good or bad, which commonly prevents the disturbance caused by strong desire from making its outward sign, from appearing in the man's behaviour. If we are sometimes tempted to say that the weakest men have the strongest desires, the plausibility of such a statement is due to the fact that the strength of the stronger man's character makes us ignore the strength of his desires.

What we call a strong character we also call a strong 'will.' This is not to be regarded as a particular endowment or faculty, like a retentive memory, or a lively imagination, or an even temper, or a great passion for society. A strong will means a strong man. It expresses a certain quality of the man himself, as distinguishable from all his faculties and tendencies, a quality which he has in relation to all of them alike. It means that it is the man's habit to set clearly before himself certain objects in which he seeks self-satisfaction, and that he does not allow himself to be drawn aside from these by the suggestions of chance desires. He need not therefore be a good man; for the objects upon which he concentrates himself may be morally bad, according to the criteria of badness which we have yet to consider. But, on the other hand, the weak man, taking his object at any time from the desire which happens to affect him most strongly, cannot be a good man. Concentration of will does not necessarily mean goodness, but it is a necessary condition of goodness.

106. According to what has been said, the proposition, current among 'determinists,' that a man's action is the joint result of his character and circumstances, is true enough in a certain sense, and, in that sense, is quite compatible with an assertion of human freedom. It is *not* so compatible, if character and circumstances are considered reducible, directly or indirectly, to

combinations and sequences of natural events. It *is* so compatible, if a 'free cause,' consisting in a subject which is its own object, a self-distinguishing and self-seeking subject, is recognised as making both character and circumstances what they are. It is not necessary to moral freedom that, on the part of the person to whom it belongs, there should be an indeterminate possibility of becoming and doing anything and everything. A man's possibilities of doing and becoming at any moment of his life are as thoroughly conditioned as those of an animal or a plant; but the conditions are different. The conditions that determine what a plant or animal or any natural agent shall do or become, are not objects that it presents to itself; not objects in which it seeks self-satisfaction. On the other hand, whatever conditions the man's possibilities does so through his self-consciousness. The climate in which he lives, the food and drink accessible to him, and other strictly physical circumstances, no doubt make a difference to him; but it is only through the medium of a conception of personal good, only so far as the man out of his relations to them makes to himself certain objects in which he seeks self-satisfaction, that they make a difference to him as a man or moral being. It is only thus that they affect his character and those moral actions which are properly so called as representing a character. Any difference which circumstances make to a man, except as affecting the nature of the personal good for which he lives, of the objects which he makes his own, is of a kind with the difference they make to the colour of his skin or the quality of his secretions. He is concerned with it, he cannot live as if it were not, but it is still not part of himself. It is still so far aloof from him that it rests with him, with his character, to determine what its moral bearing on him shall be. For that moral bearing depends not directly on the physical circumstances, but on the object which, upon occasion or in view of the circumstances, he presents to himself. The imminence of the same dangers will make a hero of one man, a rake of another, a miser of a third. The character which makes circumstances, physically the same, so diverse in their moral influence, has doubtless had its history; but the history which thus determines moral action has been a history *of* moral action, *i.e.* of action in which the agent has been an object to himself, seeking to realise an idea of his own good which he is conscious of presenting to himself.

107. The less patient reader may here be inclined to object that, in professing to oppose the naturalistic view of human action, we have given up the only position that was worth defending. 'Does not this account of moral action,' he will ask, 'though you call it a vindication of freedom, lead to all the practical ill consequences to which the strictly physical theory of the matter is said to lead? If a man's character and circumstances together necessarily determine his action, is he not entitled to say, "I have got my character, it matters not how; my circumstances are given; therefore I cannot help acting as I do"? And when once he has learnt to use this language, will there not be an end to shame and remorse, and to all effort after self-reformation?' Such an objection implies a misconception of the real meaning of the doctrine objected to, which may be partly due to the form in which it is commonly stated. That moral action is a joint result of character and circumstances is not altogether an appropriate statement of it. It would be better to say that moral action is the expression of a man's character, as it reacts upon and responds to given circumstances. We might thus prevent the impression which the ordinary statement, in default of due consideration, is apt to convey, the impression that a man's character is something other than himself; that it is an alien force, which, together with the other force called circumstances, converges upon him, moving him in a direction which is the resultant of the two forces combined, and in which accordingly he cannot help being carried.

108. It can only be by some such impression as this that the objection, just stated, is to be accounted for. It disappears upon a due consideration of what is meant by character. An action which expresses character has no *must*, in the physical sense, about it. The 'can't help it' has no application to it. Where it has any true application the action is not determined by character, any more than is a sneeze, or a twitching produced by a galvanic battery. A character is only formed through a man's conscious presentation to himself of objects as his good, as that in which his self-satisfaction is to be found. Just so far as an

action is determined by character, it is determined by an object which the agent has thus consciously made his own, and has come to make his own in consequence of actions similarly determined. He is thus conscious of being the author of the act; he imputes it to himself. The very excuses that he makes for it —not less when they take the form of an appeal to some fatalistic or 'necessarian' doctrine than in a more vulgar guise—are evidence that he does so. And in such a case the evidence of consciousness, fairly interpreted, is final. The suggestion that consciousness may not correspond with reality is, here at least, unmeaning. The whole question is one of consciousness, a question of the relation in which a man consciously stands to objects (those of desire) which exist only in and for consciousness. If the man is consciously determined by himself in being determined by those objects, he is so really: or rather this statement is a mere pleonasm, for the only reality in question is consciousness.

109. It is strictly a contradiction, then, to say that an action which a man's character determines, or which expresses his character, is one that he cannot help doing. It represents him as standing in a relation to external agency, while doing the act, in which he does not stand if his character determines it. We may say, if we like, without any greater error than that of inappropriate phraseology, that, given the agent's character and circumstances as they at any time are, the action 'cannot help being done,' if by that we merely mean that the action is as necessarily related to the character and circumstances as any event to the sum of its conditions. The meaning in that case is not untrue; but the expression is inappropriate, for it implies a kind of personification of the action. It speaks of the action, as abstracted from the agent, in terms only appropriate to an agent whose powers are directed by a force not his own.

It is probably a sort of confusion between the improper sense in which it may be said that a moral action cannot help being done, because the outcome of character in contact with certain circumstances, and the proper sense in which it is said that a man under compulsion cannot help doing something, which generates the notion that, if an action is the result of character and circumstances, the agent cannot help doing it and is a necessary agent. All results are *necessary* results. If a man's action is the result of his character and circumstances, we in effect add nothing by saying that it is their necessary result. If it is not the result of character or circumstances, or (as we prefer to say) if it is not the expression of a character in contact with certain circumstances, there must be some further element that contributes to its determination. What is that further element? 'Free-will,' some one may say. Very well; but 'free-will' is either a name for you know not what, or it is included, is the essential factor, in character. Rightly understood, the ascription of an action to character as, in respect to circumstances, its cause, is just that which effectually distinguishes it as free or moral from any compulsory or merely natural action. It is simply a confusion to suppose that, because an action is a result—and if a result, a *necessary* result—of character and circumstance, the agent is therefore a 'necessary' agent, in the sense of being an instrument of external force or a result of natural events and agencies; in other words, that 'he cannot help' acting as he does. Nay, it is more than a confusion: it is an inference positively forbidden by the proposition from which it is inferred. For to say that character is a determinant of the act, is, as we have seen, to deny that it proceeds from an agent in this sense 'necessary.'

110. The view, then, that action is the joint result of character and circumstances, if we know what we are about when we speak of character, does not render shame and remorse unaccountable and unjustifiable, any more than, in those by whom it is most thoroughly accepted, it actually gets rid of them. On the contrary, rightly understood, it alone justifies them. If a man's action did not represent his character but an arbitrary freak of some unaccountable power of unmotived willing, why should he be ashamed of it or reproach himself with it? As little does such a view render the impulse after self-reform unaccountable, or, with those who accept it *bona fide* and not as an excuse for the 'sins they have a mind to,' actually tend to weaken the impulse. There is nothing in the fact that what a man now is and does is the result (to speak pleonastically, the *necessary* result) of what he has been and has done, to prevent him from seeking to become, or from being able to become, in the future

other and better than he now is, unless the capacity for conceiving a better state of himself has been lacking to him in the past or has become lost to him at present : and that this is not so is shown by the fact that he does ask the question whether and how he can become better, even though he answer the question in the negative. The dependence of a man's present and future on his past would indeed be fatal to the possibility of that self-reform which is conditional upon the wish for it, if his past had not been one in which his conduct was determined by a conception of personal good. But because his past has been of such a kind, there has been in it, and has been continued out of it into his present, a perpetual potentiality of self-reform, consisting in the perpetual discovery by the man that he is not satisfied ; that he has not found the personal good which he sought ; that, however many pleasures he has enjoyed, he is none the better off in himself, none the nearer to that which he would wish to be.

The capacity for the conception of being better, which such an experience at once evinces and maintains, forms in itself both the inchoate impulse to realise the conception, and the possibility of its realisation. The possibility is no doubt very different from the realisation. The inchoate impulse may be constantly overborne by other impulses, with the gratification of which the man for the time, from habit or strength of passion, identifies his personal good. Its actualisation, however, depends simply on its own relative strength, not on any accessories or command of means. The *prevalent* wish to be better constitutes the being better. Whether or no in any individual case it shall obtain that prevalence, depends (to use the most general expression) on the social influences brought to bear on the man ; but the influences effective for the purpose all have their origin, ultimately, in the desire to be better on the part of other men, as carrying with it a desire for the bettering of those in whom they are interested. The 'Grace of God' works through no other channels but such as fall under this general description. If, and so far as, in the past and present of individual men and of the society which is at once constituted by them and makes them what they are, this desire is operative, the dependence of the individual's present on his past, so far from being incompatible with his seeking or being able to become better than he is, is just what constitutes the definite possibility of this self-improvement being sought and attained. If there were no such dependence, if I could be something. to-day irrespectively of what I was yesterday, or something to-morrow irrespectively of what I am to-day, the motive to the self-reforming effort furnished by regrets for a past of which I reap the fruit, that growing success of the effort that comes with habituation, and the assurance of a better future which animates it, would alike be impossible.

111. That denial, then, of the possibility of a moral new birth, which is sometimes supposed to follow logically from the ad-mission of a necessary connexion between present and past in human conduct, is in truth no consequence of this admission, but of the view which ignores the action of the self-presenting Ego in present and past alike. Once recognise this action, and it is seen that the necessary relation in which a man stands to his own past may be one of such conscious revulsion from it, on account of its failure to yield the self-satisfaction which he seeks, as amounts to what is called a conversion. But, though there is no valid reason why the acceptance of 'determinism,' in the sense explained, should debar us from looking for 'changes of heart and life' in the individual, it may yet be that a misunder-standing of the doctrine does sometimes in some degree tend to paralyse the moral initiative and weaken the power of self-reform. It is probably never fair to lay the blame of a moral deterioration or enfeeblement primarily on intellectual misap-prehension; but in a speculative age even misapprehension may tend to promote vicious tendencies, by interfering with the con-viction which would otherwise be the beginning of their cure. The form of misunderstanding on the subject now before us, most likely to be practically mischievous, will be the confusion, already noticed, between the true proposition that there is a necessary connexion between character and motive, and between motive and act, and the false proposition that man is a necessary agent, in the sense of not being his own master but an instru-ment of natural forces. Men may be found to argue, more or less explicitly, that, if that which he is depends on what he has been and has done, and if, further, whatever he may become in the future will depend on what he now is—that if this is so, as

it cannot be denied that it is, there is no good in his trying painfully to become better; that he may as well live for the pleasure of the hour as it comes. How may such self-sophistication most compendiously be met?

112. In the first place, it should be pointed out that such language implies in the highest degree, on the part of any one who uses it, a self-distinguishing and self-seeking consciousness. But for this he could not thus present to himself his own condition, as determined by what he has been in the past and determining what he will be in the future. Nor unless there were something which he sought to become, a good of himself *as himself* which he sought to attain—unless he were thus determined by himself as an object to himself—could the question, whether there was any use in trying to improve himself instead of letting things take their course, have any meaning for him.

It should be shown, secondly, that this self-distinguishing and self-seeking consciousness, with the yearning for a better state of himself, as yet unattained, which it carries with it, in a special sense makes him what he is, and has made that past history of himself, on which his present state depends, what it has been; that therefore, just so far as his future depends on his present and his past, it depends on this consciousness, depends on a direction of his inner life in which he is self-determined and his own master, because his own object.

Further, it should be shown that, so far from the dependence of his future upon what he now is and does being a reason for passivity, for letting things take their course (which means, practically, for following the desire or aversion of which the indulgence gives him most present pleasure or saves him most present pain), it would only be the absence of this dependence that could afford a reason for such passivity. If I could 'trammel up the consequence' of that which at any time I am and do; if there could be any break of continuity between what I shall be and what I am; then indeed I might be reckless of what I do, so long as it is pleasant, and, in what I allow myself to be, might take no thought of what it is desirable that I should become. It is the unthinkableness of any such break of continuity which, in the presence of the self-distinguishing and self-seeking consciousness of man, makes it impossible for the most reckless sensualist to live absolutely for the moment, and forms the standing possibility of self-improvement even in him. So long as a man presents himself to himself as possibly existing in some better state than that in which he actually is—and that he does so is implied even in his denial that the possibility can be realised—there is something in him to respond to whatever moralising influences society in any of its forms or institutions, themselves the gradual outcome through the ages of man's free effort to better himself, may bring to bear on him. The claims of the family, the call of country, the pleading of the preacher, the appeal of the Church through eye and ear, may at any time awaken in him that which we call (in one sense, truly) a new life, but which is yet the continued working of the spirit which has never ceased to work in, upon, and about him.

113. 'But what becomes of this theory,' the enlightened man of pleasure may reply, 'if it can be shown that the human agent, in that earliest stage of conscious personal being between which and all the following stages you admit that there is a necessary connexion, is a result of strictly physical forces and processes? Will it not then follow that the man's life is throughout determined in the same strictly physical way as is its earliest stage of personal consciousness; and, this being so, that it is as much a delusion for him to suppose that he can alter himself for better or for worse, as it would be for a plant or an animal to suppose so? Neither plant nor animal, indeed, is unimprovable. The produce of the plant can be modified by grafting, and improved by tillage. Animals can be trained to behave in a way in which, to begin with, they are incapable of behaving. So man, the highest of animals, is capable of improvement; but it must be by circumstance, it must be initiated from without. The improvement, the development, will not come for the wishing. It will come, for some, in the struggle for existence. To those for whom it does not so come it will not come at all, and they might as well not bother themselves about it.'

114. We answer that the improvement determined by the wish to be better on the part of the improving subject—more properly, the improvement which that wish, so far as prevalent, itself constitutes—has nothing in common with an improvement of plants or animals such as that referred to, which is

related to no such wish, and, if related to any wish at all, not to one on the part of the animal or plant improved. That there is such a wish, at any rate in the developed man, cannot be denied even by those who may profess to regard it as ineffectual. We meet them, then, by saying that the child which is to be father of the man capable of such a wish, cannot be the mere child of nature; or, conversely, that the mere child of nature cannot be father of the man, as in our own persons we know the man to be. More fully: when we say that the character of a man, and his consequent action, as it at any time stands, is the result of what his character has previously been, as gradually modified through the varying response of the character to varying circumstances, and the registration in the character of *residua* from these responses, we must assume, as the basis of the character throughout, a self-distinguishing and self-seeking consciousness.

Unless we do so, the proposition stated will not hold good. No response to circumstances of a being which has not, or is not, this consciousness, will account for its coming to have or to be it. Such a being could not be father of the moral man affiliated to it. It will have to be admitted that the consciousness necessary to a character and exhibited in moral action has supervened from without upon the supposed primitive being. No true development will be possible of the moral man from the state of being from which he is said to have been developed, because no true thread of identity can be traced between the two states. If, recognising this, we ascribe to the man or child of the past, whose character and action we suppose to have made the man of the present what he is, that self-determining consciousness which distinguishes the man as he is, the same impossibility meets us again as soon as we try to affiliate this man or child of the past to mere nature—to treat him as the outcome of natural forces and processes. It is difficult, no doubt, to understand the relation to man's self-determining consciousness of that in him which is merely natural (or, to speak more properly, of that in him which would be merely natural, if it were not related to such a consciousness); but we do not overcome the difficulty by ignoring the absolute difference between such a consciousness and everything else in the world, a difference which remains the same, whether we do or do not extend the meaning of 'nature' so as to include modes of being thus absolutely different. In its primitive, no less than in its most developed form, the self-determining consciousness as little admits of derivation from that which has or is it not, as life from that which has or is it not.

The statement then, that the human being, in the earliest stage of his conscious existence, between which and all the following stages there is a necessary connexion, is a result of forces and processes which exclude a self-determining consciousness,—though if it were admitted, it would be fatal to any doctrine of human freedom,—cannot be admitted without self-contradiction. The earlier stage will not, under any modification by circumstances, account for the latter, *if* it is the result of the processes described, or *unless* it already involves the self-determining consciousness which carries freedom with it in all modes of its existence. Should the question be asked, If this self-consciousness is not derived from nature, what then is its origin? the answer is that it has no origin. It never began, because it never was not. It is the condition of there being such a thing as beginning or end. Whatever begins or ends does so for it or in relation to it.

CHAPTER II.

115. The ground upon which, rightly or wrongly, the reducibility of moral conduct to a series of natural phenomena, and with it the possibility of a physical science of ethics, is here denied, should by this time be sufficiently plain. It lies in the view that in all conduct to which moral predicates are applicable a man is an object to himself; that such conduct, equally whether virtuous or vicious, expresses a motive consisting in an idea of personal good, which the man seeks to realise by action; and that the presentation of such an idea is not explicable by any series of events in time, but implies the action of an eternal consciousness which makes the processes of animal life organic to a particular reproduction of itself in man. The first impression of any one reading this statement may probably be that in our zeal to maintain a distinction of ethics from natural science we have adopted a view which, if significant and true, would take away the only intelligible foundation of ethics by reducing virtuous and vicious action to the same motive; a motive the rejection of which by the will we virtually declare to be impossible, by treating it as itself the act or expression of will. In order to avoid misapprehension on this point, and to explain how we understand that distinction between the good and the bad will which undoubtedly forms the true basis of ethics, it will be necessary to enter on a fuller discussion of the nature of Will, in its relation to Desire and Reason.

116. We are all familiar with the quasi-personifications of Desire, Reason, and Will, which in one form or another have governed the language of moral philosophy in all ages in which such philosophy has existed. Sometimes desire and reason have been represented as inviting the man in different directions, while the will has been supposed to decide which of the two directions shall be followed. Sometimes the opposition has been represented as lying rather between different desires, of which reason however (according to the supposition) supplies the object to the one, while some irrational appetite is the source of the other; the will being the arbiter which determines the action according to the rational or irrational desire. Meanwhile criticism has been always ready to suggest that the only possible conflict is between desires, to which reason is related only as the minister who counts the cost and calculates means, without having anything to do with their initiation or their direction to an end; that the only tenable distinction between irrational and rational desires is really one between desire for the nearer pleasure and desire for the more remote, or between desire for a pleasure which a just calculation would pronounce to be overbalanced by the pains incidental to or consequent upon its attainment, and desire for one not liable to be thus cancelled in the total result[1].

When this view is accepted, the will is naturally taken to be merely a designation for any desire that happens for the time to be strong enough to determine action. 'No doubt,' it will be said, 'there is a particular class of the phenomena observable by the inner sense—a class called acts of will—which are distinguished from other events that take place in nature as being directed by our feeling. But we are not entitled to suppose that in the case of each man there is really a single agent or power exerted in his acts of willing, a single basis of these phenomena. To do so would be of a piece with the logical fiction of "things" underlying the several groups of phenomena which we connect by a common name. Any act of willing is the result of the manifold conditions which go to constitute the feeling by which it is directed—conditions most various in the various cases of willing.'

The same criticism may be applied to our usual assumptions in regard to 'desire,' and 'intelligence' or 'reason,' which we are apt to distinguish from will, as faculties having something in common with it and yet different from it. 'No doubt,' it may be said, 'there are certain inner acts or phenomena which in virtue of certain resemblances we describe by the common name "desire;" others which on a similar ground we designate "perceptions," "conceptions" and "inferences," and afterwards reduce to the higher genus of intellectual acts. But we are deceived by a process of language if, having arrived at an abstract term to indicate the elements of likeness in these several groups of phenomena, we allow ourselves to believe in the existence of a single agent or faculty—desire as such—underlying the manifold desires of this or that man, and of another such faculty—intelligence or reason as such—underlying his manifold perceptions, conceptions and inferences.'

117. We have then first to enquire whether there is any real unity corresponding to the several terms, desire, intelligence, will, on the part of spiritual principles to which these terms are appropriate. Do they merely indicate each certain resemblances between certain sets of inner phenomena, a single point of view from which these several sets of phenomena may be regarded, and thus a unity not in the phenomena themselves but on the part of the person contemplating them? Or is there, on the other hand, a single principle which manifests itself under endless diversity of circumstance and relation in all the particular desires of a man, and is thus in virtue of its own nature designated by a single name? And, in like manner, are our acts of intelligence and will severally the expression of a single principle, which renders each group of acts possible and is entitled in its own right to the single name it bears? We shall find reason to adopt this latter view. The meaning we attach to it, however, is not that in one man there are three separate or separable principles or agents severally underlying his acts of desire, understanding, and will. We adopt it in the sense that there is one subject or spirit, which desires in all a man's experiences of desire, understands in all operations of his intelligence, wills in all his acts of willing; and that the essential character of his desires depends on their all being desires of one and the same subject which also understands, the essential character of his intelligence on its being an activity of one and the same subject which also desires, the essential character of his acts of will on their proceeding from one and the same subject which also desires and understands.

118. Let us begin with the further consideration of *desire.*
The distinction has already been pointed out between instinctive
impulse and desire of that kind which is a factor in our human
experience. The latter involves a consciousness of its object,
which in turn implies a consciousness of self. In this consciousness of objects which is also that of self, or of self
which is also a consciousness of objects, we have the distinguishing characteristic of desire (as we know it), of understanding and of will, as compared with those processes of the
animal soul with which they are apt to be confused. And this
consciousness is also the common basis which unites desire,
understanding, and will with each other. Our habitual language
for expressing the life of the soul naturally lends itself to obscure
the distinction upon which it is important here to insist. We
constantly speak of sensation as if it were in itself a consciousness of an object by which it is excited. We speak of feeling
this thing and that, which we no doubt do feel, but which we
only feel because we are self-conscious ; because in feeling we
distinguish ourselves from the feelings as their subject. The confusion is complicated by the common usage of feeling and consciousness as equivalent terms ; which makes it difficult to mark
the difference between the *feeling* of self, implied in all pleasure
and pain, and that distinguishing presentation of self, as at once
the subject of feelings and other than them, which properly constitutes self-consciousness. Nor when we have recognised the
distinction between mere feeling and feeling as it is in the self-
conscious man, is it easy to express it. If we use one set of
terms, we fail to convey the difference between sensation, as the
affection of a soul or of an individual subject properly so called,
and any affection of one material thing by another. Adopting
another set of terms, we seem to fall into the error just noticed,
of identifying mere sensation with the consciousness of self and
object.

119. The unity of an individual soul is implied in all feeling ;
or perhaps we should rather say that feeling constitutes the
unity of the individual soul. The individual animal is not
merely one for us, who contemplate the connexion between the
members organic to its life. It is one in itself, as no material
atom or material compound is, in virtue of the common feeling

through which, if one member suffer, all the members suffer with it. It is not one, as the atom is supposed to be, in the sense of being absolutely simple and excluding everything else from itself. Nor is it one, like the material universe, merely in respect of unity of relation between manifold elements. It is one in the sense that upon certain occurrences in the parts of a peculiarly constituted body there supervenes feeling, which is not any one or number of the occurrences, nor a result of their combination, in the sense of being analysable into them; which does not admit of being analysed into or explained by anything else, and would therefore be unknown but for our immediate experience of it; which, while it is not the attribute of any or all of the elements organic to it, is incommunicably private to a subject experiencing it, affected by the past and affecting the future of that particular subject, his own and not another's.

The question of the distinction between animals and plants, the question whether all 'animals' feel, whether any 'plants' do, is one of classification with which we are not here concerned. However such a question may be answered, it does not affect the importance of noticing the distinctive nature of the individuality which feeling constitutes. It is only indeed from experience of ourselves, not from observation of the animals, that we know what this individuality is; but according to all indications we are justified in ascribing it at any rate to all vertebrate animals. To say that they feel *as* men do, or that they are individual in the same sense as men, is misleading, because it is to ignore the distinctive character given to human feeling and human individuality by a self-consciousness which we have no reason to ascribe to the animals. But the assertion that they feel no less, and are no less individual, than ourselves seems to be within the mark. And if by desire we mean no more than that felt impulse after riddance from pain which pain carries with it to the individual, or that felt want which survives a feeling of pleasure; if by will we mean no more than ' activity determined by feeling ;' then we cannot do otherwise than ascribe desire and will to the animals.

120. But though feeling, in the sense explained, constitutes individuality, it does not in that sense amount to the full individuality of man. It does not make the human self what it

is. Each of us is one or individual, not merely in the sense that he feels and is *so far* conscious, but in the sense that he presents his feelings to himself, that he distinguishes himself from them, and is conscious of them as manifold relations in which he, the single self, stands to the world,—in short, as manifold facts. It is thus only as self-conscious that we are capable of knowledge, because only as self-conscious that we are aware of being in the presence of facts. Only in virtue of self-consciousness is there for us a world to be known. In that sense man's self-consciousness is his understanding. This does not of course mean that the abstract form of self-consciousness is an intelligence of facts. We know nothing of self-consciousness apart from feeling, and are probably entitled to assume that there is no such thing. The self-consciousness therefore of which we speak includes feeling; not indeed feeling as it is before the stage of self-consciousness is reached, but feeling as it is for the self-conscious soul, or feeling as manifold recognised relation to an objective world. In this reality of its existence, in this actual co-operation with the senses, self-consciousness is the *faculty* of understanding, which in its full activity, with the progressive analysis of that which the senses contain or reveal, becomes knowledge, or the actual understanding of a world. In the same way self-consciousness is the faculty or possibility of desire, in so far as it is the characteristic of desire to be directed to objects present to the mind of the person desiring them.

If this statement seems strange, it is because we are misled by our habit of abstraction. Regarding self-consciousness in unreal detachment from the sensations which to the self-conscious soul become intelligible facts, we find a paradox in the statement that it is the basis of understanding. For a like reason, because we are habituated to abstract self-consciousness from the wants and impulses which are the *sequelæ* of sensation, we stumble at the notion of our desires being founded on self-consciousness. We suppose self-consciousness, in short, apart from a soul and from the activities of sense and appetite which belong to a soul before self-consciousness supervenes. We then oppose it to those very faculties and acts of desire and understanding which are really its expression, in the sense that it is only as self-conscious that the soul exhibits them. No doubt, if self-consciousness were not the self-consciousness of a soul, if it did not supervene upon a sentient and appetitive life, it would not exhibit itself as understanding and desire; but neither would it be what it is at all. The forms of psychical activity on which it supervenes are carried on into it, though with a character altered by its supervention. They form its content, its filling; not one, however, which remains what it was upon the first manifestation of self-consciousness in the soul, but one which is constantly taking new determinations to itself through the activity of which self-consciousness is the distinguishing form.

121. Just as the action of self-consciousness in understanding becomes apparent as soon as we ask ourselves how the facts with which our intelligence deals come to be there *for us*—how occurrences of sensation come to be apprehended by us as facts—so its action in desire becomes apparent as soon as we ask ourselves how the objects to which our desires are directed, and which make them what they are, come to arise in our minds. To take an elementary instance, how do we come to desire food? Because we are hungry, is the answer that first suggests itself. But, before we accept the answer, we must enquire more carefully what we mean by the desire. Do we mean by it (1) hunger itself, as a particular sort of painful feeling; or (2) an instinctive impulse to obtain food, excited by this painful feeling but without consciousness of an object to which the impulse is directed; or (3) an impulse excited by the image of a pleasure previously experienced in eating, such as we seem to notice in a well-fed dog or cat when the dinner-bell rings; or (4) desire for an object in the proper sense; *i. e.* for something which the desiring subject presents to itself as distinct at once from itself, the subject that desires, and from other objects which might be desired but for the time are not?

It is only if we understand 'desire for food' in the second of these senses that any one can be said to desire food merely because he is hungry. In the first sense the desire, being the same thing as hunger, obviously cannot be explained by it, but only by a physiological account of the way in which hunger arises. In the two latter senses of the 'desire for food' hunger does not account for it. Hunger, whether considered simply as a painful feeling or as involving an instinctive impulse to remove that feeling, may exist without the desire for food in either of these senses. The quest and taking of food do not necessarily imply more than hunger and an instinctive impulse to remove it. They do not necessarily imply even the revival of an image of pleasure previously associated with eating some sort of food; much less desire for an object, presented as such. To begin with, even by the human infant, food must be sought and obtained instinctively, without any previous experience of it as something that will remove the pain of hunger, without any presentation to the mind of the removal of pain as an end to which means are to be sought. If the quest of food must thus in some cases be instinctive, *i. e.* carried on without consciousness of an object to which it is directed, there is nothing to show that it is not so in all, except where an experience of our own, or an experience which admits of communication to us, testifies to the contrary.

122. Now that which takes place in the soul of an animal when hungry and seeking food is not an experience of this kind. The reason, therefore, which we have for saying of ourselves or our fellow-men that we desire food as an object of which we are conscious, does not apply to animals. Those animals indeed with which we chiefly associate, exhibit all the signs of impulses to action excited by recurrent images of pleasure previously experienced, but this recurrence of the image of a past pleasure does not in itself amount to the consciousness of a desired object consisting in a particular pleasure. Self-consciousness is implied in the one as it is not in the other. The mere revival in a sentient subject of the image of a past pleasure, with the consequent impulse after the renewal of the pleasure, does not imply any consciousness by the subject of itself in distinction from the pleasure, as the subject which has enjoyed it, and may enjoy it again, and which has also enjoyed other pleasures comparable with it; nor any consciousness of an objective world to which belong the conditions of the pleasure— the means to it, and its consequences.

123. As our principal concern is to ascertain what desire in ourselves is, not what desire in the animals is not, we need not dwell on the objections which naturally suggest themselves to the view that the actions of animals in all cases admit of being

explained without the ascription to them of self-consciousness. They are objections which would probably disappear when once the difference was realised between the existence of an individual soul and the individual's presentation of his individuality to himself—his distinction of himself from relations in which he stands to a world. Even when the difference has been apprehended, the affectionate observer of the dog and the horse may be slow to admit that their behaviour represents merely the sequence of impulses upon images of pain and pleasure, without conscious reference to self or to a world; which means without either such memory or such perception, such fear or such hope, as ours. We cannot deny, at any rate of the beasts friendly to man, that in a certain sense they learn by experience; that the processes by which the trained or practised animal seeks to obtain the pleasure or avoid the pain, of which the imagination excites its impulse, imply the association with the imagined pleasure or pain of the images of many sensations which have been found to be connected with that pleasure or pain. It is readily assumed that such habitual sequence of images amounts to an experience of facts like our own; to an apprehension of an objective world, of which the necessary correlative is consciousness of self. The assumption becomes inveterate through the practice of describing the behaviour of animals in terms derived from our own experience,—a practice constantly becoming more prevalent, as the description of animal life becomes a more favourite subject of literary art. It is not to the purpose here to criticise the assumption in detail. It is enough to point out that it *is* an assumption; that the consciousness of objects as such, whether objects of knowledge or objects of desire, is more and other than any established sequence of images or any direction of desire by such sequent images; and that this consciousness of objects, whether any animals partake of it or no, is the characteristic thing in human experience, both in the experience through which we become acquainted with nature and in that through which morality arises.

124. The desire for food—to return to that primary instance— though there are senses in which it is independent of self-consciousness, is not in those senses an element in our moral experience. As a determinant of our action as men, it is a desire

for an object, of the presentation of which self-consciousness is
the condition. Whether we take the object desired to be the
removal of a particular pain or enjoyment of a particular pleasure, or the maintenance of life and strength, or some further
object for the sake of which life and strength are sought; or
whether we suppose a wish for each of these ends to be included in the unity of a will directed to the taking of food; in
any case the object is rendered an object to us by a self which
distinguishes itself from its experience. The pain of hunger,
the pleasure of eating, are alike presented as constituents in
a universe of pains and pleasures, which the subject contemplates
himself as possibly suffering and enjoying, and in relation to
which he places the pain or pleasure that for the time pre-
dominates in his imagination. There is for him a world of
feeling, however limited in its actual range yet boundless in
capacity, of which he presents himself as the centre. It is by
its relation to this world that any particular pleasure is defined
for him as an object of desire, and thus, however animal in its
origin, becomes to him, through such reference to a 'before
and after' of experience, what it is not to the animal that feels
but does not distinguish itself from its immediate feeling. This
being true even of animal pleasure, if desired as an object or as
we desire it, it is more plainly true of such an object as the
maintenance of life and strength, and of any end for the sake of
which life and strength are desired. To conceive his life as an
end, to conceive ends for which he seeks to live, are clearly the
functions only of a being who can distinguish the manifold of
his experience actual and possible from himself, and at the same
time gather it together as related to his single self.

125. Even those desires of a man, then, which originate in
animal want or susceptibility to animal pleasure, in the sense
that without such want or susceptibility they would not be,
yet become what they are in man, as desires consciously directed to objects, through the self-consciousness which is the
condition of those objects or any objects being presented. And
it is only as consciously directed to objects that they have a
moral quality or contribute to make us what we are as moral
agents. To desire food, in the sense either of being hungry or
of having an impulse excited by an imagination of some pleasure

of eating, without reference to a self which presents the pleasure to itself as a good among other possible good things, is not a function of our moral nature. If in our waking and sane life we are capable of such a merely animal experience at all, it at any rate does not affect us for the better or worse as men. It has no bearing on the state of soul or character to which the terms good or bad in the moral sense are applied. In order to have such a bearing, however dependent on susceptibilities of the animal soul, it must take its essential character from that supervention of self-consciousness upon these susceptibilities through which a man becomes aware of the pleasure derived from them as an end which he makes his own.

126. Nor can it be admitted that those desired objects which are of most concern in the moral life of the civilised and educated man, who has outgrown mere sensuality, are directly dependent on animal susceptibilities at all. It is not merely their character as objects which the man makes his good that they owe to self-consciousness. The susceptibilities in which the desires themselves originate, unlike the susceptibilities to the pain of hunger or pleasure of eating, do not arise out of the animal system, but out of a state of things which only self-conscious agents can bring about. The conflict of the moral life would be a much simpler affair than it is if it were mainly fought over those 'bodily pleasures,' in dealing with which, according to Aristotle, the qualities of 'continence and incontinence' are exhibited. The most formidable forces which 'right reason' has to subdue or render contributory to some 'true good' of man, are passions of which reason is in a certain sense itself the parent. They are passions which the animals know not, because they are excited by the conditions of distinctively human society. They relate to objects which only the intercourse of self-conscious agents can bring into existence.

This is often true of passions which on first thoughts we might be inclined to reckon merely animal appetites. The drunkard probably drinks, as a rule, not for the pleasure of drinking, but to drown pains or win pleasures—pains for instance of self-reproach, pleasures of a quickened fancy or of a sense of good fellowship—of which only the thinking man is capable. The love which is apt to be most dangerously at war with duty is not a mere sexual impulse, but the passion for a person, in which the consciousness on the lover's part both of his own individuality and of that of the beloved person is at the utmost intensity. Our envies, jealousies, and ambitions—whatever the resemblance between their outward signs and certain expressions of emotion in animals—are all in their proper nature distinctively human, because all founded on interests possible only to self-conscious beings. We cannot separate such passions from their exciting causes. Take away those occasions of them which arise out of our intercourse as persons with persons, and the passions themselves as we know them disappear. The advantages which I envy in my neighbour, the favour of society or of a particular person which I lose and he wins and which makes me jealous of him, the superiority in form or power or place of which the imagination excites my ambition — these would have no more existence for an agent not self-conscious, or not dealing with other self-conscious agents, than colour has for the blind.

127. It should further be noticed that not only do those desires and passions which form part of our moral experience depend on the action of a self-conscious soul in respect of the presentation of their objects, many of them also in respect of the conditions under which the susceptibility to them arises, but that the same action is implied in the manner in which they qualify each other. We are apt to speak of our desires for this object and that as if each operated on us singly, or as if each had its effect on us independently of the others, though our conduct may represent their combined result. But such language is not a true expression of our experience. We are never so exclusively possessed by the desire for any object as to be quite unaffected by the thought of other desired objects, of which we are conscious that the loss or gain would have a bearing on our happiness. In reflection upon our motives we abstract the predominant desire from that qualification, whether in the way of added strength or of abatement, which it derives from the belief on the part of the desiring subject that its satisfaction involves the satisfaction or frustration of other desires. But it is in fact always so qualified. Our absorption in it is never so complete but that the consideration of a possible happiness conditional upon the satisfaction of other desires makes a difference to it,

though it may not be such a difference as makes its sign in outward conduct. We do not indeed desire the objects of our ordinary interests for the sake of our general happiness, any more than for the sake of the pleasure which the satisfaction of desire constitutes. As has often been pointed out, if there were not desires for particular objects other than the desire for happiness, there could be no such thing as the desire for happiness ; for there would be nothing to constitute the happiness desired. But in every desire I so far detach myself from the desire as to conceive myself in possible enjoyment of the satisfaction of other desires, in other words, as a subject of happiness ; and the desire itself is more or less stimulated or checked, according as its gratification in this involuntary forecast appears conducive to happiness or otherwise.

128. Even with the man of most concentrated purpose, the object on which his heart is set—*e.g.* the acquisition of an estate, election to Parliament, the execution of some design in literature or art—though it may admit of description by a single phrase, really involves the satisfaction of many different desires. The several objects of these admit of distinction, but they are not to be considered so many separate forces combining to make up the actual resultant motive. No one of them apart from the rest would be what it is, because each, as it really actuates the man, is affected by the desire for personal well-being ; and that well-being presents itself to him as involving the satisfaction of them all. In the cases of concentrated purpose supposed, the man has come to identify his well-being with his success in bringing about a certain event or series of events. To him, as he forecasts his future, the possibility of that success being attained (his acquisition of the estate, his election to Parliament) presents itself as the possibility of his greatest good. It would not seem so, indeed, unless he had (or had once had) various desires, each directed to its specific object other than his well-being, and unless he contemplated the satisfaction of these desires as involved in this particular success ; but on the other hand no one of these desires would actuate him as it does, in the way of directing all his effort to the single end for which he lives, unless it were strengthened and sustained by the anticipation of a well-being, in which he conceives the satisfaction of the other desires

to be as much involved as the satisfaction of this particular one. The conception of this well-being is the medium through which each desire is at once qualified and reinforced by all the rest, in directing the man's effort to that end in which he presents to himself the satisfaction of them all. In the case of men whose effort is less concentrated in its direction, who live with more divided aims, though 'chance desires' have greater weight, yet none of these is unaffected by the idea of a happiness not to be identified with the satisfaction of any single desire.

Now it is only to the self-conscious soul, which distinguishes itself from all desires in turn, that such an idea is possible. In this further sense, then—not only as the condition (1) of the presentation of *objects*, whether desired or perceived, and (2) of the susceptibilities in which those of our desires which are of most moral importance for good or evil originate, but (3) as the source of the idea of happiness—it is self-consciousness that makes the action of desire what it really is in the life of moral beings. If it is true that no desire actuates us without qualification by the consciousness of our capacity for other experience than that which this particular desire constitutes, then, in that sense, as well as in the other senses indicated, it is true that every desire which actuates us has a character that self-consciousness gives it. The objects of a man's various desires form a system, connected by memory and anticipation, in which each is qualified by the rest; and just as the object of what we reckon a single desire derives its unity from the unity of the self-presenting consciousness in and for which alone it exists, so the system of a man's desires has its bond of union in the single subject, which always carries with it the consciousness of objects that have been and may be desired into the consciousness of the object which at present is being desired.

129. To revert then to the question from which this part of our discussion started, we shall be right in refusing to admit that particular desires are the only realities and that 'Desire' is a logical fiction; right in asserting a real existence of Desire as such, if by this we understand the one soul or subject, and that a self-conscious soul or subject, which desires in all the desires of each of us, and as belonging to which alone, as related to each other through relation to it, our several desires are what they are.

But if we mean anything else than this when we hypostatise desire—as we do when we talk of Desire moving us to act in such or such a way, misleading us, overcoming us, conflicting with Reason, &c.—then 'Desire' is a logical abstraction which we are mistaking for reality. It is thus equally important to bear in mind that there is a real unity in all a man's desires, a common ground of them all, and that this real unity or common ground is simply the man's self, as conscious of itself and consciously seeking in the satisfaction of desires the satisfaction of itself.

But the real unity underlying the operations of intelligence is also the man's self-conscious self. It is only in virtue of his self-consciousness, as has previously been pointed out, that he is aware of facts as facts, or that his experience reveals to him a world of related objects. It is clear then that we must not imagine Desire and Intellect, as our phraseology sometimes misleads us into doing, to be separate agents or influences, always independent of each other, and in the moral life often conflicting. The real agent called Desire is the man or self or subject as desiring; the real agent called Intellect is the man as understanding, as perceiving and conceiving; and the man that desires is identical with the man that understands. Yet, on the other hand, to desire is clearly not the same thing as to understand. How then is the state of the case to be truly represented?

130. We commonly content ourselves with saying that the same person has distinct faculties of desire and understanding; and to this statement, so far as it goes, no objection can fairly be made. It is equally impossible to derive desire from intellect and intellect from desire; impossible to treat any desire as a mode of understanding, or any act of understanding as a mode of desire. No reason can be given why any perception or conception should lead to desire, unless the soul has to begin with some possibility called into activity by the idea, but other than that of which the activity constitutes the idea—the perception or conception. And, conversely, we cannot explain how a desire should set intellectual activities in motion except on a corresponding supposition. This being so, we must ascribe to the self-conscious

soul or man two equally primitive, co-ordinate, possibilities of desiring and understanding. But we may not regard these as independent of each other, or suppose that one can really exist without the other, since they have a common source in one and the same self-consciousness. The man carries with him into his desires the same single self-consciousness which makes his acts of understanding what they are, and into his acts of understanding the same single self-consciousness which makes his desires what they are. No desire which forms part of our moral experience would be what it is, if it were not the desire of a subject which also understands : no act of our intelligence would be what it is, if it were not the act of a subject which also desires.

This point would not be worth insisting on, if it meant merely that desires and operations of the intellect mutually succeed each other; that in order to the excitement of desire for an object, as distinct from appetite or instinctive impulse, there must have been a perception, involving at least some elementary acts of memory and inference; and that a desire, again, commonly sets in motion an intellectual consideration of consequences and ways and means. The meaning is that every desire which is within the experience of a moral agent, involves a mode of consciousness the same as that which is involved in acts of understanding ; every act of understanding a mode of self-consciousness the same as that which is involved in desire. The element common to both lies in the consciousness of self and a world as in a sense opposed to each other, and in the conscious effort to overcome this opposition. This, however, will seem one of those dark and lofty statements which excite the suspicion of common sense. The reader's patience is therefore requested during one or two paragraphs of explanation.

131. Desire for an object may be said generally to be a consciousness of an object as already existing in and for the consciousness itself, which at the same time strives to give the object another existence than that which it thus has—to make it exist really and not merely in the desiring consciousness. A man desires, let us suppose, to taste a bottle of fine wine, to hear a certain piece of music, to see Athens, to do a service to a friend, to finish a book that he has in hand. In each case the desired

object, as such, exists merely in his consciousness, and the desire for it involves the consciousness of the difference between such existence of the desired object and that realisation of it towards which the desire strives, and which, when attained, is the satisfaction or extinction of the desire. In that sense the desire is at once a consciousness of opposition between a man's self and the real world, and an effort to overcome it by giving a reality in the world, a reality under the conditions of fact, to the object which, as desired, exists merely in his consciousness. It is true of course that the bottle of wine, the piece of music, the city of Athens, exist quite independently of the consciousness of any desiring subject; but these are not the desired objects. The experience of tasting the wine or hearing the music is the desired object; and this does not, any more than the anticipated service to the friend or the achievement of writing the book, exist while desired except in and for the consciousness of the person desiring it. So soon as it existed otherwise the desire would cease. It is true also that, though the desired object is one which for the person desiring it remains to be realised—to have reality given it—yet his desire for it is a real and definitely conditioned fact. To a superior intelligence contemplating the state of the case, the man's desire, with the unattained object which it implies, would be as real as anything else in the world. And further, while it would be apparent to such an intelligence that it was only in virtue of the man's self-consciousness that the desired object existed for him, as such; only through it that he was capable of such an experience as that of which, if the desire be not simply sensual, the forecast moves him ; on the other hand it would be no less apparent that the desire, however distinctively human, presupposes and entails some modification of the animal system. We are here considering, however, what desire for an object is to the person experiencing the desire, while experiencing it, not what it might be to another regarding it speculatively as a fact. As so experienced, the common characteristic of every such desire is its direction to an object consciously presented as not yet real, and of which the realisation would satisfy, *i. e.* extinguish, the desire. Towards this extinction of itself in the realisation of its object every desire is in itself an effort, however the effort may be prevented from making its out-

ward sign by the interference of other desires or by the circumstances of the case.

132. Such desire, then, implies on the part of the desiring
subject (a) a distinction of itself at once from its desire and from
the real world; (b) a consciousness that the conditions of the
real world are at present not in harmony with it, the subject of
the desire; (c) an effort, however undeveloped or misdirected, so
to adjust the conditions of the real world as to procure satisfaction of the desire. Let us now turn for a moment to consider
the generic nature of our thought. Here too we find the same
general characteristic, a relation between a subject and a world
of manifold facts, of which at first it is conscious simply as alien
to itself, but which it is in constant process of adjusting to itself
or making its own. This is no less true of thought in the form
of speculative understanding, the process of learning to know
facts and their relations, than it is true of it in the practical form
of giving effect and reality to ideas. We have already seen how it
is only for a self-conscious soul that the senses reveal facts or
objects at all. The same self-consciousness which arrests successive sensations as facts to be attended to, finds itself baffled and
thwarted so long as the facts remain an unconnected manifold.
That it should bring them into relation to each other is the condition of its finding itself at home in them, of its making them
its own. This establishment or discovery of relations—we
naturally call it *establishment* when we think of it as a function
of our own minds, *discovery* when we think of it as a function
determined for us by the mind that is in the world—is the
essential thing in all understanding. It is involved in those
perceptions of objects which we are apt improperly to oppose to
acts of understanding, but which all imply the discursive process
of consciousness, bringing different sensuous presentations into
relation to each other as equally related to the single conscious
subject; and it is involved in those inferences and theories of
relations between relations which we commonly treat as the
work of understanding *par excellence*. Whatever the object
which we set ourselves to understand, the process begins with
our attention being challenged by some fact as simply alien and
external to us, as no otherwise related to us than is implied in
its being there to be known; and it ends, or rather is constantly

approaching an end never reached, in the mental appropriation
of the fact, through its being brought under definite relations
with the cosmos of facts in which we are already at home.

133. Now if this is a true account of speculative thinking,
which it is our natural habit to put in stronger contrast with
desire than we do practical thinking, it is clear that between the
action of the self-conscious soul in desiring and its action in
learning to know there is a real unity. Each implies on the
part of the soul the consciousness of a world not itself or its own.
Each implies the effort of the soul in different ways to overcome
this negation or opposition—the one in the way of gathering the
objects presented through the senses into the unity of an intelligible order; the other in the way of giving to, or obtaining
for, objects, which various susceptibilities of the self-conscious
soul suggest to it and which so far exist for it only in idea, a
reality among sensible matters of fact. The unity of the self-
conscious soul thus exhibits itself in these its seemingly most
different activities.

Accordingly, if we understand by thought, as exercised *ex
parte nostra*, the consciousness in a soul of a world of manifold
facts, related to each other through relation to itself but at the
same time other than itself, and its operation in appropriating
that world or making itself at home in it, it will follow from
what has been said that thought in this sense is equally involved in the exercise of desire for objects and in the employment
of understanding about facts. In the one case it appears in the
formation of ideal objects and the quest of means to their realisation; in the other, it appears in the cognisance of a manifold
reality which it is sought to unite in a connected whole. This
community of principle in the two cases we may properly
indicate by calling our inner life, as determined by desires for
objects, practical thought, while we call the activity of understanding speculative thought.

134. Nor is this all. The exercise of the one activity is always
a necessary accompaniment of the other. In all exercise of the
understanding desire is at work. The result of any process of
cognition is desired throughout it. No man learns to know
anything without desiring to know it. The presentation of a
fact which does not on the first view fit itself into any of our

established theories of the world, awakens a desire for such adjustment, which may be effected either by further acquaintance with the relations of the fact, or by a modification of our previous theories, or by a combination of both processes. All acquisition of knowledge takes place in this way, and in every stage of the process we are moved by a forecast, however vague, of its result. The learner of course knows not how he will assimilate the strange fact till he has done so, but the idea of its assimilation as possible evokes his effort, precisely as, in a case naturally described as one of desire, the idea, let us say, of winning the love of a woman evokes the effort of the lover to realise the idea.

Thus the process of our understanding in its most distinctive sense is necessarily accompanied by desire. But can it conversely be maintained of desire, as we experience it, not only that it has in common with understanding the essential characteristics of conscious relation between self and a world, and of conscious effort to overcome the opposition between the two, but that it necessarily carries with it an exercise of understanding in the distinctive sense, as we have just seen that our exercise of understanding necessarily carries with it desire? On reflection it will appear to be only some arbitrary abridgment of our conception of desire which makes us hesitate to admit that it is so. So soon as any desire has become more than an indefinite yearning for we know not what, so soon as it is really desire *for some object of which we are conscious,* it necessarily involves an employment of the understanding upon those conditions of the real world which make the difference, so to speak, between the object as desired and its realisation. In the primary stages of desire for an object, when it is either a desire on the part of a child still feeling its way in the world, or desire for some object that has newly suggested itself, the apprehension of the conditions of its realisation may be of the most elementary kind; or, again, the person desiring may be so familiar with those conditions that he is scarcely aware of his mind dwelling on them. But in every case, if desire is consciously directed to an object, and if that object is presented as still unrealised and as dependent for its realisation upon the fulfilment of certain conditions not yet fulfilled—and otherwise it would be an object already attained, not *desired*—then a discursive action of understanding among those conditions, essentially the same as that by which we learn the nature of a matter of fact, is the necessary accompaniment of the desire. To the extent at least of an apprehension that there are conditions of which the fulfilment is necessary to the attainment of the object, it is implied in that merely inchoate desire (if it is consciously directed to an object at all) which stops short of initiating any actual exertion for the fulfilment of the conditions. Without it the consciousness of distinction between the object as desired, and those conditions of reality that would satisfy the desire, could not exist.

135. Thus these two modes of our soul's action, desire and intellect, or practical thought and speculative thought, have not merely the element in common which is expressed by the designation of each as thought, but, as has just been shown, neither action can really be exerted without calling the other into play. This is so even when the matters of fact upon which the understanding is employed are such as neither have any bearing, or are not conceived as having any, upon the improvement of man's estate, nor make any appeal to the artistic interest. It is so, again, when the object, of which the realisation is desired, is merely the enjoyment of a sensual pleasure. But in other cases the mutual involution of desire and understanding, of practical and speculative thought, is even more complete. There are processes, naturally described as intellectual, in which desire is not merely involved in the sense that the completion of the intellectual task is presented as an object which stimulates effort; while on the other hand there are processes which we naturally ascribe to desire, but in which the intellect is not merely involved as the apprehension of that reality which the desired object, as desired, lacks, or as the quest of means to its realisation. The activity of the artist, not merely in the region which we call that of the fine arts, but in any form affected by an ideal of perfect work, from that of the writer of books to that of the craftsman, we naturally and properly count intellectual. Yet it is throughout a realisation of desire. Of the mathematician or man of science it may possibly be held that he first thinks of his problem, or of facts not yet intelligible, and that the desire to solve the problem or to under-

stand the facts is a subsequent and distinguishable activity. But with the artist, of whatever kind, the intellectual conscious- ness of the ideal, which initiates and directs his work, is itself a desire to realise it. An intellectual passion is our natural designation for his state of mind.

Again, if we consider any of the more worthy practical pur- suits of men, which, as is implied in calling them pursuits, are an expression of desire, we shall find not merely that implica- tion of self-consciousness in the presentation of the object, which may not be ignored even when the object is the enjoyment of some animal pleasure, nor a mere sequence of intellectual action upon previous desire for an end; we shall find that the end itself is an object of understanding no less than of desire. It is only the fallacy of taking the pleasure that ensues on satisfac- tion of a desire to be the object of the desire, which blinds us to this. If the end of a man whose chief interest is in the better management of an estate, or the better drainage of the town where he lives, or the better education of his family, or the better administration of justice, were indeed the pleasure which he anticipates in the success of his pursuit, it might be held that, since pleasure (in distinction from the facts conditioning it) is not an object of the understanding, the understanding was not co-operant with desire in the initiation of his pursuit. But, as has often been pointed out, the possibility of pleasure in the attainment of an object presupposes a desire directed not to that pleasure but to the object; and the object in the cases supposed is plainly one that originates in intellectual conception—not in- deed in a passionless intellect, if there is such a thing, but in a soul which desires in understanding and in desiring under- stands. The same is true in regard to objects of less worthy, more selfish, ambition. The applause of a senate or a town- council, the government of an empire or a borough, are objects pursued for their own sake, not for the sake either of the plea- sure of attaining them, or of ulterior pleasures to which they may be the means; and in order to the presentation of such objects the soul must understand, in the proper and distinctive sense, no less than desire.

136. On the whole matter, then, our conclusion must be that there is really a single subject or agent, which desires in all the

desires of a man, and thinks in all his thoughts, but that the action of this subject as thinking—thinking speculatively or understanding, as well as thinking practically—is involved in all its desires, and that its action as desiring is involved in all its thoughts. Thus thought and desire are not to be regarded as separate powers, of which one can be exercised by us without, or in conflict with, the other. They are rather different ways in which the consciousness of self, which is also necessarily consciousness of a manifold world other than self, expresses itself. One is the effort of such consciousness to take the world into itself, the other its effort to carry itself out into the world; and each effort is involved in every complete spiritual act—every such act as we can impute to ourselves or count our own, whether on reflection we ascribe the act rather to intellect or rather to desire. If the 'intellectual' act implies attention—and otherwise we cannot ascribe it to ourselves—it implies desire for the attainment of an intellectual result, though the result be attained as quickly as, for instance, the meaning of a sentence in a familiar language is arrived at upon attention being drawn to it. If the desire is consciously for an object—and this again is the condition of its being imputable to ourselves—it implies, as we have seen, an intellectual apprehension at least of the difference between the object as desired and its realisation. In all the more important processes of desire the exertion of understanding is implied to a much more considerable extent, just as in every intellectual achievement of importance the action of desire is much more noticeable and protracted than in the case just instanced of intelligent attention to the import of a proposition, heard or read.

137. But if it be true that all desire is the act of a subject which thinks in desiring, all thought the act of a subject which desires in thinking, what is to be said of willing? Any identification of the will with any form of desire seems inconsistent with the apparent fact that a man has the power, however seldom he may exercise it, of willing to resist all his desires, even the strongest, and of acting accordingly. The existence of such a power has often been supposed to be the condition of any disinterested performance of duty; and the supposition is not

one to be lightly set aside. Apart from any such 'transcendental' doctrine, the difference between desire and will, it may be said, is too firmly established in the experience of men, as expressed in our habitual language (*i.e.* in such phrases as ' I should like to, but I won't '), for all the psychologists to get over it. To identify the will, again, with thought or judgment seems to imply forgetfulness of the familiar fact that a man may ' know the better and prefer the worse.' Even when it is our own action that is the object of thought, our will as evinced by action is apt not to correspond with our thought, with our judgment of what is best ; while our merely speculative thoughts seem to have as little connexion with the will as a proposition of pure mathematics has to do with the happiness or goodness of man. Our doctrine that the entire self-conscious subject, desiring as well as thinking, is concerned in every complete intellectual act, and in every desire for an object, may seem to increase the difficulty. If this is so, what are we to make of the man who is ' torn by conflicting desires ' ; who under the influence of one desire wills to do what he knows to be inconsistent with the satisfaction of another desire, which yet he strongly feels ? What of the man who has the truest thoughts, not merely on scientific matters, but about the ideal of virtuous conduct—thoughts which on our doctrine should involve desires —and who yet is led by desire to act viciously ?

138. Let us first be sure what we mean by a conflict of desires, and by the resistance of the will to desire. Does a man ever really desire, at the same time and *in the same sense*, objects which he recognises as incompatible with each other ? Our first answer will probably be : 'Yes ; we are constantly divided between conflicting desires. This is the explanation of our irresolution before action, and of our regrets in action. We are irresolute so long as the strength of competing desires is evenly matched : we act with regret when, in following the desire which prevails, we are conscious of foregoing the gratification of another, only less strong.' But the question is whether, when a man is in that state in which it can truly be said that conflicting passions are striving for the mastery in him, he actually desires an object at all ; and whether, conversely, when his desire is consciously directed to a certain object, he at the same time and

in the same sense desires another object, which is neither
included in it nor a means to it, but recognised as incompatible
with it. At any rate, if we are to allow that in the divided
state of mind supposed he desires an object at all, it is in quite a
different sense that he desires the object which, when the scale
is finally turned, he ' makes up his mind ' to pursue. And, again,
he desires this object for the time in quite a different sense
from that in which he can be supposed at the same time to
desire the object which has come off second best in his choice.
The object of his final pursuit is one which he desires in the
sensé that for the time he identifies himself with it. Living for
himself (as he necessarily does) he lives for it. The single self
of which he is conscious, the unit in which all the influences of
his life centre, but which distinguishes itself from them all, is
for the time directed to making it real. It is not in this sense
that any of the objects are desired, between which his interests
are divided while he is in the state of irresolution. If it were,
there would be no suspense of action. Nor is it thus that the
objects are desired of which he is still aware as having attractions for him after he has made up his mind to pursue another
incompatible object. If it were, he would not be pursuing the
other.

139. There are two familiar ways of dealing with the distinction here pointed out. It may be said (a) that the difference
between the sense in which a man desires sundry incompatible
objects, when he cannot make up his mind between them, and
the sense in which he finally desires the object of his ultimate
preference, is merely that in the latter case one of the competing
desires has become stronger than all the rest. The man may be
supposed still to continue to desire any of the objects which he
does not pursue, just in the same way as he desires the object
which he does prefer and pursue at the very time that he prefers
the latter. The difference may be held to lie merely in the
strength of the several desires; the satisfaction of the strongest,
when the incompatibility of their several objects has become
apparent, being that which is finally pursued. It may be said
(b) that the difference pointed out is just that between desire and
will. The desires between which we have supposed a man to be
suspended, it may be argued, are desires properly so called, while

the 'desire' with which he pursues the object to which his preference is finally given, is not properly desire but will. Thus
any of the objects which he *desired* in the state of irresolution
he may continue to *desire* when his mind is made up, though his
will is otherwise directed.

140. Neither of these views can be quite accepted. If we are
to admit that the man, suspended for the time between desires of which he knows the several satisfactions to be incompatible, desires incompatible objects, instead of rather saying
that for the time he desires no object at all, since he does not
seek to realise the idea of any object ; at any rate the inward
relation of the man towards the incompatible objects, between
which his desires are divided, is wholly different from his relation towards that which he finally prefers. His relation towards
the latter, again, is wholly different from his relation towards
that which he is supposed still to desire though not to pursue.
And this difference is not appropriately described as one between
different degrees of strength of desire.

We will suppose a man divided between hatred of a rival whom
he has opportunity of injuring, and some sense of duty (however
that is to be explained), or fear of consequences, which inclines
him to do to his rival as he would be done by. Here is a conflict
of passions or emotions by which the man, so far as any action
towards his rival goes, is for the time paralysed. Hatred of his
rival stirs him, the idea of doing the magnanimous thing attracts
him, fear of discredit deters him, but the total effect of these
influences is not such that any definite object of desire presents
itself to him of which he seeks the realisation. We will suppose
that some fresh provocation intensifies the hatred, that he finally
gives way to it and does the wrong from which he had previously
abstained ; or, on the other hand, that by some bright example or
some warning voice the counter influences are strengthened, and
that he does a service, or at least an act of justice, to the rival.
In neither case is the result truly described by saying that the
desire which the action represents is simply the continuation, in
greater relative strength, of one among several which were previously competing in the man. It differs in kind from the
competing influences. It is what none of them were while competing, what none of them are, so far as any of them survive

along with it. It implies, as did none of them, the presentation of an object with which the man for the time identifies himself or his good, and a consequent effort to realise this object. However connected with an intensification of one of the previously competing passions, it is a distinctly new motive, arising out of a changed relation of the man himself to the competing passions. He now, as he did not before, consciously directs himself to the realisation of a desired object. If he desired before, it is at any rate in another way that he desires now.

141. This is equally the case, whether the object for which he acts is that suggested by his hatred or that suggested by his conscience. When it is the pure desire to do the nobler thing, or this as reinforced by fear of discredit, that governs the man's final conduct, the impropriety of treating it as a continuation of one of the previously competing passions, which has finally gained superior strength, is most apparent. The disturbance of the inner life, caused by such passion as hatred or love, is so marked in comparison with such an emotion as a sense of duty or fear of discredit, that to speak of the latter as prevalent in virtue of its superior strength as a passion strikes us at once as unreal. It is accordingly to the example of virtuous resolution, maintained in spite of some violent passion, that the appeal is commonly made by those who would distinguish will from strongest desire. And the distinction is a true one, if it means that the motive expressed in a man's action differs in kind, and not merely in degree of strength, from passions of which the competition suspends his action or with which he has to struggle when he finally acts. But the distinction holds good just as much if, in the case supposed, the man finally acts to gratify his hatred, to realise the idea of crushing his rival, as if he takes the opposite course. Between the man's state of mind while his hatred is merely a competing passion, and his state of mind when acting for the gratification of his hatred, the difference does not lie in the degree of strength attained by the hatred, but in the fact that in the latter state the gratification of the hatred has become what it was not in the former, an object which the man seeks to realise, one which for the time he has made his good.

142. The distinction, then, between 'desires' of which the

competition suspends action, and the 'desire' which expresses itself in a morally imputable action—visible or invisible, overt or only intended—is not to be understood as lying in the greater relative strength of the latter. Rather, if the term 'desire' is to be employed in both cases, it should be understood that it is used in different senses, for in the one case the man consciously directs himself to the realisation of an ideal object (though perhaps not so as to commit an ' overt act '), in the other he does not so direct himself. On the other hand, if we say, according to the second view (*b*) mentioned above, that the final preference, represented by the actual pursuit of an object after an interval of suspense between competing passions, is not a desire but an act of will, we must say the same of the actual pursuit of an object, even though there has been no previous suspense or conflict of desires. There is nothing in the fact that the direction of the man's powers to the realisation of an object in one case supervenes upon a period of divided mind, and in another case does not, to justify us in ascribing it to desire in the latter case if we do not in the former. Yet when a man sets himself to gain the love of a woman or to save a friend's life, without another course of action suggesting itself to him as possible, who would question that he desired the object or that his action was an expression of desire ? But if the principle of action is desire in such cases, why should the fact of its being accompanied by the consciousness of a gratification, otherwise possible, having been forgone, or the fact that, before it was in operation as a principle of action, the man was for a time divided between the attractions of different objects, make it any the less desire in those cases where it is supposed to be distinctively ' will ' ? If, however, it is thus difficult to suppose the principle of action to be a will which is not desire, in the case of an action which follows upon an interval of divided mind, it is equally difficult to regard it as a desire which is not a will in the contrasted case, that of the man who is said to act upon impulse. If in such a case, being constrained to admit that the action proceeds from desire, we persist in our opposition between desire and will, we shall have to say that it is not willed. And it will follow that, just so far as a man is ' single-minded,' he has no will ; that the voluptuary who has no scruples, the saint who has no temptations, the enthusiast who never hesitates, are so far in-voluntary agents.

143. The reader may here fairly object, with some impatience, that we have had enough of disputation about the mere usage of the terms desire and will. We no doubt often use the term ' desire ' for impulses or inward solicitations of which the man is conscious, but which do not amount to a conscious direction of himself to the realisation of an object imagined or conceived. We say that a man desires what his will rejects. But we repre-sent such a state of the case quite as naturally by saying that, although such and such objects have attractions for the man, yet *on the whole* he does not desire them but only the object for which he acts. On the other hand, though we now most com-monly apply the term ' will ' to the direction of the conscious self to action, as opposed to a mere wish not amounting to such direc-tion, yet the usage has been by no means uniform. ' My poverty but not my will consents,' says the seller of poisons in ' Romeo and Juliet.' Here the consent, though said not to be of the will, might have been enough to hang for. The will is only the strong competing wish which does not suffice to determine action. Compare the outburst of St. Paul, as rendered in our authorised translation,—' To will is present with me, but how to perform that which is good I find not.' But though we cannot fix the usage of words, it is clear that the important real dis-tinction is that between the direction of the self-conscious self to the realisation of an object, its identification of itself with that object, on the one side (whether that direction and identification does or does not supervene upon a previous period of indecision, is or is not accompanied by the consciousness of attraction in an object other than that pursued), and, on the other side, the mere solicitations of which a man is conscious, but with none of which he so identifies himself as to make the soliciting object his object—the object of his self-seeking—or to direct himself to its realisation.

144. When it is urged, therefore, that the will often conflicts with and overcomes a man's desires—even if it be not necessary in order to constitute a will, as sometimes seems to be supposed, that there should be such a conflict with desire—and that an act of will therefore must be other than a desire, we answer,

Certainly it is other than any such desire as those which it is said to overcome. But it is not other than desire in that sense in which desire is ever the principle or motive of an imputable human action, of an action that has any moral quality, good or bad, that can properly be rewarded or punished, or is fit matter for praise or blame. It is not necessary to such an action that there should be any overt effect, of which other men can take note. Morally the action of a man who has made up his mind to sacrifice himself for his friend or to commit a murder is the same though he be accidentally disabled before either the good resolution or the bad one, as the case may be, has taken effect. The essential thing morally is the man's direction of himself to the realisation of a conceived or imagined object, whether circumstances allow of its issuing in *outward* action, action that affects the senses of other people, or no.

It would be a forced restriction of the term desire to refuse to apply it to such direction of the self; but unless we so restrict it, there is no ground for holding that will is other than desire. The ' desire ' which is motive to the man who barters his heritage for a mess of pottage, differs no doubt *in its object* from the ' will ' of the man who sacrifices his inclinations in adhering to a rule of abstinence which he has imposed on himself; but *in the same respect* it differs from the ' desire ' or ' impulse ' of a man who swims the Hellespont to see his mistress ; just as, again, the ' will ' described in the above instance differs in object from the ' will ' of the man who, upon cool calculation, sacrifices natural affection in order to get a better position in the world. In each of these cases the principle of action is different in respect of its object, but this is a difference to which, as we see, the distinction in the usage of the terms ' desire ' and ' will ' does not correspond ; and, apart from the difference of object, there is no difference between the principles of action in the several cases. Where it is described as will it is equally desire; where it is described as desire or impulse it is equally will. But whether described as desire or as will, it is wholly different in its relation to the subject—to the man willing or desiring—from such desires as are said to compete for mastery in the man, or from any desire that he retains when consciously acting in a way incompatible with its gratification. It is an expression or utterance of the man, as he for the time is. It begins from him, from his self-conscious self. These other 'desires' end where it begins, *viz.* in this self. They are influences or tendencies by which the man, the self, is affected, not a motion proceeding from him. They tend to move him, but *he* does not move in them; and none of them actually moves him unless the man takes it into himself, identifies himself with it, in a way which wholly alters it from what it was as a mere influence affecting him.

145. The objection to saying that will is merely a strongest desire is that, as it is apt to be understood, it leads to this difference being ignored. It is taken to imply that the principle of a man's action is no more than one of the influences to which the man in his inner life is susceptible—that one which, under the conditions of the moment, or upon consideration of the circumstances, becomes the strongest. In truth it is never any or all of these, however much it may be affected by them, but a self-distinguishing and self-realising consciousness, through which, as a transforming medium, these influences must pass before they can take effect in a moral action at all. Just as each of us is constantly having sensations which do not amount to perceptions, make no lodgment in the cosmos of our experience, add nothing to our knowledge, because not gathered into the focus of self-consciousness and through it referred to objects or determined by relation to each other; so there are impulses constantly at work in a man—the result of his organisation, of habits (his own or his ancestors'), of external excitement, &c.— of which he is more or less aware according to the degree to which their antagonism to each other calls attention to them, but which yet do not amount to principles of imputable action, or to desires of which it is sought to realise the objects, because the self-seeking, self-determining person has not identified himself with any of them. It is such impulses alone that are properly said to compete for mastery in a man before his determination to act, and that may survive along with an enacted desire that represents none of them. The 'strongest desire' or will which is realised in act is not one of them nor co-ordinate with them, though apart from them it would not be. It is a new principle that supervenes upon them through the self-conscious subject's identification of itself with one of them, just as a perception is

not a sensation or congeries of sensations, but supervenes upon certain sensations through a man's attending to them, *i.e.* through his taking them into self-consciousness and determining them, as in it, by relation to others of its contents.

146. A man, we will suppose, is acted on at once by an impulse to avenge an affront, by a bodily want, by a call of duty, and by fear of certain results incidental to his avenging the affront or obeying the call of duty. We will suppose further that each passion (to use the most general term) suggests a different line of action. So long as he is undecided how to act, all are, in a way, external to him. He presents them to himself as influences by which he is consciously affected but which are not he, and with none of which he yet identifies himself; or, to vary the expression, as tendencies to different objects, none of which is yet *his* object. So long as this state of things continues, no moral effect ensues. It ensues when the man's relation to these influences is altered by his identifying himself with one of them, by his taking the object of one of the tendencies as for the time his good. This is to *will*, and is in itself moral action, though circumstances may prevent its issuing in that sensible effect which we call an overt act. But in the act of will the man does not cease to desire. Rather he, the man, for the first time desires, having not done so while divided between the conflicting influences. His willing is not a continuation of any of those desires, if they are to be so called, that were previously acting upon him. It is that which none of these had yet become; a desire in which the man enacts himself, as distinct from one which acts upon him. Whether its object—the object to which the moral action is directed—be the attainment of revenge, or the satisfaction of a bodily want, or the fulfilment of a call of duty, it has equally this characteristic. The object is one which for the time the man identifies with himself, so that in being determined by it he is consciously determined by himself.

147. It is not necessary, however, to that putting forth of the man or self in desire which constitutes an act of will, that there should have been beforehand any conscious presentation of competing objects of desire, with consequent deliberation as to which should be pursued. When a man acts 'impulsively' or according

to a settled habit, without contemplating the possibility of a
motive that might lead him to another sort of action, it is still
only through the self-seeking and self-distinguishing self that
the inducement, or influence, or tendency, becomes a principle of
action. In such a case the man makes the object, which the
passion or habit suggests, his own, and sets himself to realise it,
just as much as in the case where he contemplates alternatives.
The evidence of this is his self-imputation of the act upon reflection. He may make excuses for it, should there be occasion to
do so, on the ground of the strength of the inducement, but
these very excuses witness that he is conscious of himself as other
than the inducements and influences of which he pleads the
strength, and conscious that it is not from them, but from himself as affected by them, that the action proceeds. When the
case is otherwise, when he is conscious of having really been but
an instrument in doing what he did, he does not make excuses
but explains the fact.

So much for the opposition, sometimes alleged, between will
and desire. It must be admitted that an act of will is never
mere desire, never a desire which has been in conflict with other
co-ordinate desires and has come out the strongest, if in speaking
of such desire we suppose abstraction to be made of the action
of a self-determining self upon and within it. But in this there
lies no difference between will and any other principle of moral
or human or imputable, as distinct from merely animal, action ;
for mere desire, of that kind to which will can properly be
opposed, never amounts to such a principle. The true distinction lies between passions as influences affecting a man—among
which we may include ' mere desires,' if we please—and the man
as desiring, or putting himself forth in desire for the realisation
of some object present to him in idea, which is the same thing
as willing.

148. The recognised opposition between Will and Intellect
stands on a different footing. We have already pointed out that,
though a man in desiring (in the sense of consciously directing
himself to the realisation of objects) necessarily exercises intellect,
and in exercising intellect desires, yet such desire and such
speculative thought are differently directed activities of the self-

conscious subject. It is to be remembered further that the understanding employed in the exercise of desire relates to the desired object and to the conditions of its realisation, while the desire involved in a process of thinking has for its object the completion of that process. It is therefore not to the purpose to insist on the obvious fact that a man morally excellent, in the sense that his desires are habitually directed to good practical objects, may be 'stupid,' unskilled, and uninterested in the exercise of intellect on all matters of literature, science, and art, as well as lacking in power of expression upon the matters in which he is interested; or conversely, that a man whose thoughts are habitually occupied, and occupied to great effect, in the region of literature, science, and art, may be deficient in moral interests. From a certain point of view, no doubt, this apparent discrepancy between moral interests or objects, and those of the artist and the man of science or letters, presents a serious difficulty. If we were forming a theory of the universe, or trying to regard the facts of human nature and history as the realisation of one idea (and the effort thoroughly to understand them doubtless implies such an attempt), then it would be a necessary problem to show that these seemingly discrepant interests and objects have some ultimate point of meeting. Our present concern, however, is with the individual consciousness and its objects—the objects of this or that man, as he is actually conscious of them, not as they may be combined with other objects in an idea which is not consciously his though it may be operative in him.

For the consciousness of the individual the direction of himself to such objects as, e. g., the settlement of a vexed question in philology, or the perfect rendering of certain atmospheric effects in landscape painting, has nothing in common with the direction of himself to such objects as, e.g., the discipline of his own tongue, or the promotion of sobriety among his neighbours. It is easy indeed to see that, even within the experience and sphere of action of the individual, interests of the one kind are not without a bearing—at any rate in the result—on interests of the other kind. The effect of 'moral' interests appears in habits without which the scholar or artist is not properly free for his work, nor exempt from the temptation to be showy instead of thorough in

it. Conversely, the effect of scientific and artistic interests may
be to neutralise to some extent the attractions which compete
most actively with reverence for moral law and devotion to the
service of men. There is also such a thing as a consciousness of
the ultimate unity of all pursuits that contribute to the perfection of man, which may import a certain enthusiasm of humanity
into the devotion with which the scholar or artist applies himself
to his immediate object, and which may keep the practical mind
open to interests in literature and art. Still the immediate difference, for the consciousness of the individual, between the
kinds of object distinguished is such that the employment of
thought upon objects of a non-practical kind, though it necessarily carries with it a direction of desire to the realisation of the
intellectual ideal, may very well go along with an absence of
desire for the realisation of any moral ideal; while, on the other
hand, the direction of desire to the latter object, though it
necessarily implies an exercise of intellect in the conception of
the moral object and of the conditions of its attainment, may
very well go along with a want of inclination to think, and of
ability to think well, about other things.

149. It is clear then that a particular act of will does not, on
the part of the person willing, involve thought except about the
object of the act of will—such thought as is implied in the conception of self, of an object present to the self in idea as desired,
of a world in which that object awaits realisation, of conditions
under which it is to be realised. Now when we oppose thinking
and willing, we may have in view the distinction between the
speculative and the practical employment of the human spirit,
the distinction between its work as directed to that discovery of
relations between existing things which enables it to regard
them as one, and its work as bringing conceived or imagined
objects into real existence. This is a valid distinction, though
it must be borne in mind, as previously pointed out, that the
speculative employment is necessarily accompanied by willing—
for we only find unity in the world because we have an idea that
it is there, an idea which we direct our powers to realise—and
that throughout any *practical* process ideas operate and are
operated upon (to use the most general expression) in a manner
which we should describe as thought, if the term had not come

to be specially associated with the *speculative* exercise of thought. But if this is the distinction that we have in view when we oppose thinking and willing, it is improper to say that *mere* thinking is not willing, or that willing is *more* than thinking. Speculation and moral action are co-ordinate employments of the same self-conscious soul, and of the same powers of that soul, only differently directed. Speculative thinking is not an element of moral action, requiring the addition of something else to constitute moral action. But when we say that *mere* thinking is not willing, we imply that the thinking of which we speak does stand in this relation to moral action—that some complementary element needs to be added to it in order to constitute moral action. And of the speculative exercise of thought this is not true.

150. If then the proposition in question is to be to the purpose at all, it must relate to such thinking as is involved in or presupposed by an act of will. If we say, *e. g.*, that the act of willing to pay a debt is more than mere thinking, what we wish to point out is certainly not that thinking about a mathematical theorem is not equivalent to willing to pay the debt. We probably mean to say that the mere thinking about paying the debt falls short of willing to pay it. But here our rejoinder will be that this depends on what we mean by the thinking. If thinking about payment of the debt means merely an otiose contemplation of a possible event, the proposition may be true but is little to the purpose. Such thought does not amount to either of those activities of the thinking self which have been described above. Just as sensuous impressions are constantly occurring to us which tell us nothing, suggest nothing, because they do not fit into any context of ideas, so ideas are constantly, as we say, passing through our minds without forming part of any process of thought speculative or practical, as defined by reference to an end. The possibility of paying his debts may thus pass through the mind of the debtor without really amounting to an object of thought at all, either in the sense in which a fact that I am trying to understand, or that I am applying to other facts in order to understand them, is an object of thought, or in the sense in which an undertaking that interests me is so. At any rate the object thought of in such thinking, such otiose contemplation,

is not the object willed in the will to pay the debt. The object thought of is a possible occurrence—an object of speculative thought, if of thought at all. The man presents to himself the payment of his debt as an event that may happen, with its various incidents. But it is not such a possible event that a man *wills* in willing to pay the debt. To will an event, as distinguished from an act, is a contradiction. The object willed is the realisation of an idea—an idea of relief from annoyance, of satisfying one's neighbours' expectations, of what self-respect requires, or of a good in which all these ends are included.

151. Thus, though such an object of thought as the possible event of the debt being paid is not the object willed, the object willed is yet an object of thought. There is always thinking in willing. A thoughtless will would be no will. Without the thought of self and a world as mutually determined, of an object present to the self in a desire felt by it, but awaiting realisation in the world, there would be no will but only blind impulse. Even in cases where the will is said to be governed by animal appetite, it is still the realisation of an idea that is the object willed. The pleasure incidental to the gratification of the appetite exists ideally or in anticipation for me, and what I will is the realisation of this idea. Otherwise it would be no longer *I* that did the act, but an appetite dwelling in me. The act would not be mine; I should not impute it to myself, any more than, *e. g.*, an operation which I find the animal system has performed while I have been asleep. But if in all cases of willing the object willed is the realisation of an idea, the object of will is also an object of thought. It is only for a subject which thinks, and so far as thinking, that it can exist.

The question accordingly arises whether thinking, of the kind which is thus essential to willing, can properly be regarded as merely a *part* of, or an *element* in, willing, to which something must be added in order to constitute an act of will. Unless this is so, the proposition that *mere* thinking is not willing, that willing is *more* than thinking, conveys a false impression. And it would seem not to be so. The act of willing is not *in part* one of thinking. It is an act of thought, though not of thought speculatively directed, wholly and throughout. There is no factor or element in it separable (except verbally) from thought, and of which the addition to thought makes up the whole called an act of will. Is it not, we may perhaps ask, the addition of desire to thought that constitutes will? But the answer must be, No, will is not thought *plus* desire. Desire of the kind which enters into willing involves thought; thought of the kind which enters into willing involves desire; for the desire is the direction of a self-conscious subject to the realisation of an idea, while the thought is the presence of an idea in such a subject impelling to its own realisation. We cannot say that the thought is separate from the desire and supervenes upon it, or that the desire is so related to the thought.

152. The notion of their being separate elements which together make up an act of will arises from thought and desire being severally supposed to be something which, *as in will*, they are not. We have already seen that when, on the one hand, different *desires* are said to compete for mastery in a man, or when it is said that one object is *desired* but another willed, and when, on the other hand, a moral action is said to proceed from or represent some *desire*, 'desire' is being used in different senses. In one sense it means desire as it affects a man, in the other the desire which proceeds from a man or in which he expresses himself. Desire of the one sort ends where the other begins, *viz.* in the direction of the man's self to an object. In the one case he does, in the other he does not, put himself forth to the realisation of the desired object, as one in the realisation of which he seeks self-satisfaction. In like manner our thoughts may mean either thoughts that, as we say, occur to us, or thoughts to the realisation of which we direct ourselves. It is thought only in the latter of the two senses distinguished, desire likewise in the latter of its two senses, that enters into willing.

No doubt, both thought in the other sense and desire in the other sense are presupposed by willing, as *conditions antecedent*; and in the sense in which they are severally conditions antecedent of the act of willing but do not enter into it, they are clearly separable. There may very well be one without the other. I may, *e.g.*, contemplate payment of a debt as a possible event, consider how much money would be required for the purpose, how the creditor would behave when he got his money, and so on, without being affected by any desire to pay; and conversely

I may feel that I should be more at ease if I paid, without my thoughts running further on the event. But in the sense in which thought and desire enter into an act of will, each is the whole act; and we can only distinguish them by describing one and the same act of the inner man, which thought and desire equally constitute, as in respect of desire the direction of a self-conscious subject to the realisation of an idea, in respect of thought the action of an idea in such a subject impelling to its realisation.

153. Will then is equally and indistinguishably desire and thought—not however *mere* desire or *mere* thought, if by that is meant desire or thought as they might exist in a being that was not self-distinguishing and self-seeking, or as they may occur to a man independently of any action of himself; but desire and thought as they are involved in the direction of a self-distinguishing and self-seeking subject to the realisation of an idea [1]. If so, it must be a mistake to regard the will as a faculty which a man possesses along with other faculties—those of desire, emotion, thought, &c.—and which has the singular privilege of acting independently of other faculties, so that, given a man's character as it at any time results from the direction taken by those other faculties, the will remains something apart which may issue in action different from that prompted by the character. The will is simply the man. Any act of will is the expression of the man as he at the time is. The motive issuing in his act, the object of his will, the idea which for the time he sets himself to realise, are but the same thing in different words. Each is the reflex of what for the time, as at once feeling, desiring, and thinking, the man is. In willing he carries with him, so to speak, his whole self to the realisation of the given idea. All the time that he so wills, he may feel the pangs of conscience, or (on the other hand) the annoyance, the sacrifice, implied in acting conscientiously. He may think that he is doing wrong, or that it is doubtful whether after all there is really an objection

---

[1] It may prevent possible misapprehension, if I say that the term idea is here and in all similar passages used in the wide sense generally attached to it by English writers, who have followed the definition of it by Locke as 'the immediate object of the mind in thinking.' In this sense it seems pretty much equivalent to the German 'Vorstellung.'

to his acting as he has resolved to do. He may desire some one's good opinion which he is throwing away, or some pleasure which he is sacrificing. But for all that it is only the feeling, thought, and desire represented by the act of will, that the man recognises as for the time himself. The feeling, thought, and desire with which the act conflicts are influences that he is aware of, influences to which he is susceptible, but they are not *he*.

BOOK III.

THE MORAL IDEAL AND MORAL PROGRESS.

CHAPTER I.

GOOD AND MORAL GOOD.

154. WE are now in a position to return to the difficulty which was raised at the beginning of the last chapter, and which led to our attempt to ascertain the nature of Will, in its relation to desire and thought. That difficulty was as to the ground of distinction between the good and the bad will; a distinction which in some form or other—whether we consider the goodness of a will to be an attribute which it possesses on its own account, or to be relative to some result to which it contributes beyond the will itself—must lie at the root of every system of Ethics. What becomes of this distinction, we supposed an objector to ask, if the doctrine previously stated is admitted, 'that in all conduct to which moral predicates are applicable a man is an object to himself; that such conduct, equally whether virtuous or vicious, expresses a motive consisting in an idea of personal good which the man seeks to realise by action' (§ 115)? Further consideration has confirmed this statement. If it is a genuine definition that we want of what is common to all acts of willing, we must say that such an act is one in which a self-conscious individual directs himself to the realisation of some idea, as to an object in which for the time he seeks self-satisfaction. Such being an act of willing, the will in actuality must be the self-conscious individual as so directing himself, while the will in possibility, or as a faculty, will be the self-conscious individual as capable of so directing himself.

The above, however, is merely a *formal* account of willing and the will. It does not tell us the real nature of any act of will, or of any man as willing, or of any national will—if there be such a thing as one will operating in or upon the several members of a nation—or of the human will, if again there be such a thing as one will operating throughout the history of mankind. For the real nature of any act of will depends on the particular nature of the object in which the person willing for the time seeks self-satisfaction; and the real nature of any man as the subject of will—his character—depends on the nature of the objects in which he mainly tends to seek self-satisfaction. Self-satisfaction is the form of every object willed; but the filling of that form, the character of that in which self-satisfaction is sought, ranging from sensual pleasure to the fulfilment of a vocation conceived as given by God, makes the object what it really is. It is on the specific difference of the objects willed under the general form of self-satisfaction that the quality of the will must depend. It is here therefore that we must seek for the basis of distinction between goodness and badness of will.

155. The statement that the distinction between the good and bad will must lie at the basis of any system of Ethics, and the further statement that this distinction itself must depend on the nature of the objects willed, would in some sense or other be accepted by all recognised 'schools' of moralists, but they would be accepted in very different senses. On the one side the modern Utilitarian would only accept the former statement in the sense that, unless an action is done *intentionally*, it is not the subject of moral predicates. The action, in his view, derives its moral quality not from the motive or character which it expresses, but from the effects which it produces. Those effects, indeed, do not entitle the act to be reckoned morally good or bad, unless it is one which the agent intends or wills to do; but, given the intentional act, it is not on the motive which leads to its being intended, but on its effects in the way of pleasure or pain, that its morality depends. This is very plainly put by J. S. Mill: 'The morality of the action depends entirely upon the intention—that is, upon what the agent *wills to do*. But the motive, that is, the feeling which makes him will so to do, when it makes no difference in the act, makes none in the morality: though it makes a great difference in our moral

estimation of the agent, especially if it indicates a good or a bad habitual *disposition*—a bent of character from which useful or from which hurtful actions are likely to arise[1].' In other words, while there are two distinct objects of moral approbation or disapprobation, or two objects which admit of the designation morally good or bad, (*a*) intentional action, (*b*) the motive or character of an agent, the latter is only to be judged relatively to the former, just as the former is only to be judged relatively to its effects as producing pleasure or pain. The motive or character is morally good, if likely on the whole to issue in intentional actions which are good in the sense of producing on the whole, one person taken with another and one time with another, an excess of pleasure over pain.

Clearly, upon this view, our statement that Ethics is founded on the distinction between the good and bad will could only be accepted under the proviso that by good and bad will is understood good and bad intentional action, and further that intentional action is understood to be good or bad according to its relation to an ultimate good and evil, which are constituted not by any kind of action, intention, or character, but by pleasure and pain. The other statement that 'the distinction between the good and bad will must depend on the nature of the objects willed' would be subjected by the Utilitarian to a similar qualification. He could accept it if by ' will ' is understood intention, and if by 'the objects willed' are understood the effects of the intentional act in the way of producing pleasure and pain. If by ' will ' is meant ' habitual disposition,' and by ' objects willed ' motives, he could only accept the statement on the understanding that the ' nature of the objects willed ' is itself taken to depend on the tendency of the motives to issue in actions productive of a preponderance of pleasure or pain as the case may be.

It is in a precisely opposite sense that the propositions in question would have to be understood, in order to be approved by a strict follower of Kant. With him an act of will would never be understood merely of an intention to do a certain deed, in abstraction from the motive or object for the sake of which the deed is done; and with him again the good will is good, not in

---

[1] Utilitarianism, p. 27, note.

virtue of any effects extrinsic to it, but in virtue of what it is in itself, not as a means, but as an absolute end. The first of the above statements, therefore, he would accept in the sense which it naturally bears. In the second he might see a loophole for error. To say that a will is good in virtue of the nature of the objects willed, does not exclude the notion that it may be good in virtue of desired effects other than its own goodness, or as directed to objects which are willed otherwise than for the reason of their being prescribed by a universal practical law. So far as the statement in question is understood according to any such notion as this, Kant—at any rate if interpreted according to the reiterated letter of his doctrine—would reckon it fundamentally erroneous.

156. It is not according to the plan of the present treatise to examine critically either the moral doctrine of Kant as stated by himself, or that of Utilitarianism as stated by leading authorities, until it has been attempted to give the outline of a positive doctrine in regard to the nature of goodness and of our moral progress [1]. This done, the criticism may be undertaken with less liability to its drift being misunderstood, and without conveying the impression that no truth is thought to remain where some error has been detected. What then are the questions naturally raised for us by the considerations which we have so far pursued, and which a positive ethical doctrine should begin by attempting to answer? The first of them may perhaps be stated thus. Granted that, according to our doctrine, in all willing a self-conscious subject seeks to satisfy itself—seeks that which for the time it presents to itself as its good—how can there be any such intrinsic difference between the objects willed as justifies the distinction which 'moral sense' seems to draw between good and bad action, between virtue and vice? And if there is such a difference, in what does it consist?

A possible answer to the question would of course be a denial that there is any such difference at all. By an *intrinsic* difference between the objects willed we mean a difference between them in respect of that which is the motive to the person willing them, as distinct from a difference constituted by any effects which the

---

[1] [See Preface].

realisation of the objects may bring about, but of which the anticipation does not form the motive. Now according to all strictly Hedonistic theories the difference between objects willed is, according to this sense of the terms, extrinsic, not intrinsic. The motive to the persons willing is supposed to be in all cases the same, *viz.* desire for some pleasure or aversion from some pain. The conditions of the pleasures which different men desire, or which the same man desires at different times, are of course most various; but it is not the conditions of any pleasure but the pleasure itself that a man desires, if pleasure is really his object at all. On the Hedonistic supposition, therefore, every object willed is on its inner side, or in respect of that which moves the person willing, the same. It moves him as anticipated pleasure, or anticipated escape from pain. The difference between objects willed lies on their outer side, in effects which follow from them but are not included in them as motives to the persons willing. Two objects having been equally willed as so much anticipated pleasure, the realisation of the one does in the event produce a preponderance of pleasure over pain to the agent himself or to others, while the realisation of the other produces a preponderance of pain over pleasure. Thus and thus only, according to this theory—extrinsically not intrinsically—is the difference constituted between a good object of will and a bad one.

157. A detailed criticism of this doctrine would be out of place till we come to the examination of Utilitarianism. If the αἴτιον τοῦ ψευδοῦς can be explained, it will not stand seriously in our way; for though excellent men have argued themselves into it, it is a doctrine which, nakedly put, offends the unsophisticated conscience. Whatever the process may have been, we have reached a state in which we seem to know that the desires we think well of in ourselves differ absolutely as desires, or in respect of the objects desired in them, from those which we despise or condemn. If asked straight out to admit that all objects of desire, as desired, are alike, since it is pleasure that is equally the desired thing in them all; that it is only in the effects of the actions arising out of them, not in what they are for the desiring consciousness, that good desires differ from bad ones; upon first thoughts we should certainly refuse to do so. Hesitation would

only ensue if the enlightened enquirer asked us to reflect, whether we ever find ourselves desiring any thing from which we do not anticipate pleasure of some sort, and whether it is not this anticipation that makes us desire it. Thus challenged, we feel ourselves in a difficulty. This account of desire has a plausibility which we do not at once see our way to explaining. Yet to accept it seems to involve us logically [1] in an admission of the intrinsic identity of all desires, good and bad, which offends our moral conviction. If we could explain away the apparent cogency of the plea that it is some anticipated pleasure, as such, which we always find ourselves desiring, the conviction of the difference between good and bad desires, as states of consciousness on the part of the persons desiring, would hold its own undisturbed.

158. Now, according to the account previously given of desire, it is not difficult to explain the confusion which makes pleasure seem to be its only object. We saw that, in all such desire as can form the motive to an imputable act, the individual directs himself to the realisation of some idea, as to an object in which he seeks self-satisfaction. It is the consciousness that self-satisfaction is thus sought in all enacted desire, in all desire that amounts to will, combined with the consciousness that in all self-satisfaction, if attained, there is pleasure, which leads to the false notion that pleasure is always the object of desire. Whether in any case it really is so, or no, depends on whether pleasure is the object with which a man is seeking to satisfy himself. If it is not, pleasure is not the object of his dominant desire. However much pleasure there may prove to be in the self-satisfaction, if any, which the attainment of his object brings with it—and our common experience is that the objects with which we seek to satisfy ourselves do not turn out capable of satisfying us—it cannot be *this* pleasure that is the object which he desires. Its possibility presupposes the desire and its fulfilment. It cannot therefore be the exciting cause of the desire, any more than the pleasure of satisfying hunger can be the exciting cause of hunger.

[1] The attempt to combine the doctrine that pleasure as such is the sole object of desire, with the assertion of an *intrinsic* difference between good and bad desires, on the ground that pleasures differ in quality, will be considered below.

Only if the idea which in his desire the man seeks to realise is the idea of enjoying some pleasure—whether a pleasure of the kind which we commonly call sensual in a special sense, *i.e.* one incidental to the satisfaction of animal appetite, or a pleasure of pure emotion—can we truly say that pleasure is the object of his desire.

159. When the idea of which the realisation is sought is not that of enjoying any pleasure, the fact that self-satisfaction is sought in the effort to realise the idea of the desired object does not make pleasure the object of the desire. It may very well be that a man pursues an object in which he seeks self-satisfaction with the clear consciousness that no enjoyment of pleasure can yield him satisfaction, and that there must be such pain in the realisation of the idea to which he devotes himself as cannot be compensated, in any scale where pleasure and pain alone are weighed, by any enjoyment of an end achieved[1]. So it is in the more heroic forms of self-sacrifice. Self-satisfaction is doubtless sought in such sacrifice. The man who calmly faces a life of suffering in the fulfilment of what he conceives to be his mission could not bear to do otherwise. So to live is his good. If he could attain the consciousness of having accomplished his work, if he could 'count himself to have apprehended'—and probably just in proportion to the elevation of his character he is unable to do so—he would find satisfaction in the consciousness, and with it a certain pleasure. But supposing this pleasure to be attained, only the exigencies of a theory could suggest the notion that, as so much pleasure, it makes up for the pleasures forgone and the pains endured in the life through which it has been reached. Such a notion can only be founded on the see-saw process which first assumes that preference in every case is determined by amount of anticipated pleasure, and then professes to ascertain the relative amount of pleasure which a given line of action affords a man by the fact that he prefers so to act.

160. Even if it were the case, however, that self-satisfaction was more attainable than it is, and that the pleasure of success

---

[1] Cf. Arist. Eth. Nic. III. ix. 5. Οὐ δὴ ἐν ἁπάσαις ταῖς ἀρεταῖς τὸ ἡδέως ἐνεργεῖν ὑπάρχει, πλὴν ἐφ᾽ ὅσον τοῦ τέλους ἐφάπτεται. 'Thus the rule that the exercise of virtue is pleasant does not hold of all the virtues, except in so far as the end is attained.'

to the man who has 'spurned delights and lived laborious days' really admitted of being set against the pleasure missed in the process, it would none the less be a mere confusion to treat this pleasure of success as the desired object, in the realisation of which the man seeks to satisfy himself. A man may seek to satisfy himself with pleasure, but the pleasure of self-satisfaction can never be that with which he seeks to satisfy himself. This is equally true of the voluptuary and of the saint. The voluptuary must have his ideas of pleasures, unconnected with self-satisfaction, before he can seek self-satisfaction (where it is not to be found) in the realisation of those ideas; just as much as the saint must have ideas, not of pleasures but of services due to God and man, before he can seek self-satisfaction in their fulfilment. Most men, however, at least in their ordinary conduct, are neither voluptuaries nor saints; and we are falling into a false antithesis if, having admitted (as is true) that the quest of self-satisfaction is the form of all moral activity, we allow no alternative (as Kant in effect seems to allow none) between the quest for self-satisfaction in the enjoyment of pleasure, and the quest for it in the fulfilment of a universal practical law. Ordinary motives fall neither under the one head nor the other. They are interests in the attainment of objects, without which it seems to the man in his actual state that he cannot satisfy himself, and in attaining which, because he has desired them, he will find a certain pleasure, but only because he has previously desired them, not because pleasures are the objects desired.

161. Such interests, though not mere appetites because conditioned by self-consciousness, correspond to them as not having pleasure for their object. This point was sufficiently made out in the controversy as to the 'disinterestedness' of benevolence, carried on during the first part of the eighteenth century. When philosophers of the 'selfish school' represented benevolence as ultimately desire for some pleasure to oneself, Butler and others met them by showing that this was the same mistake as to reckon hunger a desire for the pleasure of eating. The appetite of hunger must precede and condition the pleasure which consists in its satisfaction. It cannot therefore have that pleasure for its exciting object. 'It terminates upon its object,' and is not relative to anything beyond the taking of food; and in the same

way benevolent desires terminate upon their objects, upon the
benefits done to others. In the 'termination' in each case there
is pleasure, but it is a confusion to represent this as an object
beyond the obtaining of food or the doing a kindness, to which
the appetite or benevolent desire is really directed. What is
true of benevolence is true of motives which we oppose to it,
as the vicious to the virtuous, *e.g.* of jealousy or the desire for
revenge. Iago does not work upon Othello for the sake of any
pleasure that he expects to experience when his envy is gratified,
but because in his envious state an object of which the realisation
seems necessary to the satisfaction of himself is Othello's ruin,
just as the consumption of food is necessary to the satisfaction
of hunger. What he desires is to see Othello down, not the
pleasure he will feel when he sees him so—a pleasure which he
could not feel unless he had desired the object independently of
such anticipation.

It is true that any interest or desire for an object may come
to be reinforced by desire for the pleasure which, reflecting
upon past analogous experience, the subject of the interest may
expect as incidental to its satisfaction. In this way 'cool self-
love,' according to the terminology of the last century, may
combine with 'particular desires or propensions.' If there is to
be any chance, however, of the expected pleasure being really
enjoyed, the 'self-love' of which pleasure is the object must not
supersede the 'particular propension' of which pleasure, in the
case of ordinary healthy interests, is *not* the object. The pleasure
incidental to the satisfaction of an interest cannot be attained
after loss of the interest itself, nor can the interest be revived by
wishing for a renewal of the pleasure incidental to its satisfaction. Hence just so far as 'cool self-love,' in the sense of a
calculating pursuit of pleasure, becomes dominant and super-
sedes particular interests, the chances of pleasure are really lost;
which accounts for the restlessness of the pleasure-seeker, and
for the common remark that the right way to get pleasure is
not to seek it.

162. It may seem presumptuous to charge clear-headed
moralists with the mistake of supposing that a desire can be
excited by the anticipation of its own satisfaction. But such a
mistake certainly seems to be accountable for the acceptance of

the doctrine that pleasure is the sole object of desire by so powerful a writer as J. S. Mill. He, as is well known, differs from the older Utilitarians in holding that, although pleasure and freedom from pain are the only things desirable as ends, some *kinds* of pleasure are more desirable and valuable than others, not as involving a greater amount of pleasure, but in their intrinsic nature[1]. Every one must feel that the Utilitarian theory receives a certain exaltation from his treatment of it, and especially from his assertion of this point. But the question is whether the admissions which he has to make in order to establish it do not virtually amount to a departure from the doctrine that pleasure or freedom from pain is the only object of desire; a departure which he only disguises from himself and his reader by virtually assuming that a desire may have for its object the pleasure, or deliverance from pain, involved in its satisfaction. It will be useful to dwell a little longer on this question, not for the sake of picking holes in a writer from whom we have all learnt much, but in order to bring out more clearly the distinction between the quest for self-satisfaction which all moral activity is rightly held to be, and the quest for pleasure which morally *good* activity is not.

163. No one of course can doubt that pleasures admit of distinction in quality according to the conditions under which they arise. So Plato and Aristotle distinguished pleasures incidental to the satisfaction of bodily wants from pleasures of sight and hearing, and these again from the pleasures of pure intellect. So too we might distinguish pleasures of satisfied desire from pleasures of pure emotion, and subdivide each sort according to the various conditions under which desire or emotion is excited. No one pretends that the pleasures of a sot are not really different from those of a man of refined taste. The question is in what sense, upon the principle that pleasure is the ultimate good by relation to which all other good is to be tested, these differences of kind between pleasures may be taken to constitute any difference in the degree of their goodness or desirability. All Utilitarians would hold that on one ground

[1] Utilitarianism, pp. 10–12.

or another they might be so taken, but they would not all agree upon the ground. The strict Benthamites hold that such differences of kind between pleasures as arise from differences in their exciting causes only affect their value or the degree of their goodness, in so far as they affect the amount of pleasure enjoyed on the whole; while Mill holds that these differences affect the value of pleasures independently of the effect they have on their amount. The estimation of pleasures should not depend on quantity alone: quality is to be considered as well as quantity [1].

164. For an explanation and defence of this variation from the doctrine of his master, Mill appeals to the ' unquestionable fact that those who are equally acquainted with, and equally capable of appreciating and enjoying, both, do give a most marked preference to the manner of existence which employs their higher faculties,' as compared with one involving more sensual pleasures. They do this, ' even though knowing it to be attended with a greater amount of discontent.' We naturally accept such an appeal because we cannot help thinking of the man whose preference Mill describes, as *better in himself* than one more ' sensual,' and of the ' higher faculties ' as intrinsically of more value; in other words, because we regard the attainment of a certain type of character or some realisation of the possibilities of man, not pleasure, as the end by relation to which goodness or value is to be measured. But, on the principle that pleasure is the only thing good ultimately or in its own right, we are not justified in so doing. On this principle one man can be better, one faculty higher than another, only as a more serviceable instrument for the production of pleasure. On this ground it is open to the Utilitarian to argue that a man who devotes himself to the exercise of such ' higher faculties ' as Mill is here thinking of, produces a greater amount of pleasure on the whole, all circumstances affecting that amount being taken into account, than does the man who does not trouble himself about his ' higher faculties.' But it is altogether against Utilitarian principles that a pleasure should be of more value because the man who pursues it is better. They only entitle us to argue back from the amount of pleasure to the worth of the man who acts so as to produce it.

[1] *Utilitarianism*, pp. 10–12.

If we rid ourselves then of all presuppositions, illegitimate on Utilitarian principles, in regard to the superiority of the man or the faculties exercised in what we call the highest pursuits, and if we admit that all desire is for pleasure, the strongest desire for the greatest pleasure, what is proved by the example of the man who, being 'competently acquainted with both,' prefers the life of moral and intellectual effort to one of healthy animal enjoyment? Simply this, that the life of effort brings more pleasure to the man in question than *he* would derive from the other sort of life. It outweighs for him any quantity of other pleasure *of which his nature is capable*. The fact that he is 'competently acquainted with both' sorts of pleasure can give no significance beyond this to his preference of one above the other. He may be 'competently acquainted' with animal enjoyments; but it does not follow that the pleasure they afford him is as intense and unmixed as that which they afford to the man who makes them his principal pursuit. The question of value then between the two sorts will have to be settled by a calculation of amount, the intensity of each kind, as experienced by those to whom it is most intense, being weighed against its duration and its degree of purity, productiveness, and extent[1]. The calculation is certainly very hard to make—whether it can be made at all is a question to be touched on when we come to a more detailed examination of Utilitarianism [2]—but it is the only possible way, if pleasure is the sole and ultimate good, of measuring the comparative worth of pleasures. The example of a certain man's preference, unless we have some other standard of his excellence than such as is relative to pleasure as the ultimate good, proves nothing as to the superiority of the pleasure which he chooses to another sort of pleasure preferred by some one else. It only proves that it is more of a pleasure *to him* than is that to which he prefers it; and this it only proves on supposition that the stronger desire is always for the greater pleasure.

165. Now it will be found, we think, that with Mill this supposition really rests on a confusion between the pleasure or

[1] Cf. Dumont's version of the Principles of Morals and Legislation (Hildreth's translation), p. 31.
[2] [See Book IV. chap. iii.]

removal of pain which ensues upon the satisfaction of any desire and the object of that desire. In an eloquent passage he illustrates the unwillingness of any one acquainted with the 'higher' pleasures to exchange them for any quantity of the lower :—

'Now it is an unquestionable fact that those who are equally acquainted with, and equally capable of appreciating and enjoying, both, do give a most marked preference to the manner of existence which employs their higher faculties. Few human creatures would consent to be changed into any of the lower animals, for a promise of the fullest allowance of a beast's pleasures; no intelligent human being would consent to be a fool, no instructed person would be an ignoramus, no person of feeling and conscience would consent to be selfish and base, even though they should be persuaded that the fool, the dunce, or the rascal is better satisfied with his lot than they are with theirs. They would not resign what they possess more than he, for the most complete satisfaction of all the desires which they have in common with him. If they ever fancy they would, it is only in cases of unhappiness so extreme, that to escape from it they would exchange their lot for almost any other, however undesirable in their own eyes. A being of high faculties requires more to make him happy, is capable probably of more acute suffering, and is certainly accessible to it at more points, than one of an inferior type; but in spite of these liabilities, he can never really wish to sink into what he feels to be a lower grade of existence. We may give what explanation we please of this unwillingness ; we may attribute it to pride, a name which is given indiscriminately to some of the most and to some of the least estimable feelings of which mankind are capable ; we may refer it to the love of liberty and personal independence, an appeal to which was with the Stoics one of the most effectual means for the inculcation of it ; to the love of power, or to the love of excitement, both of which do really enter into and contribute to it : but its most appropriate appellation is a sense of dignity, which all human beings possess in one form or other, and in some, though by no means in exact, proportion to their higher faculties ; and which is so essential a part of the happiness of those in whom it is strong, that nothing which conflicts with it could be, otherwise than momentarily, an object of desire to them[1].'

It appears from this passage that there is a motive, which has been variously described as ' pride,' ' love of liberty,' ' love of power,' ' love of excitement,' but of which the most appropriate designation is ' sense of dignity,' that makes a man of a certain sort refuse to accept any amount of such pleasure as a fool, or a dunce, or a rascal might share, in lieu of the exercise of the higher faculties, however much suffering this may entail. This refusal is appealed to as showing that the pleasure attending this exercise is intrinsically preferable to such as may be shared with a dunce or a rascal. That it is intrinsically preferable those who are not Utilitarians will readily agree. But unless it is a greater pleasure on the whole, it is not on Utilitarian principles

[1] Utilitarianism, pp. 12–13.

more really desirable or the greater good, and the fact that by the sort of person in contemplation it is preferred does not show that it is even for him, much less that it is on the whole, the greater pleasure, unless his preference is necessarily for what is to him the greater pleasure.

166. But with what plausibility can the motive described as a sense of dignity be reckoned a desire for pleasure at all? Mill indeed calls it 'an essential part of the happiness of those in whom it is strong'; but no desire as such, since it must rather be painful than pleasant, can properly be called a 'part of happiness.' It may be suggested therefore that by the 'sense of dignity' spoken of Mill understands an emotion, as distinct from desire, which he would no doubt be justified in calling a part of happiness, an ingredient in the sum of a man's pleasures. In that case we must suppose that it is desire for the pleasure of this emotion which makes the man, who is capable of the pleasure attending the exercise of the higher faculties, prefer this to the pleasure which he might share with the dunce. If this indeed were the true account of the matter, the strict Benthamite who will recognise no distinction in quality as distinct from quantity of pleasure, might say that it was simply a case of the pleasure preferred being more 'productive.' The intellectual pleasure brings the additional pleasure, consisting in the emotion called sense of dignity, which the animal pleasure does not. It is scarcely however a plausible account of the motive which makes an intelligent person unwilling to be a fool, a person of feeling and conscience unwilling to be selfish or base, though persuaded that the change would save him much discontent, to say that it is desire for the preponderating pleasure involved in the sense of being a superior person. Nor, if it were, would there be any ground for holding the man so actuated to be really happier than the fool or the selfish man, who, according to his standard of measurement, has as good a chance of feeling the pleasure of superiority without corresponding discontent. The truth is that Mill does not really regard this 'sense of dignity' as an emotion in distinction from desire. He regards it as a counter motive to desires for animal pleasure, which mere emotion could not be. Nor does he mean that the preference determined by it is preference for the pleasure of

feeling superior to the pleasures shared with average men. The
motive which he has in view is a desire to be worthy, not a
desire to feel the pleasure of being worth more than others; and
he only regards it as desire for pleasure at all, because he fancies
that a desire, of which the disappointment makes me unhappy,
is therefore a desire for happiness—that a desire is for the
pleasure which ensues upon its satisfaction.

167. The real ground then of Mill's departure from the stricter
Utilitarian doctrine, that the worth of pleasure depends simply
on its amount, is his virtual surrender of the doctrine that all
desire is for pleasure; but he does not recognise this surrender,
because he thinks that to call a desired object part of the happiness of the person desiring it is equivalent to saying that the
desire for the object is a desire for pleasure. Yet little reflection
is needed to show that it is not so. The latter proposition can
only mean that a possible action or experience is contemplated
as likely to be pleasant, and is then desired for the sake of the
pleasure. It means that the anticipation of pleasure determines
desire. But the other proposition, that a desired object is part
of the happiness of the person desiring it, rather means that
desire determines the anticipation of pleasure; that, given desire
for an object, however different from pleasure that object may
be, there results pleasure, or at least a removal of pain, in the
satisfaction of the desire; that the man feeling the desire necessarily looks forward to this result as part of a possible happiness
to come, and cannot be completely happy till the object is attained. This is equivalent to saying, as has been so often
mentioned above, that to desire an object is to seek self-satisfaction in its attainment, but it does not in the least imply that
pleasure is the object in which self-satisfaction is sought.

168. The same is true of the other forms in which Mill expresses the conception on which he considers the proof of Utilitarianism to rest. 'Desiring a thing and finding it pleasant . . .
are two parts of the same phenomenon.' 'To think of an object
as desirable . . . and to think of it as pleasant are one and
the same thing[1].' Both statements are ambiguous. Each
is in a sense true, but not in the sense which would imply that
a pleasure is the only possible object of desire. In the latter

[1] Utilitarianism, p. 58.

statement what is meant by 'thinking of an object as desirable'?
Does it mean thinking of it as one that *should be* desired? Thus
understood, the statement would lose all plausibility. No one
would pretend that to think of an object as one which he *should*
desire is the same thing as thinking of it as pleasant. Rather,
so long as he thinks of it as one in which he finds pleasure, it is
impossible for him to place it in any such relation to himself as
could be represented by saying that he thinks of it as an object
which he should desire. Nor is there any sign that Mill uses
the terms 'desired' and 'desirable' except as pretty much equivalent. To 'think of an object as desirable,' means with him to
reflect on it as one that is desired. Now it is quite true that
I cannot reflect on an object as one that I desire without thinking of it as pleasant, in the sense that I cannot reflect on my
desire for it without thinking of the pleasure there would be in
the satisfaction of the desire. But this in no way implies that
the desire is a desire for that or any other pleasure.

As regards the other statement, if the 'phenomenon' under
consideration is taken to include both the desire for an object
and the satisfaction of that desire in the attainment of its object,
then to desire the object and to find its *attainment* pleasant are
doubtless parts of that one phenomenon. If, on the other hand,
the phenomenon is held to be confined to the desire, and not to
include its satisfaction, then 'to find a thing pleasant' is no part
of the phenomenon; for unsatisfied desire involves no pleasure.
We may suppose, however, that 'to find it pleasant' is here
hastily written for 'to anticipate pleasure from it.' Thus interpreted, the statement is indisputable so far as it goes. To desire
an object, and to anticipate pleasure from its attainment, are
certainly parts of one and the same phenomenon. But the question remains of the relation in which the two parts of the
phenomenon stand to each other. Is it always the anticipation
of pleasure from an object that excites the desire for it, or are
there cases in which the anticipation of pleasure in the satisfaction of desire arises out of an independent desire for an object
which is not pleasure at all? The former is the view which
Mill believed himself to hold, and which his 'Proof of Utilitarianism' requires; but the proposition under consideration is
equally compatible with the latter view, and it may be doubted

whether it would have seemed so self-evident to most readers, or even to Mill himself, if it were not so.

169. The reason for this doubt as regards Mill himself is that he insists upon the reality of desires which, as he describes them, are only desires for *pleasure* in the improper and illogical sense; which are not determined by an antecedent imagination of pleasure; but from which there results pleasure in the attainment of the desired object, pain in its absence. Thus, having pointed out that the Utilitarian doctrine requires us to consider happiness, or pleasure, the only thing desirable as an end, he goes on to say[1] that 'it maintains not only that virtue is to be desired, but that it is to be desired disinterestedly,' *i. e.*, as he explains, not as a means to 'any end beyond it.' The mind, he tells us, is 'not in a right state, not in a state conformable to Utility,' unless it so desires virtue. But such desire for virtue is clearly not determined by any antecedent imagination of pleasure. It is of course open to any one to argue that what is called desire for virtue is really desire for pleasures that are to be obtained in a certain way; but in that case virtue is not an ultimate object of desire, the desire for it is not disinterested. That presentation of virtue which determines any disinterested desire for it, can only be a presentation of a possible state of character or mode of action as an ideal object which we seek to realise; and the object thus presented cannot be identified with any pleasant feeling or series of feelings, which, having experienced it, we imagine and desire to experience again. If, then, the presentation of virtue as an ultimate object, and not merely as a means, does determine desire, there are desires which are not excited by the anticipation of pleasure, though in such cases as much as in any other the desired object, just so far as desired, is 'part of the happiness' of the person desiring it, in the sense that, having desired it, he cannot be happy without it.

There are other objects of desire recognised by Mill—money, power, fame—which he admits are not pleasures (though to power and fame, he thinks 'there is a certain amount of immediate pleasure annexed[2]'), but which have yet come to be desired for their own sake. In regard to them, as in regard to virtue, he suggests that they were originally desired as means,

[1] *Utilitarianism*, p. 54.   [2] *Ibid.* p. 55.

as conducive to pleasure or to protection from pain, but he does not pretend that, by those who desire them most strongly, they are so desired any longer. 'What was once desired as an instrument for the attainment of happiness has come to be desired for its own sake.' That the desire for them originated in a desire *for pleasure* is, indeed, a view founded on the assumption that pleasures alone are wished for. To aid in the attainment of our wishes, as these things do, is with Mill the same thing as to aid in the attainment of pleasure. But we may waive this point, for questions as to the history of any desire do not affect its present relation to its object. If money, fame, and power are desired not as a means to pleasure but for their own sake—and this Mill admits—then there are desires, whatever their history, which are not desires for pleasure, however essential their gratification may be to the happiness of those who so desire.

170. As against the view, therefore, that all desire is for some pleasure or other, from which it would seem to follow that the good will cannot differ intrinsically, or as desire, from the bad, but only in virtue of effects in the way of pleasure and pain, we may adduce the involuntary evidence of the most eminent modern advocate of that view. We find him explicitly recognising desires which, as they exist, however they may have originated, are not desires for pleasure, and which he only brings under his general theory of desire on the ground that the objects of such desires are desired by us as part of our happiness. But this, as we have seen, is no more than saying that they are desired by a self-conscious subject, who in all desire, or at any rate in all that amounts to will, is seeking self-satisfaction, and who, so far as he reflects on any desire, reflects also on the pleasure of its possible fulfilment. It leaves the question open what the ideal object is, in the realisation of which self-satisfaction is sought. It does not exclude the possibility of its being even the endurance of pain, as perhaps, under sterner conditions of society than ours, or under the influence of fanatical belief, it not unfrequently has been. The formula is at any rate elastic enough to allow of the strong assertion by Mill himself, that the attainment of a certain disposition may be an object of desire in itself, irrespectively of any pleasures that flow from it. We may return then to examine the question whether there is any *intrinsic* distinction

between objects willed, on which the difference between a good and a bad will may rest, without allowing ourselves to be stopped *in limine* by a denial of the possibility of such distinction and a reduction of all motives, however various in their effects, to desire for some pleasure or other on the part of the person desiring.

171. It will have appeared from the foregoing discussion that the primary difference between the view here advanced and that of 'Hedonistic' philosophers relates to the generic definition of the good—not only of the morally good, but of good in the wider sense. Whereas with them the good generically is the pleasant, in this treatise the common characteristic of the good is that it satisfies some desire. In all satisfaction of desire there is pleasure, and thus pleasantness in an object is a necessary incident of its being good. We cannot think of an object as good, *i.e.* such as will satisfy desire, without thinking of it as in consequence such as will yield pleasure; but its pleasantness depends on its goodness, not its goodness upon the pleasure it conveys. This pleasure, according to our view, so far as it is a necessary incident of any good, presupposes desire and results from its satisfaction, while according to the Hedonistic view desire presupposes an imagination of pleasure. The importance of this distinction, which may at first sight seem somewhat finely drawn, will appear as soon as we consider its bearing on the question of the distinguishing nature of the moral good, or on that other form of the same question—the form in which it seems to have been first raised by philosophy—in which it is enquired, how the true good differs from the merely apparent.

If the generic definition of good is that it is pleasure, the moral good as distinct from the natural can only be pleasure obtained in a particular way; either simply pleasure experienced as a result of intentional action, in distinction from such pleasure as comes to us in a natural course of events which we have not contributed to bring about, or such pleasure as, in Locke's language, 'is not the natural product and consequence of the action itself,' but is attached to it by some positive law, either the law of God, or civil law, or the law of opinion[1]. This at any rate is what

[1] See Locke's Essay, Book II. ch. xxviii. § 5 : 'Good and evil are nothing but

'moral good' according to this view must mean, so long as it is understood to be the designation of an end. As a designation of means, it will be applicable to actions which tend to produce the pleasure obtainable in the particular manner described. From the same point of view the apparent good can only be distinguished from the true as a pleasure of which the enjoyment in its consequences yields a preponderance of pain over pleasure, whether to the individual enjoying it or (according to the Utilitarian view) to the majority of persons or of sentient beings. On the other hand, regarding the good generically as that which satisfies desire, but considering the objects we desire to be by no means necessarily pleasures, we shall naturally distinguish the moral good as that which satisfies the desire of a moral agent, or that in which a moral agent can find the satisfaction of himself which he necessarily seeks. The true good we shall understand in the same way. It is an end in which the effort of a moral agent can really find rest.

172. It will at once be objected that this account of moral good either tells us nothing at all about it, or only tells us anything in virtue of some assumption in regard to moral good involved in our notion of a moral agent. The objection is in a certain sense a valid one. The question, What is our moral nature or capability?—in other words, What do we mean by calling ourselves moral agents?—is one to which a final answer cannot be given without an answer to the question, What is moral good? For the moral good is the realisation of the moral capability, and we cannot fully know what any capability is till we know its ultimate realisation. It may be argued therefore that we either know what the moral good in this sense is, and accordingly have no need to infer what it is from our moral nature, or else we do not know what it is, in which case neither

pleasure or pain, or that which occasions or procures pleasure or pain to us. Moral good and evil, then, is only the conformity or disagreement of our voluntary actions to some law, whereby good or evil [*i. e.* pleasure or pain] is drawn on us by the will and power of the law-maker.' Here it will be seen that the terms 'good and evil,' when qualified as 'moral,' are transferred from end to means. But, according to the general definition of 'good and evil' as equivalent to pleasure and pain, we must suppose that Locke considered the 'conformity of our voluntary actions to some law' to constitute 'moral good' only because it brings about the pleasure which, by one or other of the laws which he recognises, is attached to such conformity.

can we know what the moral nature is from which we profess to infer what the moral good is.

The answer is that from a moral capability which had not realised itself at all nothing could indeed be inferred as to the moral good which can only consist in its full realisation; but that the moral capability of man is not in this wholly undeveloped state. To a certain extent it has shown by actual achievement what it has in it to become, and by reflection on the so far developed activity we can form at least some negative conclusion in regard to its complete realisation. We may convince ourselves that this realisation can only be attained in certain directions of our activity, not in others. We cannot indeed describe any state in which man, having become all that he is capable of becoming—all that, according to the divine plan of the world, he is destined to become—would find rest for his soul. We cannot conceive it under any forms borrowed from our actual experience, for our only experience of activity is of such as implies incompleteness. Of a life of completed development, of activity with the end attained, we can only speak or think in negatives, and thus only can we speak or think of that state of being in which, according to our theory, the ultimate moral good must consist. Yet the conviction that there must be such a state of being, merely negative as is our theoretical apprehension of it, may have supreme influence over conduct, in moving us to that effort after the Better which, at least as a conscious effort, implies the conviction of there being a Best. And when the speculative question is raised as to what this Best can be, we find that it has not left itself without witness. The practical struggle after the Better, of which the idea of there being a Best has been the spring, has taken such effect in the world of man's affairs as makes the way by which the Best is to be more nearly approached plain enough to him that will see. In the broad result it is not hard to understand how man has bettered himself through institutions and habits which tend to make the welfare of all the welfare of each, and through the arts which make nature, both as used and as contemplated, the friend of man. And just so far as this is plain, we know enough of ultimate moral good to guide our conduct; enough to judge whether the prevailing interests which make our character are or are not in the direction which tends further to realise the capabilities of the human spirit.

173. But here again it may be urged that we are going too fast, that we are making huge assumptions. We seem to be taking for granted that there is some best state of being for man —best in the sense that in it lies the full realisation of his capabilities, and that in it therefore alone he can satisfy himself, though as a matter of fact in his efforts after self-satisfaction he constantly acts in a manner inconsistent with his attaining it. We seem to be taking for granted, further, that this best state of man is already present to some divine consciousness, so that it may properly be said to be the vocation of man to attain it; that some unfulfilled and unrealised, but still operative, idea of there being such a state has been the essential influence in the process by which man has so far bettered himself; and that a continued operation of the same idea in us, with that growing definiteness which is gathered from reflection on the actions and institutions in which it has so far manifested itself, is the condition of character and conduct being morally good in the proper sense of the words. How are such assumptions to be justified?

174. In order to justify them, we must in the first place recall the conclusions arrived at in an earlier stage of this treatise. We saw reason to hold that the existence of one connected world, which is the presupposition of knowledge, implies the action of one self-conditioning and self-determining mind; and that, as our knowledge, so our moral activity was only explicable on supposition of a certain reproduction of itself, on the part of this eternal mind, as the self of man—'a reproduction of itself to which it makes the processes of animal life organic, and which is qualified and limited by the nature of those processes, but which is so far essentially a reproduction of the one supreme subject, implied in the existence of the world, that the product carries with it under all its limitations and qualifications the characteristic of being an object to itself' (§ 99). Proof of such a doctrine, in the ordinary sense of the word, from the nature of the case there cannot be. It is not a truth deducible from other established or conceded truths. It is not a statement of an event or matter of fact that can be the object of experiment or observation.

It represents a conception to which no perceivable or imaginable object can possibly correspond, but one that affords the only means by which, reflecting on our moral and intellectual experience conjointly, taking the world and ourselves into account, we can put the whole thing together and understand how (not *why*, but *how*) we are and do what we consciously are and do. Given this conception, and not without it, we can at any rate express that which it cannot be denied demands expression, the nature of man's reason and man's will, of human progress and human short-coming, of the effort after good and the failure to gain it, of virtue and vice, in their connection and in their distinction, in their essential opposition and in their no less essential unity.

175. The reason and will of man have their common ground in that characteristic of being an object to himself which, as we have said, belongs to him in so far as the eternal mind, through the medium of an animal organism and under limitations arising from the employment of such a medium, reproduces itself in him. It is in virtue of this self-objectifying principle that he is determined, not simply by natural wants according to natural laws, but by the thought of himself as existing under certain conditions, and as having ends that may be attained and capabilities that may be realised under those conditions. It is thus that he not merely desires but seeks to satisfy himself in gaining the objects of his desire; presents to himself a certain possible state of himself, which in the gratification of the desire he seeks to reach; in short, wills. It is thus, again, that he has the impulse to make himself what he has the possibility of becoming but actually is not, and hence not merely, like the plant or animal, undergoes a process of development, but seeks to, and does, develop himself. The conditions of the animal soul, 'servile to every skiey influence,' no sooner sated than wanting, are such that the self-determining spirit cannot be conscious of them as conditions to which it is subject—and it is so subject and so conscious of its subjection in the human person—without seeking some satisfaction of itself, some realisation of its capabilities, that shall be independent of those conditions.

176. Hence arises the impulse which becomes the source,

according to the direction it takes, both of vice and of virtue. It is the source of vicious self-seeking and self-assertion, so far as the spirit which is in man seeks to satisfy itself or to realise its capabilities in modes in which, according to the law which its divine origin imposes on it and which is equally the law of the universe and of human society, its self-satisfaction or self-realisation is not to be found. Such, for instance—so self-defeating— is the quest for self-satisfaction in the life of the voluptuary. Animals are not voluptuaries; for, if they seek pleasure at all, they do so in the sense that they are stimulated to action by the images of this pleasure and that, as those images recur. They are not objects to themselves, as men are, and therefore cannot set themselves, as the voluptuary does, to seek self-satisfaction in the enjoyment of all the pleasures that are to be had. It is one and the same principle of his nature—his divine origin, in the sense explained—which makes it possible for the voluptuary to seek self-satisfaction, and thus to live for pleasure, at all, and which according to the law of its being, according to its inherent capability, makes it impossible that the self-satisfaction should be found in any succession of pleasures. So it is again with the man who seeks to assert himself, to realise himself, to show what he has in him to be, in achievements which may make the world wonder, but which in their social effects are such that the human spirit, according to the law of its being which is a law of development in society, is not advanced but hindered by them in the realisation of its capabilities. He is living for ends of which the divine principle that forms his self alone renders him capable, but these ends, because in their attainment one is exalted by the depression of others, are not in the direction in which that principle can really fulfil the promise and potency which it contains.

How in particular and in detail that fulfilment is to be attained, we can only tell in so far as some progress has actually been made towards its attainment in the knowledge, arts, habits, and institutions through which man has so far become more at home in nature, and through which one member of the human family has become more able and more wishful to help another. But the condition of its further fulfilment is the will in some form or other to contribute to its fulfilment. And hence the differentia of the virtuous life, proceeding as it does from the same self-objectifying principle which we have just characterised as the source of the vicious life, is that it is governed by the consciousness of there being some perfection which has to be attained, some vocation which has to be fulfilled, some law which has to be obeyed, something absolutely desirable, whatever the individual may for the time desire; that it is in ministering to such an end that the agent seeks to satisfy himself. However meagrely the perfection, the vocation, the law may be conceived, the consciousness that there is such a thing, so far as it directs the will, must at least keep the man to the path in which human progress has so far been made. It must keep him loyal in the spirit to established morality, industrious in some work of recognised utility. What further result it will yield, whether it will lead to a man's making any original contribution to the perfecting of life, will depend on his special gifts and circumstances. Though these are such, as is the case with most of us, that he has no chance of leaving the world or even the society immediately about him observably better than he found it, yet in 'the root of the matter'—as having done loyally, or 'from love of his work' (which means under consciousness of an ideal), or in religious language 'as unto the Lord,' the work that lay nearest him—he shares the goodness of the man who devotes a genius to the bettering of human life.

177. It may seem that in the preceding section we have gone off prematurely into an account of virtue and vice, in respect at once of the common ground of their possibility and of their essential difference, without the due preliminary explanation of the relation between reason and will. A very little reflection, however, on what has been said will show the way in which this relation is conceived. By will is understood, as has been explained, an effort (or capacity for such effort) on the part of a self-conscious subject to satisfy itself: by reason, in the practical sense, the capacity on the part of such a subject to conceive a better state of itself as an end to be attained by action. This is what will and reason are severally taken to imply in the most primitive form in which they appear in us. A being without capacity for such effort or such conception would not, upon our theory, be considered to have will or reason. In this most

primitive form they are alike modes of that eternal principle of self-objectification which we hold to be reproducing itself in man through the medium of an animal organism, and of which the action is equally necessary to knowledge and to morality. There is thus essentially or in principle an identity between reason and will; and widely as they become divergent in the actual history of men (in the sense that the objects where good is actually sought are often not those where reason, even as in the person seeking them, pronounces that it is to be found), still the true development of man, the only development in which the capabilities of his 'heaven-born' nature can be actualised, lies in the direction of union between the developed will and the developed reason. It consists in so living that the objects in which self-satisfaction is habitually sought contribute to the realisation of a true idea of what is best for man—such an idea as our reason would have when it had come to be all which it has the possibility of becoming, and which, as in God, it is.

178. Such a life, as in vague forecast conceived, has always been called, according to a usage inherited from the Greek fathers of moral philosophy, a life according to reason. And this usage is in harmony with the definition just given of reason at its lowest potency in us. For any truest idea of what is best for man that can guide our action is still a realisation of that capacity for conceiving a better state of himself, which we must ascribe to every child whom we can regard as 'father of the man' capable of morality, to any savage to whom we would affiliate the moral life that we inherit. Nay, even if we mean by a 'true idea of what is best for man' such an adequate and detailed idea of our perfection as we cannot conceive ourselves to have—since to have it would imply that the perfection was already attained, and the conception of ourselves in perfection is one that we cannot form—still such an idea would be but the completed expression of that self-realising principle of which the primary expression is the capacity, distinctive of the 'animal rationale' in all its forms, of conceiving itself in a better state than it is.

On the other hand it must be borne in mind that this same capacity is the condition, as has been pointed out, no less of the vicious life than of the virtuous. The self-objectifying principle cannot exert itself as will without also exerting itself as reason, though neither as will nor as reason does it, in the vicious life, exert itself in a direction that leads to the true development of its capacity. That a man should seek an object as 'part of his happiness,' or as one without which in his then state he cannot satisfy himself,—and this is to will—implies that he presents himself to himself as in a better state with the object attained than he is without it; and this is to exercise reason. Every form of vicious self-seeking is conditioned by such presentation and, in that sense, by reason. Why then, it may be asked, should the moralising influence in man, the faculty through which the paths of virtue are marked out, whether followed or no, be specially called reason? We answer: because it is through the operative consciousness in man of a possible state of himself better than the actual, though that consciousness is the condition of the possibility of all that is morally wrong, that the divine self-realising principle in him gradually fulfils its capability in the production of a higher life. With this consciousness, directed in the right path, *i.e.* the path in which it tends to become what according to the immanent divine law of its being it has in it to be—and it is as so directed that we call it 'practical reason'—rests the initiative of all virtuous habit and action.

179. It is true that, just so far as this consciousness is operative in the direction supposed, it carries an improvement of the will with it. Men come to seek their satisfaction, their good, in objects conceived as desirable because contributing to the best state or perfection of man; and this change we describe by saying that their will becomes conformable to their reason. For the self-realisation of the divine principle in man this change of will is just as necessary as the development of practical reason, and to an intelligence which could view the process as a whole would appear inseparable from it. But to us who view the process piecemeal, ourselves representing certain stages in it, it is natural to treat the development of practical reason, *i. e.* the gradual filling up and definition of the idea of human perfection, as a separate process, upon which the corresponding conformation of will may or may not ensue. We see that in the individual the idea of what is good for him in his actual state of passion

and desire—the idea which in fact he seeks to realise in action—
is apt not to correspond to his conviction of what is truly good.
That conviction is the echo in him of the expression which
practical reason has so far given to itself in those institutions,
usages, and judgments of society, which contribute to the perfection of life, but his desires and habits are not yet so far conformed to it that he can seek his good in obeying it, that he can
will as it directs. He knows the better—knows it, in a sense,
even as better for himself, for he can think of himself as desiring
what he *does not*, but feels that he *should*, desire—but he prefers
the worse. His will, we say, does not answer to his reason.

It is thus natural for us to treat will and reason as separate
and even as conflicting faculties, though when we reflect on
moral action in its real integrity we see that it involves each
alike, and that it is only some *better* reason with which in
vicious action a man's will conflicts, while there is an exercise of
reason by him which is the very condition of his viciousness.
The 'better' reason is his capacity for conceiving a good of his
own, so far as that capacity is informed by those true judgments
in regard to human good which the action of the eternal spirit
in man has hitherto yielded; while the reason which shows
itself in his actual vice is the same capacity, as taking its object
and content from desires of which the satisfaction is inconsistent
with the real bettering of man. But just because it is this
capacity in a man which, while it alone renders selfishness in all
its forms possible, is the medium through which alone ideas of a
better life than he is living are brought home to him—ideas
themselves arising from the development of this capacity as it
has so far gone in men—we are right, when once we have
allowed ourselves to treat reason and will as separate faculties,
in regarding reason as the one which has the initiative in the
bettering of life. In the same way of thinking we may properly
ascribe to reason—not as gradually unfolding itself in us, but as
in the perfection to which that process tends, and which we must
suppose to be actually attained in the eternal mind—a fully
articulated idea of the best life for man, and accordingly speak
of life according to reason as the goal of our moral effort. Meanwhile the error which lies in the treatment of reason and will as
separate faculties we may correct by bearing in mind that it is

one and the same self of which reason and will are alike capacities; that in every moral action, good or bad, each capacity is exerted as much as the other; and that every step forward in the self-realisation of the divine principle in man involves a determination of will no less than of reason, not merely a conception of a possible good for man, but the adoption by some man or men of that good as his or theirs.

CHAPTER II.

CHARACTERISTICS OF THE MORAL IDEAL.

A. *The Personal Character of the Moral Ideal.*

180. LET us pause here to take stock of the conclusions so far arrived at. It will be convenient to state them in dogmatic form, begging the reader to understand that this form is adopted to save time, and does not betoken undue assurance on the part of the writer. Through certain *media*, and under certain consequent limitations, but with the constant characteristic of self-consciousness and self-objectification, the one divine mind gradually reproduces itself in the human soul. In virtue of this principle in him man has definite capabilities, the realisation of which, since in it alone he can satisfy himself, forms his true good. They are not realised, however, in any life that can be observed, in any life that has been, or is, or (as it would seem) that can be lived by man as we know him; and for this reason we cannot say with any adequacy what the capabilities are. Yet, because the essence of man's spiritual endowment is the consciousness of having it, the idea of his having such capabilities, and of a possible better state of himself consisting in their further realisation, is a moving influence in him. It has been the parent of the institutions and usages, of the social judgments and aspirations, through which human life has been so far bettered; through which man has so far realised his capabilities and marked out the path that he must follow in their further realisation. As his true good is or would be [1] their complete realisation, so his goodness is proportionate to his

---

[1] We say that his true good *is* this complete realisation when we think of the realisation as already attained in the eternal mind. We say that it *would be* such realisation when we think of the realisation as for ever problematic to man in the state of which we have experience.

habitual responsiveness to the idea of there being such a true good, in the various forms of recognised duty and beneficent work in which that idea has so far taken shape among men. In other words, it consists in the direction of the will to objects determined for it by this idea, as operative in the person willing; which direction of the will we may, upon the ground stated, fitly call its determination by reason.

181. Our next step should be to explain further how it is that the idea in man of a possible better state of himself, consisting in a further realisation of his capabilities, has been the moralising agent in human life; how it has yielded our moral standards, loyalty to which—itself the product of the same idea—is the condition of goodness in the individual. Before we attempt this explanation, however, it will be well to clear up an ambiguity which will probably be thought to lurk in the doctrine already advanced. We have spoken of a certain 'divine principle' as the ground of human will and reason; as realising itself in man; as having capabilities of which the full development would constitute the perfection of human life; of direction to objects contributory to this perfection as characteristic of a good will. But what, it will be asked, is to be understood in regard to the relation of this 'divine principle' to the will and reason of individuals? Does it realise itself in persons, in you and me, or in some impersonal Humanity? Do the capabilities spoken of admit of fulfilment in individuals, or is the perfection of human life some organisation of society in which the individual is a perfectly adjusted means to an end which he is not in himself? Until these questions have been dealt with, a suspicion may fairly be entertained that we have been playing fast and loose with the conception of man as in himself an end to himself. We have been taking advantage, it may be said, of a speculation in regard to the development of the human race, which is quite a different thing from what is naturally understood by a moral progress of the individual, to justify a theory which that speculation, fairly interpreted, tends rather to invalidate. The theory we want to maintain is one that would found a supposed duty, and a supposed possible effort, on the part of the individual to make himself better, upon an ideal in him of a possible moral perfection, upon a conception actuating him of something that he

may possibly become as an absolute end in himself. Does not the belief in a development of the human race, which individuals indeed unwittingly promote but perish in promoting, logically involve the complete negation of such a theory?

182. It is clearly of the very essence of the doctrine above advanced that the divine principle, which we suppose to be realising itself in man, should be supposed to realise itself in persons, as such. But for reflection on our personality, on our consciousness of ourselves as objects to ourselves, we could never dream of there being such a self-realising principle at all, whether as implied in the world or in ourselves. It is only because we are consciously objects to ourselves, that we can conceive a world as an object to a single mind, and thus as a connected whole. It is the irreducibility of this self-objectifying consciousness to anything else, the impossibility of accounting for it as an effect, that compels us to regard it as the presence in us of the mind for which the world exists. To admit therefore that the self-realisation of the divine principle can take place otherwise than in a consciousness which is an object to itself, would be in contradiction of the very ground upon which we believe that a divine principle does so realise itself in man. Personality, no doubt, is a term that has often been fought over without any very precise meaning being attached to it. If we mean anything else by it than the quality in a subject of being consciously an object to itself, we are not justified in saying that it necessarily belongs to God and to any being in whom God in any measure reproduces or realises himself. But whatever we mean by personality, and whatever difficulties may attach to the notion that a divine principle realises itself through a qualifying medium in the persons of men, it is certain that we shall only fall into contradictions by substituting for persons, as the subject in which the divine self-realisation takes place, any entity to which self-consciousness cannot intelligibly be ascribed. If it is impossible that the divine self-realisation should be complete in such persons as we are or can conceive ourselves coming to be, on the other hand in the absence of self-objectification, which is at least the essential thing in personality, it cannot even be inchoate.

183. This consideration has an important bearing upon certain

ways of thinking or speaking in which we are apt to take
refuge when, having adopted a theory of the moral life as the
fulfilment in the human spirit of some divine idea, we are called
upon to face the difficulty of stating whether and how the fulfilment is really achieved. Any life which the individual can
possibly live is at best so limited by the necessities of his position, that it seems impossible, on supposition that a divine self-
realising principle is at work in it, that it should be an adequate
expression of such a principle. Granted the most entire devotion
of a man to the attainment of objects contributory to human
perfection, the very condition of his effectually promoting that
end is that the objects in which he is actually interested, and
upon which he really exercises himself, should be of limited
range. The idea, unexpressed and inexpressible, of some absolute and all-embracing end is, no doubt, the source of such devotion, but it can only take effect in the fulfilment of some
particular function in which it finds but restricted utterance.
It is in fact only so far as we are members of a society, of which
we can conceive the common good as our own, that the idea has
any practical hold on us at all, and this very membership implies confinement in our individual realisation of the idea. Each
has primarily to fulfil the duties of his station. His capacity for
action beyond the range of those duties is definitely bounded,
and with it is definitely bounded also his sphere of personal
interests, his character, his *realised* possibility. No one so confined, it would seem, can exhibit all that the Spirit, working
through and in him, properly and potentially is. Yet is not
such confinement the condition of the only personality that we
know? It is the condition of social life, and social life is to
personality what language is to thought. Language presupposes thought as a capacity, but in us the capacity of thought is
only actualised in language. So human society presupposes persons in capacity—subjects capable each of conceiving himself
and the bettering of his life as an end to himself—but it is only
in the intercourse of men, each recognised by each as an end,
not merely a means, and thus as having reciprocal claims, that
the capacity is actualised and that we really live as persons. If
society then (as thus appears) is the condition of all development
of our personality, and if the necessities of social life, as alone

we know or can conceive it, put limits to our personal development, can we suppose it to be in persons that the spirit operative
in men finds its full expression and realisation ?

184. It is from this difficulty that we are apt to seek an
escape by speaking as if the human spirit fulfilled its idea in the
history or development of mankind, as distinct from the persons
whose experiences constitute that history, or who are developed
in that development; whether in the achievements of great
nations at special epochs of their history, or in some progress
towards a perfect organisation of society, of which the windings
and back-currents are too complex for it to be surveyed by us as
a whole. But that we are only disguising the difficulty, not
escaping it, by this manner of speech, we shall see upon reflecting that there can be nothing in a nation however exalted
its mission, or in a society however perfectly organised, which is
not in the persons composing the nation or the society. Our
ultimate standard of worth is an ideal of *personal* worth. All
other values are relative to value for, of, or in a person. To
speak of any progress or improvement or development of a
nation or society or mankind, except as relative to some greater
worth of persons, is to use words without meaning. The saying
that 'a nation is merely an aggregate of individuals' is indeed
fallacious, but mainly on account of the introduction of the
emphatic 'merely.' The fallacy lies in the implication that the
individuals could be what they are, could have their moral and
spiritual qualities, independently of their existence in a nation.
The notion is conveyed that they bring those qualities with
them ready-made into the national existence, which thereupon
results from their combination; while the truth is that, whatever moral capacity must be presupposed, it is only actualised
through the habits, institutions, and laws, in virtue of which
the individuals form a nation. But it is none the less true that
the life of the nation has no real existence except as the life of
the individuals composing the nation, a life determined by their
intercourse with each other, and deriving its peculiar features
from the conditions of that intercourse.

Nor, unless we allow ourselves to play fast and loose with the
terms 'spirit' and 'will,' can we suppose a national spirit and
will to exist except as the spirit and will of individuals, affected

in a certain way by intercourse with each other and by the history of the nation. Since it is only through its existence as our self-consciousness that we know anything of spirit at all, to hold that a spirit can exist except as a self-conscious subject is self-contradictory. A 'national spirit' is not something in the air; nor is it a series of phenomena of a particular kind; nor yet is it God—the eternal Spirit or self-conscious subject which communicates itself, in measure and under conditions, to beings which through that communication become spiritual. It would seem that it could only mean one of two things; either (*a*) some type of personal character, as at any time exhibited by individuals who are held together and personally modified by national ties and interests which they recognise as such; or (*b*) such a type of personal character as we may suppose *should* result, according to the divine idea of the world, from the intercourse of individuals with each other under the influence of the common institutions which make a particular nation, whether that type of character is actually attained or no. At any rate, if a 'national spirit' is held to be a form in which an eternal Spirit, in the only sense in which we have reason to think there is such a thing, realises itself, then it can only have its being in persons, though in persons, of course, specially modified by the special conditions of their intercourse with each other. The degree of perfection, of realisation of their possibilities, attained by these persons is the measure of the fulfilment which the idea of the human spirit attains in the particular national spirit. If the fulfilment of the idea is necessarily incomplete in them, it can be no more complete in the national spirit, which has no other existence, as national, than that which it has in them.

185. A like criticism must apply to any supposition that the spirit which is in man could fulfil its capability—the capability which belongs to it as a self-realisation of the eternal mind through the medium of an animal soul—in some history of mankind or some organisation of society, except in respect of a state of personal being attained by the individuals who are subjects of the history or members of the society. It does not appear how any idea should express or realise itself in an endless series of events, unless the series is relative to something beyond itself, which abides while it passes; and such a mere

endless series the history of mankind must be, except so far as its results are gathered into the formation of the character of abiding persons. At any rate the idea of a spirit cannot realise itself except in spirits. The human spirit cannot develope itself according to its idea except in self-conscious subjects, whose possession of the qualities—all implying self-consciousness—that are proper to such a spirit, in measures gradually approximating to the realisation of the idea, forms its development. The spiritual progress of mankind is thus an unmeaning phrase, unless it means a progress *of* personal character and *to* personal character—a progress of which feeling, thinking, and willing subjects are the agents and sustainers, and of which each step is a fuller realisation of the capacities of such subjects. It is simply unintelligible unless understood to be in the direction of more perfect forms of personal life.

There may be reason to hold that there are capacities of the human spirit not realisable in persons under the conditions of any society that we know, or can positively conceive, or that may be capable of existing on the earth. Such a belief may be warranted by the consideration on the one hand of the promise which the spirit gives of itself, both in its actual occasional achievement and in the aspirations of which we are individually conscious, on the other hand of the limitations which the necessity of confinement to a particular social function seems to impose on individual attainment. We may in consequence justify the supposition that the personal life, which historically or on earth is lived under conditions which thwart its development, is continued in a society, with which we have no means of communication through the senses, but which shares in and carries further every measure of perfection attained by men under the conditions of life that we know. Or we may content ourselves with saying that the personal self-conscious being, which comes from God, is for ever continued in God. Or we may pronounce the problem suggested by the constant spectacle of unfulfilled human promise to be simply insoluble. But meanwhile the negative assurance at any rate must remain, that a capacity, which is nothing except as personal, cannot be realised in any impersonal modes of being.

186. It is not, of course, to be denied that the facts of human

life and history put abundant difficulties in the way of any theory whatever of human development, as from the less to the more perfect kind of life, in distinction from mere generalisations as to the nature of the changes which society has undergone. If it were not for certain demands of the spirit which is ourself, the notion of human progress could never occur to us. But these demands, having a common ground with the apprehension of facts, are not to be suppressed by it. They are an expression of the same principle of self-objectification without which, as we have seen, there could be no such thing as facts for us, for our consciousness, at all. Their strength is illustrated by the persistency with which, in spite of the rebuff they for ever seem to be receiving from observations of nature and history, they for ever reassert themselves. It is the consciousness of possibilities in ourselves, unrealised but constantly in process of realisation, that alone enables us to read the idea of development into what we observe of natural life, and to conceive that there must be such a thing as a plan of the world. That we can adjust all that we observe to this idea is plainly not the case. When we have traced processes of development in particular regions of organic life, we are scarcely nearer the goal. For, in order to satisfy the idea which sets us upon the search for development, we should be able to connect all particular processes of development with each other, the lower as subservient to the higher, and to view the world, including human history, as a whole throughout which there is a concerted fulfilment of capabilities. This we cannot do; but neither our inability to do it, nor the appearance of positive inconsistency between much that we observe and any scheme of universal development, can weaken the authority of the idea, which does not rest on the evidence of observation but expresses an inward demand for the recognition of a unity in the world answering to the unity of ourselves—a demand involved in that self-consciousness which, as we have seen, alone enables us to observe facts as such. The important thing is that we should not, in eagerness to reconcile the idea of development with facts known only bit by bit and not in their real integrity, lose sight of the essential implications of the idea itself.

187. Of these implications one is the eternal realisation for,

or in, the eternal mind of the capacities gradually realised in time. Another is that the end of the process of development should be a real fulfilment of the capacities presupposed by the process. When we speak of any subject as in process of development according to some law, we must mean, if we so speak advisedly, that that into which the subject is being developed already exists for some consciousness. We express the same thing by saying that the subject is something, in itself or potentially, which it has not yet in time actually become; and this again implies that in relation to some conscious being it is eternally that which in some other relation it is in time coming to be. A state of life or consciousness not yet attained by a subject capable of it, *in relation to that subject* we say *actually is not;* but if there were no consciousness for which it existed, there would be no sense in saying that *in possibility it is,* for it would simply be nothing at all. Thus, when we speak of the human spirit being in itself, or in possibility, something which is not yet realised in human experience, we mean that there is a consciousness for and in which this something really exists, though, on the other hand, for the consciousness which constitutes human experience it exists only in possibility.

It would not be enough to say ' a consciousness *for* which it really exists.' That might merely mean that this undeveloped capability of the human spirit existed as an object of consciousness to the eternal mind, in the same way in which facts that I contemplate exist for me. Such a statement would suffice, were the subject of development merely a natural organism. But when that which is being developed is itself a self-conscious subject, the end of its becoming must really exist not merely *for,* but *in* or *as,* a self-conscious subject. There must be eternally such a subject which is all that the self-conscious subject, as developed in time, has the possibility of becoming ; in which the idea of the human spirit, or all that it has in itself to become, is completely realised. This consideration may suggest the true notion of the spiritual relation in which we stand to God ; that He is not merely a Being who has made us, in the sense that we exist as an object of the divine consciousness in the same way in which we must suppose the system of nature so to exist, but that He is a Being in whom we exist; with whom we are in principle one; with whom the human spirit is identical, in the sense that He *is* all which the human spirit is capable of becoming.

188. In regard to the other principle which we have noticed as implied in the idea of development—that the end of the process of development should be a real fulfilment of the capacities pre-supposed by the process—it may be argued that, however indisputable, it can afford us little guidance in judging of the ultimate end to which any process of development is tending. In cases where end or function are matter of observation, and capacity or faculty are inferred from them, it has no application; and if it is to be available in other cases, we must have some means of ascertaining the nature of capacities, independently of observation of the ends to which they are relative. But have we any such means? And in their absence, since the ultimate end of human progress must be beyond the reach of observation, are not our conclusions as to capacities of men which must be fulfilled in the course of human development mere arbitrary guess-work? May it not turn out that what we have been regarding as permanent capacities of men, from which something might be inferred as to the end of human development, on the ground that this end must be such as really to fulfil them, are temporary phases of some unknown force, working in we know not what direction, and that their end may be simply to disappear, having borne their part in the generation of an unknowable future?

189. To such questions we should reply as follows. We must be on our guard against lapsing into the notion that a process *ad infinitum*, a process not relative to an end, can be a process of development at all. If the history of mankind were simply a history of events, of which each determines the next following, and so on in endless series, there would be no progress or development in it. As we cannot sum an infinite series, there would be nothing in the history of mankind, so conceived, to satisfy that demand for unity of the manifold in relation to an end, which alone leads us to read the idea of development into the course of human affairs. If there is a progress in the history of men it must be towards an end consisting in a state

of being which is not itself a series in time, but is both comprehended eternally in the eternal mind and is intrinsically, or in
itself, eternal. Further : although any other capacity may be of
a kind which, having done its work in contributing to the attainment of such a state of being, passes away in the process of its
attainment—as the particular capacities of myriads of animals,
their function fulfilled, pass away every hour—yet a capacity
consisting in a self-conscious personality cannot be supposed so
to pass away. It partakes of the nature of the eternal. It is
not itself a series in time; for the series of time exists for it.
We cannot believe in there being a real fulfilment of such a
capacity in an end which should involve its extinction, because
the conviction of there being an end in which our capacities are
fulfilled is founded on our self-conscious personality—on the idea
of an absolute value in a spirit which we ourselves are. And for
the same reason we cannot believe that the capacities of men—
capacities illustrated to us by the actual institutions of society,
though they could not be so illustrated if we had not an independent idea of them—can be really fulfilled in a state of
things in which any rational man should be treated merely as a
means, and not as in himself an end. On the whole, our conclusion must be that, great as are the difficulties which beset the
idea of human development when applied to the facts of life, we
do not escape them but empty the idea of any real meaning, if
we suppose the end of the development to be one in the attainment of which persons—agents who are ends to themselves—are
extinguished, or one which is other than a state of self-conscious
being, or one in which that reconciliation of the claims of persons,
as each at once a means to the good of the other and an end to
himself, already partially achieved in the higher forms of human
society, is otherwise than completed.

190. Meanwhile, as must constantly be borne in mind, in
saying that the human spirit can only realise itself, that the
divine idea of man can only be fulfilled, in and through persons,
we are not denying but affirming that the realisation and fulfilment can only take place in and through society. Without
society, no persons : this is as true as that without persons,
without self-objectifying agents, there could be no such society
as we know. Such society is founded on the recognition by

persons of each other, and their interest in each other, *as persons,*
i. e. as beings who are ends to themselves, who are consciously
determined to action by the conception of themselves, as that for
the sake of which they act. They are interested in each other
as persons in so far as each, being aware that another presents his
own self-satisfaction to himself as an object, finds satisfaction for
himself in procuring or witnessing the self-satisfaction of the other.
Society is founded on such mutual interest, in the sense that
unless 'it were operative, however incapable of expressing itself
in abstract formulae, there would be nothing to lead to that
treatment by one human being of another as an end, not merely
a means, on which society even in its narrowest and most primitive forms must rest. There would be nothing to countervail
the tendency, inherent in the self-asserting and self-seeking
subject, to make every object he deals with, even an object of
natural affection, a means to his own gratification. The combination of men as ἴσοι καὶ ὅμοιοι for common ends would be impossible. Thus except as between persons, each recognising the
other as an end in himself and having the will to treat him as
such, there can be no society.

But the converse is equally true, that only through society, in
the sense explained, is personality actualised. Only through
society is any one enabled to give that effect to the idea of
himself as the object of his actions, to the idea of a possible
better state of himself, without which the idea would remain
like that of space to a man who had not the senses either of
sight or touch. Some practical recognition of personality by
another, of an 'I' by a 'Thou' and a 'Thou' by an 'I,' is necessary to any practical consciousness of it, to any such consciousness of it as can express itself in act. On the origin of such
recognition in the past we speculate in vain. To whatever
primitive groupings, as a matter of history or of imagination,
we can trace our actual society, these must already imply it.
But we know that we, who are born under an established system
of family ties, and of reciprocal rights and obligations sanctioned
by the state, learn to regard ourselves as persons among other
persons because we are treated as such. From the dawn of
intelligence we are treated, in one way or another, as entitled
to have a will of our own, to make ourselves the objects of our

actions, on condition of our practically recognising the same title in others. All education goes on the principle that we are, or are to become, persons in this sense. And just as it is through the action of society that the individual comes at once practically to conceive his personality—his nature as an object to himself—and to conceive the same personality as belonging to others, so it is society that supplies all the higher content to this conception, all those objects of a man's personal interest, in living for which he lives for his own satisfaction, except such as are derived from the merely animal nature.

191. Thus it is equally true that the human spirit can only realise itself, or fulfil its idea, in persons, and that it can only do so through society, since society is the condition of the development of a personality. But the function of society being the development of persons, the realisation of the human spirit in society can only be attained according to the measure in which that function is fulfilled. It does not follow from this that all persons must be developed in the same way. The very existence of mankind presupposes the distinction between the sexes; and as there is a necessary difference between their functions, there must be a corresponding difference between the modes in which the personality of men and women is developed. Again, though we must avoid following the example of philosophers who have shown an *a priori* necessity for those class-distinctions of their time which after ages have dispensed with, it would certainly seem as if distinctions of social position and power were necessarily incidental to the development of human personality. There cannot be this development without a recognised power of appropriating material things. This appropriation must vary in its effects according to talent and opportunity, and from that variation again must result differences in the form which personality takes in different men. Nor does it appear how those reciprocal services which elicit the feeling of mutual dependence, and thus promote the recognition by one man of another as an 'alter ego,' would be possible without different limitations of function and ability, which determine the range within which each man's personality developes, in other words, the scope of his personal interests.

Thus, under any conditions possible, so far as can be seen, for human society, one man who was the best that his position allowed, would be very different from another who was the best that *his* position allowed. But, in order that either may be good at all in the moral sense, *i.e.* intrinsically and not merely as a means—in order that the idea of the human spirit may be in any sense fulfilled in him—the fulfilment of that idea in some form or other, the contribution to human perfection in some way or other, must be the object in which he seeks self-satisfaction, the object for which he lives in living for himself. And it is only so far as this development and direction of personality is obtained for all who are capable of it (as presumably every one who says 'I' is capable), that human society, either in its widest comprehension or in any of its particular groups, can be held to fulfil its function, to realise its idea as it is in God.

B. *The Formal Character of the Moral Ideal or Law.*

192. Having thus endeavoured to explain the relation in which the development of the human race must stand to the personal perfection of individuals, we return to the problem which was postponed to make way for that explanation. We have seen how there is a real identity between the end for which the good man consciously lives—the end of fulfilling in some way his rational capacity, or the idea of a best that is in him— and the end to which human development, if there is such a thing, must be eternally relative in the eternal mind. It may be no more than such an identity as there is between the mere consciousness *that* there is an object and the consciousness *what* the object is. More precisely, it may be no more than the identity between the idea that a man has, in virtue of his rational capacity, of something, he knows not what, which he may and should become, and the idea, perfectly articulated and defined in the divine consciousness, of a state of being in which the capacities of all men are fully realised. But the idea as it is in the individual man, however indefinite and unfilled, is a communication in germ or principle of the idea as it is in God, and the communication is the medium through which the idea as in God determines the progressive development of human capacities in time. Alike as in God, as communicated in principle to men,

and as realising itself by means of that communication in a certain development of human capacities, the idea can have its being only in a personal, *i.e.* a self-objectifying, consciousness. From the mere idea in a man, however, ' of something, he knows not what, which he may and should become,' to the actual practice which is counted morally good, it may naturally seem a long step. We have therefore to explain in further detail how such an idea, gradually taking form and definiteness, has been the moralising agent in human life, yielding our moral standards and inducing obedience to them.

193. Supposing such an idea to be operative in man, what must be the manner of its operation? It will keep before him an object, which he presents to himself as absolutely desirable, but which is other than any particular object of desire. Of this object it can never be possible for him to give a sufficient account, because it consists in the realisation of capabilities which can only be fully known in their ultimate realisation. At the same time, because it is the fulfilment of himself, of that which he has in him to be, it will excite an interest in him like no other interest, different in kind from any of his desires and aversions except such as are derived from it. It will be an interest as in an object conceived to be of unconditional value; one of which the value does not depend on any desire that the individual may at any time feel for it or for anything else, or on any pleasure that, either in its pursuit or in its attainment or as its result, he may experience. The conception of its desirableness will not arise, like the conception of the desirableness of any pleasure, from previous enjoyment of it or from reflection on the desire for it. On the contrary, the desire for the object will be founded on a conception of its desirableness as a fulfilment of the capabilities of which a man is conscious in being conscious of himself.

In such men and at such times as a desire for it does actually arise—a desire in that sense which implies that the man puts himself forth for the realisation of the desired object—it will express itself in their imposition on themselves of rules requiring something to be done irrespectively of any inclination to do it, irrespectively of any desired end to which it is a means, *other than this end, which is desired because conceived as absolutely desirable.* With the men in whom, and at the times when, there is no such desire, the consciousness of there being something absolutely desirable will still be a qualifying element in life. It will yield a recognition of those unconditional rules of conduct to which, from the prevalence of unconformable passions, it fails to produce actual obedience. It will give meaning to the demand, without which there is no morality and in which all morality is virtually involved, that ' something be done merely for the sake of its being done [1],' because it is a consciousness of the possibility of an action in which no desire shall be gratified but the desire excited by the idea of the act itself, as of something absolutely desirable in the sense that in it the man does the best that he has in him to do.

194. But, granted the conception of an unconditional good for man, with unconditional rules of conduct which it suggests, what in particular will those rules enjoin? We have said that man can never give a sufficient account of what his unconditional good is, because he cannot know what his capabilities are till they are realised. This is the explanation of the infirmity that has always been found to attach to attempted definitions of the moral ideal. They are always open to the charge that there is employed in the definition, openly or disguisedly, the very notion which profession is made of defining. If, on being asked for an account of the unconditional good, we answer either that it is the good will or that to which the good will is directed, we are naturally asked further, what then is the good will? And if in answer to this question we can only say that it is the will for the unconditional good, we are no less naturally charged with ' moving in a circle.' We do but slightly disguise the circular process without escaping from it if, instead of saying directly that the good will is the will for the unconditional good, we say that it is the will to conform to a universal law for its own sake or because it is conceived as a universal law; for the recognition of the authority of such a universal law must be founded on the conception of its relation to an unconditional good.

---

[1] ' So gewiss der Mensch ein Mensch ist, so gewiss äussert sich in ihm eine Zunöthigung, einiges ganz unabhängig von äusseren Zwecken zu thun lediglich damit es geschehe, und andres eben so zu unterlassen lediglich damit es unterbleibe.'—J. G. FICHTE.

It is one of the attractions of Hedonistic Utilitarianism that it seems to avoid this logical embarrassment. If we say that the unconditional good is pleasure, and that the good will is that which in its effects turns out to produce most pleasure on the whole, we are certainly not chargeable with assuming in either definition the idea to be defined. We are not at once explaining the unconditional good by reference to the good will, and the good will by reference to the unconditional good. But we only avoid doing so by taking the good will to be relative to something external to itself; to have its value only as a means to an end wholly alien to, and different from, goodness itself. Upon this view the perfect man would not be an end in himself; a perfect society of men would not be an end in itself. Man or society would alike be only perfect in relation to the production of feelings which are felt, with whatever differences of quantity, by good men and bad, by man and brute, indifferently. By such a theory we do not avoid the logical embarrassment *attending the definition of a moral ideal;* for it is not a moral ideal, in the sense naturally attached to that phrase, that we are defining at all. By a moral ideal we mean some type of man or character or personal activity, considered as an end in itself. But, according to the theory of Hedonistic Utilitarianism, no such type of man or character or personal activity is an end in itself at all.

195. It may not follow that the theory is false on this account. That is a point which would have to be considered in a full critical discussion of Hedonism. What has to be noticed here is that such a theory is not available for our purpose. It affords no help when once we have convinced ourselves that man can only be an end to himself; that consequently it is only in himself as he may become, in a complete realisation of what he has it in him to be, in his perfect character, that he can find satisfaction; that in this therefore alone can lie his unconditional good. When we are seeking for a definition of the moral ideal in accordance with this view, we should be aware what we are about. It is as well to confess at once that, when we are giving an account of an agent whose development is governed by an ideal of his own perfection, we cannot avoid speaking of one and the same condition of will alternately as means and as end. The goodness of the will or man as a means must be described as

lying in direction to that same goodness as an end. For the end is that full self-conscious realisation of capabilities to which the means lies in the self-conscious exercise of the same capabilities—an exercise of them in imperfect realisation, but under the governing idea of the desirability of their fuller realisation. If we had knowledge of what their fuller realisation would be, we might so describe it as to distinguish it from that exercise of them in less complete development which is the means to that full realisation. We might thus distinguish the perfection of man as end from his goodness as means to the end, though the perfection would be in principle identical with the goodness, differing from it only as the complete from the incomplete. But we have no such knowledge of the full realisation. We know it only according to the measure of what we have so far done or are doing for its attainment. And this is to say that we have no knowledge of the perfection of man as the unconditional good, but that which we have of his goodness or the good will, in the form which it has assumed as a means to, or in the effort after, the unconditional good; a good which is not an object of speculative knowledge to man, but of which the idea—the conviction of there being such a thing—is the influence through which his life is directed to its attainment.

196. It is therefore not an illogical procedure, because it is the only procedure suited to the matter in hand, to say that the goodness of man lies in devotion to the ideal of humanity, and then that the ideal of humanity consists in the goodness of man. It means that such an ideal, not yet realised but operating as a motive, already constitutes in man an inchoate form of that life, that perfect development of himself, of which the completion would be the realised ideal itself. Now in relation to a nature such as ours, having other impulses than those which draw to the ideal, this ideal becomes, in Kant's language, an imperative, and a categorical imperative. It will command something to be done universally and unconditionally, irrespectively of whether there is in any one, at any time, an inclination to do it. But when we ask ourselves what it is that this imperative commands to be done, we are met with just the same difficulty as when asked to define the moral ideal or the unconditional good. We can only say that the categorical imperative commands us to

obey the categorical imperative, and to obey it for its own sake. If—not merely for practical purposes but as a matter of speculative certainty—we identify its injunction with any particular duty, circumstances will be found upon which the bindingness of that duty is contingent, and the too hasty identification of the categorical imperative with it will issue in a suspicion that, after all, there is no categorical imperative, no absolute duty, at all. After the explanations just given, however, we need not shrink from asserting as the basis of morality an unconditional duty, which yet is not a duty to do anything unconditionally except to fulfil that unconditional duty. It is the duty of realising an ideal which cannot be adequately defined till it is realised, and which, when realised, would no longer present itself as a source of duties, because the *should be* would be exchanged for the *is*. This is the unconditional ground of those particular duties to do or to forbear doing, which in the effort of the social man to realise his ideal have so far come to be recognised as binding, but which are each in some way or other conditional, because relative to particular circumstances, however wide the range of circumstances may be to which they are relative.

197. At the same time, then, that the categorical imperative can enjoin nothing *without liability to exception* but disinterested obedience to itself, it will have no lack of definite content. The particular duties which it enjoins will *at least* be all those in the practice of which, according to the hitherto experience of men, some progress is made towards the fulfilment of man's capabilities, or some condition necessary to that progress is satisfied. We say it will enjoin these *at least*, because particular duties must be constantly arising out of it for the individual, for which no formula can be found before they arise, and which are thus extraneous to the recognised code. Every one, however, of the duties which the law of the state or the law of opinion recognises must in some way be relative to circumstances. The rule therefore in which it is conveyed, though stated in the most general terms compatible with real significance, must still admit of exceptions. Yet is there a true sense in which the whole system of such duties is unconditionally binding. It is so as an expression of the absolute imperative to seek the absolutely desirable, the ideal of humanity, the fulfilment of man's vocation.

Because an expression (though an incomplete one) of this absolute imperative, because a product of the effort after such an unconditional good, the requirements of conventional morality, however liable they may be to exceptions, arising out of circumstances other than those to which they are properly applicable, are at least liable to no exception for the sake of the individual's pleasure. As against any desire but some form or other of that desire for the best in conduct, which will, no doubt, from time to time suggest new duties in seeming conflict with the old—against any desire for this or that pleasure, or any aversion from this or that pain—they are unconditionally binding.

198. Upon this view, so far from the Categorical Imperative having no particular content, it may rather seem to have too much. It enjoins observance of the whole complex of established duties, as a means to that perfection of man of which it unconditionally enjoins the pursuit. And it enjoins this observance as unconditionally as it enjoins the pursuit of the end to which this observance is a means, *so long as it is such a means.* It will only allow such a departure from it in the interest of a fuller attainment of the unconditional end, not in the interest of any one's pleasure. The question indeed is sure to suggest itself, what available criterion such a doctrine affords us, either for distinguishing the essential from the unessential in the requirements of law and custom, or for the discernment of duty in cases to which no recognised rule is applicable. So far as it can be translated into practice at all, must not its effect be either a dead conformity to the code of customary morality, anywhere and at any time established, without effort to reform or expand it, or else unlimited license in departing from it at the prompting of any impulse which the individual may be pleased to consider a higher law? These questions shall be considered in due course[1]; but before we enquire into the practical bearings of our doctrine as to the relation between the system of duties anywhere recognised and the unconditional ground of all duties— before we ask how it affects our criteria of what in particular we should do or not do—we have further to make good the doctrine

[1] [See Book IV.]

itself.   We have to revert to the question, still left unanswered, how the mere idea of something absolutely desirable—an idea which, we confess, does not primarily enable us to say anything of its object but that there must be such a thing—should have gradually defined itself, should have taken body and content, in the establishment of recognised duties, in the formation of actual virtues, among men.

CHAPTER III.

The Origin and Development of the Moral Ideal.

A. *Reason as Source of the Idea of a Common Good.*

199. That an idea of something absolutely desirable, which we cannot identify with any particular object of desire without soon discovering our mistake in the dissatisfaction which ensues upon the attainment of the particular object—that such an idea of a supreme good, which is no good thing in particular, should express itself in a system of social requirements and expectations, of which each would seem to have reference to a definite social need, may naturally at first be thought an extravagant supposition. Further consideration, however, may change our view. The idea of the absolutely desirable, as we have seen, arises out of, or rather is identical with, man's consciousness of himself as an end to himself. It is the forecast, proper to a subject conscious at once of himself as an absolute end, and of a life of becoming, of constant transition from possibility to realisation, and from this again to a new possibility—a forecast of a well-being that shall consist in the complete fulfilment of himself. Now the self of which a man thus forecasts the fulfilment, is not an abstract or empty self. It is a self already affected in the most primitive forms of human life by manifold interests, among which are interests in other persons. These are not merely interests dependent on other persons for the means to their gratification, but interests in the good of those other persons, interests which cannot be satisfied without the consciousness that those other persons are satisfied. The man cannot contemplate himself as in a better state, or on the way to the best, without contemplating others, not merely as a means to that better state, but as sharing it with him.

200. It may seem unphilosophical now-a-days to accept this

distinctive social interest on our part as a primary fact, without attempting to account for it by any process of evolution. Any history indeed that might be offered of it, which should enable us to connect its more complex with its simpler forms, would be much to be welcomed. But the same could not be said for a history which should seem to account for it by ignoring its distinctive character, and by deriving it from forms of animal sympathy from which, because they have no element of identity with it, it cannot in the proper sense have been developed. What the real nature may be of the sympathy of the higher animals with each other, we have probably no means of knowing. *If* it is merely an excitement of pleasure or pain in one animal, upon sign of pleasure or pain being given by another; *if* it is merely an impulse on the part of one animal to act so as to give pleasure to another, with whose pleasure its own is thus associated; then what we know as the social interest of men is more and other than a development of it. For it is characteristic of this interest that, to the man who is the subject of it, those who are its objects are ends, in the same sense in which he is an end to himself. Or, more properly, they are included in the end for which he lives in living for himself. The feeling of pleasure or pain in response to manifested pleasure or pain on the part of another sentient being does not contain the germ of such an interest, unless the subject of the feeling is conscious of himself as other than the feeling which he experiences, and of the agent occasioning it as an 'alter ego.' Only on that condition can desire for a renewal of the pleasure become, or give place to, desire for a good, to be shared by the person desiring it with another whose good is as his own.

However dependent therefore the social interest, as we know it, may be upon feelings of animal origin, such as sexual feelings, or feelings of want in the offspring which only the parent can supply, it is not a product of those feelings, not evolved from them. In order to issue in it they must have taken a new character, as feelings of one who can and does present to himself a good of himself as an end in distinction from any particular pleasure, and a like good of another or others as included in that end. To ignore the distinctive character which our sympathies thus derive, and must have derived in any being to whom we can reasonably affiliate ourselves, from the action of a self-objectifying consciousness, is as misleading an abstraction from the reality of human nature as it would be, on the other hand, to separate that consciousness from those sympathies and interests, without which the formal idea in a man of a possible better state of himself would have no actual filling.

201. We may take it, then, as an ultimate fact of human history—a fact without which there would not be such a history, and which is not in turn deducible from any other history—that out of sympathies of animal origin, through their presence in a self-conscious soul, there arise interests as of a person in persons. Out of processes common to man's life with the life of animals there arise for man, as there do not apparently arise for animals,

> 'Relations dear and all the charities
> Of father, son, and brother':

and of those relations and charities self-consciousness on the part of all concerned in them is the condition. At the risk of provoking a charge of pedantry, this point must be insisted on. It is not any mere sympathy with pleasure and pain that can by itself yield the affections and recognised obligations of the family. The man for whom they are to be possible must be able, through consciousness of himself as an end to himself, to enter into a like consciousness as belonging to others, whose expression of it corresponds to his own. He must have practical understanding of what is meant for them, as for himself, by saying 'I.' Having found his pleasures and pains dependent on the pleasures and pains of others, he must be able in the contemplation of a possible satisfaction of himself to include the satisfaction of those others, and that a satisfaction of them as ends to themselves and not as means to his pleasure. He must, in short, be capable of conceiving and seeking a permanent well-being in which the permanent well-being of others is included.

202. Some sort of community, founded on such unity of self-consciousness, on such capacity for a common idea of permanent good, must be presupposed in any groupings of men from which the society that we know can have been developed. To the man living under its influence the idea of the absolutely desirable, the effort to better himself, must from the first express itself in some form of social requirement. So far as he is set on making

his way to some further fulfilment of himself, he must seek to carry those in whom he is interested with him in the process. That 'better reason'[1] which, in antagonism to the inclinations of the moment, presents itself to him as a law for himself, will present itself to him as equally a law for them; and as a law for them on the same ground and in the same sense as it is a law for him, *viz.* as prescribing means to the fulfilment of an idea of absolute good, common to him with them—an idea indefinable indeed in imagination, but gradually defining itself in act.

The conception of a moral law, in its strict philosophical form, is no doubt an analogical adaptation of the notion of law in the more primary sense—the notion of it as a command enforced by a political superior, or by some power to which obedience is habitually rendered by those to whom the command is addressed. But there is an idea which equally underlies the conception both of moral duty and of legal right; which is prior, so to speak, to the distinction between them; which must have been at work in the minds of men before they could be capable of recognising any kind of action as one that *ought* to be done, whether because it is enjoined by law or authoritative custom, or because, though not thus enjoined, a man owes it to himself or to his neighbour or to God. This is the idea of an absolute and a common good; a good common to the person conceiving it with others, and good for him and them, whether at any moment it answers their likings or no. As affected by such an idea, a man's attitude to his likes and dislikes will be one of which, in his inward converse, the 'Thou shalt' or 'Thou must' of command is the natural expression, though of law, in the sense either of the command of a political superior or of a self-imposed rule of life, he may as yet have no definite conception.

And so affected by it he must be, before the authority either of custom or of law can have any meaning for him. Simple fear cannot constitute the sense of such authority nor by any process of development, properly so called, become it. It can only spring from a conviction, on the part of those recognising the authority, that a good which is really their good, though in constant conflict with their inclinations, is really served by the power in which they recognise authority. Whatever force may be

[1] See above, § 179.

employed in maintaining custom or law, however 'the interest of the stronger,' whether an individual or the few or the majority of some group of people, may be concerned in maintaining it, only some persuasion of its contribution to a recognised common good can yield that sort of obedience to it which, equally in the simpler and the more complex stages of society, forms the social bond.

203. The idea, then, of a possible well-being of himself, that shall not pass away with this, that, or the other pleasure; and relation to some group of persons whose well-being he takes to be as his own, and in whom he is interested in being interested in himself—these two things must condition the life of any one who is to be a creator or sustainer either of law or of that prior authoritative custom out of which law arises. Without them there might be instruments of law and custom; intelligent co-operating subjects of law and custom there could not be. They are conditions at once of might being so exercised that it can be recognised as having right, and of that recognition itself. It is in this sense that the old language is justified, which speaks of Reason as the parent of Law. Reason is the self-objectifying consciousness. It constitutes, as we have seen, the capability in man of seeking an absolute good and of conceiving this good as common to others with himself : and it is this capability which alone renders him a possible author and a self-submitting subject of law.

In saying this we are saying nothing for or against any theory of the conditions under which, as a matter of history, laws may have been first established. It is easy, and for certain purposes may be advisable, to define a sense of the term in which 'laws' do not exist till an advanced stage of civilisation, when sovereignties of ascertained range and scope have been established, and when the will of the sovereign has come to be expressed in general and permanent forms. In proportion as we thus restrict our usage of the term 'law' we shall have to extend our view of the effect upon human life of social requirements, which are not 'laws,' but to which the good citizen renders an obedience the same in principle as that which he renders to 'laws'; an obedience at once willing and constrained —willing, because recognised as the condition of a social good, which is his own highest good; constrained, in so far as it prevents him from doing what he would otherwise like to do. It is with the ground of this obedience that the moralist is concerned, as having been rendered when as yet 'law' in the restricted sense was not, and as still rendered equally by the good citizen to the law which the state enforces, and to that of which the sanction is a social sentiment shared by him.

204. This ground the moralist finds in Reason, according to the sense explained. He will listen respectfully to any account, for which historians can claim probability, of the courses of events by which powers, strong enough to enforce general obedience, have been gathered into the hands of individuals or groups of men; but he will reflect that, though the exercise of force may be a necessary incident in the maintenance of government, it cannot of itself produce the state of mind on which social union in any of its forms depends. He will listen, further, to all that the anthropologist can tell him of the earliest forms in which such union can be traced; but here again he will reflect that, when the phenomena of some primitive usage have been duly established, the interpretation of the state of mind which they represent is a further question, and one that cannot be answered without reference to the developed consciousness which is ours. When the anthropologist has gathered all the results he can from a collation of the sayings and doings of such uncivilised people as can now be observed, with records and survivals from the lives of our ancestors, his clue for the interpretation of his material will depend in the last resort on his analysis of that world of feeling, thought, and desire, in which he himself lives. Unless the fragmentary indications obtainable of the life of primitive humanity can be interpreted as expressing a consciousness in germ or principle the same as ours, we have no clue to their inner significance at all. They are at best no more to us than the gestures of animals, from which we may conjecture that the animal is pleased or pained, but by which no consciousness in its intrinsic nature is conveyed to us, as it is conveyed in the speech of another man. We may, of course, take this view of them. We may hold that no inference is possible from them to any state of mind on the part of primitive man. But we cannot interpret them as expressing a state of mind without founding our conception of the state of mind on our own consciousness.

Even if it were possible on any other plan to read a state of mind in them at all, we certainly could not read in them a consciousness from which our own has been developed, without assuming an identity, under whatever variety of modification, between the less and the more developed consciousness.

Thus, though our information about primitive man were very different from what it is, it could never be other than a contradiction to found upon it a theory of the state of mind underlying the earliest forms of social union, which should represent this state of mind as different in kind from that which, upon fair analysis of the spiritual life now shared by us, we find to be the condition of such social union as actually exists. If we are right in ascribing to Reason a function of union in the life that we know; if we are right in holding that through it we are conscious of ourselves, and of others as ourselves,—through it accordingly that we can seek to make the best of ourselves and of others with ourselves, and that in this sense Reason is the basis of society, because the source at once of the establishment of equal practical rules in a common interest, and of self-imposed subjection to those rules; then we are entitled to hold that Reason fulfilled a function intrinsically the same in the most primitive associations of man with man, between which and the actual institutions of family and commune, of state and nation, there has been any continuity of development.

205. The foundation of morality, then, in the reason or self-objectifying consciousness of man, is the same thing as its foundation in the institutions of a common life—in these as directed to a common good, and so directed not mechanically but with consciousness of the good on the part of those subject to the institutions. Such institutions are, so to speak, the form and body of reason, as practical in men. Without them the rational or self-conscious or moral man does not exist, nor without them can any being have existed from whom such a man could be developed, if any continuity of nature is implied in development. No development of morality can be conceived, nor can any history of it be traced (for that would imply such a conception), which does not presuppose some idea of a common good, expressing itself in some elementary effort after a regulation of life. Without such an idea the development would be

as impossible as it is impossible that sight should be generated when there is no optic nerve. With it, however restricted in range the idea may be, there is given 'in promise and potency' the ideal of which the realisation would be perfect morality, the ideal of a society in which every one shall treat every one else as his neighbour, in which to every rational agent the well-being or perfection of every other such agent shall be included in that perfection of himself for which he lives. And as the most elementary notion in a rational being of a personal good, common to himself with another who is as himself, is in possibility such an ideal, so the most primitive institutions for the regulation of a society with reference to a common good are already a school for the character which shall be responsive to the moral ideal.

It has become a common-place among us that the moral susceptibilities which we find in ourselves, would not exist but for the action of law and authoritative custom on many generations of our ancestors. The common-place is doubtless perfectly true. It is only misleading when we overlook the rational capacities implied in the origin and maintenance of such law and custom. The most elementary moralisation of the individual must always have arisen from his finding himself in the presence of a requirement, enforced against his inclinations to pleasure, but in an interest which he can recognise as being his own, no less than the interest of those by whom the requirement is enforced. The recognition of such an interest by the individual is an outcome of the same reason as that which has led to the maintenance of the requirement by the society he belongs to. All further development of morality—all articulation of duties, all education of conscience in response to them—presupposes this primary recognition. Of the principal movements into which the development may be analysed we shall now go on to speak in more detail, only premising that the necessity of describing them separately should not lead us to forget that they are mutually involved.

B. *The Extension of the Area of Common Good.*

206. The first of the movements into which the development of morality may be analysed consists in a gradual extension, for

the mental eye of the moral subject, of the range of persons to whom the common good is conceived as common; towards whom and between whom accordingly obligations are understood to exist. What may have been the narrowest restrictions on this range within which the process of moralisation has gone on, we have no means of saying. We only know that the earliest ascertainable history exhibits to us communities, relatively very confined, within any one of which a common good, and in consequence a common duty, is recognised as between the members of the community, while beyond the particular community the range of mutual obligation is not understood to extend. Among ourselves, on the contrary, it is almost an axiom of popular Ethics that there is at least a potential duty of every man to every man—a duty which becomes actual so soon as one comes to have any dealing with the other. It is true that plenty of pretexts, some under very philosophical disguise, are always forthcoming when it is wished to evade the duty; but, when we are free from private bias, we do not seriously dispute its validity. Conscience is uneasy at its violation, as it would not have been, according to all indications, in the case, let us say, of a Greek who used his slave as a chattel, though according to his lights the Greek might be as conscientious as any of us. Yet the language in which we most naturally express our conception of the duty of all men to all men indicates the school—that of tribal, or civil, or family obligation—in which we have been trained to the conception. We convey it in the concrete by speaking of a human family, of a fraternity of all men, of the common fatherhood of God; or we suppose a universal Christian citizenship, as wide as the Humanity for which Christ died, and in thought we transfer to this, under certain analogical adaptations, those claims of one citizen upon another which have been actually enforced in societies united under a single sovereignty.

207. It is not uncommon indeéd with men to whom a little philosophy has proved a dangerous thing, to make much of the distinction between an obligation that admits of being enforced between persons subject to a common sovereign, and what is alleged to be due from man to man, as such; to extenuate the claims of humanity, and even to make merry over the fraternity

of men and nations. The distinction is easily drawn, and, so
long as there continue to be men who will not observe obligations unless enforced, it cannot be considered practically unim-
portant. But for the moralist it is more important to observe
the real fusion, in the conscience of those citizens of the modern
world who are most responsive to the higher influences of their
time, of duties enforced by legal penalties and those of which
the fulfilment cannot be exacted by citizen of citizen, or by
sovereign of subjects, but is felt to be due from man to man.
It is not more certain that a man would not recognise a duty,
e.g. of educating his poor neighbours or helping to liberate
a slave, unless, generations before him, equal rights had been
enforced among men who could not have understood the wrong
of slavery or the claim of the labourer to a chance of raising
himself, than that there are men now to whom such duties
present themselves with just the same cogency as legal obligations; men to whom the motive for fulfilling the latter has
been so entirely purged from any fear of penalties, that the
absence of such fear, as a motive to the fulfilment of humanitarian duties, makes no difference to the felt necessity of fulfilling them.

No gradual modification of selfish fear or hope could yield a
disposition of this kind; and if these were the sole original
motives to civil or tribal or family obedience, it would be unintelligible that a state of mind should result, in which a man
imposes duties on himself quite beyond the range of such obedience. But if at the root of such obedience, as well as of the
institutions to which it has been rendered, there has been an
idea of good, suggested by the consciousness of unfulfilled possibilities of the rational nature common to all men, then it is
intelligible that, as the range of this idea extends itself—as it
comes to be understood that no race or religion or status is a
bar to self-determined co-operation in its fulfilment—the sense
of duty which it yields, and which has gained its power over
natural desires and aversions through generations of discipline
in the family and the state, should become a sense of what is
due to man as such, and not merely to the members of a particular community. The change is not necessarily in the
strength, in the constraining power, of the feeling of duty—

perhaps it is never stronger now than it may have been in an Israelite who would have yet recognised no claim in a Philistine, or in a Greek who would yet have seen no harm in exposing a sickly child—but in the conceived range of claims to which the duty is relative. Persons come to be recognised as having claims who would once not have been recognised as having any claim, and the claim of the ἴσοι καὶ ὅμοιοι comes to be admitted where only the claim of indulged inferiors would have been allowed before. It is not the sense of duty to a neighbour, but the practical answer to the question Who is my neighbour? that has varied.

208. The extension of this process has indeed often been looked on with suspicion by practical men. It has been suggested that the friend of man is apt to be the friend of no one in particular. 'Enthusiasm for humanity' is thought to interfere with the ties of country and fellow-citizenship, without putting any influence in their place which can be relied on for controlling the selfish inclinations of the individual. The suspicion is probably groundless. The excuses which selfishness makes for itself in the mouths of cultivated men will, no doubt, vary according to the philosophical tendencies of the time; and it would be hard to deny that it may take advantage of a cant of Humanitarianism, as of any other cant that may be in vogue. But if this illustrates the old lesson—too familiar to need illustration—that there are no intellectual formulae of which the adoption will serve as a substitute for discipline of character, it argues nothing against the view that, given the discipline of character by which alone our selfish or pleasure-seeking tendencies can be controlled or superseded, the practical value of a man's morality increases with the removal of limitations upon his view of the kind of humanity which constitutes a claim equal with his own. If the fundamental readiness to forgo pleasure for duty cannot be produced merely by a wider view of the claims which others have on us, it can scarcely suffer from such a view. Indeed, if habit is strengthened by exercise, it would seem that the habit on which the fulfilment of known duties depends, once partially formed, must be strengthened rather than otherwise by that more constant call for the practice of duty which naturally arises from recognition of a wider range

of persons to whom duties are due. Self-indulgent tendencies which often tend to revive, as life goes on, in those who have mastered themselves enough for 'respectability,' but to whom the range of duties implied in respectability is a narrow one, will be more constantly challenged by situations in which unfamiliar duties have to be met. And if the dutiful disposition must thus gain rather than lose in strength from the enlightenment before which the exclusive dependence of moral claims on relations of family, status, or citizenship disappears, it would seem that with this disappearance its effect in furthering the social realisation of human capabilities must greatly increase. Faculties which social repression and separation prevent from development, take new life from the enlarged co-operation which the recognition of equal claims in all men brings with it. Nor is it the case, as we are apt to suppose, that the gain in this respect is confined merely to the majority, while the few favoured by the system of privileged status and national antagonism proportionately lose. We only imagine this to be the case from a misleading association of greater capability with more distinctive supremacy. The special qualities of command are, no doubt, less highly developed as the idea of the brotherhood of men comes to be more fully carried out in the institutions of the world, but meanwhile the capabilities implied in social self-adjustment become what they could not be before. If we admire these capabilities less than the qualities of command, it is perhaps because we have not adjusted our admirations to what we must yet admit to be the divine plan of man's development.

209. The very possibility, however, of raising the question whether men are really the better for the acceptance of humanitarian ideas, indicates the extent of their actual currency. Their influence may be traced alike in the positive laws, and institutions maintained by law, of civilised nations; in the law of opinion, the social sentiments and expectations, prevalent among them; and in the formulae by which philosophers have sought to methodise this law of opinion. It would be superfluous here to follow in detail the process by which the law of Christendom has gradually come to conform to the 'Jus naturale' already recognised by Ulpian and the Institutes, according to which 'omnes homines aequales sunt.' Nor is it to the purpose to

discuss the share which Stoic philosophers, Roman jurists, and Christian teachers may severally have had in gaining acceptance for the idea of human equality. It is only some spirit of partisanship that can lead us to put one set of teachers or institutions into competition with another for the credit of having contributed most to what, after all, is but the natural fulfilment of a capability given in reason itself—a fulfilment which only special selfish interests can withstand. Given the idea of a common good and of self-determined participators in it—the idea implied, as we have seen, in the most primitive human society—the tendency of the idea in the minds of all capable of it must be to include, as participators of the good, all who have dealings with each other and who can communicate as ' I ' and ' Thou.' With growing means of intercourse and the progress of reflection the theory of a universal human fellowship is its natural outcome. It is rather the retardation of the acceptance of the theory that the historian has to explain ; its retardation by those private interests which have made it inconvenient for powerful men and classes to act upon it, and have led them to welcome any counter-theory which might justify their practice; such, *e.g.*, as the interests which led some of the American communities, after claiming their own independence on the ground that ' all men are born free and equal,' to vindicate negro slavery for nearly a hundred years and only to relinquish it after a tremendous war in its defence.

210. However retarded, equality before the law has at length been secured, at least ostensibly, for all full-grown and sane human beings throughout Christendom. Under ordinary circumstances the right to free movement, and to the free enjoyment and disposal of the fruits of his labour, is guaranteed to every one, on condition of his respecting the like freedom in others. Social sentiment not merely responds to the requirements of law in this respect and secures their general observance, but often demands, on the ground of a common humanity, some positive contribution to the service of others where law can merely prevent a violation of rights, and some abatement from the strict exaction of a claim which law sanctions. It would almost everywhere condemn the refusal of help to a man, however alien in blood, language and religion, whose life depended

on the help being given him, or the exaction of a debt legally
due at the cost of the debtor's starvation.   The necessities of
war indeed are treated as practically suspending the claims of a
common humanity.   The processes by which the general conscience reconciles itself to their so doing cannot be considered
here; but the fact that it is only when in conflict with the apparent claims of a common country that the claims of a common
humanity are thought to be superseded, shows what a strong
hold the latter have obtained on social sentiment.

211. For an abstract expression of the notion that there is
something due from every man to every man, simply as men,
we may avail ourselves of the phrase employed in the famous
definition of Justice in the Institutes :—' Justitia est constans
et perpetua voluntas suum cuique tribuendi.'   Every man both
by law and common sentiment is recognised as having a ' suum,'
whatever the ' suum ' may be, and is thus effectually distinguished
from the animals (at any rate according to our treatment of
them) and from things.   He is deemed capable of having something of his own, as animals and things are not.   He is treated
as an end, not merely as a means.   It is obvious indeed that the
notion expressed by the ' suum cuique,' even when it carries with
it the admission that every man, as such, has a ' suum,' is a most
insufficient guide to conduct till we can answer the question
what the ' suum ' in each case is, and that no such answer is
deducible from the mere principle that every one has a ' suum.'
In fact, of course, this principle is never wrought into law or
general sentiment without very precise, though perhaps insufficient and ultimately untenable, determinations of what is due
from one to another in the ordinary intercourse of those habitually associated.   Particular duties to this man and that have
been recognised long before reflection has reached the stage in
which a duty to man as such can be recognised.   How far upon
reflection we can find in these particular duties—in the detail
of conventional morality—a permanent and universal basis for
right conduct, is a separate question.   For the present we wish
to follow out the effect exerted upon the responsive conscience
by life in a society where a capacity for rights, some claim on
his fellow-men, has come to be ascribed to every man.   Given
that readiness to recognise a duty and to act upon the recog-

nition, which is the proper outcome in the individual of family and civil discipline as governed by an idea of common good, what sort of rule of conduct will the individual, upon unbiassed reflection, obtain for himself from the establishment in law and general sentiment of the principle that every man can claim something as his due? How will it tend to define for him the absolutely desirable, and the ideal of conduct as directed thereto?

212. The great result will be to fix it in his mind, as a condition of such conduct, that it should be *alike* for the real good of all men concerned in or affected by it, as estimated on the same principle. This rule has indeed become so familiarised to our consciences, however frequently we violate it, that at first sight it may seem to some too trivial to be worthy a philosopher's attention, while by others it may be remarked that, till we have decided what the real good of all men is, and have at least some general knowledge of the effect upon it, under certain conditions, of certain lines of conduct, the rule will not tell us how we ought to act in particular cases. Such a remark would be plainly true. For the present, however, we are considering the importance to the conscientious man of this recognition of a like claim in all men, taken simply by itself, irrespectively of those criteria of the good and of those convictions as to the means of arriving at it by which the recognition is in fact always accompanied. It is the source of the refinement in his sense of justice. It is that which makes him so over-curious, as it seems to the ordinary man of the world, in enquiring, as to any action that may suggest itself to him, whether the benefit which he might gain by it for himself or for some one in whom he is interested, would be gained at the expense of any one else, however indifferent to him personally, however separated from him in family, status, or nation. It makes the man, in short, who will be just before he is generous; who will not merely postpone his own interest to his friend's, but who, before he gratifies an 'altruistic' inclination, will be careful to enquire how in doing so he would affect others who are not the object of the inclination. This characteristic of the man who is just in the full light of the idea of human equality is independent of any theory of well-being on his part. Whether he has any theory on the matter at all,

whether he is theoretically an 'Ascetic' or a 'Hedonist,' makes little practical difference. The essential thing is that he applies no other standard in judging of the well-being of others than in judging of his own, and that he will not promote his own well-being or that of one whom he loves or likes, from whom he has received service or expects it, at the cost of impeding in any way the well-being of one who is nothing to him but a man, or whom he involuntarily dislikes; that he will not do this knowingly, and that he is habitually on the look-out to know whether his actions will have this effect or not.

On supposition that a man has really attained this habit of practical justice, that it is his constant and uniform state, he has in him at least the negative principle of all virtue; a principle that will effectually restrain him from doing all that he ought not, if it does not move him to do all that he ought. We cannot indeed be sure that it will prevent the possibility of his doing acts which in the general result yield more pain than pleasure. The most equitable intentions, most carefully carried out, will not, for instance, save a man from liability to do something, in ignorance of its consequences, which will in fact promote a dangerous disease. If however we do not speak of a man doing an action which he ought not except in contemplation of his state of mind, as at any rate intending consequences which he might have known to be mischievous, then the man who is just in the sense described will be safe from doing what he ought not.

213. Such a man perhaps would not, even at this day and in the most Christianised and civilised society, command universal or very hearty admiration. Moral emotions have not been so far wrought into accord with that principle of right in man as man, which has been established in law and recognised (though by no means in its full application) by social opinion. There may indeed be a well-founded suspicion that the plea of justice before generosity is often rather made an excuse for deficient generosity than a ground for scrupulosity of justice. But, more than this, the duty of treating all men equally, even to the extent of not serving a friend or kinsman or countryman in a manner prejudicial to any one else, though it would no longer be in words denied, has yet little hold on the 'hearts' even of educated and

respectable men. It has been for this reason, far more than from its being founded on a Hedonistic psychology, which in fact was common to it with nearly all the Moral Philosophy of England, that Utilitarianism has encountered so much popular dislike. The principle embodied in the formula, that 'every one should count for one and no one for more than one' in the calculation of felicific consequences, has been the source at once of its real beneficence in the life of modern society and of the resistance, far more formidable than that of 'Ascetic' philosophy, which it has met with. It has been the source of its beneficence because, quite independently of the identification of the highest good with a greatest possible sum of pleasures—perhaps indeed, as we shall see later on, inconsistently with that identification—it has practically meant for Utilitarians that every human person was to be deemed an end of absolute value, as much entitled as any one else to have his well-being taken account of in considering the justifiableness of an action by which that well-being could be affected. And it is precisely this that has brought the Utilitarian into conflict with every class-prejudice, with every form of family or national pride, with the inveterate and well-reputed habit of investing with a divine right the cause of the friend or the party or the institution which happens to interest us most, without reference to its bearings on the welfare of others more remote from our sympathies.

214. For practical purposes the principle that, in the estimate of the resulting happiness by which the value of an action is to be judged, 'every one should count for one and no one for more than one,' yields very much the same direction as that one of the formulae employed by Kant for the statement of the Categorical Imperative, which has probably always commended itself most to readers alive to the best spirit of their time :—'Act so as to treat humanity, whether in your own person or in that of others, always as an end, never merely as a means.' We say *for practical purposes*, because, as strictly interpreted, the one by a Benthamite, the other by a Kantist, the significance of the two formulae is wholly different. The Benthamite would repudiate or pronounce unintelligible the notion of an absolute value in the individual person. It is not every person, according to him, but every pleasure, that is of value in itself; and in

accordance with this view he has to qualify the formula we have been dwelling on, so as to empty it, if not of all practical significance, at any rate of the significance which we have ascribed to it, and which has been the real guide to the reforming Utilitarian.

Upon Hedonistic principles it will only be as 'supposed equal in degree'[1] that one person's happiness, *i. e.* his experience of pleasure, is to count for as much as another's. Now as the ascertainment of this equality in degree between the happiness of one man and that of another is practically impossible, and as there is every reason to think that different men are susceptible of pleasure in most different degrees, it is hard to see how the formula, thus interpreted, can afford any positive ground for that treatment of all men's happiness as entitled to equal consideration, for which Utilitarians have in practice been so laudably zealous. The most that could be deduced from it would be some very general condemnation of those fixed class-distinctions which, by interfering with the free pursuit of pleasure on the part of unprivileged persons, would seem to lessen the aggregate of pleasure resulting on the whole. Under it a superior race or order could plead strong justification, not indeed for causing useless pain to the inferior, but for systematically postponing the inferior's claims to happiness to its own. Certainly no absolute rule could be founded on it, prohibiting all pursuit of happiness by one man which interferes with the happiness of another, or what we commonly call the oppression of the weaker by the stronger; for, the stronger being presumably capable of pleasure in higher degree, there could be nothing to show that the quantity of pleasure resulting from the gain to the stronger through the loss to the weaker was not greater than would have been the quantity resulting if the claims of each had been treated as equal. Instead of such a rule as that on which Utilitarians have been among the forwardest to act—'We that are strong ought to bear the infirmities of the weak, and not to please ourselves'—we should be logically entitled at most to a counsel of prudence, advising much circumspection on the part of the strong before he assumes that an addition to his pleasure, which involves a subtraction from the pleasure of the weak, would neutralise the subtraction in the hedonistic calculus.

[1] See Mill's Utilitarianism, p. 93.

215. There is reason to hold, then, that Kant's formula affords a better expression than does Bentham's, as interpreted according to Bentham's notion of the good, for the rule on which the ideally just man seeks to act. That rule, as we have seen, is one that such a man gathers for himself from the lessons which law and conventional morality have taught him. It is his ἐπανόρθωμα νόμου, ᾗ ἐλλείπει διὰ τὸ καθόλου[1], his articulation, and application to the particulars of life, of that principle of an absolute value in the human person as such, of a like claim to consideration in all men, which is implied in the law and conventional morality of Christendom, but of which the application in law is from the nature of the case merely general and prohibitory, while its application in conventional morality is in fact partial and inconsistent. 'The recognition of the claims of a common humanity' is a phrase that has become so familiar in modern ears that we are apt to suspect it of being cant. Yet this very familiarity is proof of the extent to which the idea represented by it has affected law and institutions. The phrase is indeed cant in the mouth of any one in whom there is no conscientious will giving vitality and application to the idea which, as merely embodied in laws and institutions, would be abortive and dead. But if it is only the conscience of the individual that brings the principle of human equality into productive contact with the particular facts of human life, on the other hand it is from the embodiment of the principle in laws and institutions and social requirements that the conscience itself appropriates it. The mistake of those who deny the *a priori* character of such 'intuitions'[2] of the conscience as that represented by Kant's formula, does not lie in tracing a history of the intuitions, but in ignoring the immanent operation of ideas of the reason in the process of social organisation, upon which the intuitions as in the individual depend. A short summary of the view which we have been seeking to oppose to theirs will make this view clearer,

[1] I. e. his 'rectification of law, where law fails through being general.' Arist. Eth. Nic. V. x. 6.

[2] I use the term 'intuition' here, in the sense commonly attached to it by recent English writers on Morals, for a judgment not derived deductively or inductively from other judgments. The reader should be on his guard against confusing this sense of the term with that in which it is used as an equivalent for the German 'Anschauung,' or apprehension of an object.

as it affects the intuition on which the practice of justice is founded.

216. The individual's conscience is reason in him as informed by the work of reason without him in the structure and controlling sentiments of society. The basis of that structure, the source of those sentiments, can only be a self-objectifying spirit; a spirit through the action of which beings such as we are, endowed with certain animal susceptibilities and affected by certain natural sympathies, become capable of striving after some bettering or fulfilment of themselves, which they conceive as an absolute good, and in which they include a like bettering or fulfilment of others. Without such spiritual action, in however elementary a form, there can be no society, in the proper human sense, at all; no community of persons, however small, to whom the treatment in any respect by each of the other as himself would be intelligible.

On the other hand, given any community of persons rendered possible by such a spiritual principle, it is *potentially* a community of all men of whom one can communicate with the other as 'I' with 'Thou.' The recognition of reciprocal claims, established as between its own members within each of a multitude of social groups, admits of establishment between members of all the groups taken together. There is no necessary limit of numbers or space beyond which the spiritual principle of social relation becomes ineffective. The impediments to its action in bringing about a practical recognition of universal human fellowship, though greater in degree, are the same in kind as those which interfere with the maintenance of unity in the family, the tribe, or the urban commonwealth. They are all reducible to what we may conveniently call the antagonism of the natural to the spiritual man. The prime impediment, alike to the maintenance of the narrower and to the formation of wider fellowships, is selfishness: which we may describe provisionally (pending a more thorough enquiry into the relation between pleasure and the good) as a preference of private pleasure to common good. But the wider, the more universal the fellowship that is in question, the more serious become those impediments to it, of which selfishness may and does take advantage, but which are so far independent of it that they bring the most self-devoted members of one tribe or state into what seems on both sides inevitable hostility with those of another. Such are ignorance, with the fear that springs from ignorance; misapprehension of the physical conditions of well-being, and consequent suspicion that the gain of one community must be the loss of another; geographical separations and demarcations, with the misunderstandings that arise from them. The effect of these has often been to make it seem a necessary incident of a man's obligation to his own tribe or nation that he should deny obligations towards men of another tribe or nation. And while higher motives have thus co-operated with mere selfishness in strengthening national separation and antagonism, it would be idle to deny a large share, in the process by which such influences have been partially overcome, to forces—*e. g.* the force of conquest and, in particular, of Roman conquest—which, though they have been applied and guided in a manner only possible to distinctively rational agents, have been very slightly under the control of any desire for social good on the part of the persons wielding them.

But where the selfishness of man has proposed, his better reason has disposed. Whatever the means, the result has been a gradual removal of obstacles to that recognition of a universal fellowship which the action of reason in men potentially constitutes. Large masses of men have been brought under the control each of a single system of law; and while each system has carried with it manifold results of selfish violence and seeming accident, each has been essentially an expression of reason, as embodying an idea of permanent well-being which the individual conceives to be common to his nation with himself. Each has maintained alike, under whatever differences of form, the institutions of the family and of property; and there has thus arisen, along with an order of life which habituates the individual to the subordination of his likes and dislikes to social requirements, a sort of common language of right, in which the idea of universal human fellowship, of claims in man as man— itself the outcome of the same reason which has yielded the laws of particular communities—can find the expression necessary to its taking hold on the minds of men.

217. In the light of these considerations we may trace a

history, if we like to call it so, of the just man's conscience—of the conscience which dictates to him an equal regard to the well-being, estimated on the same principle as his own, of all whom his actions may affect. It is a history, however, which does not carry us back to anything beyond reason. It is a history of which reason is the beginning and the end. It is reason which renders the individual capable of self-imposed obedience to the law of his family and of his state, while it is to reason that this law itself owes its existence. It is thus both teacher and learner of the lesson through which a conscience of any kind, with the habit of conformity to conscience, is first acquired, and the individual becomes capable of a reverence which can control inclinations to pleasure. Reason is equally the medium of that extension of one system of law over many communities, of like systems over a still wider range, which, in prophetic souls reflecting on it, first elicits the latent idea of a fellowship of all, and furnishes them with a mode of expression through which the idea may be brought home to ordinary men. When it is so brought home, the personal habits which are needed to give practical effect to it, and which on their part only needed the leaven of this idea to expand into a wider beneficence, are already there. But they are there through the action of the same reason, as already yielding social order and obedience within narrower forms of community.

Thus in the conscientious citizen of modern Christendom reason without and reason within, reason as objective and reason as subjective, reason as the better spirit of the social order in which he lives, and reason as his loyal recognition and interpretation of that spirit—these being but different aspects of one and the same reality, which is the operation of the divine mind in man—combine to yield both the judgment, and obedience to the judgment, which we variously express by saying that every human person has an absolute value; that humanity in the person of every one is always to be treated as an end, never merely as a means; that in the estimate of that well-being which forms the true good every one is to count for one and no one for more than one; that every one has a 'suum' which every one else is bound to render him.

CHAPTER IV.

C. *The Determination of the Idea of Common Good.*

218. THE development of morality, which we have been considering, has been a development from the primary recognition of an absolute and common good—a good common as between some group of persons interested in each other, absolute as that of which the goodness is conceived to be independent of the likes and dislikes of individuals; but we have so far considered the development only with reference to the extension of the range of persons between whom the good is conceived to be common, and who on this ground come to recognise equivalent duties to each other. The outcome of the process, when treated in this one-sided way, exhibits itself merely as the intuition of the educated conscience that the true good must be good for all men, so that no one should seek to gain by another's loss, gain and loss being estimated on the same principle for each. It has not appeared so far how the conscience is trained in the apprehension of what in particular the good is, and in the consequent imposition on itself of particular duties. We have treated the precept 'suum cuique' as if the just man arrived at the idea of its applicability to all men, and at the corresponding disposition to apply it, without any such definite enlightenment in regard to the good proper to every one with whom he may have to do, as is necessary for his practical guidance. Some such defect of treatment is unavoidable so long as abstraction of some kind is the condition of all exposition; so long as we can only attend to one aspect of any reality at a time, though quite aware that it is only one aspect. We have now to make up for the defect by considering the gradual determination of the idea of good,

which goes along with the growth of the conviction that it is good for all men alike, and of the disposition to act accordingly.

219. In doing so we must first recall some conclusions previously arrived at. The idea of a good, we saw, is the idea of something that will satisfy a desire. In no case is to think of a pleasure the same thing as to think of a good. Only if some pleasure is the object of desire does the anticipation of the satisfaction of the desire yield the idea of the pleasure as a good. When, as is constantly the case, the object of strongest desire to a man—the object to which he is actually directing himself—is not any pleasure, then it is not any pleasure that is thought of as a good, for it is not any pleasure that is the object with which the man thinks of satisfying himself. In that case it is only so far as the man in desiring contemplates the pleasure, or relief from pain, that will be constituted by satisfaction of the desire—a pleasure of which the imagination cannot from the nature of the case have excited the desire—that any idea of pleasantness enters into the idea of the object as good at all. Taken by itself, then, if it could be taken by itself, the mere succession of desires in a man, as reflected on, would yield the presentation of many different good things, in which the satisfaction of those desires had been found and was expected to recur. Many of these would be pleasures, because many objects of desire are pleasures (though the thought even of these as pleasures is different from the thought of them as good); but many would not be pleasures, because there are many objects of desire which are not imagined pleasures, and which, though pleasure may be anticipated in their attainment, cannot be desired on account of that pleasure. That very reflection on desires, however, which is necessary to the idea of the several objects satisfying them as good, implies that the subject of the desires distinguishes himself from them. Hence there necessarily accompanies or supervenes upon the idea of manifold good things, in which manifold satisfactions have been or may be found, the idea of a possible object which may yield satisfaction of the desiring man or self, as such, who, as satisfaction of each particular desire is attained, still finds himself anew dissatisfied and wanting.

220. Such an idea is implied in the most elementary moral judgments. It must be operative in every one who judges of

actions or dispositions as virtuous or vicious, and must be supposed by him to be operative in every one to whom he ascribes
virtue or vice. For an agent merely capable of seeking the
satisfaction of successive desires, without capacity for conceiving
a satisfaction of himself as other than the satisfaction of any
particular desire, and in consequence without capacity for conceiving anything as good permanently or on the whole, there
could be no possibility of judging that any desire should or
should not be gratified. No such judgment can be formed of
any desire, unless the desire is considered with reference to a
good other than such as passes with the satisfaction of a desire.
Even if the judgment involved no more than a comparison of
the pleasures that had been experienced in the gratification of
different desires, and a decision that one should not be gratified
because interfering with the gratification of another from which
more pleasure was expected, this very comparison would imply
that the person making it distinguished himself from his desires
and was cognisant of something good for himself on the whole—
though for himself only in respect of his capacity for pleasure—
to which good he expects the gratification of one desire to contribute more than that of another. Now the capacity for
regarding certain desires as desires which should not be gratified, must be supposed in any one who is either to form moral
judgments or to have them applied to him. This must be
equally admitted whether we consider action or disposition to
be the proper object of moral judgment; whether we hold it to
be by effects or by motives that actions are rendered morally
good or bad. Unless a man could think of himself as capable
of governing his actions by the consideration that of his desires
some should, while others should not, be gratified, the distinction of praise-worthy and blame-worthy actions would be unmeaning to him. He could not apprehend the distinction, nor
could it with any significance be applied to his actions.

221. It will scarcely be disputed, then, that the possibility of
moral judgments implies some idea of a good, other than any
particular pleasure or satisfaction of passing desire, with the
superior value of which the value of any such pleasure or satisfaction may be compared. But we are apt to look upon the idea
of superior good as formed merely by the combination in thought

of the many particular pleasures and satisfactions, as an imagined sum of them. Every one has experience of certain pleasures, of which he retains the memory and desires the recurrence. Their recurrence in the largest quantity and with the greatest intensity that he can imagine, forms for him, it is supposed, when he thinks calmly of the matter, that greatest good by reference to which he can estimate the value of the pleasures which from time to time he desires, counting them objects of which the desire should or should not be gratified, according as their enjoyment is found upon experience to be compatible or otherwise with the enjoyment of that greatest sum of imaginable pleasures.

Now the question is whether the practical idea of something good on the whole, of a true or chief or highest or ultimate good —the idea implied in the capacity for moral judgment—could even in its earliest stages be formed in this way. The process by which on first thoughts we are led to suppose that it can be and is so formed, would seem to be as follows. The good we rightly identify with the desired. We at the same time accept the notion that the object of desire is always some imagined pleasure—a notion which would not commend itself as it does, but for the confusion into which we readily fall between the pleasure, or relief from pain, constituted by the satisfaction of any desire, and the object exciting the desire. Every particular good being thus supposed to be some pleasure, we infer that the greatest good for any individual must be the greatest quantity of pleasure possible for him, and that the greatest good of which the idea can affect him must be the greatest sum of pleasures that he can imagine.

It is the latter part of the inference that is here specially in question. Upon reflection it will appear that, from the supposition that every desire has some imagined pleasure for its object, it not only is no legitimate inference that a greatest sum of imaginable pleasures is most desired and therefore presents itself to the individual as his greatest good ; it rather follows that no such sum of pleasures can be desired at all. If the supposition is admitted, we are justified indeed in arguing that, in one sense of the term, the greatest pleasure is most desired, but only in the sense in which the greatest pleasure means the most intense particular pleasure that can be remembered or imagined. To argue from it that a greatest sum of imaginable pleasures is the object most desired, or one that can be desired at all, is to argue from desire for a state of feeling to desire for something which is not a possible state of feeling. There can be no such thing as a state of feeling made up of a sum of pleasures; and if the only possible object of desire is a state of pleasant feeling, as remembered or imagined, there can be no such thing as desire for a sum of pleasures. A sum of pleasures is not a pleasure, nor is the thought of it a remembrance or imagination of pleasure, such as on the supposition excites desire. It can only exist for the thought of a person considering certain pleasures as addible quantities, but neither enjoying them nor imagining their enjoyment. For the feeling of a pleased person, or in relation to his sense of enjoyment, pleasures cannot form a sum. However numerous the sources of a state of pleasant feeling, it is one, and is over before another can be enjoyed. It and its successors can be added together in thought, but not in enjoyment or in imagination of enjoyment. If then desire is only for pleasure, *i.e.* for an enjoyment or feeling of pleasure, we are simply the victims of words when we talk of desire for a sum of pleasures, much more when we take the greatest imaginable sum to be the most desired. We are confusing a sum of pleasures as counted or combined in thought, with a sum of pleasures as felt or enjoyed, which is a nonentity.

222. In the above it is not intended to deny that there may be in fact such a thing as desire for a sum or contemplated series of pleasures, or that a man may be so affected by it as to judge that some particular desire should not be gratified, if its gratification would interfere with the attainment of that more desirable object. The contention is merely that there could not be such a desire if desire were solely for pleasure, in the sense of being always excited by an imagination of some feeling of pleasure. As there cannot be a feeling of a sum of pleasures, neither can there be an imagination of such a feeling. Desire for a sum or series of pleasures is only possible so far as upon sundry desires, each excited by imagination of a particular pleasure, there supervenes in a man a desire not excited by any such imagination; a desire for self-satisfaction. The man thinks of himself—he

cannot be properly said to imagine himself—as the permanent
subject of these successive desires and of the successive pleasures
by imagination of which they have been excited; and a desire
to satisfy himself in their successive enjoyment, unless counter-
acted by a desire to satisfy himself in some other way (whether
with some particular pleasure imagined, or with some object that
is not pleasure at all), may arise in consequence. Thus, in order
to account for the transition from desire for imagined pleasures
to desire for a sum or series of pleasures, we must suppose the
action of a principle wholly different from desire for imagined
pleasures. We must suppose a determination of desire by the
conception of self, its direction to self-satisfaction. The idea of
something good on the whole, even if nothing but a sum of
pleasures entered into the idea as present to the mind of one
whom it renders capable of moral judgment, could yet not result
from the recurrence of images of pleasure or from a combination
of desires each excited by such an image. A desire to satisfy
oneself, then, as distinct from desire for a feeling of pleasure,
being necessary even to desire for a sum of pleasures, the question is whether it can be a contemplated possibility of satisfying
oneself *with pleasures* that yields the idea of a true or highest
good, with which particular gratifications of desire may be
contrasted.

223. Now it is not in dispute that we may and constantly do
seek self-satisfaction for the moment in some imagined pleasure,
though in our calmer mind we know that the pleasure cannot
afford the self-satisfaction sought. We could not deny this, according to the account previously given of the will, without
denying that the will is often directed to the attainment of
pleasure. To deny it would be as untrue as to say of any one
that his object is always a pleasure, even the habitual ' pleasure-
seeker' being liable to particular propensions excited quite otherwise than by imaginations of pleasure. But, though self-satisfaction is constantly being sought in some pleasure or another,
without reflection on the impossibility of its being found there,
it is clear that interest in the attainment of a pleasure cannot
suggest an idea, such as can control action, of something truly
good or good on the whole—an idea of which the import lies in
contrast with the pleasure of which the attraction is for the

moment most strongly felt, and which presupposes some consideration of the question where self-satisfaction is really to be found. Reflecting on his desires for certain pleasures, a man may, no doubt, judge one of them to be more of a good than another, on the ground of its greater present attraction for him; but such a judgment neither implies nor could yield the contrast of the desired with the desirable, of good for the moment with good on the whole. It does indeed imply in any one so judging a distinction of himself from his feelings, which, at a further stage of its action, yields the idea of something good on the whole. This idea arises from a man's thought of himself as there to be satisfied when any feeling, in the enjoyment of which he may have sought satisfaction, is over. It is the idea of something in which he may be satisfied, not for this time and turn merely, but at least *more* permanently. Could a contemplated succession of pleasures, then, seem to him to offer this relatively permanent satisfaction? Could he, while reflecting on himself so far as to conceive the need of a lasting good, fail to reflect also on the fleeting nature of the pleasures of which he contemplates the succession? Could he be deluded by his own faculty of summing the stages of a succession into supposing that a series of pleasures, of which only one will be in enjoyment at each stage of the series, and none at all at the end, is the more lasting good of which he is in search, and for the sake of which he calls in question the value of the pleasure for the time most attractive in imagination?

224. To answer these questions in the negative may seem unwarrantable, if for no other reason, in presence of the deliberate judgment of so many enlightened persons who tell us that their only conception—the only conception which seems to them possible—of a true good is just that of a greatest sum of pleasures; that when they decide against the pursuit of a particular pleasure as not good on the whole, they simply mean that its enjoyment would be incompatible with the attainment of a larger sum of pleasures which it is open to them to enjoy. Can we doubt that such persons really form their judgments of the good as they suppose themselves to do; and is it not absurd to deny that those conceptions of the true good, which we inherit and which affect our consciences, *may* at any rate have been formed in the same way?

Now undoubtedly, if we must accept as true the account which most persons, under the influence of the current philosophy, give of the ultimate moral idea which actuates them; if we are to admit that well-being means for them a sum of pleasures, the highest well-being the largest possible sum of pleasures; it is useless further to argue the question before us. But there are reasons for not accepting that account. It rests on a supposition that all desire is for pleasure. This supposition chiefly commends itself, as has been previously pointed out, through the confusion into which we readily fall, in reflecting on any desire, between the object of which the idea excites the desire, and the pleasure we anticipate in the fulfilment of the desire—the pleasure, as it is sometimes called, of success. If an ordinarily unselfish man, unaccustomed to precise analysis of mental experiences, is appealed to by a Hedonistic philosopher to say whether in calm moments of reflection, when exempt from the pressure of appetite or of any particular passion, the good for which he finds himself wishing is not always pleasure—not any single pleasure, but a quantity of pleasures more or less distinctly articulated in thought, or perhaps simply pleasurable existence—he is apt to assent. He does so because, being interested in certain objects, and being aware that, when he reflects on his interests, he often says to himself 'how pleasant it will be when such or such an object is attained,' he mistakes the desire to satisfy himself in the attainment of the objects for a desire to satisfy himself with the pleasure of the attainment.

No doubt this pleasure of attainment is one which, upon self-reflection, the man really contemplates himself as enjoying; there is really a desire for it which co-operates with his various interests; but it could not take the place of the objects of these various interests without destroying the interests and with them its own possibility. This however does not prevent men who are in fact deeply absorbed in the pursuit of objects other than pleasures from being argued into the belief that, because they are conscious of anticipating pleasures of attainment, pleasure is the object of their pursuit. The further step is then easily taken of interpreting this pleasure as made up of those several pleasures to which, through the confusion above noticed, it has come to be supposed that all desires are directed. Thus we settle down into the notion that our motive principles are on the one hand particular passions, each excited by imagination of some pleasure or some pain, and on the other a deliberate desire for a good made up of as many particular desired pleasures as, after deduction for incidental pains, we deem ourselves capable of obtaining. This deliberate desire is taken to be the source of our disapproval of certain pleasures as not good on the whole, because not compatible with the acquisition of that larger sum of pleasures which is more deliberately desired.

225. As to the mistake of supposing all desires to have some pleasure or other for their object, enough has perhaps been said. But writers who have fully recognised this mistake, who have most strenuously asserted that particular desires terminate upon their objects, and that those objects in many cases are not pleasures, have adhered to the notion that the deliberate desire for what is good on the whole is equivalent to desire for a greatest possible quantity of pleasure. They have indeed generally expressed this as a desire for happiness, but they have also been generally ready to accept the identification of happiness with a sum of pleasures, of greatest happiness with a greatest sum of pleasures. It might perhaps have been otherwise if the convenient ambiguity attaching to the term 'happiness' did not tend to hide from us the difficulty of dealing upon this theory with that desire for the good of others, the genuineness of which we should be slow to dispute. Clearly a desire for the good of others, though that greatest good be understood to consist for them in pleasures, is not a desire for pleasure on the part of the person who entertains it, unless he desires the production of pleasure to others, not as an end, but as a means to his own. Now that benevolence is not to be considered as a desire for any pleasure to oneself, other than that of doing the benevolent act, is one of the few points—and it speaks well for the improvement of our time that it should be so—on which moralists seem to have come almost to an agreement. But to consider it a desire for the pleasure of doing the benevolent act is to fall into the fallacy of supposing a desire to be excited by imagination of its own satisfaction—a fallacy from which such writers as Butler and Hutcheson, and in recent years Mr. H. Sidgwick[1], have kept themselves clear.

[1] Methods of Ethics, Book I. chap. iv.

226. A desire for the good of others, then, though it be a desire to produce pleasure in them, is not a desire for pleasure. We
may, if we like, apply both to it and to the desire for our own
true well-being the common designation 'desire for happiness;'
but, if the desire for our own well-being consists in a desire for
a sum of pleasures, we are applying the common designation
to the two kinds of desire in absolutely different senses. We
shall have to take it that there are two co-ordinate principles, ' Benevolence ' and ' Reasonable Self-Love,' alike, according to the phraseology of the last century, in being calm or
settled or deliberate principles, but wholly different as desires in
respect of the objects to which they are directed, since one is,
while the other is not, a desire for pleasure ; and we shall have
to suppose that these serve indifferently as grounds for moral
approbation and disapprobation, the reason for rejecting desired
pleasures as not good on the whole being sometimes that they
are incompatible with the object sought by Benevolence, sometimes that they are incompatible with that sought by Reasonable Self-Love.

That our practical judgments as to the true good rest on
two such different principles is a conclusion which, once clearly
faced, every enquirer would gladly escape, as repugnant both to
the philosophic craving for unity, and to that ideal of ' singleness
of heart ' which we have been accustomed to associate with the
highest virtue. The method of escaping it generally favoured
by Utilitarians involves the fallacy, already sufficiently noticed,
of supposing benevolent desires to have for their object the
pleasure of their own satisfaction. This fallacy once discerned,
the conclusion can only be avoided either by a bolder denial of
the existence of a deliberate and disinterested benevolence than
we are generally prepared for—by a return, in short, to the
position of Hobbes—or by reconsideration of the view that
' Reasonable Self-Love,' desire for one's own true good, is equivalent to desire for a sum of pleasures.

227. Such a reconsideration is forced upon us from a different
quarter so soon as we take account of the fact, already noticed,
that pleasures do not admit of being accumulated in enjoyment.
A man who is enjoying a pleasure for the thousandth time *has*
no more pleasure, however much more an enumerator might

reckon him to have *had*—nay, if novelty adds a charm to
pleasure, he has less—than the man who is enjoying it for the
first time. We may talk, if we like, of a larger sum of pleasures
as more of a good than a less sum, of a largest possible sum as
the greatest or highest good, but in doing so we are bound to
remember, if we would not be misled by words, that we are
talking of 'goods' of which, from the nature of the case, there
can be neither possession nor any approach to possession. Now
when any one is deliberately judging what is for his good on
the whole, in the light of the experience presupposed by such a
judgment, it would seem that he can scarcely help being alive to
this state of the case and being affected by it in his judgment.
Reflection upon the perishing nature of pleasures suggests itself
to every one unsophisticated in his 'moralising' and unbiassed by
philosophical systems. It is traceable in literature as far back
as the literature of reflection extends. It would be far more
reasonable to suppose that it was the source of the deliberate
quest for something good on the whole, than that it could be set
aside in such a quest. And if it cannot be set aside, it must
effectually prevent the man who has practically asked himself
what it is that can satisfy him, from seeking a sum of pleasures,
even 'the greatest possible,' in expectation that it can satisfy or
tend to satisfy him ; in other words, under the persuasion that
it is that truly or ultimately desirable object for the sake of
which a particular desired pleasure should be rejected. He cannot really look forward to any millionth repetition of a pleasant
feeling as bringing him nearer to the satisfaction of himself than
he was the first time the pleasure was felt. It will not at all
follow that such a person, if challenged by a philosopher to say
what the ultimate good is, of which the idea actuates him, might
not, under pressure of the impossibility of adequately defining
it, be drawn into accepting an account of it as a greatest sum of
pleasures. The action of the idea in him, however, is not dependent on the account he may give of it. The question is
whether the idea, as it really actuates him, can be the idea of a
sum of pleasures, of which he must be aware—and have become
aware before the idea could consciously actuate him—that each
perishes in the enjoyment. To the present writer it seems that
this question, once plainly put, carries a negative answer with it.

228. 'But why,' it may be objected, 'should the fact that a greatest sum of pleasures cannot be enjoyed as a sum, *i. e.* all at once, prevent a man from wishing to enjoy this greatest sum, as it may be enjoyed, successively, and from regarding this successive enjoyment as the object supremely desirable ?' Now undoubtedly, as already admitted, a man may think of himself as enjoying many pleasures in succession, may desire their successive enjoyment and, reflecting on his desire, esteem the enjoyment a good. But it is not the pleasures *as a sum* that attract him. He cannot imagine them as a sum, for the imagination of pleasure must always be of some specific feeling of pleasure, which must have ceased to possess the imagination before another can possess it. What affects him is the thought of himself as capable of a state of continuous enjoyable existence, and on the contrary as liable to a like continuity of pain. The consideration how many pleasures there will be in the course of the enjoyable existence, what their sum will amount to, does not at all enter into or affect the thought of it as desirable. If he judges a pleasure, which now attracts him, to be not truly a good on the ground of its incompatibility with ulterior pleasure, it is not because he presents to himself two possible sums of pleasure—one as the result would be if the pleasure now attracting him were enjoyed, the other as it would be if that pleasure were forgone—and pronounces the latter the larger. It is because he believes the pleasure which he disapproves to entail an unnecessary breach in the enjoyable existence, which he wishes for without reference to any sum of pleasures that an enumerator might find it to contain.

This, we say, is the case *if* a particular imagined pleasure is 'in a calm hour' condemned on account of its known incompatibility with ulterior pleasure, which must mean not any imagined pleasure but a conceived succession of pleasures. But while not denying that an attractive pleasure *may* be disapproved on this account, we could not admit that the ordinary reference of a healthy moral man to his own true happiness, as a reason for rejecting present pleasure, was to be thus explained. If it were, it would not have much effect upon conduct. The thought of oneself as in a state of enjoyable existence, if it were not a thought of anything else than this, could scarcely countervail the attraction of an imagined pleasure, here and now intensely desired. An imagination of pain might be effectual for the purpose, but hardly a thought of pleasure, which is not an imagination of any pleasure in particular. In truth a man's reference to his own true happiness is a reference to the objects which chiefly interest him, and has its controlling power on that account. More strictly, it is a reference to an ideal state of well-being, a state in which he shall be satisfied; but the objects of the man's chief interests supply the filling of that ideal state. The idea of such a state, indeed, neither is, nor is conceived as being, fully realisable by us. The objects of which we contemplate the attainment as necessary to its fulfilment are not contemplated as completely fulfilling it. In our contemplation of them as truly good the forecast of an indefinable Better is always present. But in any consideration of true happiness which is other than the vague discontent of the sated or baffled voluptuary, the consciousness of objects which we are seeking to realise, of ideas to which we are trying to give effect, holds the first place. Just because we wish for the attainment of such objects, we are unhappy till we attain them; and thus, owing to the difficulty of mentally articulating them, we are apt to lump them in our thoughts as happiness. But they do not consist in pleasures. The ideas of them, which we are seeking to realise, are not ideas of pleasures. Though we may look forward to our life in attaining them, or when they are attained, as a pleasant one—and certainly we cannot look forward to it as otherwise— this anticipation is quite secondary. It is only brought into distinct consciousness, if at all, during intervals of relaxed energy or under the pressure of an argumentative Hedonist. In short, it is the realisation of those objects in which we are mainly interested, not the succession of enjoyments which we shall experience in realising them, that forms the definite content of our idea of true happiness, so far as it has such content at all.

229. Our conclusion then is that it is a misinterpretation of consciousness, arising in a manner not inexplicable, to regard the idea of a truer or higher good, with which the good of any particular pleasure or the gratification of any particular passion may be contrasted—an idea necessary to the capacity for moral

judgment—as equivalent or reducible to the idea of a larger sum of pleasures enjoyable by the person entertaining the idea. In the mind at least of those persons over whom the idea has any controlling power, its filling is supplied by ideal objects to which they are seeking to give reality, and of which the realisation forms their prevailing interest. Such an ideal object [1], for example, is the welfare of a family. In those forms of human life which we can know, either from the intercourse of present society or from the record of the past, this object has probably had the largest share in filling up the idea of true or permanent good. As a man reflects—perhaps quite inarticulately—on the transitoriness of the pleasures by imagination of which his desires are from hour to hour excited; as he asks (practically, if without formal expression) what can satisfy the self which abides throughout and survives those desires; the thought of the well-being of a family, with which he identifies himself and of which the continuity is as his own, possesses his mind. It is interest in this well-being which forms the most primitive and universal countervailing influence, apart from imagination of pain, to the attraction of imagined pleasures. If not strong enough to prevent such pursuit of pleasures as has been found incompatible with the well-being of a family, it at least awakens self-reproach in the pursuit, a consciousness that it should not be.

Now whatever difficulty there may be in adequately defining this interest—as there must be, for it is an interest which, though fundamentally always the same, is constantly actualising itself in new ways—there is one thing which it clearly is not. It is not, directly or indirectly, an interest, on the part of the person influenced by it, either in winning any particular pleasure, or in securing an enjoyable existence, or in getting as much pleasure as he can. Doubtless in looking forward to a well-being of his family, he thinks of himself as conscious of it and sharing in it, even though he may expect to be 'laid in the grave' before his idea of the family well-being is realised. Every one thus immortalises himself, who looks forward to the realisation of ideal objects, with which on the one hand he identifies himself, and which on the other hand he cannot think

---

[1] It will be understood that by an ideal object is meant an object present in idea but not yet given in reality.

of as bounded by his earthly life,—objects in which he thinks of himself as still living when dead. But to suppose, because a man looks forward to a satisfaction of his interest in the well-being of his family and contemplates enjoyment in that satisfaction, that therefore such enjoyment is the object of the interest, would be to repeat the mistake of supposing a desire to be excitable by the idea of its own satisfaction. The fact, if it be a fact, that the man's conception of the well-being of his family is nothing but a conception of it as possessing the means to a sustained succession of pleasures, does not affect the case in this respect. It remains equally true that his desire for the family well-being is absolutely different from a desire for pleasure.

230. There may not be the means of proving that, as a matter of fact, the form in which true good, or good on the whole, was first conceived was that of family well-being. The earliest forms in which the most essential practical ideas have taken effect must always, from the nature of the case, remain beyond the reach of historical investigation. We are warranted however by simple consideration of its nature, in holding that the idea of true good could only become matter of definite consciousness in view of its possible realisation in an object which at once excites a strong interest, and can at the same time be regarded as having the permanence necessary to satisfy the demand arising from a man's involuntary contemplation of his own permanence. The idea of the good, it must be remembered, like all practical ideas, is primarily a demand. It is not derived from observation of what exists but from an inward requirement that something should be ; something that will yield self-satisfaction of the kind that is sought when we think of ourselves as surviving each particular desire and its gratification. It is this requirement or demand that first sets us upon seeking to bring objects into existence, in which some sort of abiding satisfaction may be found; but it is only in contemplation of these objects as in some measure realised or in process of realisation, that the demand arrives at any clear consciousness of itself, or that it can yield the idea of something as truly good, in contrast with something else that is not so.

231. Now among the objects thus brought into existence by

demand for the satisfaction of an abiding self, and of which the contemplation first supplied some definite content to the idea of a true good, it would seem that the most primitive and elementary must have been those that contribute to supply the wants of a family—to keep its members alive and comfortably alive. If it is asked by what warrant we carry back the institution of the family into the life of the most primitive men, we answer that we carry it back no further than the interest in permanent good. From beings incapable of such an interest, even though connected by acts of generation with ourselves, we cannot in any intelligible sense have been developed. They cannot have had any such essential community with ourselves as would be implied in calling them men. But the capacity for such an interest is also the capacity which renders possible the family bond. That determination of an animal organism by a self-conscious principle, which makes a man and is presupposed by the interest in permanent good, carries with it a certain appropriation by the man to himself of the beings with whom he is connected by natural ties, so that they become to him as himself and in providing for himself he provides for them. Projecting himself into the future as a permanent subject of possible well-being or ill-being—and he must so project himself in seeking for a permanent good—he associates his kindred with himself. It is this association that neutralises the effect which the anticipation of death must otherwise have on the demand for permanent good. At a stage of intellectual development when any theories of immortality would be unmeaning to them, men have already, in the thought of a society of which the life is their own life but which survives them, a medium in which they carry themselves forward beyond the limits of animal existence.

232. Thus we conclude that, in the earliest stages of human consciousness in which the idea of a true or permanent good could lead any one to call in question the good of an immediately attractive pleasure, it was already an idea of a social good—of a good not private to the man himself, but good for him as a member of a community. We conclude that it must have been so, because it is a man's thought of himself as permanent that gives rise to the idea of such a good, and because

the thought of himself as permanent is inseparable from an identification of himself with others, in whose continued life he contemplates himself as living; and because further, as a consequence of this, the objects which the effort to realise this thought brings into being, and in contemplation of which the idea of permanent good passes from the more blindly operative to the more clearly conscious stage, are arrangements of life, or habits of action, or applications of the forces and products of nature, calculated to contribute to a common well-being. Hence the distinction commonly supposed to exist between considerate Benevolence and reasonable Self-Love, as co-ordinate principles on which moral approbation is founded, is a fiction of philosophers.

In saying this we must not be understood either to be denying that reasonable Self-Love is a source of moral approbation, or to be seeking to reduce Benevolence in any way to desire for pleasure to oneself. The meaning is that the distinction of good for self and good for others has never entered into that idea of a true good on which moral judgments are founded. It must have been held to do so, no doubt (except upon the selfish hypothesis), if the actuating idea of a true good, as for oneself, had been founded on desire for a sum of pleasures; since a desire for pleasure, though it may' be balanced by a desire to produce pleasure, and though the two desires may suggest in certain cases the same course of outward action, must always be absolutely different from it as a motive. But in fact the idea of a true good as for oneself is not an idea of a series of pleasures to be enjoyed by oneself. It is ultimately or in principle an idea of satisfaction for a self that abides and contemplates itself as abiding, but which can only so contemplate itself in identification with some sort of society; which can only look forward to a satisfaction of itself as permanent, on condition that it shall also be a satisfaction of those in community with whom alone it can think of itself as continuing to live. For practical purposes, or as it ordinarily affects a man, it is an idea of an order of life, more or less established, but liable to constant interference from actions prompted by passion or desire for pleasure; an order in the maintenance and advancement of which he conceives his permanent well-being to consist. This well-being he doubtless conceives as his own, but that he should conceive it as exclusively his own—his own in any sense in which it is not equally and co-incidentally a well-being of others—would be incompatible with the fact that it is only as living in community, as sharing the life of others, as incorporated in the continuous being of a family or nation, of a state or a church, that he can sustain himself in that thought of his own permanence to which the thought of permanent well-being is correlative. His own permanent well-being he thus necessarily presents to himself as a social well-being. The rule of action, which a consideration of this well-being suggests, may sometimes forbid the indulgence of generous impulses, as it will constantly forbid the pursuit of an attractive pleasure; but between it and the rule of considerate Benevolence there can never be a conflict, for they are one and the same rule, founded on one and the same quest for a self-satisfaction which shall abide, but which no man can contemplate as abiding except so far as he identifies himself with a society whose well-being is to him as his own.

233. After all this argumentation, however, which may already seem too prolix, we may be sure that the old objection will here return. This permanent well-being, what is it—what is it conceived as being by the person who desires it—but a succession of pleasures, or of states in which pleasure predomi-nates over pain, whether it is of himself or of others that the man thinks as enjoying this succession? We can best finally answer this question by gathering into a summary form the view which it is sought to oppose to that suggested by the question. But before doing so it will be well also to put in a final 'caveat' against two misapprehensions, which may be lurking in our minds when we put the question. Though we answered it in the affirmative, we should be none the nearer to a reduction of the moral life to an origin in mere succession of feel-ings. As has already been pointed out [§ 222], a desire for one's own permanent well-being, though the well-being looked for-ward to consisted merely in a succession of pleasures, would still be quite a different thing, would imply a consciousness of quite a different nature, from desire excited by an imagined pleasure. Nor, if we answer it in the affirmative, will any recognition of sympathy bring us nearer to an identification of self-regarding

and 'altruistic' motives. It is clear that desire for a well-being as consisting in a succession of pleasures to oneself, is quite different from desire for a well-being that consists in a succession of pleasures to others. The fact that one man may be pleased or pained by the knowledge of another's pleasure or pain does not alter the fact that each man's pleasure or pain is private to himself. Desires are determined by their objects; and desire for pleasure, having an absolutely different object, is an absolutely different desire from desire for the production of pleasure to others. If therefore a man's desire for his own true well-being is essentially a desire that he may enjoy a succession of pleasures, and that for the well-being of others a desire to convey to them a succession of pleasures, the two desires are opposite, though perhaps reconcilable principles of action, and we must fall back on the view, which we have been seeking to set aside, of the co-ordination, as distinct from the identity, of Benevolence and Reasonable Self-Love.

234. This premised, to the question, What is the well-being which in a calm hour we desire but a succession of pleasures? we reply as follows. The ground of this desire is a demand for an abiding satisfaction of an abiding self. In a succession of pleasures there can be no such satisfaction, nor in the longest prolongation of the succession any nearer approach to it than in the first pleasure enjoyed. If a man, therefore, under the influence of the spiritual demand described, were to seek any succession of pleasures as that which would satisfy the demand, he would be under a delusion. Such a delusion may be possible, but we are not to suppose that it takes place because many persons, through a mistaken analysis of their inner experience, affirm that they have no idea of well-being but as a succession of pleasures. The demand for an abiding self-satisfaction has led to an ordering of life in which some permanent provision is made, better or worse, for the satisfaction of those interests which are not interests in the procuring of pleasure, but which may be described most generally as interests in the development of our faculties, and in the like development of those for whom we care.

When a man 'sits down in a calm hour' to consider what his permanent well-being consists in, what it is that in desiring it he really desires, it is not indeed to be supposed that he traces the desire back to its ultimate source in his self-objectifying personality, or that he thinks of its object in the abstract form of that which will satisfy the demand arising from such a personality. But, if unbiassed either by particular passions or by philosophical prepossessions, he will identify his well-being with an order of life which that demand has brought into existence. The thought of his well-being will be to him the thought of himself as living in the successful pursuit of various interests which the order of society—taking the term in its widest sense —has determined for him ; interests ranging, perhaps, from provision for his family to the improvement of the public health or to the production of a system of philosophy. The constituents of the contemplated well-being will be the objects of those various interests, objects (*e.g.* the provision for a family or the sanitation of a town) in process of realisation, which, when realised, take their place as permanent contributions to an abiding social good. In them therefore the man who carries himself forward in thought along the continued life of a family or a nation, a state or a church, anticipates a lasting and accumulating possession, as he cannot do in successive enjoyments. In them he can think of himself as really coming nearer to an absolute good. Just so far as he is interested in such objects, he must indeed anticipate pleasure in their realisation, but the objects, not the pleasure, form the actuating content of his idea of true well-being. A transfer of his interest from the objects to the pleasure would be its destruction.

235. If this answer is accepted to the question, what it is that we desire in desiring our own true or permanent well-being, it would seem that we have already answered the question, what it is that we desire in desiring the true well-being of others. It is the same common well-being, the same good of a society which we also desire as our own. No doubt, there are generous impulses consisting in desires to convey pleasures, simply as such, to others, or to lessen their pains. These are as little to be ignored as they are to be identified with desires for pleasures to oneself. But the desire for the well-being, whether as of others or as of oneself, is no more to be identified with such generous impulses, with which it may very well conflict, than those

impulses that are excited by the imagination of pleasure. The objects of which a man anticipates the realisation in looking forward to such well-being, are objects, as we have seen, which he necessarily thinks of as realised for a society no less than for himself, for himself only as a member of a society. The opposition of self and others does not enter into the consideration of a well-being so constituted. Generous impulses and desires for pleasures may indeed co-operate with the desire for it, though never equivalent to that desire, and may do so in different degrees in different cases. The objects most prominent in a man's working idea of true well-being will vary, no doubt, according to circumstances and his idiosyncrasy. To revert to instances previously given, in one case the sanitation of a town, in another the composition of a book on an abstruse subject, may hold the largest place in a man's mind when he sets himself to enquire what in particular forms the content of the idea of true well-being, as he individually is actuated by it. In the former case it can be understood that the impulse to convey pleasures to particular persons, or to relieve their pains, might effectually co-operate with the idea as it actuates the individual, while it scarcely could do so in the latter case. In both cases, again, anticipated pleasures of achievement might stimulate the work which interest in a well-being not constituted by pleasures initiates and directs, though that they should become the main objects of interest would be fatal to the work. But however the idea of a true good may vary in the particular aspect which it presents to the individual according to the special nature of his higher interests, and in whatever measures impulsive benevolence or any desire for pleasure may respectively further its operation in him, it remains true that, in its actuation of the individual, no less than in that ordering of society which at once is effected through that actuation of individuals and in turn conditions it, the idea does not admit of the distinction between good for self and good for others. As the source of moral action and of moral judgment, it has equally to control, and in controlling must be equally independent of, the desire for pleasure and the desire to please.

236. But granting that in a man's idea of well-being as true or permanent there is such an identification of his own and

others' well-being, he must still think of it as standing in some definite relation to others as to himself. He may think of their true good as also his and of his as also theirs, but how, it will be asked, does he conceive of the true good for others, if not as their happiness, *i.e.* as the most unbroken succession of pleasures possible for them ? We answer that the happiness which, under influence of the idea of permanent good, a man seeks for others is of the same kind as the happiness which, under influence of the same idea, he seeks for himself. We have seen that true happiness, as he conceives it for himself, consists in the realisation of the objects of various interests by which he is possessed —interests of which he is only capable through self-identification with a society. True happiness, as he conceives it for others, consists in the realisation for them of the same objects. His own interest in these objects carries with it an ascription of a like interest to others, and in the realisation of the objects he anticipates a happiness to them, just as he anticipates it to himself. Now the interest, as he experiences it in himself, is an interest, not in pleasure, but in the objects—these not being pleasures; and what he seeks to procure for others is a satisfaction of a like interest, which is not an interest in pleasures. He seeks to help them in attaining objects which he supposes to be common to them with him, and these objects, not being pleasures in his case, cannot be pleasures in theirs. In the realisation of the objects there must be pleasure for the others, on supposition of their interest in the objects, as for himself, and in anticipating their realisation of the objects he will doubtless also anticipate the pleasure incidental to it; but it is primarily the objects which he seeks to help them in gaining, the pleasure only as incidental to the attainment of those particular objects. Pleasures incidental to the attainment of other objects, though equally pleasures, he would have no interest in conveying to them. It is a *true* happiness which he seeks for them, and the truth of their happiness depends on the nature of the desired objects, not themselves pleasures, to the realisation of which it is incidental.

237. By way of illustration, we may again revert to the instance of a man supremely interested in the sanitation of a town. Such a man would naturally be described as devoted to

the true happiness of his fellow-creatures. No doubt his great
object is to help the men whom he sees about him to live more
happily, and, absorbed in his work, he is not likely to analyse
very accurately what it is that he presents to himself when he
thinks of their living more happily. It is not at all essential
that he should do so. If in confusion or haste he pronounces
that the happiness he is seeking for them consists merely in a
succession of pleasures, the mistake is probably of little practical
importance. It matters less than if he made the same speculative mistake in regard to the end which he seeks for himself.
A theory that his object for himself was pleasure—the pleasure,
as perhaps he might say, of successful work—might strengthen the
pleasure-seeking tendency, by which such a man, like all the
rest of us, must really be affected, till there might be danger of
its weakening or supplanting the interest which is, in fact, the
condition of his pleasure in his work. A misinterpretation of
the happiness which he seeks for others can have no such mischievous effect. Even if, through the notion that his motive
was desire for the mere pleasure of others, it really became so,
he would not have become a pleasure-seeker. He would have become a practically less wise and useful, but not a selfish man.

None the less, however, such a beneficent person would be
really misinterpreting the object which mainly moves him in so
describing it. It is not pleasure, as such, to be enjoyed by other
persons, that he seeks to bring about, but an improvement of the
persons, of which pleasure is the incident and the sign. He
conceives them, like himself, as having objects which it is their
vocation to realise, which health is the condition of their
realising, and which form part of one great social end, the same
for himself as for them. What this end is he conceives, like the
rest of us, very dimly, though, but for the power which the idea
of there being such an end exercises over him, not only directly
but indirectly through those institutions of society which are
its product, he would not live the life which he does. Pressed
to give an account of it, he readily in his description puts the
pleasure, which is the incident of realisation, in place of that
realisation of worthy objects to which he is in fact seeking to
help his neighbours. He speaks as if that 'happiness' of others
which he is seeking to promote were merely pleasure irrespec-

tively of the conditions of the pleasure, whereas in truth it is a fulfilment of capabilities which, without clear analysis of what they are, but on the strength of his own experience, he assigns to the others.

238. There are two questions, however, of which the consideration might make him more clearly aware what his mind on the matter really is; might convince him that, not pleasure as such, but the attainment of objects other than pleasures though involving pleasure in their attainment, is the end to which he seeks to help other men. Let him ask himself whether he can look upon the value of the pleasure, which he supposes himself to be labouring to produce, as depending simply on its amount; whether he does not, for others as for himself, distinguish between higher and lower pleasures according to the nature of the pursuit out of which they arise, or according to the state of mind to which they are relative. If he does, it must follow that it is not pleasure as such, or by itself, that he is seeking to produce, but pleasure as an incident of a life of which the value or desirability does not consist in its pleasantness. Let him ask himself, further, whether the ideal end which he seeks for others as for himself, though it be an end never realised, is not something in which a permanent satisfaction can be found; whether he himself could find true happiness in a succession of pleasures of which each, having been enjoyed, leaves him with the consciousness of being no nearer satisfaction than he was before; whether on the contrary he does not count it an essential condition of every contribution to his own true happiness that it should bring him nearer to the fulfilment of his mission, to a completion of his capacities, as no enjoyment of pleasure can be held to do; and whether his final object in working for the true happiness of others can be to help them to a succession of pleasures, which would be no contribution to a true happiness as he seeks it for himself.

239. These considerations might make such a man aware that his interest in true happiness as for himself, and his interest in it as for others, are not two interests but one interest, of which the object is not a succession of pleasures but a fulfilment of itself, a bettering of itself, a realisation of its capabilities, on the part of the human soul. These capabilities

are not distinctively capabilities of pleasure. The pleasure of their realisation does not differ as pleasure, except perhaps in respect of its less intensity, from any animal enjoyment. They are capabilities of certain kinds of life and action, of which (as previously explained) no adequate account can be given till they are attained. Of what ultimate well-being may be, therefore, we are unable to say anything but that it must be the complete fulfilment of our capabilities, even while the idea that there is such an ultimate well-being may be the guiding idea of our lives. But of particular forms of life and action we can say that they are better, or contribute more to true well-being than others, because in them there is a further fulfilment of man's capabilities, and therefore a nearer approach to the end in which alone he can find satisfaction for himself.

That interest in a true good which leads us to reject attractive pleasures as pleasures which should not be enjoyed, and to endure repellent pains as pains which should be undergone, is interest in the furtherance of such better forms of life and action—in their furtherance because they are better. The special features of the object in which the true good is sought will vary in different ages and with different persons, according to circumstances and idiosyncracy. There are circumstances in which it cannot present itself to the individual as anything else than the work of keeping a family comfortably alive, without reference to the well-being of any wider society in which the family is included, or to any other form of family well-being than such as consists in the decent satisfaction of animal wants. From such a form of the interest in true good to one in which it mainly expresses itself in the advancement of some branch of knowledge, or the improvement of the public health, or the endeavour after 'personal holiness,' there may seem to be a great step. But in all its forms the interest has the common characteristic of being directed to an object which is an object for the individual only so far as he identifies himself with a society, and seeks neither an imagined pleasure nor a succession of pleasures, but a bettering of the life which is at once his and the society's.

240. We have dwelt thus at length on the difference between the interest in a true good or permanent well-being in all its

forms, and the desire to experience any succession of pleasures, even such a succession as an imaginary enumerator might find to make up the largest possible sum, in order to avoid misapprehension in consideration of the process by which the idea of a true good defines itself and, in defining itself, gives rise to the conception of particular duties. This process, we saw, was really inseparable from that of which the main features have already been considered ; the extension, namely, of the range of persons between whom the good is conceived to be common, and who on this ground recognise equivalent duties to each other. Following out that extension as if it were a separate process, we found that its outcome was the intuition of the educated conscience that the true good must be good for all men, so that no one should seek to gain by another's loss, gain and loss being estimated on the same principle for each. But it had not so far appeared how the conscience is trained in the apprehension of what in particular the good is, and in the consequent imposition on itself of particular duties. This defect was to be made up by considering the gradual determination of the idea of good, which goes along with the growth of the conviction that it is good for all men alike.

We committed ourselves a little way back to the familiar opinion—more likely to find acceptance than many here advanced—that the idea of a true good first took hold of men in the form of a consideration of what was needed to keep the members of a family alive and comfortably alive. Now between a state of mind in which the idea of good is only operative in this form, and one which can at least naturally express itself in the proposition that the only true good is the good will, can there be anything in common ? Is it not idle to attempt to connect them as phases in the operation of a single spiritual principle ? It would be so, no doubt, if interest in provision for the necessities of a family really exhausted the spiritual demand from which it arises. But this is not the case. It must be remembered that provision for the wants of a family, of the kind we are contemplating, cannot have been a merely instinctive process. It cannot have been so, at least, on supposition that it was a process of which we can understand the nature from our own experience, or that it was a stage in the development of

the men that we are and know. It would not have had anything in common with the family interests by which we are
ourselves influenced, unless it rested not on instinct but on self-
consciousness—on a man's projection of himself in thought into
a future, as a subject of a possibly permanent satisfaction, to be
found in the satisfaction of the wants of the family with which
he identifies himself. Now this power of contemplating himself
as possibly coming to be that which he is not, and as so coming
to be in and through a society in which he lives a permanent
life, is in promise and potency an interest in the bettering of
mankind, in the realisation of its capabilities or the fulfilment of
its vocation, conceived as an absolutely desirable end.

Between the most primitive and limited form of the interest,
as represented by the effort to provide for the future wants of a
family, and its most highly generalised form, lie the interests of
ordinary good citizens in various elements of a social well-being.
All have a common basis in the demand for abiding self-satisfaction which, according to the theory we have sought to maintain, is yielded by the action of an eternal self-conscious principle
in and upon an animal nature. That demand however only
gradually exhibits what it has in it to require. Until life has
been so organised as to afford some regular relief from the
pressure of animal wants, an interest in what Aristotle calls
τὸ εὖ ζῆν, as distinct from τὸ ζῆν[1], cannot emerge. Yet that
primitive organisation of life through which some such relief is
afforded, being rational not instinctive, would be impossible
without the action of the same self-objectifying principle which
in a later stage exhibits itself in the pursuit of ends to which
life is a means, as distinct from the pursuit of means of living.
The higher interest is latent in the lower, nor would it be
possible to draw a line at which the mere living of the family
ceases to be the sole object and its well-being begins to be
cared for.

241. But, when a supply of the means of living has been
sufficiently secured to allow room for a consideration of the ends
of living, what are those ends taken to be? Can any such
progress be noted in men's conception of them as could justify
us in speaking of a development of the idea of duty? If the

---

[1] 'Living well,' or 'well-being,' as distinct from merely 'living.'

idea of good were simply equivalent to the idea of a maximum of pleasure, a growth of moral ideas would simply mean a progressive discovery of means to pleasure. A development of the idea of duty, in the sense of a process affecting our conception of the ends of action, there could not be. If on this hypothesis we are to speak of a moral development at all, it can only be in the sense of an increasing enlightenment as to what should be done, in order to an end of which itself the idea undergoes no modification. It is otherwise if the idea of the good is an idea of something which man should become for the sake of becoming it, or in order to fulfil his capabilities and in so doing to satisfy himself. The idea of the good, according to this view, is an idea, if the expression may be allowed, which gradually creates its own filling. It is not an idea like that of any pleasure, which a man retains from an experience that he has had and would like to have again. It is an idea to which nothing that has happened to us or that we can find in existence corresponds, but which sets us upon causing certain things to happen, upon bringing certain things into existence. Acting in us, to begin with, as a demand which is ignorant of what will satisfy itself, it only arrives at a more definite consciousness of its own nature and tendency through reflection on its own creations—on habits and institutions and modes of life which, as a demand not reflected upon, it has brought into being. Moral development then will not be merely progress in the discovery and practice of means to an end which throughout remains the same for the subject of the development. It will imply a progressive determination of the idea of the end itself, as the subject of it, through reflection on that which, under influence of the idea but without adequate reflection upon it, he has done and has become, comes to be more fully aware of what he has it in him to do and to become.

242. Of a moral development in this sense we have evidence in the result; and we can understand the principle of it; but the stages in the process by which the principle thus unfolds itself remain obscure. As has been already pointed out, such an end as provision for the maintenance of a family, if pursued not instinctively but with consciousness of the end pursued, implies in the person pursuing it a motive quite different from

desire either for an imagined pleasure or for relief from want. It implies the thought of a possibly permanent satisfaction, and an effort to attain that satisfaction in the satisfaction of others. Here is already a moral and spiritual, as distinct from an animal or merely natural, interest—an interest in an object which only thought constitutes, an interest in bringing about something that should be, as distinct from desire to feel again a pleasure already felt. But to be actuated by such an interest does not necessarily imply any reflection on its nature; and hence in men under its influence there need not be any conception of a moral as other than a material good. Food and drink, warmth and clothing, may still seem to them to be the only good things which they desire for themselves or for others.

This may probably still be the case with some wholly savage tribes; it may have once been the case with our own ancestors. If it was, of the process by which they emerged from it we know nothing, for they have already emerged from it in the earliest state of mind which has left any record of itself. All that we can say is that an interest moral and spiritual in the sense explained—however unaware of its own nature, however unable to describe itself as directed to other than material objects —must have been at work to bring about the habits and institutions, the standards of praise and blame, which we inherit, even the remotest and most elementary which our investigations can reach. We know further that *if* that interest, even in the form of interest in the mere provision for the material support of a family, were duly reflected upon, those who were influenced by it must have become aware that they had objects independent of the gratification of their animal nature; and, having become aware of this, they could not fail with more or less distinctness to conceive that permanent welfare of the family, which it was their great object to promote, as consisting, at any rate among other things, in the continuance in others of an interest like their own; in other words, as consisting in the propagation of virtue.

243. When and how and by what degrees this process of reflection may have taken place, we cannot say. It is reasonable to suppose that till a certain amount of shelter had been secured from the pressure of natural wants, it would be im-

possible. The work of making provision for the family would be too absorbing for a man to ask himself what was implied in his interest in making it, and thus to become aware of there being such a thing as a moral nature in himself and others, or of a moral value as distinct from the value of that which can be seen and touched and tasted. However strong in him the interest in the welfare of his society—which, as we have seen, is essentially a moral interest—until some relief had been won from the constant care of providing for that welfare in material forms, he would have no time to think of any intrinsic value in the persons for whom the provision was made, or in the qualities which enabled it to be made. Somehow or other, however—by what steps we know not—with all peoples that have a history the time of reflection has come, and with it the supervention upon those moral interests that are unconscious of their morality, of an interest in moral qualities as such. An interest has arisen, over and above that in keeping the members of a family or tribe alive, in rendering them persons of a certain kind; in forming in them certain qualities, not as a means to anything ulterior which the possession of these qualities might bring about, but simply for the sake of that possession; in inducing in them habits of action on account of the intrinsic value of those habits, as forms of activity in which man achieves what he has it in him to achieve, and so far satisfies himself. There has arisen, in short, a conception of good things of the soul, as having a value distinct from and independent of the good things of the body, if not as the only things truly good, to which all other goodness is merely relative.

Already in the earliest stages of the development of the human soul, of which we have any recorded expression, this distinction is virtually recognised. Such a formal classification as that which Aristotle assumes to be familiar, between τὰ ἐκτὸς ἀγαθὰ, τὰ περὶ ψυχὴν, and τὰ περὶ σῶμα[1], is, of course, only the product of what may be called reflection upon reflection. It is the achievement of men who have not only learnt to recognise and value the spiritual qualities to which material things serve as instruments or means of expression, but have formed the abstract conception of a universe of values which may be

[1] External goods, goods of the soul, and goods of the body. Eth. Nic. I. viii. 2.

exhaustively classified. But independently of such abstract conceptions, we have evidence in the earliest literature accessible
to us of the conception and appreciation of impalpable virtues
of the character and disposition, standing in no direct relation to the senses or to animal wants—courage, wisdom,
fidelity, and the like. The distinction is at least apprehended
between the sensible good things that come to a man, or
belong or attach to him as from without, and the good qualities
of the man. It may be that the latter are chiefly considered
in relation to the former, as qualities contributing to the
material welfare of a society; but, though there may be as yet
no clear notion of virtue as a pure good in itself independently
of anything extraneous that it may obtain, it is understood that
prosperity and the desert of prosperity are different things.
And the recognition of desert is in itself a recognition of a
moral or spiritual good, as distinct from one sensible or material.
It is evidence that the moral nature, implied in the interest in
a social well-being, has so far reflected on itself as to arrive at
moral conceptions.

244. Whenever and wherever, then, the interest in a social
good has come to carry with it any distinct idea of social merit
—of qualities that make the good member of a family, or good
tribesman, or good citizen—we have the beginning of that
education of the conscience of which the end is the conviction
that the only true good is to be good. This process is properly
complementary to that previously analysed, of which the end
was described as the conviction that the true good is good for
all men, and good for them all in virtue of the same nature and
capacity. The one process is complementary to the other, because the only good in the pursuit of which there can be no
competition of interests, the only good which is really common
to all who may pursue it, is that which consists in the universal
will to be good—in the settled disposition on each man's part to
make the most and best of humanity in his own person and in
the persons of others. The conviction of a community of good
for all men can never be really harmonised with our notions of
what is good, so long as anything else than self-devotion to an
ideal of mutual service is the end by reference to which those
notions are formed.

245. In fact we are very far, in our ordinary estimates of good, whether for ourselves or for others, from keeping such a standard before us, and just for that reason the conviction of the community of good for all men, while retaining its hold on us as an abstract principle, has little positive influence over our practical judgments. It is a source of counsels of perfection which we do not 'see our way' to carrying out. It makes itself felt in certain prohibitions, *e.g.* of slavery, but it has no such effect on the ordering of life as to secure for those whom we admit that it is wrong to use as chattels much real opportunity of self-development. They are left to sink or swim in the stream of unrelenting competition, in which we admit that the weaker has not a chance. So far as negative rights go—rights to be let alone—they are admitted to membership of civil society, but the good things to which the pursuits of society are in fact directed turn out to be no good things for them. Civil society may be, and is, founded on the idea of there being a common good, but that idea in relation to the less favoured members of society is in effect unrealised, and it is unrealised because the good is being sought in objects which admit of being competed for. They are of such a kind that they cannot be equally attained by all. The success of some in obtaining them is incompatible with the success of others. Until the object generally sought as good comes to be a state of mind or character of which the attainment, or approach to attainment, by each is itself a contribution to its attainment by every one else, social life must continue to be one of war—a war, indeed, in which the neutral ground is constantly being extended and which is itself constantly yielding new tendencies to peace, but in which at the same time new vistas of hostile interests, with new prospects of failure for the weaker, are as constantly opening.

CHAPTER V.

D. *The Greek and the Modern Conceptions of Virtue.*

246. OUR next business will be to consider more in detail how that gradual spiritualisation or dematerialisation (in the sense explained) of the idea of true good, through which alone it can come to answer the inward demand which is its source, exhibits itself in the accepted standards of virtue and in the duties which the candid conscience recognises. The conception of virtue is the conception of social merit as founded on a certain sort of character or habit of will. Every form of virtue arises from the effort of the individual to satisfy himself with some good conceived as true or permanent, and it is only as common to himself with a society that the individual can so conceive of a good. He must in some way identify himself with others in order to conceive himself as the subject of a good which can be opposed to such as passes with his own gratification. Thus both the practice of virtue and the current standard of virtue, which on the one hand presupposes the practice and on the other reacts upon and sustains it, have a history corresponding to the gradual development and determination of the idea of what social good consists in.

The virtue which is practised and esteemed with reference to a common well-being, constituted by such good things as, according to the distinction above noticed, would fall under the head of 'external' or 'bodily goods,' has indeed an element of identity with the virtue practised or esteemed with reference to a well-being of which the virtue itself is an integral element, but has also an important difference from it. The identity between the two kinds of virtue consists in the fact that the good to which each is relative is a *common* good and is desired as such. In both cases the virtue rests upon an interest which is effectually distinguished from any desire for pleasure, from any egoistic passion, by being directed to an object which the individual presents to himself as common to him with others and as desirable on that account. The difference lies in the degree of truth and adequacy with which the common good is conceived in one case as compared with the other.

When the end with reference to which social merit is judged of is merely some form of material well-being, the moral effort is being directed to an end of merely relative value as if it were of absolute value. That effort rests, as we have seen, on the inward demand for a true or abiding self-satisfaction, and this is not to be found in the possession of means to a succession of pleasures any more than in the succession itself, not in the possession of anything which one man or group of men can possess to the exclusion of another. A common good conceived as consisting in such possession is inadequately conceived—conceived in a manner which must ultimately lead to the self-defeat of the moral effort—and the virtue directed by the conception, though it has the root of identity, just pointed out, with a higher virtue, is so far inferior. Considered merely as ' self-devotion' it may be on a level with the highest virtue. There may be as genuine self-devotion in the act of the barbarian warrior who gives up his life that his tribe may win a piece of land from its neighbours, as in that of the missionary who dies in carrying the gospel to the heathen. But it is a falsely abstract view of virtue to take no account of the end in pursuit of which the self is devoted. The real value of the virtue rises with the more full and clear conception of the end to which it is directed, as a character not a good fortune, as a fulfilment of human capabilities from within not an accession of good things from without, as a function not a possession. The progress of mankind in respect of the standard and practice of virtue has lain in such a development of the conception of its end.

247. We cannot so write without being reminded of the famous opening of Kant's 'Foundation of the Metaphysic of Morals,'—' Nothing can be conceived in the world, or even out of it, which can be called good without qualification, but a Good

Will.' In describing the development in question, however, as a growth of the conviction that the only unconditional good is a good will, and a consequent more definite reference of virtue to this unconditional good as its end, we run a risk of misapprehension. Can it be intended, the reader may ask, that no action is morally good, or directed as it should be, unless the object of the doer is to promote goodness or to become good? Has this been the object with reference to which, as a matter of fact, the habits and dispositions ordinarily reputed virtuous have come to be so reputed? If the ultimate dictum of the enlightened conscience is to be that, just as according to St. Paul 'whatsoever is not of faith is sin,' so no action is morally good unless done for the sake of its goodness, shall we not have to make out some wholly new διαγραφὴ or 'table' of the virtues, incapable of natural adjustment to the actual usage of our terms of praise and blame? Is it not more rational to say with Hume that 'no action can be virtuous, or morally good, unless there be in human nature some motive to produce it, distinct from the sense of its morality'?[1]

The formula quoted from Kant is certainly liable to be understood in a way which challenges these objections. The good will may be taken to mean a will possessed by some abstract idea of goodness or of moral law; and, if such possession were possible at all, except perhaps during moments of special spiritual detachment from the actualities of life, it would amount to a paralysis of the will for all effectual application to great objects of human interest. It would no longer be the will of the good workman, the good father, or the good citizen. But it is not thus that we understand the good will. The principle which it is here sought to maintain is that the perfection of human character—a perfection of individuals which is also that of society, and of society which is also that of individuals—is for man the

---

[1] *Treatise on Human Nature*, Book III. Part II. § 1. The ground for the proposition in the text is thus put by Hume in the sequel: ' It is a plain fallacy to say, that a virtuous motive is requisite to render an action honest, and at the same time that a regard to the honesty is the motive of the action. We can never have a regard to the virtue of an action, unless the action be antecedently virtuous. No action can be virtuous but so far as it proceeds from a virtuous motive. A virtuous motive therefore must precede the regard to the virtue; and 'tis impossible that the virtuous motive and the regard to the virtue can be the same.'

only object of absolute or intrinsic value; that, this perfection consisting in a fulfilment of man's capabilities according to the divine idea or plan of them, we cannot know or describe in detail what it is except so far as it has been already attained; but that the supreme condition of any progress towards its attainment is the action in men, under some form or other, of an interest in its attainment as a governing interest or will; and that the same interest—not in abstraction from other interests, but as an organising influence upon and among them —must be active in every character which has any share in the perfection spoken of or makes any approach to it, since this perfection, being that of an agent who is properly an object to himself, cannot lie in any use that is made of him, but only in a use that he makes of himself.

248. We hold that in fact the estimation of virtue, the award of praise and blame, has always had reference to man himself, not to anything adventitious to man, as the object of ultimate value from which the value of any virtue was derived. In those primitive conditions of society, in which attention was so necessarily concentrated on the simple maintenance of life that there was no room for the virtues of culture and reflection to develope, we have no reason to doubt that it was a contemplation of possible persons who should exist in the family which gave the family interest its real meaning to those who were actuated by it; just as now, to the poor person whose waking hours are spent in the struggle to keep his family respectable, it is not any abstraction of the family, but the contemplation of sons and daughters, as persons living decent lives in the future, that is the moving influence. The primitive virtue that meant merely valour in the struggle for a life of which others were to share the benefit had yet its animating principle in the idea of something which the valorous man and the others, in and for themselves, were to become. As the horizon of man's possibilities expands upon the view, as new forms of social merit relative to the fulfilment of those capabilities come to be recognised, the conception of virtue becomes proportionately complex. With an Athenian in the period of the bloom of Hellas, the term which we can only render 'virtue' was apparently used for any eminent faculty

exercised in any of the regions of human achievement [1]—regions
scarcely less wide and various then than now—so that Aristotle
found it necessary to distinguish 'intellectual virtues' from those
of habit and character. But however discrepant may seem to us
to have been the kinds of excellence or ability that were alike
spoken of as the 'virtue' of men, however little they may have
been affected by any conception of moral law, of any duty owed
by man to God or his neighbour, as such, they were still dependent both for their estimation and for their practice on the
conception of intrinsic value, as lying not in anything that might
happen to a man, in his pleasure or his good fortune, but in what
he might do and might become. Virtue was a δύναμις ἐνεργετικὴ,
a faculty of beneficence [2]. The range of recognised beneficence
was wide, as the range of capabilities of which men were becoming conscious was wide. There was a 'virtue' to be exhibited
in handicraft no less than in the functions of a magistrate or
citizen-soldier or head of a family; but it was some interest in the
achievement by men of what they had it in them to do, in their
becoming the best they had it in them to become, that at once
governed the estimation of virtue in all these cases and inspired
or sustained the practice.

249. There were ages, no doubt, in which this interest,
though active enough, took little account of itself; ages in which
the question was never raised how far the forms of action which
commonly excited praise were really co-operative with each other,
or really contributory to the end which was being pursued with
little reflection on its nature. When and how the period of
reflection is reached, what are the conditions which enable some
nations to reach it while others apparently do not, we do not
know; but when it is reached, there arises a quest for some
definite and consistent conception of the main ends of human
achievement. Is there some one direction, common to all the
forms of activity esteemed as virtuous, which explains and justifies that estimation? This question, it is to be observed, is in its
effect by no means merely a speculative one. In the process of
bringing into clear and harmonious consciousness the nature of
ends previously pursued under the influence of some idea of value

---

[1] Thuc. I. xxxiii. 2; II. xl. 6 (Arnold's note); Arist. Rhet. I. ix. 2.
[2] Arist. *loc. cit.*

which could give no account of itself, the incompatibility of some of these ends with others becomes apparent, and the possibility suggests itself of so methodising life as to avoid the misdirection of activity and keep it to channels in which it may really contribute to the one end of supreme value, however that may be conceived. Hence along with the conviction of the unity of virtue, which finds so clear and strong an expression in the Greek philosophers, we find an attempt both to reform the current estimation of the several practices and dispositions counted virtuous, and to introduce a systematic order of living for individuals and communities, corresponding to the idea of the unity of the end.

The habit of derogation from the uses of 'mere philosophy,' common alike to Christian advocates and the professors of natural science, has led us too much to ignore the immense practical service which Socrates and his followers rendered to mankind. From them in effect comes the connected scheme of virtues and duties within which the educated conscience of Christendom still moves, when it is impartially reflecting on what ought to be done. Religious teachers have no doubt affected the hopes and fears which actuate us in the pursuit of virtue or rouse us from its neglect. Religious societies have both strengthened men in the performance of recognised duties, and taught them to recognise relations of duty towards those whom they might otherwise have been content to treat as beyond the pale of such duties; but the articulated scheme of what the virtues and duties are, in their difference and in their unity, remains for us now in its main outlines what the Greek philosophers left it.

250. In their Ethical teaching, however, the greatest of the Greek philosophers—those to whom Christendom owes, not indeed its highest moral inspiration, but its moral categories, its forms of practical judgment—never professed to be inventors. They did not claim to be prophets of new truth, but exponents of principles on which the good citizen, if he thought the matter out, would find that he had already been acting. They were seeking a clearer view of the end or good towards which the βίος πολιτικὸς, the citizen-life, was actually directed. And this conception of their vocation was not less true than, in its

superiority to personal self-assertion, it was noble. They were really organs through which reason, as operative in men, became more clearly aware of the work it had been doing in the creation and maintenance of free social life, and in the activities of which that life is at once the source and the result. In thus becoming aware of its work the same reason through them gave a further reality to itself in human life. The demand for an abiding satisfaction, for a true or permanent good, in action upon the wants and fears and social impulses of men, had yielded the institutions of the family and the state. These again had brought into play certain spiritual dispositions and energies, recognised as beneficent and stimulated by the effect of that recognition on the social man, but not yet guided by any clear consciousness of the end which gave them their value. In arriving at that consciousness of itself, as it did specially through the Greek philosophers, the same spiritual demand which had given rise to the old virtue yielded a virtue which was in a certain important sense new; a character which would not be satisfied without understanding the law which it obeyed, without knowing what the true good was, for which the demand had hitherto been more blindly at work.

251. We speak of the change advisedly as consisting not merely in a new theory about virtue, but in a higher order of virtue itself. Socrates and his followers are not rightly regarded as the originators of an interesting moral speculation, such, for instance, as Hume may have started as to the nature of ' moral sense,' or the evolutionists as to its hereditary development. They represent, though it might be too much to say that they introduced, a new demand, or at least a fuller expression of an old demand, of the moral nature. Now though our actual moral attainment may always be far below what our conscience requires of us, it does tend to rise in response to a heightened requirement of conscience, and will not rise without it. Such a requirement is implied in the conception of the unity of virtue, as determined by one idea of practical good which was to be the conscious spring of the perfectly virtuous life—an idea of it as consisting in some intrinsic excellence, some full realisation of the capabilities, of the thinking and willing soul. Here we have—not indeed in its source, but in

that first clear expression through which it manifests its life—
the conviction that every form of real goodness must rest on a
will to be good, which has no object but its own fulfilment.
When the same conviction came before the world, not in the
form of a philosophy but in the language of religious aspiration
—'Blessed are the pure in heart, for they shall see God'—and
when there seemed to be a personal human life which could be
contemplated as one in which it had been realised, it appealed
to a much wider range of persons than it had done in the
schools of Greece, and moved the heart with a new power. But
if those affected by it came to ask themselves what it meant
for them—in what the morality resting on purity of heart
consisted—it was mainly in forms derived, knowingly or un-
knowingly, from the Greek philosophers that the answer had
to be given.

252. The purity of the heart can only consist in the nature
of its motives or governing interests. Actions, the same outwardly, represent a heart more or less pure, according as the
motive which prompts them is more or less singly or predominantly an interest in some form or other of that which is
truly good; or—to say the same thing in a manner less liable
to be misunderstood, since motives do not admit of isolation—
according as the motive belongs to a character more or less
thoroughly governed by such an interest. This distinction of
true from seeming virtue, as dependent on the motive of each,
was brought out by Plato and Aristotle with a clearness which
was in fact final. Their account of the true good itself was
indeed but formal and provisional, as, for reasons already indicated, every such account must be; though, unless mankind has
lived its last two thousand years in vain, the formal and provisional account of the good should mean more for us than it
could mean for the Greeks. But that a conscious direction to
this good—a 'purity of heart' in this sense—was the condition
of all true virtue and constituted the essential unity between one
form of virtue and another, this they taught with all the consistency and directness which a Christian teacher could desire,
which indeed stands in strong contrast with the appeal to semi-
sensual motives that has been common, and perhaps necessary
for popular practical effect, in the Christian Church. Τοῦ καλοῦ

ἕνεκα· κοινὸν γὰρ τοῦτο ταῖς ἀρεταῖς [1], is the formula in which Aristotle sums up the teaching of himself and his master as to the basis of goodness. Like every formula, it may have come to be used as cant, but in its original significance it conveyed the great principle that a direction of a man's will to the highest possible realisation of his faculties is the common ground of every form of true virtue. This direction of the will, according to both Aristotle and Plato, was to be founded on habit; but the habit even in its earliest and least reflective stage was to be under the direction of reason, as embodied in law or acting through a personal educator, and through appropriate teaching was in due time to pass into a fully intelligent and appreciative conformity to the reason which was its source. Given this direction of the will, uniting intellectual apprehension with strongest desire, all virtue was given [2] : without it there was, in the proper sense, none, but at best only such a possibility of virtue as may be afforded by tendencies and habits, directed from without to higher ends than the subject has intelligently made his own.

253. This view of the essential principle of all virtue at once distinguishes the doctrine of Plato and Aristotle from any form of Hedonism, or of Utilitarianism so far as Hedonistic. The condition of virtuous action according to them did not lie in its production of a certain effect, but in its relation to a certain object, as rationally desired by the agent; and this was an object of which the nature, as desired, was not that which according to the Hedonist alone excites desire. It was not an imagined pleasure. But a student of these philosophers will be apt to remark that, although clearly the quality which, according to them, makes an action good is not that which makes it good according to the Utilitarian, and is relative to some other end than the pleasure which the Utilitarian deems alone either desired or desirable, it is not so clear what this other end is. And this indefiniteness, he will argue, in the conception of the

---

[1] 'Desire for what is beautiful or noble ; this is the common characteristic of all the virtues.' Arist. Eth. Nic. IV. ii. 7.

[2] Cf. Arist. Eth. Nic. VI. xiii. 6. Ἅμα τῇ φρονήσει μιᾷ οὔσῃ πᾶσαι ὑπάρξουσιν (*sc. αἱ ἀρεταί*). 'The single virtue of practical wisdom implies the presence of all the moral virtues.'

end, on conscious direction to which virtue is made to depend, must be just so far an indefiniteness in the conception of virtue itself.   An end, which is not pleasure, is to be desired for its own sake ; so far 'purity of heart' is insisted on ; but, unless we know what the end is, we are still in the dark as to the real characteristics of the heart purely devoted to it.   If from the Hedonistic point of view 'purity of heart' can have no meaning at all, can the Greek philosophers on the other hand, it may be asked, do more than assure us that there must be such a thing and that it is morally all-important, without being able to point to any real interest corresponding to this formal idea ?   Did not 'purity of heart' acquire a meaning in the Christian Church, other than it could have borne in the schools of philosophy, because the Christian revelation supplied this interest ?

Now that there are senses in which a higher moral standard is possible for the Christian citizen than was possible for the Greek of Aristotle's age, will not be disputed.   We have already dwelt on an important difference, arising out of the fact that a practical conviction of the brotherhood of all men, such as was impossible to the Greek, brings with it for us a new standard of justice—not indeed a new conception of what is due towards those who have claims of right upon us, but a new view of the range of persons who have such claims.   As we proceed we shall see how the interests of the 'pure heart' have become really more determinate, its demands upon itself fuller, in the Christian society than they were to the most enlightened and conscientious Greek.   But for the present our concern is rather to point out the greatness—in a certain sense the completeness and finality— of the advance in spiritual development which the Greek philo- sophers represent.   Once for all they conceived and expressed the conception of a free or pure morality, as resting on what we may venture to call a disinterested interest in the good ; of the several virtues as so many applications of that interest to the main relations of social life ; of the good itself not as anything external to the capacities virtuously exercised in its pursuit, but as their full realisation.   This idea was one which was to govern the growth of all the true and vital moral conviction which has descended to us.   It had indeed still to acquire fulness and determinateness with the formation of habits and institutions corresponding to it, but it was itself the source of that formation. It was not indeed ever to become such a definitely presentable rule of life as we often sigh for, but we must bear in mind that, so far as the shortcomings which we are apt to complain of in it arise from the impossibility either of envisaging or of exhaustively defining the good which it presupposes, they are inseparable from the very nature of morality, as an effort not an attainment, a progressive construction of what should be, not an enjoyment of what is, governed not by sight but by faith. They are shortcomings, in fact, to which it is only through illusions that we can claim superiority.

254. Aristotle, as we know, with all the wisdom of Plato before him, which he was well able to appropriate, could find no better definition of the true good for man than the full exercise or realisation of the soul's faculties in accordance with its proper excellence, which was an excellence of thought, speculative and practical. The pure morality then, which we credit him with having so well conceived, must have meant morality determined by interest in such a good. But what real import or filling, it will be asked, can such an interest have? Is not the conception of morality, as determined by this interest, if it is really no more than it professes to be, essentially an empty conception? To this we answer that it would have been an empty conception, if there had not already taken place such a realisation of the soul's faculties as gave a meaning, though not its full and final meaning, to the definition of the good. In fact, however, as we have already seen, the same spiritual principle which yielded the demand for an account of what was good in itself, and the conception of true goodness as determined by interest in that good, had also yielded a realisation of the soul's faculties in certain pursuits and achievements, and in a certain organisation of life. Already there were arts and sciences, already families and states, with established rules of what was necessary for their maintenance and furtherance. Thus such a definition of the good as Aristotle gives us was more than explanatory of the meaning of a name. It was rather the indication of a spiritual problem, of which some progress had been made in the solution. The realisation of the soul's faculties had not to wait to begin; the desire for, the interest in, such a good had not still to be initi-

ated. The philosopher had not to bring before men an absolutely new object of pursuit, but to bring them to consider what
gave its value to an object already pursued.

255. From that very consideration, it is true, the object took
a new character for the consciousness of the person pursuing it.
It began to be for him what it had previously been only in itself,
or in idea, or for some divine spirit working through him but
without his knowledge. The realisation of the soul's faculties in
the state, for instance, though in one sense it has already been
an object to every one who duly performs his functions as a
citizen, becomes an object in a new sense to one who is conscious
of his citizen's work as contributing in some humble way to an
end which is the bettering of the citizens, and who does it or
seeks to do it, not for incidental pleasure or reward, but for the
sake of that end. To awaken such a consciousness in men, and
thus to enable them to do old work in a spirit that made it new,
was the function of the Socratic philosophers. They had not to
create wisdom, or fortitude, or temperance, or justice. They had
not to direct the habits of action, recognised as laudable under
those names, to any other object than that in relation to which
they had always had their value; but they had to make it clear
that this object, being a perfection of the rational man, an
unfolding of his capacities in full harmonious activity, was not
one to which the virtuous practices were related as means to an
external end, but itself included their exercise. To do so was to
establish the principle of the conviction that goodness is to be
sought for its own sake and, as so sought, is itself and alone the
good; but it was not to leave the conception of goodness without definite content. On the contrary it was to determine it
further, as a conception of the modes of action hitherto counted
virtuous, with the added qualification that, in order to be truly
virtuous, they must be brought into harmony with each other
as jointly contributing to a perfection of life, and must each
have their root in a character of which the governing interest
was an interest in that perfection.

256. In the development of that reflective morality which
our own consciences inherit, both the fundamental principle and the mode of its articulation have retained the form
which they first took in the minds of the Greek philosophers.

To whatever alien speculative influences we may have been subject—and of late no doubt the influences of evolutionary Hedonism have been strongly alien—we do not get rid of the conviction that to be good in one of the many forms of goodness is for the individual the good; that, inexhaustibly various as those forms may be, each of them must be founded on a will, of which the good in one or other of these forms is the object; and that the good for man, in that universal sense in which it is beyond the reach of the individual's realisation, must yet be of a kind which is related to all forms of individual goodness as the life of a body to the various vital functions, at once resulting from them and rendering them possible. And when we come to ask ourselves what are the essential forms in which, however otherwise modified, the will for true good (which is the will to be good) must appear, our answer follows the outlines of the Greek classification of the virtues. It is the will to know what is true, to make what is beautiful; to endure pain and fear, to resist the allurements of pleasure (*i.e.* to be brave and temperate), if not, as the Greek would have said, in the service of the state, yet in the interest of some form of human society; to take for oneself, to give to others, of those things which admit of being given and taken, not what one is inclined to but what is due.

257. It was not, of course, by accident that, when reflective morality first took shape among the Greeks, it became aware of these main lines through which the good was to be pursued. As was said above, the effort after a true good had already worked in these lines and was to continue to work in them, and it is the continuity of that work as carried on by us—the actual progressive realisation of human capacities in knowledge, in art, and in social life—that has been the ground of identity between the first systematic reflection on the goodness exhibited in those lines, and all reflection on the same subject that has followed. And just as it has been the continuity in the actual pursuit of the true good that has kept those standards of virtue, which arise in reflection upon the pursuit, the same through succeeding ages, so it has been in sequence upon variations in the actual pursuit, which have taken place independently of reflection, that variations in the standards implying reflection have arisen.

On the whole the variations in the object pursued as good, though there have been periods apparently of mere loss and shrinkage, have consisted in its acquisition of greater fulness and determinateness. In like manner the differences between our standards of virtue and those recognised by the Greek philosophers arise from the greater fulness of conditions which we include in our conception of the perfecting of human life. The realisation of human capacities has, in fact, taken a far wider range with us than in the most advanced of ancient states. As actually achieved, it is a much more complete thing than it was two thousand years ago, and every progress achieved opens up a further vista of possibilities still unrealised. In consequence the attainment of true good presents itself to men under new forms. The bettering of human life, though the principle of it is the same now as in the Socratic age, has to be carried on in new ways; and the actual pursuit of true good being thus complicated, reflection on what is implied in the pursuit yields standards of virtue which, though identical in principle with those recognised by Aristotle, are far more comprehensive and wide-reaching in their demands. This will appear more clearly if we consider how Aristotle's account of fortitude and temperance would have to be modified in order to answer the requirements of the Christian conscience.

258. If a ' Christian worker' who devotes himself, unnoticed and unrewarded, at the risk of life and at the sacrifice of every pleasure but that of his work, to the service of the sick, the ignorant and the debased, were told that his ideal of virtue was in principle the same as that of the ἀνδρεῖος, ' the brave man,' described by Aristotle, and if he were induced to read the description, he would probably seem to himself to find nothing of his ideal in it. Yet the statement would be true. The principle of self-devotion for a worthy end in resistance to pain and fear is the same in both cases. But Aristotle could only conceive the self-devotion in some form in which it had actually appeared. He knew it in no higher form than as it appeared in the citizen-soldier, who faced death calmly in battle for his State. In that further realisation of the soul's capacities which has taken place in the history of Christendom, it has appeared in a far greater wealth of forms.

In Aristotle's view the βίος πρακτικὸς—the life of rational self-determined activity—was only possible for a few among the few. It presupposed active participation in a civil community. Such communities could only exist in certain select nations, and, where they existed, only a few of the people contributing to their maintenance and living under their direction were fit to share in civil functions. These alone had moral claims or capabilities. The rest were instruments of their convenience. In modern Christendom it is not merely our theories of life but the facts of life that have changed. 'Weak things of the world and things that are despised hath God called.' With the recognition of rights in human beings as such, on which we have previously dwelt (§ 201 and foll.), there comes a new realisation of human capacities, not only for the emancipated multitude, but for those whom Aristotle would have allowed to be previously sharers in the βίος πρακτικός. The problems of life become for them far more difficult indeed, but, just on account of their greater range and complication, they become of such a kind as to elicit powers previously unused.

We are apt to speak as if the life of the Greek or Roman citizen, in the full bloom of municipal civilisation, was much fuller and richer than that of the modern citizen under a régime of universal freedom and equal rights. For the many we admit the modern system may be a gain, but for the few we take it to be a corresponding loss. Yet this is surely a very superficial view. The range of faculties called into play in any work of social direction or improvement must be much wider, when the material to be dealt with consists no longer of supposed chattels but of persons asserting recognised rights, whose welfare forms an integral element in the social good which the directing citizen has to keep in view. Only if we leave long-suffering, considerateness, the charity which 'beareth all things, believeth all things, hopeth all things,' with all the art of the moral physician, out of account in our estimate of the realisation of the soul's powers, can we question the greater fulness of the realisation in the present life of Christendom, as compared with the highest life of the ancient world.

259. It is a consequence of this change in the realities of social life that the conception of moral heroism has greatly

widened—widened not in the sense of more attenuated abstraction but of more concrete filling—so that it requires some patience of reflection to trace the identity of principle through all its forms. The Quaker philanthropist can scarcely recognise a brother in the citizen-soldier, or the soldier a brother in the philanthropist. It is indeed in one sense a new type of virtue that has come into being with the recognition of the divine image, of spiritual functions and possibilities, in all forms of weak and suffering humanity. The secondary motives, which assist self-devotion in war or in the performance of functions of recognised utility before the eyes of fellow-citizens, are absent when neither from the recipients of the service done nor from any spectators of it can any such praise be forthcoming as might confirm in the agent the consciousness of doing nobly. Yet every day and all about us pain is being endured and fear resisted in rendering such service. The hopelessly sick are being tended; the foolish and ignorant are being treated as rational persons; human beings whom a Greek would have looked on as chattels, or as a social encumbrance to be got rid of, are having pains bestowed on them which only a faith in unapparent possibilities of their nature could justify. In the whole view of life which this work implies, in the objects which inspire it, as those whom they influence would describe them, in the qualities of temper and behaviour which it calls into play, it seems to present a strong contrast to that which the Greek philosopher would have looked for from his ideally brave man. It implies a view of life in which the maintenance of any form of political society scarcely holds a place; in which lives that would be contemptible and valueless, if estimated with reference to the purposes of the state, are invested with a value of their own in virtue of capabilities for some society not seen as yet. Its object, whether described simply as the service of the suffering and ignoble, or as the service of God manifested in suffering and ignobility, is one which the philosophic Greek would scarcely have recognised as a form of the καλόν. The qualities of self-adjustment, of sympathy with inferiors, of tolerance for the weak and foolish, which are exercised in it, are very different from the pride of self-sufficing strength which with Aristotle was inseparable from heroic endurance.

260. Yet beneath these differences lies a substantial identity. The willingness to endure even unto complete self-renunciation, even to the point of forsaking all possibility of pleasure, or, as Aristotle puts it, of passing the point beyond which there seems no longer to be either good or evil[1]; the willingness to do this in the service of the highest public cause which the agent can conceive—whether the cause of the state or the cause of the kingdom of Christ—because it is part of the noble life, of the 'more excellent way,' so to do; this is common to the ideal of fortitude equally as conceived by Aristotle and as it has been pursued in the Christian Church. If we cannot ignore, on the one hand, the limitations in Aristotle's view of the conditions under which his ideal could be realised[2]—conditions which would have rendered it wholly unrealisable in the chief occupations of Christian charity—on the other hand it is only fair to notice how free it is from debasement by any notion of a compensation which the brave man is to find in pleasures of another world for present endurance. The fact, indeed, that Christian preachers have not been ashamed to dwell upon such compensation as a motive to self-renunciation, ought not to be taken to imply that the heroism of charity exhibited in the Christian Church has really been vitiated by pleasure-seeking motives. Religious rhetoric is apt to be far in arrear of the motives which it seeks to express, and to strengthen by expression. 'Unspeakable joys' has been but a phrase to convey the yearning of the soul for that perfection which is indescribable except so far as attained. Joys that are unspeakable are unimaginable, and the desire which really has such joys for its object is quite different from a desire excited by an imagination of pleasure.

In short, we are not entitled to say that the Aristotelian ideal of fortitude has been either more or less *pure* than that which has been operative in Christendom; but there is no doubt that the latter has become far more comprehensive, and it has become so in correspondence with an enhanced fulness in our conception of the ends of living. Faculties, dispositions, occupations, persons, of which a Greek citizen would have taken

[1] Eth. Nic. III. vi. 6; ix. 4, 5.
[2] Ib. III. vi. 7, and foll.

no account, or taken account only to despise, are now recognised as having their place in the realisation of the powers of
the human soul, in the due evolution of the spiritual from the
animal man. It is in consequence of this recognition that the
will to endure even unto death for a worthy end has come to
find worthy ends where the Greek saw nothing but ugliness and
meanness, and to express itself in obscure labours of love as well
as in the splendid heroism at which a world might wonder.

261. Alongside of 'fortitude' in the reflective morality of
Greece was placed 'temperance,' as that habit of will which
stands to the allurements of pleasure in the same relation as
'fortitude' to pain and fear. If we wish to compare the
standard of self-denial in respect of pleasures, which the conscience of Christendom in its highest forms has come to
prescribe, with the standard recognised by the Greek philosophers, it is to the account which the latter give of σωφροσύνη
that we must turn. The first impression of any one who came
to this account, having his mind charged with the highest
lessons of Christian self-denial, would be of its great poverty—
a poverty more striking, as it will probably appear, in the case
of 'temperance' than in the case of 'courage.' He finds 'temperance' restricted by Aristotle to control over the mere animal
appetites; or, more exactly, to control over desire for the pleasures incidental to the satisfaction of those appetites. The
particular usage of a name, indeed, is of slight importance. If
Aristotle had reasons for limiting σωφροσύνη to a certain meaning, and made up elsewhere for what is lacking in his account of
the virtue described under that name, no fault could be found.
But σωφροσύνη and ἀνδρεία between them have to do duty for
the whole of what we understand by self-denial. However little
we may have cleared up the moral demand which we express to
ourselves as the duty of self-denial, we cannot get rid of the
conviction that it is a demand at any rate of much wider significance in regard to indulgence in pleasures than that which
Aristotle describes as actuating the 'temperate' man, nor do we
find the deficiency made good in any account which he gives of
other forms of virtue.

262. If we look a little closer, however, we shall notice the
identity between the habit of will of which 'temperance,' as

conceived by Aristotle, is an expression, and that on which every renunciation of pleasures, even the widest and completest, if it is to be of moral value, must rest. No 'ascetic' moralist, so far as known, has supposed such renunciation to be possible, or, if possible, to be of value merely on its own account. It becomes possible only through the prevalence of desire for some object other than the enjoyment of pleasure. It is this desire alone, not the renunciation of pleasures except as an incident or sign of such desire, that can be of moral value; just as, on the other side, it is not desires for pleasure that are in themselves morally evil, but the occupation of the will by them—the direction of a man's self to this or that pleasure as his good—to the exclusion of those higher interests which cannot possess the man along with them, and which can only themselves be accounted desires for pleasure through the fallacy, previously dwelt upon, of supposing a desire to have for its object the pleasure of its own satisfaction. Perhaps, under a true conviction of the essential immorality of the pleasure-seeking character, certain moralists may have sometimes spoken as if there were intrinsic evil in desires for pleasure apart from their competition with other desires, and again some intrinsic good in the renunciation of pleasures apart from interest in the higher object for the sake of which they are renounced; but this has only been through unguardedness in expression. With Kant, for instance, whatever his rigour in identifying moral badness with selfishness and this with pleasure-seeking, it was never doubtful that the goodness of the good will lay in the prevalence of interest in a worthy object, badness in such a failure of the worthy interest as enables the desire for pleasure to prevail. His error consisted in his too abstract view of the interest on which he held that true goodness must depend, and which he seems to reduce to interest in the fulfilment of moral law according to the most abstract possible conception of it. Of this no more can be said here. For the present our concern is to point out the agreement between the motive which the reflective Greek regarded as the basis of the virtue manifested in control over certain desires for pleasure, and the source of that self-denial which our own consciences require of us.

263. It must be admitted that, when Aristotle treats most

methodically of σωφροσύνη, he does little to specify the particular form of that interest in the καλὸν which he considered to be the basis of the virtue. He seems more intent on specifying the psychological nature of the pleasures, over desire for which the term σωφροσύνη, as strictly applied, implies due control. But to a Greek who was told that the virtue of temperance was a mastery over certain desires, exercised τοῦ καλοῦ ἕνεκα, there would be no practical doubt what the motive was to be, what was to be the object in which a prevailing interest was to enable him to exercise this mastery. In his view it could only be reverence for the divine order of the state, such a desire to fulfil his proper function in the community as might keep under the body and control the insolence of overweening lust. The régime of equal law, the free combination of mutually respecting citizens in the enactment of a common good, was the 'beautiful thing' of which the attraction might, through a fitting education, become so strong as to neutralise every lust that tended to disqualify a man for the effectual rendering of service to his state, or tempted him to deal wantonly with his neighbour. It was this character of the motive or interest on which it was understood to rest, that gave to σωφροσύνη an importance in the eyes of the Greek moralist which, if we looked simply to the very limited range of pleasures—pleasures of the merely animal nature—in regard to which Aristotle supposes the 'temperate man' to exercise self-restraint, would scarcely be intelligible. Not the mere sobriety of the appetites, but the foundation of that sobriety in a truly civil spirit, in the highest kind of rational loyalty, gave the virtue its value. And hence it was—because it was associated with such a basis—that σωφροσύνη came to be regarded as carrying with it a group of virtues with which control of the animal impulses might seem to us to have little to do. As it is put by a writer of the Aristotelian school, παρέπεται τῇ σωφροσύνῃ εὐταξία, κοσμιότης, αἰδὼς, εὐλάβεια[1].

264. When we compare this conception of 'temperance' with the demand for self-denial which the enlightened Christian conscience makes on itself, we are struck alike with the unity of principle and the difference of range or comprehension in the

[1] De virt. et vit. 1250 b. 12.   'With temperance go orderliness, regularity, the feeling of shame, discreetness.'

application of the principle. The idea of the subjection in us of a lower or animal man to a higher appeals to us as it did to the Greek. We too think of the higher man as the law-abiding, law-reverencing man. An abstinence or temperance dictated merely by fear of some painful result of indulgence we do not count a virtue. The true virtue of self-denial we deem to be only reached when it is through interest in the performance of some public duty or other, in the fulfilment of some function or other which falls to us as members of a community, that we come practically to forbid ourselves the pursuit of certain plea-sures, or to reach a state in which the prohibition is unnecessary because the inclination to them is neutralised by higher inter-ests. On the other hand, we present to ourselves the objects of moral loyalty which we should be ashamed to forsake for our pleasures, in a far greater variety of forms than did the Greek, and it is a much larger self-denial which loyalty to these objects demands of us. It is no longer the state alone that repre-sents to us the 'melior natura' before whose claims our animal inclinations sink abashed. Other forms of association put restraints and make demands on us which the Greek knew not. An indulgence, which a man would otherwise allow himself, he forgoes in consideration of claims on the part of wife or children, of men as such or women as such, of fellow-Christians or fellow-workmen, which could not have been made intelligible in the ancient world. It is easy, no doubt, in making such com-parisons to be misled by names. We must not conclude, be-cause to a Greek all duty was summed up in what he owed to his πόλις, that he recognised no duties but such as we should naturally call duties to the state. The term 'state' is generally used by us with a restricted meaning which prevents it from being a proper equivalent for πόλις. But, apart from any question of names, it is certain that the requirements founded on ideas of common good, which in our consciences we recognise as calling for the surrender of our inclinations to pleasure, are more far-reaching and penetrate life more deeply than did such re-quirements in the ancient world, and that in consequence a more complete self-denial is demanded of us.

265. Even if we confine our view to 'temperance' as Aristotle conceived it, *i. e.* as a virtue exhibited only in dealing with the

pleasure ἣ γίνεται ἐν σιτίοις καὶ ἐν ποτοῖς καὶ τοῖς ἀφροδισίοις λεγο-
μένοις[1]—waiving the consideration of other forms of self-denial
—we shall find that the highest Greek standard, as represented
by the philosophers, falls short of that which a conscience, duly
responsive to the highest claims, would now require of us.   The
principles from which it was derived, so far as they were
practically available and tenable, seem to have been twofold.
One was that all indulgence should be avoided which unfitted
a man for the discharge of his duties in peace or war ; the other,
that such a check should be kept on the lusts of the flesh as
might prevent them from issuing in what a Greek knew as ὕβρις
—a kind of self-assertion, and aggression upon the rights of
others in respect of person and property, for which we have not
an equivalent name, but which was looked upon as the antithesis
of the civil spirit.

We speak of these as the only practically available and tenable
principles that were recognised for the regulation of ' temperance.'   There is indeed another notion which is perhaps the
one most constantly and distinctly alleged by the philosophers
as a reason for being ' temperate.'   This is the notion that the
kind of pleasure with which temperance has to do is in some way
unworthy of man, because one of which the other animals are
susceptible.   It is not very likely, however, to have represented
a conviction of the general conscience, nor does it appear how
any practical standard of temperance could have been derived
from such a notion.   The conviction that there is a lower and a
higher—that there are objects less and more worthy of man—is
no doubt one of the most fundamental of our moral nature ; or
rather it is one of the simplest expressions for the demand
which is that nature.   This conviction must carry with it a
disapproval of indulgences which interfere with the pursuit of
the more worthy objects—such, e.g., as disqualify for efficient
citizenship—but it is a false philosophical gloss on this disapproval to treat it as grounded on the fact that these indulgences are of a kind which are not distinctive of man, but are
shared by the ' lower animals.'   Just in that respect in which
they are matter of disapproval, in so far, that is to say, as they

[1] 'The pleasures of eating, drinking, and sexual intercourse.'   Eth. Nic. III.
x. 10.

interfere with the fulfilment of some higher human function, they are not indulgences of a kind in which the animals are found to partake. The animals do not, so far as we know, gratify their appetites in a way that interferes with the attainment of any object that they are capable of presenting to themselves[1]. If the gratification of appetites, therefore, called for our disapproval on the ground of its being common to us with them, it should be disapproved in itself and altogether, not on account of any obstruction which it offers to other and higher ends (for in the case of the animals there is no such obstruction), but on account of some intrinsic quality belonging to it. The conclusion would be that we should aim at an entire suppression of animal gratification, which would entail the extinction of the human race. We should have no measure of excess in such gratification—for one degree of it is no more 'brutal' than another—but a reason, practically inoperative, for rejecting it altogether.

On the other hand, a little consideration would show that the attraction of pleasures, 'of which the other animals partake,' has really little to do with the practices condemned by the philosophers and by our conscience as 'intemperate.' It is probably never the pleasure of drinking, strictly so called, that leads a man to get drunk. The mere pleasures of eating, apart from the gratification of vanity and undefinable social enjoyments, have but a slight share in promoting the 'excesses of the table.' The temptations to sexual immorality would be much less formidable than they are, if the attractive pleasure consisted merely in the satisfaction of sexual appetite. Thus, without including in our conception of intemperance any other vices than Aristotle had in view when applying the name, we must still maintain (1) that these vices are not in fact mainly due to the attraction of pleasures of which other animals, so far as we know, are susceptible, and (2) that, if they were, this would afford no intelligible ground for treating such practices as vices, which might not equally be urged as a reason for an abstinence incompatible with the continuance of our race.

266. Returning, then, to those really tenable principles of

---

[1] So Aristotle remarks that temperance and its opposite are not predicable of brutes. Eth. Nic. VII. vi. 6.

temperance, περὶ σιτίων καὶ ποτῶν καὶ τῶν ἀφροδισίων, specified above, with which the Greek philosophers supply us, do we find that, as applied by the philosophers, they afford a standard of temperance adequate either to the recognised ideal, or to the highest practice, of the modern world ? The answer must be that on the most important point, περὶ τῶν ἀφροδισίων, they do not. The limit which, on the strength of them, the philosophers would have drawn between lawful and lawless love, would not have been that which our consciences would call on us to observe. It would not have excluded all indulgence of the sexual passion except as between man and woman in monogamous married life. The failure, however, was not in the intrinsic nature of the principles recognised by the philosophers, for there is no true foundation for the strictest sexual morality other than that social duty which they asserted. The failure arose from the structure of existing society, which determined their application of their principles. As we have more than once pointed out, while there is one sense in which moral ideas must precede practice, there is another in which they follow and depend upon it. The moral judgment at its best in any age or country—*i. e.* in those persons who are as purely interested in the perfection of mankind and as keenly alive to the conditions of that perfection as is then possible—is still limited in many ways by the degree of progress actually made towards the attainment of that perfection. It was thus the actual condition of women, the actual existence of slavery, the fact that as yet there had been no realisation, even the most elementary, of the idea of there being a single human family with equal rights throughout—it was this that rendered the Greek philosophers incapable of such an idea of chastity as any unbrutalised English citizen, whatever his practice, if he were honest with himself would acknowledge. To outrage the person of a fellow-citizen, to violate the sanctity of his family rights, was for the Greek as much as for us a blamable intemperance. In the eye of the philosophers it meant a subjection of the higher, or civil, or law-reverencing, man to that lower man in us which knows not law; and they were quite aware that not merely the abstinence from such acts, but the conquest of the lusts which lead to them by a higher interest, was the condition of true virtue. To the

spirit of our Lord's re-enactment of the seventh commandment
in the sermon on the Mount, to the substitution of the rule of
the pure heart for that of mere outward observance, they were
no strangers. What they had still to learn was not that the
duty of chastity, like any other, was to be fulfilled from the
heart and with a pure will, but the full extent of that duty.

267. And this they failed to appreciate because the practical
realisation of the possibilities of mankind in society had not
then reached a stage in which the proper and equal sacredness
of all women, as self-determining and self-respecting persons,
could be understood. Society was not in a state in which the
principle that humanity in the person of every one is to be
treated always as an end, never merely as a means, could be
apprehended in its full universality; and it is this principle
alone, however it may be stated, which affords a rational ground
for the obligation to chastity as we understand it. The society
of modern Christendom, it is needless to say, is far enough from
acting upon it, but in its conscience it recognises the principle
as it was not recognised in the ancient world. The legal in-
vestment of every one with personal rights makes it impossible
for one whose mind is open to the claims of others to ignore the
wrong of treating a woman as the servant of his pleasures at the
cost of her own degradation. Though the wrong is still habitually done, it is done under a rebuke of conscience of which a
Greek of Aristotle's time, with most women about him in
slavery, and without even the capacity (to judge from the
writings of the philosophers) for an ideal of society in which
this should be otherwise, could not have been sensible. The
sensibility could only arise in sequence upon that change in the
actual structure of society through which the human person, as
such, without distinction of sex, became the subject of rights.
That change was itself, indeed, as has been previously pointed
out in this treatise, the embodiment of a demand which forms
the basis of our moral nature—the demand on the part of the
individual for a good which shall be at once his own and the
good of others. But this demand needed to take effect in laws
and institutions which give every one rights against every one,
before the general conscience could prescribe such a rule of
chastity, founded on the sacredness of the persons of women,

as we acknowledge. And just as it is through an actual change
in the structure of society that our ideal in this matter has come
to be more exacting than that of the Greek philosophers, so it
is only through a further social change that we can expect a
more general conformity to the ideal to be arrived at. Only
as the negative equality before the law, which is already established in Christendom, comes to be supplemented by a more
positive equality of conditions and a more real possibility for
women to make their own career in life, will the rule of
chastity, which our consciences acknowledge, become generally
enforced in practice through the more universal refusal of women
to be parties to its violation.

268. In this matter of chastity, then, there is a serious inferiority of the highest Greek ideal to the highest ideal of
Christendom, but it is important to notice where the inferiority
lies. We have no right to disparage the Greek ideal on the
ground of any inferiority in the motive which the Greek philosophers would have considered the true basis of this, as of every,
form of temperance. There can be no higher motive to it than
that civil spirit, in the fullest and truest sense, on which they
conceived it to rest. But we may fairly disparage their ideal in
respect of the kind of life which the realisation of this motive
was considered to require. The sexual temperance which they
demanded, they demanded on the true ground, but not in full
enough measure. In that respect their ideal had certain inevitable shortcomings—inevitable, because no ideal can go
more than a certain distance, in the detail of conduct which it
requires, beyond the conditions of the given age.

And this comparative poverty of the Greek ideal becomes
more apparent when we reflect that, as has been pointed out
above, the only form in which the virtuous renunciation of
pleasures presents itself to the philosophers is that of temperance περὶ σιτίων καὶ ποτῶν καὶ τῶν ἀφροδισίων. Temperance, thus
limited, has in their systems to do duty for the whole of what
we should call self-denial. Under no other title than that of
the σώφρων is the self-denying man described by the philosophers. And it may fairly be argued that, in respect of the
governing principle of the will, the σώφρων, as they conceive
him, does not differ from the highest type of self-denial known

to Christian society. But the range of action which they looked for from him, as the expression of this principle, was very limited in comparison with the forms of self-denial with which we are practically familiar; and it was so limited because great part of the objects, by which in the society of modern Christendom self-denial is in fact elicited, in Greek society was not there to elicit it.

269. If we consider, in regard to any person whom we credit with a high degree of habitual self-denial, what are the pleasures which we suppose him to deny himself, it will appear that those, in relation to which alone Aristotle supposed 'temperance' to be exercised, form a very small part of them. In determining the province of 'temperance' Aristotle, following the psychology of Plato [1], expressly excludes two kinds of pleasure: (1) 'pleasures of the soul,' as instances of which he gives the pleasures of gratified ambition and love of learning; (2) such 'pleasures of the body' as are received through the senses of hearing, sight, or smell. It is not such pleasures as these that the temperate man forgoes. Now, as has been already said, this exclusion would be a very small matter if it merely concerned the usage of the name 'temperance.' The important point is that the ancient philosophers seemingly give no place to that type of virtuous character in which devotion to some form of true good leads to a renunciation of such pleasures as those included in the above classes. Yet it is just such pleasures as these of which the renunciation is involved in that self-denial which in our impartial and unsophisticated judgment we most admire—that which in our consciences we set before ourselves as the highest ideal. It would seem no great thing to us that in the service of mankind one should confine himself to necessary food and drink, and should observe the strictest limitations of Christian morality in the matter of sexual indulgence; and it is such indulgence alone, we must remember, not the enjoyments of family life, that would fall within the class of pleasures in which, according to the Greek philosophers, temperance is exercised. We have examples about us of much severer sacrifice. There are men, we know, who with the keenest sensibility to such pleasures as those of 'gratified ambition and love of learning,' yet deliberately forgo

[1] Eth. Nic. III. x. 2, 3; Plato, Philebus, 51.

them; who shut themselves out from an abundance of æsthetic enjoyments which would be open to them, as well as from those of family life; and who do this in order to meet the claims which the work of realising the possibilities of the human soul in society—a work a hundred-fold more complex as it presents itself to us than as it presented itself to Aristotle—seems to make upon them. Such sacrifices are made now, as they were not made in the days of the Greek philosophers, and in that sense a higher type of living is known among us; not because there are men now more ready to fulfil recognised duties than there were then, but because with the altered structure of society men have become alive to claims to which, with the most open eye and heart, they could not be alive then.

270. To an ancient Greek a society composed of a small group of freemen, having recognised claims upon each other and using a much larger body of men with no such recognised claims as instruments in their service, seemed the only possible society. In such an order of things those calls could not be heard which evoke the sacrifices constantly witnessed in the nobler lives of Christendom, sacrifices which would be quite other than they are, if they did not involve the renunciation of those 'pleasures of the soul' and 'unmixed pleasures,' as they were reckoned in the Platonic psychology, which it did not occur to the philosophers that there could be any occasion in the exercise of the highest virtue to forgo. The calls for such sacrifice arise from that enfranchisement of all men which, though in itself but negative [1] in its nature, carries with it for the responsive conscience a claim on the part of all men to such positive help from all men as is needed to make their freedom real. Where the Greek saw a supply of possibly serviceable labour, having no end or function but to be made really serviceable to the privileged few, the Christian citizen sees a multitude of persons, who in their actual present condition may have no advantage over the slaves of an ancient state, but who in un-developed possibility, and in the claims which arise out of that possibility, are all that he himself is. Seeing this, he finds a necessity laid upon him. It is no time to enjoy the pleasures of

---

[1] Negative, because amounting merely to the denial to any one of a right to use others as his instruments or property.

eye and ear, of search for knowledge, of friendly intercourse, of applauded speech or writing, while the mass of men whom we call our brethren, and whom we declare to be meant with us for eternal destinies, are left without the chance, which only the help of others can gain for them, of making themselves in act what in possibility we believe them to be. Interest in the problem of social deliverance, in one or other of the innumerable forms in which it presents itself to us, but in which it could not present itself under such a state of society as that contemplated by the Greek, forbids a surrender to enjoyments which are not incidental to that work of deliverance, whatever the value which they, or the activities to which they belong, might otherwise have.

271. There thus arise those forms of self-denial which did not enter within the horizon of the ancient moralists, and in which, if anywhere, we are entitled to trace the ethical progress of our own age. Questions whether we are better than our fathers are idle enough, but it is not so idle—indeed it is a necessity of our moral nature—to endeavour, through whatever darkness and discouragement, to trace 'some increasing purpose through the ages,' of which the gradual fulfilment elicits a fuller exertion of the moral capabilities of individuals. Such a purpose we may not unreasonably hold to be directed to the development of society into a state in which all human beings shall be treated as, actually or in promise, persons—as agents of whom each is an end equally to himself and to others. The idea of a society of free and law-abiding persons, each his own master yet each his brother's keeper, was first definitely formed among the Greeks, and its formation was the condition of all subsequent progress in the direction described; but with them, as has been often enough remarked, it was limited in its application to select groups of men surrounded by populations of aliens and slaves. In its universality, as capable of application to the whole human race, an attempt has first been made to act upon it in modern Christendom. With every advance towards its universal application comes a complication of the necessity, under which the conscientious man feels himself placed, of sacrificing personal pleasure in satisfaction of the claims of human brotherhood. On the one side the freedom of every one to shift for himself—a freedom

to a great extent really secured—on the other, the responsibility of every one for every one, acknowledged by the awakened conscience; these together form a moral situation in which the good citizen has no leisure to think of developing in due proportion his own faculties of enjoyment. The will to be good is not purer or stronger in him than it must have been in any Greek who came near to the philosopher's ideal, but the recognition of new social claims compels its exercise in a new and larger self-denial.

272. An objection, indeed, is pretty sure to be made to the whole principle upon which we reckon such self-denial as is here contemplated a higher virtue than entered into the Greek ideal. 'Are we entitled,' it may be asked, 'to make a virtue out of the renunciation of anything intrinsically good, and are not the pleasures which we suppose to be renounced by the self-denying servant of mankind intrinsically good? We may indeed, upon the principles of "universalistic Hedonism," admire the conduct of such a person, as suited to the times of present distress. The general capacity for pleasure being so limited by the faulty conditions of society, we may admit it to be the best thing in the long run that there should be men ready to forgo the most really desirable pleasures for the sake of rendering others ultimately more capable of them. The public spirit, the altruistic enthusiasm, of such men is of great value, as a means to the end which consists in the maximum of pleasure obtainable by human (or perhaps all sentient) beings, taken together; and for that reason it is rightly counted virtuous. But it is not more virtuous in proportion to the amount and desirability of the pleasure sacrificed by those under its influence; nor is it any inferiority of the Greek ideal of virtue to that here put forward as characteristic of modern Christendom, that it did not imply any sacrifice of "pure" pleasures, i.e. of such pleasures as carry no pain in their train. It would be another matter if it could be alleged against the Greek ideal that it did not imply public spirit; but this is not pretended. The fault alleged is merely that public spirit, as the Greek conceived it, involved a less costly sacrifice on the part of the individual than do those forms of altruistic enthusiasm to which we are now taught to aspire.

But if the allegation is true, so much the better for the Greek ideal. If the conditions of modern life are such that the completest fulfilment of social duty does often call for the renunciation of much pure pleasure on the part of the individual, this may put difficulties in the way of an optimistic view of human history, but it cannot make the ideal of virtue as more painful higher than the ideal of it as more pleasant. The only pleasures of which a limitation is properly included in the conception of the highest virtue, are those of which the enjoyment beyond a certain point either interferes with the individual's health, and thus with his capacity for other enjoyment, or involves some aggression upon the rights of others, and thus lessens the possibility of enjoyment on their part. It was just these pleasures of which a due limitation was taken to be implied in that constituent of the virtuous character which the ancients call temperance. It was not their defect, but their merit, that they did not conceive the highest virtue to involve properly a rejection of normal pleasures of any other kind.'

273. From the point of view of Hedonistic Utilitarianism such an objection is inevitable and unanswerable. It is well to allow full weight to it, were it only for the sake of forcing ourselves to consider whether the actual admiration of our consciences, which we can hardly doubt is most fully commanded by the life of the largest self-denial, is in accord with such Utilitarianism. The answer which must be given to it, according to the theory previously set forth in this treatise, can easily be anticipated. It is not because it involves the renunciation of so much pleasure that we deem the life of larger self-denial, which the Christian conscience calls for, a higher life than was conceived of by the Greek philosophers; but because it implies a fuller realisation of the capacities of the human soul. It is not the renunciation, as such, but the spiritual state which it represents, that constitutes the value of the life spent in self-devoted service to mankind; and it represents, we must remember, not merely a certain system of desires and interests, on the part of the persons who make the renunciation, but a certain social development in consequence of which those desires and interests are called into play.

As we have seen, it is the emancipation of the multitude, and the social situations arising out of it, that call forth the energies of the self-denying life as we now witness it. When we compare the realisation of human capabilities implied in that life with the realisation of them implied in the highest type of citizenship contemplated by the ancient philosophers, we must take account not merely of some typical representative of Christian charity on the one side, and of the ideal Greek citizen on the other, each in his separate individuality, but of the moral and spiritual conditions of other men, to which these several types of character are relative. For it is human society as a whole that we must look upon as the organism in which the capacities of the human soul are unfolded. Human society indeed is essentially a society of self-determined persons. There can be no progress of society which is not a development of capacities on the part of persons composing it, considered as ends in themselves. But in estimating the worth of any type of virtue, as implying or tending to bring about a realisation of man's spiritual capacities, we must not confine our view to some particular group of men exhibiting the virtue. We must consider also those relations between them and other men, by which the particular type of virtue is determined. We must enquire whether any apparent splendour in that virtue is due to a degradation of human society outside the particular group, or whether, on the contrary, the virtue of the few takes its character from their assistance in the struggle upward of the many.

274. Now, when we compare the life of service to mankind, involving so much sacrifice of pure pleasure, which is lived by the men whom in our consciences we think best, and which they reproach themselves for not making one of more complete self-denial, with the life of free activity in bodily and intellectual exercises, in friendly converse, in civil debate, in the enjoyment of beautiful sights and sounds, which we commonly ascribe to the Greeks, and which their philosophers certainly set before them as an ideal, we might be apt, on the first view, to think that, even though measured not merely by the quantity of pleasure incidental to it but by the fulness of the realisation of human capabilities implied in it, the latter kind of life was the higher of the two. Man for man, the Greek who at all came up to the ideal of the philosophers might seem to be

intrinsically a nobler being—one of more fully developed powers —than the self-mortifying Christian, upon whom the sense of duty to a suffering world weighs too heavily to allow of his giving free play to enjoyable activities, of which he would otherwise be capable. But such a comparison of man with man, in abstraction from the rest of mankind, is not the way to ascertain the real value of the virtue of either in its relation to the possibilities of the human soul. If (as would seem to be the case) the free play of spiritual activity in the life of the Greek citizen, with its consequent bright enjoyableness, depended partly on the seclusion of the Greek communities from the mass of mankind, partly on their keeping in slavery so much of the mass as was in necessary contact with them; if the seclusion and the slavery were incidental to a state of things in which the powers of the human soul, considered as the soul of universal human society, were still in their nonage; then, whatever value we may ascribe to the highest type of Greek life, as suggesting an ideal of ' liberty, equality and fraternity,' afterwards to be realised on a wider scale, we cannot regard its exemption from the impeding cares, which the intercommunication of mankind on terms of recognised equality brings with it, as constituting a real superiority.

275. Though it is not to be pretended, then, that the life of the self-denying Christian citizen is morally the better on account of the burden of care and the manifold limitations, which the acknowledged claims of human brotherhood impose on it, it must be maintained on the other hand that the life of the Greek citizen was not morally the better for the freedom from such burden and limitations which he enjoyed; because this freedom was correlative to an undeveloped condition on the part of the rest of mankind. The title of the modern or Christian type of virtue to a positive superiority is not to be found in the burden, unknown to the Greeks, which it bears, but in that which the presence of this burden implies; the new spiritual activity, namely, on the part of the multitude, now conscious of their claims and set free to assert them practically, and the wider range of interests in human good which in response to those claims are awakened in the hearts of the virtuous. That this enhanced activity, these enlarged interests, should involve

for the virtuous much voluntary curtailment of the innocent pleasures which, but for such disturbing claims and interests, would be open to them, is, as regards the attainment of moral good, a matter of indifference. For the curtailment in itself they are neither the better nor the worse; but in the actual order of things, so far as appears, it is a necessary incident of progress towards that full development of what man has it in him to be, that satisfaction of the demand of the human soul for its own perfection, which is for us the good; and for that reason it is the part of the highest virtue to welcome it.

276. We may speculate, indeed, on the possibility of a state of things in which the most entire devotion to the service of mankind shall be compatible with the widest experience of pleasure on the part of the devoted person. We may argue that the perfection of the human soul implies its unimpeded activity, which is pleasure; and that therefore, though in certain stages of the progress towards such perfection there may be for certain persons an abridgment of pleasure, its attainment must be pure enjoyment. Or again we may comfort ourselves with surmising that, though to this or that individual citizen his self-devotedness may mean a large sacrifice of pleasure, yet to others, who have the benefit of his devotion without sharing in it, there is in consequence such an accession of pleasure that the result is a large addition to the sum of enjoyment on the whole. All speculation of this kind, however, provokes much counter-speculation. By what right, it may be asked, do we assume that the more developed or perfect state of the human soul is one in which a larger aggregate of pleasure is enjoyed than in the less perfect state? There is pleasure, no doubt, in all satisfaction of desire, there is pleasure in all unimpeded activity. So far therefore as a man has desired the perfection of the human soul, there will be pleasure to him in the consciousness of contributing to that perfection, but not necessarily a greater amount than he has to forgo in order to the contribution. So far as the perfection is attained, again, there will be less impediment to the activity directed to its attainment, and therefore more pleasure in the exercise of the activity. But it would seem at least possible that, according to the plan of the world, the perfection of the human soul may involve the constant presence of

a lower nature, consisting in certain tendencies, never indeed dominant, but in conflict with which alone the higher energies of man can emerge. In that case it may very well be that the desire for human perfection, which is the desire for true good, though gradually coming to taste more of the particular pleasure incidental to its satisfaction and to the free play of the action which it moves, as it more fully attains its end, may never be destined to carry men, even in its fullest satisfaction, into a state of pure enjoyment, or into one in which they will be exempt from large demands for the rejection of possible pleasure.

277. At any rate, whatever may be the future in store for it, we should scarcely question the loss of otherwise possible pleasure which the dominance of such a desire entails on those who are possessed by it, were it not for the confusion which leads us to assume that the satisfaction of a strongest desire must always convey to the subject of it a pleasure greater than any which he would otherwise have enjoyed. It is true, of course, that for any one in whom the desire for goodness or the love of mankind, or however else we may describe the impulse to a life of sacrifice, is really the dominant motive, it would be impossible really to enjoy those pleasures, however innocent, which interfere with his giving effect to the desire and which he rejects for that reason. But it does not follow from this that he would not have had more enjoyment on the whole if the dominant desire had been different, and if he had been free to take his fill of the innocent pleasures from which it has withheld him. According to all appearances and any fair interpretation of them, he certainly would have had more.

Whether the loss of pleasure in the life of such a man through the disturbing action of his altruistic enthusiasm is or is not compensated by a consequent accession of pleasure to others, who have the benefit of the results of his enthusiasm without sharing in the disturbance or self-denial, may be more open to doubt. If our nature were such that the saint or reformer could set himself to confer happiness on others without seeking to communicate a character like his own; if we could take advantage of the services of such an one without admiring and aspiring in some measure to become like him, the gain to the general sum of pleasures as the result of his activity would be less doubtful than it is.   But if, as we must hold to be the case, the character and activity of the altruistic enthusiast, under ordinary conditions of temperament and circumstance, is not preponderatingly pleasure-giving to the enthusiast himself ; and if his effect upon others is always in greater or less degree to disturb their acquiescence in the life of ordinary enjoyment; then the case is at least not clear in favour of the assumption that the effect of such character and activity is an addition to the aggregate of human pleasure, one man taken with another. He must be much stiffened in hedonistic theory who could maintain that the life which ended on the cross was one of more enjoyment than that which would have been open to the Cruci- fied but for the purpose which led to this end ; and the Crucified himself foresaw that he came not to send peace on earth but a sword.   It would be unwarrantable indeed to found a general ethical argument on this example, but it may be fairly used to bring home to our minds that question as to the sufficiency of the hedonistic justification of the self-denying life, which is all that it would be to our purpose here to suggest.

278. These considerations have arisen from our noticing that the practical attitude towards pleasures, which in our con- sciences we regard as belonging to the highest virtue, is one of larger renunciation than was contemplated by the Greek philo- sophers as entering into the ideal of virtue.   In this respect we claim a superiority for the modern or Christian ideal, inde- pendently of all attempts to show that conduct in accordance with it is more productive of pleasure in the long run or to mankind on the whole.   The success of such attempts we hold to be at least very questionable.   It is not by their aid that we seek to show the more self-denying (or pleasure-renouncing) type of virtue to be the higher ; nor, on the other hand, is this view founded on any impression that a virtue is more of a virtue for being painful.   We give the advantage to the Christian type because it implies, directly on the part of those by whom it is exhibited, a wider range of interest and activity in the work of perfecting mankind, and indirectly, on the part of the multitude by whose claims it is elicited, a liberation of their powers unknown to the ancient world.

279. This conclusion, it will be remembered, has been arrived at in the process of comparing those manifestations of the good will which the Greek philosophers presented to themselves, under the names ἀνδρεία and σωφροσύνη, as specially related to the endurance of pain and the rejection of certain pleasures for worthy objects, with the self-denying disposition which our consciences acknowledge as the best. In the root of the matter the Greek conception of these virtues is thoroughly sound. They are considered genuine only when resting on a pure and good will, which is a will to be good—a will directed not to anything external, or anything in respect of which it is passive, but to its own perfection, to the attainment of what is noblest in human character and action. In this respect that which we may call, after its first clear enunciators, the Platonic or Aristotelian conception of virtue, as has been said above, is final. It marks the great transition, whenever and however achieved, in the development of the idea of true good from the state of mind in which it is conceived as a well-being more or less independent of what a man is in himself, to that in which it is conceived as a well-being constituted by character and action. Its defects, as compared with the standard which we now acknowledge, arose from the actual shortcoming in the then achievement of the human soul—the soul of human society—as compared with that of which we are ourselves partakers.

As has been previously pointed out, an explicit or reflective ideal[1] of the true good, or of virtue as a habit of will directed to it, can only follow upon a practical pursuit of the good, arising indeed out of the same spiritual demand which is the source of the ideal, but not yet consciously regulated by any theoretical form of it. In this pursuit have arisen institutions and arrangements of life, social requirements and expectations, conventional awards of praise and blame. It is in reflection upon these—in the effort to extract some common meaning from them, to reject what is temporary and accidental in them, while retaining what is essential—that there is formed such an explicit ideal of the good and of virtue as we find in the Greek philosophers. Any one who really conformed to their ideal of virtue would, no doubt, have lived a better life than any one was actually living,

[1] *I. e.* an ideal which the persons affected by it have reflected on.

because he would have been pursuing, sustainedly and upon a principle of which he was aware, a line of conduct which in fact the best men were only pursuing with frequent lapses through defect either of will or judgment. But in their determinate conception or filling up of the ideal, and in their consequent conception of the sort of behaviour in which the virtuous will was to be exhibited, they were necessarily limited by the actual state of human society. 'Human brotherhood' had no meaning for them. They had no adequate notion of the claims in response to which the good will should be exercised. In respect of the institutions and arrangements of life, of the social requirements, etc., just spoken of, a great range of new experience has come into being for us which did not exist for them. The soul of human society has realised its capacities in new ways. We know that it can achieve, because it has done so, much of which the Greek philosophers did not dream.

280. Hence has resulted a change in the ideal of what its full realisation would be, and consequently a change in the conception of what is required from the individual as a contribution to that realisation. In particular the idea has been formed of the possible inclusion of all men in one society of equals, and much has been actually done towards its realisation. For those citizens of Christendom on whom the idea of Christendom has taken hold, such a society does actually exist. For them—according to their conscientious conviction, if not according to their practice—mankind is a society of which the members owe reciprocal services to each other, simply as man to man. And the idea of this social unity has been so far realised that the modern state, unlike the ancient, secures equality before the law to all persons living within the territory over which its jurisdiction extends, and in theory at least treats aliens as no less possessed of rights. Thus when we come to interpret that formal definition of the good, as a realisation of the powers of the human soul or the perfecting of man, which is true for us as for Aristotle, into that detail in which alone it can afford guidance for the actions of individuals, the particular injunctions which we derive from it are in many ways different from any that Aristotle could have thought of. For us as for him the good for the individual is to be good, and to be good is to contribute in some way disinterestedly,

or for the sake of doing it, to the perfecting of man. But when we ask ourselves how we should thus contribute, or what are the particular forms of virtuous life to which we should aspire, our answer is determined by the consciousness of claims upon us on the part of other men which, as we now see, must be satisfied in order to any perfecting of the human soul, but which were not, and in the then state of society could not be, recognised by the Greek philosophers. It is the consciousness of such claims that makes the real difference between what our consciences require of us, or our standards of virtue, and the requirements or standards which Greek Ethics represent.

281. It must be borne in mind, however, that the social development, which has given the idea of human brotherhood a hold on our consciences such as it could not have for the Greeks, would itself have been impossible but for the action of that idea of the good and of goodness which first found formal expression in the Greek philosophers. It implies interest in an object which is common to all men in the proper sense,—in the sense, namely, that there can be no competition for its attainment between man and man; and the only interest that satisfies this condition is the interest, under some form or other, in the perfecting of man or the realisation of the powers of the human soul. It is not to be pretended, indeed, that this in its purity, or apart from other interests, has been the only influence at work in maintaining and extending social union. It is obvious, for instance, that trade has played an important part in bringing and keeping men together; and trade is the offspring of other interests than that just described. The force of conquest, again, such as that which led to the establishment for some centuries of the ‘Pax Romana’ round the basin of the Mediterranean, has done much to break down estranging demarcations between different groups of men; and conquest has generally originated in selfish passions. But neither trade nor conquest by themselves would have helped to widen the comprehension of political union, to extend the range within which reciprocal claims are recognised of man on man, and ultimately to familiarise men with the idea of human brotherhood. For this there must have been another interest at work, applying the immediate results of trade and conquest to other ends than those which the trader

and conqueror had in view; the interest in being good and doing good. Apart from this, other interests might tend to combine certain men for certain purposes and for a time, but because directed to objects which each desires for himself alone and not for another—objects which cannot really be attained in common—they divide in spirit, even when they combine temporarily in outward effect; and, sooner or later, the spiritual division must make its outward sign.

282. It is sometimes supposed, indeed, that desires of which the object on each man's part is his own pleasure, may gradually produce a universal harmony and adjustment of claims, as it comes to be discovered that the means by which each may get most pleasure for himself are also the means which serve to yield most pleasure to every one else. The acceptance of this view probably arises from a combination of two notions; one, the notion that in the long run, or on the whole, the greatest amount of pleasure results to each individual from that order of life and society which yields most pleasure in the long run to every other individual; the other, the notion that a man's desire for pleasure is or may become a desire for pleasure on the whole, as distinct from any particular pleasure. Putting these two notions together, we conclude that men, having no other motive than desire for pleasure, may, after sufficient experience, be led by their several desires each to act in a way productive of most pleasure to all the rest.

But while the first of these notions is fairly arguable, the second is certainly false. To be actuated by a desire for pleasure is to be actuated by a desire for some specific pleasure to be enjoyed by oneself. No two or more persons whose desires were only of this kind could really desire anything in common. Under the given institutions of society one man's desire for pleasure may, no doubt, lead to a course of action which will incidentally produce pleasure to another; as in trade, when A's desire for the pleasure to be got by the possession of some article leads him to give B a price for it, which enables B in turn to obtain some pleasure that he desires. But even in this case it is clear not only that the desires of A and B, as desires for pleasures, are not directed to a common object, but that, if left to their natural course, they would lead to conflict. A desires the pleasure which he obtains by buying the article of B, but (*qua* desiring pleasure) he does not desire, he has an aversion to, the loss of means to other pleasures involved in paying a price for it. He only pays the price, and so adjusts his desire for pleasure to B's, because under the given social order he can obtain the article in no other way. The desires, in short, of different men, so far as directed each to some pleasure, are in themselves tendencies to conflict between man and man. In many cases, through the action of society, there has come to be some established means of compromise between them, such as that of buying and selling; but the cases in which no such settled means of compromise is available, and in which there-fore A cannot gratify his particular desire for pleasure without depriving B of the chance of gratifying his, occur constantly enough to show us what is the natural tendency of a desire for pleasure, if left to itself [1].

283. If we are enquiring, then, for an interest adequate to account for the existence of an ever-widening social union, in

---

[1] Kant (Werke, ed. Rosenkranz, viii. p. 138) illustrates the fallacy, as he con-siders it, of supposing that a moral harmony can result from the desire on the part of each man for his own greatest pleasure, by the story of the pledge given by King Francis to the Emperor Charles, 'was mein Bruder Karl haben will (Mailand), das will ich auch haben.' It will naturally be retorted on Kant that the illustration is inapt, because, while Charles and Francis could not each pos-sess the duchy of Milan, the pleasures desired by men of well-regulated minds are such that each can gratify his desire without interfering with the gratification of the other. On reflection, however, it will appear that this possibility of adjust-ing the desires for pleasure of different men (as in buying and selling) depends on the presence of controlling agencies which are themselves not the product of desires for pleasures; and that on the estranging tendency of these desires, if left to themselves, Kant is substantially right. There are, no doubt, social pleasures, pleasures which are like all others in that each man who desires them desires them for himself alone, but which can only be enjoyed in company, and which therefore bring men together. But though desires for such pleasures might lead men to associate temporarily for the purpose of their gratification, the association would itself tend to bring them into collision with other men associated for a like purpose, and would be liable to perpetual disruption, as desires for pleasures of a different kind arose in the persons so associated. There are also pleasures, such as the enjoyment of the common air and sunshine, of which the sources cannot be appropriated, and for which therefore, under the simplest conditions of life, the desire as entertained by different men cannot tend to conflict. Under any other conditions, however, the opportunity for enjoying such pleasures, though not the sources of them, would become matter of competition, and thereupon the desire even for them would become a tendency to conflict.

which the claims of all are acknowledged by the loyal citizen as the measure of what he may claim for himself, it is not in the desire for pleasure that we can find it, or in those 'particular passions,' such as ambition, which are wrongly supposed to have pleasure for their object, but which resemble the desire for pleasure in being directed to some object private in each case to the person under the influence of the passion. Given a social authority strong enough to insist on respect for general convenience in the individual's pursuit of his ends, and minded to do so, then desire for pleasure, aversion from pain, and the various egoistic passions, may adjust themselves to its requirements and even be enlisted in its service; but they cannot be the source of such an authority. It can have its origin only in an interest of which the object is a common good; a good in the effort after which there can be no competition between man and man; of which the pursuit by any individual is an equal service to others and to himself. Such a good may be pursued in many different forms by persons quite unconscious of any community in their pursuits ; by the craftsman or writer, set upon making his work as good as he can without reference to his own glorification ; by the father devoted to the education of his family, or the citizen devoted to the service of his state. No one probably can present to himself the manner of its pursuit, as it must have been pursued in order to the formation of the most primitive tribal or civil society. If we would find an expression applicable to it in all its forms, 'the realisation of the capacities of the human soul,' or 'the perfecting of man,' seems best suited for the purpose. To most men, indeed, engaged in the pursuit of any common good, this expression might convey no meaning. Nevertheless it is as part of, or as contributing to, such a realisation, that the object of their pursuit has its attraction for them; and it is for the same reason that it has the characteristic described, of being an object for which there can be no competition between man and man, and of which the pursuit is of general service.

284. Of such a good there had, of course, been pursuit ages before the Greek philosophers began to reflect on it and seek to define it. A proof of this was the very existence of the communities in which the philosophers lived, and of which they

themselves only professed to explain the true idea. But it is one thing for men to be actuated by an inward demand for—to make spiritual effort after—a good which in its intrinsic nature is universal or common to all men; another thing for them to conceive it in its universality. It was because it helped men to such a conception of the good in its universality that the teaching of the philosophers was of so much practical importance in the social history of man. The Greek citizen who loyally served his state, or sought to know the truth for its own sake, was striving for a good not private to himself but in its own nature universal; yet he had no notion of there being any identity in the ends of living, for himself on the one side, and for slaves and barbarians on the other. The philosophers themselves—such was the practical limitation of their view by the conditions of life around them—would not have told him that there was. But when they told him that the object of his life should be duly to fulfil his function as a man, or to contribute to a good consisting in a realisation of the soul's faculties, they were directing him to an object which in fact was common to him with all men, without possibility of competition for it, without distinction of Greek or barbarian, bond or free. Their teaching was thus, in its own nature, of a kind to yield a social result which they did not themselves contemplate, and which tended to make good the practical shortcomings of their teaching itself.

285. It would not be to the purpose here to enter on the complicated and probably unanswerable question of the share which different personal influences may have had in gaining acceptance for the idea of human brotherhood, and in giving it some practical effect in the organisation of society. We have no disposition to hold a brief for the Greek philosophers against the founders of the Christian Church, or for the latter against the former. All that it is sought to maintain is this; that the society of which we are consciously members— a society founded on the self-subordination of each individual to the rational claims of others, and potentially all-inclusive— could not have come into existence except (1) through the action in men of a desire of which (unlike the desire for pleasure) the object is in its own nature common to all; and (2) through the formation in men's minds of a conception of what this object is,

sufficiently full and clear to prevent its being regarded as an object for any one set of men to the exclusion of another. It was among the followers of Socrates, so far as we know, that such a conception was for the first time formed and expressed— for the first time, at any rate, in the history of the traceable antecedents of modern Christendom. Inevitable prejudice, arising from the condition of society about them, prevented them from apprehending the social corollaries of their own conception. But the conception of the perfecting of man as the good for all, of a habit of will directed to that work in some of its forms as the good for each, had been definitely formed in certain minds, and only needed opportunity to bear its natural fruit. When through the establishment of the 'Pax Romana' round the basin of the Mediterranean, or otherwise, the external conditions had been fulfilled for the initiation of a society aiming at universality; when a person had appeared charging himself with the work of establishing a kingdom of God among men, announcing purity of heart as the sole condition of membership of that kingdom, and able to inspire his followers with a belief in the perpetuity of his spiritual presence and work among them; then the time came for the value of the philosophers' work to appear.

They had provided men with a definite and, in principle, true conception of what it is to be good—a conception involving no conditions but such as it belongs to man as man, without distinction of race or caste or intellectual gifts, to fulfil. When the old barriers of nation and caste were being broken down; when a new society, all-embracing in idea and aspiration, was forming itself on the basis of the common vocation 'Be ye perfect as your Father in Heaven is perfect,' there was need of conceptions, at once definite and free from national or ceremonial limitations, as to the modes of virtuous living in which that vocation was to be fulfilled. Without them the universal society must have remained an idea and aspiration, for there would have been no intellectual medium through which its members could communicate and co-operate with each other in furtherance of the universal object. It was in consequence of Greek philosophy, or rather of that general reflection upon morality which Greek philosophy represented, that such conceptions were forth-

coming. By their means men could arrive at a common understanding of the goodness which, as citizens of the kingdom of
God, it was to be their common object to promote in themselves
and others. The reciprocal claim of all upon all to be helped
in the effort after a perfect life could thus be rendered into a
language intelligible to all who had assimilated the moral culture
of the Graeco-Roman world. For them conscious membership
of a society founded on the acknowledgement of this claim
became a definite possibility. And as the possibility was realised,
as conscious membership of such a society became an accomplished spiritual fact, men became aware of manifold relations,
unthought of by the philosophers, in which the virtues of
courage, temperance and justice were to be exercised, and from
the recognition of which it resulted that, while the principle of
those virtues remained as the philosophers had conceived it, the
range of action understood to be implied in being thus virtuous
became (as we have seen) so much wider.

286. It will be well here to recall the main points to which
our enquiry in its later stages has been directed. Our theory
has been that the development of morality is founded on the
action in man of an idea of true or absolute good, consisting in
the full realisation of the capabilities of the human soul. This
idea, however, according to our view, acts in man, to begin
with, only as a demand unconscious of the full nature of its
object. The demand is indeed from the outset quite different
from a desire for pleasure. It is at its lowest a demand for
some well-being which shall be common to the individual desiring it with others; and only as such does it yield those
institutions of the family, the tribe, and the state, which further
determine the morality of the individual. The formation of
more adequate conceptions of the end to which the demand is
directed we have traced to two influences, separable for purposes
of abstract thought but not in fact: one, the natural development,
under favouring conditions, of the institutions, just mentioned,
to which the demand gives rise; the other, reflection alike upon
these institutions and upon those well-reputed habits of action
which have been formed in their maintenance and as their effect.
Under these influences there has arisen, through a process of

which we have endeavoured to trace the outline, on the one hand an ever-widening conception of the range of persons between whom the common good is common, on the other a conception of the nature of the common good itself, consistent with its being the object of a universal society co-extensive with mankind. The good has come to be conceived with increasing clearness, not as anything which one man or set of men can gain or enjoy to the exclusion of others, but as a spiritual activity in which all may partake, and in which all must partake, if it is to amount to a full realisation of the faculties of the human soul. And the progress of thought in individuals, by which the conception of the good has been thus freed from material limitations, has gone along with a progress in social unification which has made it possible for men practically to conceive a claim of all upon all for freedom and support in the pursuit of a common end. Thus the ideal of virtue which our consciences acknowledge has come to be the devotion of character and life, in whatever channel the idiosyncrasy and circumstances of the individual may determine, to a perfecting of man, which is itself conceived not as an external end to be attained by goodness, but as consisting in such a life of self-devoted activity on the part of all persons. From the difficulty of presenting to ourselves in any positive form what a society, perfected in this sense, would be, we may take refuge in describing the object of the devotion, which our consciences demand, as the greatest happiness of the greatest number; and until we puzzle ourselves with analysis, such an account may be sufficient for practical purposes. But our theory becomes false to the real demand of conscience, if it interprets this happiness except as including and dependent upon the unimpeded exercise by the greatest number of a will, the same in principle with that which conscience calls upon the individual to aim at in himself.

287. No sooner, however, has such a statement been made in regard to the end of moral effort than one becomes aware how liable it is to be understood in an abstract sense, wholly inadequate to the meaning which it is intended to convey. It seems to reduce the life of thoroughly realised spiritual capacity, in which we must suppose all that is now inchoate in the way of art and knowledge, no less than of moral efforts, to have reached

completion, to a level with that effort as we know it under those conditions of impeded activity which alone (as it might seem) give a meaning to such phrases as 'self-sacrifice' or a 'devoted will.' The student of Aristotle will naturally recall his saying, ἀσχολούμεθα ἵνα σχολάζωμεν, καὶ πολεμοῦμεν ἵν᾽ εἰρήνην ἄγωμεν[1], and will object to us that, while professing to follow in principle Aristotle's conception of virtue as directed to the attainment of a good consisting in a realisation of the soul's powers, we are forgetting Aristotle's pronounced judgment that the highest form of this realisation, and with it complete 'happiness,' was to be reached not in the exercise of the 'practical virtues' with their attendant pains and unrest, but in the life of pure contemplation, which, whatever difficulty there may be in forming any positive conception of it, was certainly understood as excluding self-denial and all the qualities which we naturally take to be characteristic of moral goodness. Even those who may be disposed to think that Aristotle's language about the blessedness of the contemplative life expresses little more than a philosopher's conceit; that, if applied to the pursuit of science and philosophy as we in fact painfully pursue them, it is quite untrue; and that, in any attempt to translate it into an account of some fruition of the Godhead higher than we can yet experience, we pass at once into a region of unreality—even such persons may be ready to accept his view in its negative application. They may think that he makes out his case unanswerably against the supposition that moral goodness in any intelligible sense can be carried on into, or be a determining element in, the life in which ultimate good is actually attained.

288. In meeting this objection it must be once more admitted that our view of what the life would be, in which ultimate good was actually attained, can never be an adequate view. It consists of the idea that such a life must be possible, filled up as regards particulars, in some inadequate measure, by reflection on the habits and activities, on the modes of life and character, which through influence of that idea have been brought into being. If the idea, as it actuates us, carried with it a full consciousness of what its final realisation would be, the distinction

[1] *I.e.* 'We give up leisure in order to enjoy it, and we make war for the sake of having peace.' Eth. Nic. X. vii. 6.

between idea and realisation would be at an end. But while for this reason it is impossible for us to say what the perfecting of man, of which the idea actuates the moral life, in its actual attainment might be, we can discern certain conditions which, if it is to satisfy the idea, it must fulfil. It must be a perfecting of *man*—not of any human faculty in abstraction, or of any imaginary individuals in that detachment from social relations in which they would not be men at all. We are therefore justified in holding that it could not be attained in a life of mere scientific and artistic activity, any more than in one of 'practical' exertion from which those activities were absent; in holding further that the life in which it is attained must be a social life, in which all men freely and consciously co-operate, since otherwise the possibilities of their nature, as agents who are ends to themselves, could not be realised in it; and, as a corollary of this, that it must be a life determined by one harmonious will —a will of all which is the will of each—such as we have previously called, in treating it as the condition of individual virtue, a devoted will; *i.e.* a will having for its object the perfection which it alone can maintain.

When we speak of the formation of such a will in all men as itself constituting that true end of moral effort, relation to which gives the virtues their value, we understand it, not as determined merely by an abstract idea of law, but as implying (what it must in fact imply) a whole world of beneficent social activities, which it shall sustain and co-ordinate. These activities, as they may become in a more perfect state of mankind, we cannot present to ourselves; but they would not be the activities of a more perfect mankind, unless they were the expression of a will which pursues them for their own sake, or as its own fulfilment. Such a will therefore we may rightly take to be *in principle* that perfect life, unknown to us except in its principle, which is the end of morality; a like will being the condition of those virtues, known to us not in principle merely but in some imperfect exercise, which form the means to that end.

289. This explanation made, we return to our statement that 'the ideal of virtue which our consciences acknowledge has come to be the devotion of character and life to a perfecting of man,

which is itself conceived as consisting in a life of self-devoted activity on the part of all persons.' This statement naturally suggests two further lines of objection and enquiry. If we are to accept it as a true account of the ideal of virtue, what is to be said, it may be asked, of those activities, those developed faculties, in the pursuit of knowledge and in the practice of art, which we undoubtedly value and admire, and which the ancient philosophers for that reason rightly reckoned virtues, but which would not commonly be thought to have anything to do with such devotion of character and life to a perfecting of man as is here made out to be at once the essence and the end of virtue, either in the way of implying it on the part of the man of science and the artist, or as tending to promote it in others? That they tend to general pleasure may perhaps be admitted, but can it be seriously held that they contribute to a true good consisting in self-devoted activity on the part of all persons? Must we not either be content to accept the account of true good as consisting in that general pleasure to which the practice of the moral virtues and the pursuit of science and art may, at least with much plausibility, be alike considered means; or, if we will not accept this account of the end of morality, must we not admit that the value of the moral virtues on the one side, and that of intellectual excellence, scientific or artistic, on the other, cannot be deemed relative to one common good?

290. To any one who has accepted the reasons given for rejecting the notion that pleasure is the true good, and who at the same time recognises the necessity of conceiving some ultimate unity of good, to which all true values are relative, these questions present a serious difficulty. It shall be dealt with in the sequel, and is noticed here in order to record the writer's admission that it cannot be passed over[1]. But for the present,

---

[1] [The question is not discussed in the *Prolegomena to Ethics*, and from a mark at this point in the Author's manuscript it is almost certain that he had abandoned the idea of dealing with it in the present volume. It has however been thought best to print the section in its entirety. The reader will probably gather from Book III a general idea of the way in which the difficulty would have been met, especially if he remembers that the end has been throughout defined as the realisation of the possibilities of human nature, and that devotion to such objects as the well-being of a family, the sanitation of a town, or the composition of a book, has been described as an unconscious pursuit of this end. In other words, the pursuit

considering the readiness with which most people acquiesce in the distinction of moral from other excellence, as if it were relative to an end of its own with which science and art, as such, have nothing to do, it may be advisable to give precedence to another order of objections with which our doctrine is likely to be challenged.

Of what avail, it will be asked, is the theory of the good and of goodness here stated for the settlement of any of the questions which a moralist is expected to help us to settle? We want some available criterion of right and wrong in action. We want a theory of Duty which, as applied to the circumstances of life, can be construed into particular duties, so that we may be able to judge how far our own actions and lives (to say nothing of those of others) are what they should be, and may have some general guide to the line of conduct we should adopt in circumstances where use and wont will either not guide us at all, or will lead us astray. But the theory advanced above, construed in the natural way, would seem too severe to admit of practical use, for it would offer nothing but unrealisable counsels of perfection; while, construed in another way, it would seem to allow of our treating any and every action as having its measure of good. If it is meant that, in order to be morally good—in order to satisfy a duly exacting conscience—an action must have for its motive a desire consciously directed to human perfection, we shall have a standard of goodness which might indeed serve the purpose, so far as we acknowledged it, of keeping us in perpetual self-abasement; but, if we were not to act till we acted from such a motive, should we ever act at all? If, on the other hand, our theory of the good practically means no more than that the morality of actions represents the operation in human society of an impulse after self-realisation on the part of some impersonal spirit of mankind, it will yield no

of such objects for their own sakes is considered to have a latent reference to the whole of which they are parts, a reference which would become conscious if the whole and the parts were ever opposed to each other; and this point of view would no doubt have been worked out with regard to the pursuit of art and science as ends in themselves (cf. § 370 sub fin.). The question becomes more complicated when the person who devotes himself to art or science is supposed to have formed a philosophical conception of the ultimate end; and on this question the concluding pages of the volume should be consulted.]

criterion of the good and bad in action; for we must hold every distinctively human action, good and bad alike, to be characterised by the results of such operation. Even if our theory be correct in regard to the spiritual impulse, other than desire for pleasure, implied in the formation of morality and the susceptibility to moral ideals, is it not after all by a calculation of pleasure-giving consequences that we can alone decide whether an action which has been done should or should not have been done, or which of the courses of action open to us under any given complication of circumstances should or should not be adopted?

These questions will be considered in our next Book.

BOOK IV.

THE APPLICATION OF MORAL PHILOSOPHY TO THE GUIDANCE OF CONDUCT.

CHAPTER I.

THE PRACTICAL VALUE OF THE MORAL IDEAL.

291. IN considering whether our theory of the good and of goodness can be of use in helping us to decide what ought to be done and whether we are doing it, it is important to bear in mind the two senses—the fuller and the more restricted—in which the question, What ought to be done? may be asked. It may either mean—and this is the narrower sense in which the question may be asked—What ought an action to be as determined in its nature by its effects? or it may be asked with the fuller meaning, What ought the action to be with reference to the state of mind and character which it represents? in which case the simple τί δεῖ πράττειν; becomes equivalent to πῶς ἔχων πράττει ὁ τὸ δέον πράττων; The former is the sense in which the question is asked, when it is not one of a self-examining conscience, but of perplexity between different directions in which duty seems to call. The latter is the sense in which a man asks it when he is comparing his practice with his ideal. We reckon the latter sense the fuller, because a man cannot properly decide whether, in respect of character and motives, he is acting as he ought, without considering the effects of the course of action which he is pursuing, as compared with the effects of other courses of action which it is open to him to pursue [1]; while he can compare the value of one set of effects with another without considering the nature of the motives which

---

[1] [This statement should be taken in connection with § 304 and foll.]

might prompt him to the adoption of the several courses of
action leading to the several effects. Thus, whereas the question in the latter sense includes the question as asked in the
former sense, the question can be dealt with in the former sense
without raising it in the latter.

292. It is clear, however, that in whichever of these distinguishable senses we ask the question, What ought to be done ?
the answer to it must be regulated by one and the same conception of the good. If we hold, according to the explanation
previously given, that the one unconditional good is the good
will, this must be the end by reference to which we estimate the
effects of an action. The circumstances in which the question is
raised, whether such or such an action ought to be done, may be
of a kind, as we shall see presently, which prevent any reference
to the character of an agent, and shut us up in our moral judgment of the act to a consideration of its effects; but the effects
which we look to, according to our theory, must still be effects
bearing on that perfection of human character which we take to
be the good. In like manner the consistent Utilitarian will
answer the question of 'ought or ought not' in both the distinguished senses upon one and the same principle. He decides
what ought to be done under any given circumstances by considering what will be the effects, in the way of producing
pleasure or pain, of the several courses of action possible under
the circumstances; and for the same reasons upon which he
decides what the action, as measured by its effects, should be, he
will hold that it should be done—will be of more value, according
to the same standard, if done—in a state of mind which itself
involves pleasure; cheerfully and 'disinterestedly,' not under any
kind of constraint. But it will only be indirectly, according to
him, that the question of the motive—of the ultimate object which
the man sets before himself in doing the act—will come into
account. The act will not depend for its goodness or moral
value, for being such an act as ought to be done, upon this motive
or object. For this it depends simply, according to the Utilitarian view, upon its pleasure-giving effects. The question
whether the motive from which the act proceeds is good or bad,
a motive which a man ought or ought not to have, is a separate
question, and one to which the answer depends on that given to

the question whether the actions to which such a motive ordinarily incites are or are not actions which, on the ground of their pleasure-giving effects, ought to be done. The motives which we ought to have, the dispositions which we ought to cultivate (if indeed the term 'ought,' according to the Utilitarian view, can be applied in this connection at all), will be so because they lead to actions productive of preponderating pleasure [1].

293. Upon the view of the moral end or good adopted in this treatise, the question of motive and the question of effects hold quite a different relative position to that which they hold in the Utilitarian system. If the good is a perfection of mankind, of which the vital bond must be a will on the part of all men, having some mode of that perfection for its object, it will only be in relation to a state of will, either as expressing it or as tending to promote it, or as doing both, that an action can have moral value at all. The actions which *ought* to be done, in the fullest sense of the word, are actions expressive of a good will, in the sense that they represent a character of which the dominant interest is in conduct contributory to the perfection of mankind, in doing that which so contributes for the sake of doing it. We cannot say with *complete* truth of any action which has been done, that it has been what it ought to have been, unless it represents such a character, or of any action contemplated as possible, that it will be what it ought to be, except on supposition that it will fulfil the same condition.

But it is clear that even among past actions it is only of his own, if of them, that a man has really the means of judging whether they represent such a character. Of prospective actions for which we are not personally and immediately responsible, we

---

[1] Cf. Mill's Utilitarianism, p. 26, note. 'The morality of the action depends entirely upon the intention—that is, upon what the agent *wills to do* ' (as distinct from the end which he seeks in doing it). ' But the motive, that is, the feeling which makes him will so to do, when it makes no difference in the act, makes none in the morality: though it makes a great difference in our moral estimation of the agent, especially if it indicates a good or a bad habitual *disposition*—a bent of character from which useful or from which hurtful actions are likely to arise.' 'Useful' of course here means pleasure-giving. 'When it makes no difference in the act.' means, when it makes no difference in the act *as measured by its outward effects.* That the motive should make no difference to an act, in its true or full nature, we should pronounce, according to the view stated in the text, to be an impossibility.

could never say that they are such as ought to be done, if we considered them to depend for being so on the disposition of the
agent; since we cannot foresee what the disposition with which
any agent will do them will be. When we say that restraints
ought to be put upon the liquor-traffic, or that a mistress ought
to look carefully after her servants, or that our neighbour ought
to give his children a better education, we are not making any
reference in thought to any motive or disposition from which we
suppose that the obligatory act will proceed. In such cases, as
in all where we apply the predicates 'ought' and 'ought not'
otherwise than in reflection upon our own acts, or in some interpretation of the acts of others founded on an ascription to them
of motives which we think their acts evidence, we are not contemplating the acts in their full nature. The full nature, for
instance, of a father's act in providing for the education of his
children depends on the character or state of will which it
represents; and what this is in any particular case no one can
tell. But the action has a nature, though not its whole nature,
in respect of its effect upon the children, and through them
upon others; and we can abstract this nature from its nature
in relation to the will of the father, without error resulting
in our judgment as to the former, just as we can judge correctly
of the mechanical relations of a muscular effort without taking
account of the organic processes on which the effort really
depends.

It is an abstraction of this kind that we have to make in all
cases where we judge, without reference to ourselves, that a
certain sort of action, not yet done, is one that ought to be done;
and it might be well if we could make up our minds that we are
not warranted in going further when we judge the actions of
others. Histories, no doubt, would be much shortened, and
would be found much duller, if speculations about the motives
(as distinct from the *intentions*) of the chief historical agents were
omitted; nor shall we soon cease to criticise the actions of contemporaries on the strength of inferences from act to motive.
But in all this we are on very uncertain ground. It is clearly
quite right in judging either of historical or contemporary
actions to take account, so far as possible, of all the circumstances—to appreciate the bearings of any act as presented to

those who were or are concerned in doing it, to consider what the effects of it, as probably contemplated by them, were or are. But this is a different thing from trying to ascertain the state of character on the part of the agents which the actions represent, and in ignorance of which the full moral nature of the acts is not known. It is wiser not to make guesses where we can do no more than guess, and to confine ourselves, *where no question of self-condemnation or self-approval is involved,* to measuring the value of actions by their effects without reference to the character of the agents ; as we must do (subject to a reservation to be stated below) where the question is whether an action, not yet done, ought to be done or not.

294. After this statement we shall naturally be called on to explain in what cases and in what way, according to our theory, a man should endeavour, when it is an action which he has him-self done, or thinks of doing, that is in question, to consider it in what we have called its full moral nature, *i. e.* with reference not merely to effects which it has had or is likely to have, but to the state of mind on the part of the agent which it expresses or would express. Before doing so, however, let us make sure that the reader is under no misapprehension as to the points at issue with the Utilitarians, with whom we agree in holding that ordinary judgments upon the moral value of actions must be founded on consideration of their effects alone. To the Utilitarian the virtu-ous character is good simply as a means to an end quite different from itself, namely a maximum of possible pleasure. An action is good, or has moral value, or is one that ought to be done, upon the same ground. If two actions, done by different men, are alike in their production of pleasure, they are alike in moral value, though the doer of one is of virtuous character and the doer of the other is not so. In our view the virtuous character is good, not as a means to a 'summum bonum' other than itself, but as in principle identical with the 'summum bonum'; and accordingly, if two actions could be alike in their moral effects (as they very well may be in production of pleasure) which represent, the one a more virtuous, the other a less virtuous character, they would still be quite different in moral value. The one would be more, the other less, of a good, according to the kind of character which they severally represent. But it is only

an action done by himself that a man has the means of estimating in relation to the character represented by it. Actions done by others, if similar outwardly or in effect, can only be referred to similar states of character, though the states which they represent may in fact be most different; and in regard to actions simply contemplated as possible the question of the character represented by them cannot be raised at all. When from the nature of the case, however, a consideration of effects can alone enter into the moral valuation of an act, the effects to be considered, according to our view, will be different from those of which the Utilitarian, according to his principles, would take account. They will be effects, not in the way of producing pleasure, but in the way of contributing to that perfection of mankind, of which the essence is a good will on the part of all persons. These are the effects which, in our view, an action must in fact tend to produce, if it is one that *ought to be done*, according to the most limited sense of that phrase; just as these are the effects *for the sake of which* it must be done, if it is done *as* it ought to be done.

295. For an omniscient being, indeed, the distinction—unavoidable for us—between the judgment that an action ought to be done, and the judgment that an action is done as it ought to be done, would not exist. It is occasioned by a separation in the moral judgment of act from motive, only possible for an imperfect intelligence. An omniscient being could not contemplate a future action as merely possible, or apart from the motive which must really cause it when it comes to be done, any more than it could fail to know the motive of every act that has been done. Knowing the state of will from which every future act will proceed, as well as that from which every past act has proceeded, it would not regard any act as being what it should be, unless the character expressed by it were what it should be. It would trace the effect of any fault on the part of the character in the actual consequences of the action. For it is only to our limited vision that there can seem to be such a thing as good effects from an action that is bad in respect of the will which it represents, and that in consequence the question becomes possible, whether the morality of an action is determined by its motive or by its consequences. There is no real reason to doubt that the good or evil in the motive of an action is exactly measured by

the good or evil in its consequences, as rightly estimated—
estimated, that is, in their bearing on the production of a good
will or the perfecting of mankind. The contrary only appears
to be the case on account of the limited view we take both of
action and consequences. We notice, for instance, that selfish
motives lead an able man to head a movement of political reform
which has beneficent consequences. Here, we say, is an action
bad in itself, according to the morality of the ' good will,' but
which has good effects : is it to be judged according to its motive,
or according to its effects ? But, in fact, if we look a little more
closely, we shall find that the selfish political leader was himself
much more of an instrument than of an originating cause, and
that his action was but a trifling element in the sum or series of
actions which yielded the political movement. The good in the
effect of the movement will really correspond to the degree of
good will which has been exerted in bringing it about ; and the
effects of any selfishness in its promoters will appear in some
limitation to the good which it brings to society.

It is seldom indeed that the most conspicuous actors on the
world's stage are known to us enough from the inside, or that
the movements in which they take part can be contemplated
with sufficient completeness, to enable us very certainly to verify
this assurance in regard to them. But the more we learn of such
a person, for instance, as Napoleon, and of the work which seemed
to be his, the more clearly does it appear how what was evil in
it arose out of his personal selfishness and that of his contemporaries, while what was good in it was due to higher and purer
influences of which he and they were but the medium. And
within the more limited range of affairs which each of us can
observe for himself a like lesson is being constantly learnt. If
the ' best motives ' seem sometimes to lead to actions which are
mischievous in results, it is because these ' best motives ' have
not been good enough. If there has been no other taint of selfishness about them, yet they have been acted on inconsiderately ;
which means that the agent has been too selfish to take the
trouble duly to think of what his action brings with it to others.
It is only, in short, the unavoidably abstract nature of our judgments upon conduct that leads to distinction between good in
motive and good in effect. We infer a motive from the action

of another; but, if the inference be correct so far as it goes, we still do not know the motive in its full reality,—in its relation, so to speak, to the universe of a character, and to the influences which have made and are making that character. The effects of the action, again, we only contemplate in a like fragmentary way. With the whole spiritual history of the action before us on the one side, with the whole sum and series of its effects before us on the other, we should presumably see that just so far as a good will, *i. e.* a will determined by interest in objects contributory to human perfection, has had more or less to do with bringing the action about, there is more or less good, *i. e.* more or less contribution to human perfection, in its effects.

296. Granting, then, that the moral value of an action really depends on the motives or character which it represents, the question remains whether for us the consideration of motives can be of any avail in deciding whether an action ought to be done or to have been done. It must be admitted at once that, in judging of another's action, we have not enough insight into motive (as distinct from intention) to be warranted in founding our moral estimate on anything but the effects of the action. At the same time we are bound to remember that an estimate so founded is necessarily imperfect, and to be cautious in our personal criticism accordingly. Only if the agent himself describes his motives, as interesting persons are apt to do, are we warranted in judging them, and then *only as described by him.* Again, when the question is whether an action ought to be done, which we are not ourselves responsible for doing or preventing, a consideration of motives can plainly have no bearing on it. There remain the cases (1) of reflection on past actions of our own, (2) of consideration whether an act should be presently done, which it rests with ourselves to do or not to do. In both these cases the question of the character or state of will which an action represents may be raised with a possibility of being answered. Given an ideal of virtue, such as has been delineated above, a man may ask himself, Was I, in doing so and so, acting as a good man should, with a pure heart, with a will set on the objects on which it should be set?—or again, Shall I, in doing so and so, be acting as a good man should, goodness being understood in the same sense? The question may be reasonably asked, and

there is nothing in the nature of the case to prevent a true answer being given to it. It remains to be considered, however, whether it can be raised with advantage; whether our ideal of virtue can in this way be practically applied with the result of giving men either truer views of what in particular they ought to do, or a better disposition to do it.

297. The habit in a man of raising such questions about himself as those just indicated, is what we have mainly in view when we call him conscientious. Now it must certainly be admitted that there have been men, great in service to their kind, to whom we should not naturally apply this epithet; and again that although, in most cases where a man is complained of as ' over-conscientious,' the complaint merely indicates his superiority to the level of moral practice about him, it may sometimes indicate a real fault. There is a kind of devotion to great objects or to public service, which seems to leave a man no leisure and to afford no occasion for the question about himself, whether he has been as good as he should have been, whether a better man would not have acted otherwise than he has done. And again there is a sense in which to be always fingering one's motives is a sign rather of an unwholesome preoccupation with self than of the eagerness in disinterested service which helps forward mankind. A man's approach to the ideal of virtue is by no means to be measured by the clearness or constancy of his reflection upon the ideal. A prevalent interest in some work which tends to make men what they should be may be found in those who seldom entertain the question whether they are themselves what they should be, and who in those regions of their life which lie off the line of the prevailing interest—perhaps also in their choice of means by which to give effect to that interest—are the worse for not entertaining it. With all their sins of omission and commission such men may be nearer the ideal of virtue than others, who pride themselves on conformity to a standard of virtue (which cannot be the highest, or they would not credit themselves with conforming to it), and who so hug their reputation with themselves for acting conscientiously that in difficult situations they will not act at all.

298. This admission made, it remains true that the com-

parison of our own practice, as we know it on the inner side in relation to the motives and character which it expresses, with an ideal of virtue, is the spring from which morality perpetually renews its life. It is thus that we 'lift up our hearts, and lift them up unto the Lord.' It is thus alone, however insufficient, however 'dimly charactered and slight,' the ideal, that the initiative is given in the individual—and it can be given nowhere else—to any movement which really contributes to the bettering of man. It is thus that he is roused from acquiescence in the standard of mere respectability. No one, indeed, who recognises in their full extent the results of disinterested spiritual effort on the part of a forgotten multitude, which the respectability of any civilised age embodies, or who asks himself what any of us would be but for a sense of what respectability requires, will be disposed to depreciate its value. But the standard of respectability by which any age or country is influenced could never have been attained, if the temper which acquiesces in it had been universal—if no one had been lifted above that acquiescence —in the past. It has been reached through the action of men who, each in his time and turn, have refused to accept the way of living which they found about them, and to which, upon the principle of seeking the greater pleasure and avoiding the greater pain, they would naturally have conformed. The conception of a better way of living may have been on a larger or a smaller scale. It may have related to some general reformation of society, or to the change of some particular practice in which the protesting individual had been concerned. But if it has taken effect in any actual elevation of morality, it is because certain men have brought it home to themselves in a contrast between what they should be and what they are, which has awakened the sense of a personal responsibility for improvement.

In so doing they may not have raised the question of personal goodness, in the form in which it presents itself to the self-examining conscience of one who lives among a highly moralised society and conforms as a matter of course to its standards. They may not have asked themselves, Have we, in doing what was expected of us, been doing it from the right motives? In that form the question presupposes the establishment of a definite standard of conventional morality. In the days when such morality was still in making, and in the minds of the forgotten enthusiasts to whom we owe it, this would scarcely be the way in which the contrast between an ideal of virtue and current practice would present itself. Under such conditions it would present itself less as a challenge to purify the heart than as a call to new courses of overt action, the relation of which to motives and character it would not occur to any one to consider. But in principle it is the same operation in the individual of an idea of a perfect life, with which his own is contrasted, whether it take the form of a consciousness of personal responsibility for putting an end to some practice which, to a mind awakening to the claims of the human soul, seems unjust or unworthy, or the form of self-interrogation as to the purity of the heart from which a walk and conduct, outwardly correct, proceeds.

299. It may be objected, however, that in thus identifying the motive power at work in the practical reformer of morality with that which sets the introspective conscience upon the enquiry whether the heart is as pure as it should be, we are obscuring the real question as to the practical value of the latter. No one doubts that a man who improves the current morality of his time must be something of an Idealist. He must have an idea, which moves him to seek its realisation, of a better order of life than he finds about him. That idea cannot represent any experienced reality. If it did, the reformer's labour would be superfluous; the order of life which he seeks to bring about would be already in existence. It is an idea to which nothing real as yet corresponds, but which, as actuating the reformer, tends to bring into being a reality corresponding to itself. It is in this sense that the reformer must be an Idealist. But the idea which he seeks to realise is an idea of definite institutions and arrangements of life, of courses of action, each producing their outward sensible effects. What real identity is there between the influence of such an idea—an ideal of virtue, if we like to call it so—producing a visible alteration in man's life, and that of an ideal which sets a man upon asking, not what there is which he ought to do and is not doing, but whether, in that which he has been doing and will (as he ought) continue to do, his heart has been sufficiently pure?

The identity will appear, when we reflect that it is not a

'mere idea' of a better order of life that ever set any one upon a work of disinterested moral reform, in that sense of the term in which one of us might have 'an idea' of the Lord Mayor's show, or of a debate in Parliament, without having been present at them. The idea which moves the reformer is one that he feels a personal responsibility for realising. This feeling of personal responsibility for its execution is part and parcel of the practical idea itself, of the form of consciousness which we so describe. It is that which distinguishes it as a *practical* idea. The reformer cannot bear to think of himself except as giving effect, so far as may be, to his project of reform; and thus, instead of merely contemplating a possible work, he does it. He presents himself to himself on the one hand as achieving, so far as in him lies, the contemplated work, on the other hand as neglecting it for some less worthy object; and he turns with contempt and aversion from the latter presentation. Now it is because, to the real reformer, the thought of something which should be done is thus always at the same time the thought of something which he should be and seeks to be, but would not be if he did not do the work, that there is a real unity between the spiritual principle which animates him, and that which appears in the self-questioning of the man who, without charging himself with the neglect of any outward duty, without contemplating any particular good work which he might do but has not done, still asks himself whether he has been what he should be in doing what he has done.

300. But, granted the unity of the spiritual principle at work in the two supposed cases, is there any real unity in the effects which it produces in the person of the moral reformer and in the person of the self-questioning 'saint'? In the one case the effect is the recognition and fulfilment of certain specific duties, previously not recognised or not fulfilled, by the moral reformer and those whom he influences. He and they come to deal differently with their fellow-men. But in the other case, if we enquire what specific performance follows from the self-questioning as to purity of heart, we find it difficult to answer. Among the respectable classes of a well-regulated society there is little in outward walk and conduct to distinguish the merely respectable from the most anxiously conscientious.

As a rule, it will only be to a man already pretty thoroughly moralised by the best social influences that it will occur to reproach himself with having unworthy motives even in irreproachable conduct; and, as a rule, when such a man comes thus to reproach himself in presence of some ideal of a perfect Will, he will already have been fulfilling, under the feeling that it is expected of him, all the particular duties which the consciousness of such an ideal might otherwise challenge him to fulfil. Unless he has leisure for philanthropy, or a gift of utterance, there will be little in outward act to distinguish his converted state—if we may so describe the state in which he learns to contrast his personal unworthiness with an ideal of holiness—from that of moral self-complacency, in which he may have previously been living, and which is the state of most of the dutiful citizens about him.

301. If we could watch him closely enough, indeed, even in outward conduct there would appear to be a difference. Doing the work expected of him 'not with eye-service, as a man-pleaser, but in singleness of heart, as unto the Lord,' he will rise to a higher standard of doing it. Into the duties which he is expected to fulfil he will put much more meaning than is put by those who claim their fulfilment, and will always be on the look-out for duties which no one would think the worse of him for not recognising. But in so doing, he probably will not seem to himself to be acting according to a higher standard than those about him. And in fact, although in a certain sense he transcends the 'law of opinion,' of social expectation, he only does so by interpreting it according to its higher spirit. That law, being, as we have seen, the result of the past action in human consciousness of an ideal of conduct, will yield different rules according as it is or is not interpreted by a consciousness under the same influence. It speaks with many voices according as men have ears to hear, and the spirit of the conscientious man shows itself in catching the purest of them. He is like a judge who is perpetually making new law in ostensibly interpreting the old. He extracts the higher meaning out of the recognised social code, giving reality to some requirements which it has hitherto only contained potentially. He feels the necessity of rules of conduct which, though they necessarily

arise out of that effort to make human life perfect which has brought conventional morality into existence, are not yet a recognised part of that morality, and thus have no authority with those whose highest motive is a sense of what is expected of them.

302. This is true; but it is not merely on this account—not merely on account of certain effects in outward conduct which, upon sufficient scrutiny, it might be found to yield—that we claim for the temper of genuine self-abasement in presence of an ideal of holiness an intrinsic value, the same in kind with that which all would ascribe to a zeal for moral reform. We claim such a value for it—a value independent of any that it might possess as a means to a good other than itself—on the ground that it is a component influence in the perfect human life; on the ground that, whatever the universe of activities in which that life displays itself may prove to be, the self-abasing, which is also the aspiring or God-seeking, spirit, must always be their source and spring. The character exhibited by the moral reformer has a like value, in so far as it is not merely a means to the perfect life, but a phase of the same spiritual principle as must govern that life. But whereas we cannot but suppose that, if the perfect life of mankind were attained, this spiritual principle must have passed out of the phase in which it can appear as a reforming zeal—for in that event there could no longer be wrongs to redress, or indulged vices to eradicate—on the other hand we cannot suppose that, while human life remains human life, it can even in its most perfect form be superior to the call for self-abasement before an ideal of holiness.

There is no contradiction in the supposition of a human life purged of vices and with no wrongs left to set right. It is indeed merely the supposition of human life with all its capacities realised. In such a life the question of the reformer, What ought to be done in the way of overt action that is not being done? would no longer be significant. But so long as it is the life of men, *i. e.* of beings who are born and grow and die; in whom an animal nature is the vehicle through which the divine self-realising spirit works; in whom virtue is not born ready-made but has to be formed (however unfailing the process may

come to be) through habit and education in conflict with opposing tendencies; so long the contrast must remain for the
human soul between itself and the infinite spirit, of whom it
must be conscious, as present to itself but other than itself, or
it would not be the human soul. The more complete the realisation of its capacities, the clearer will be its apprehension at
once of its own infinity in respect of its consciousness of there
being an infinite spirit—a consciousness which only a self-
communication of that spirit could convey—and of its finiteness
as an outcome of natural conditions; a finiteness in consequence
of which the infinite spirit is for ever something beyond it, still
longed for, never reached. Towards an infinite spirit, to whom
he is thus related, the attitude of man at his highest and completest could still be only that which we have described as self-
abasement before an ideal of holiness; not the attitude of knowledge, for knowledge is of matters of fact or relations, and the
infinite spirit is neither fact nor relation; not the attitude of
full and conscious union, for that the limitation of human nature
prevents; but the same attitude of awe and aspiration which
belongs to all the upward stages of the moral life. He must
think of the infinite spirit as better than the best that he can
himself attain to, but (just for that reason) as having an essential community with his own best. And, as his own best rests
upon a self-devoted will, so it must be as a will, good not under
the limitation of opposing tendencies but in some more excellent,
though not by us positively conceivable, way, that he will set
before himself the infinite spirit.

303. The spiritual act, then, which in different aspects may
be described either as self-abasement or self-exaltation—the act
in which the heart is lifted up to God, in which the whole inner
man goes forth after an ideal of personal holiness—this act,
while it is in principle one with the whole course of man's moral
endeavour, may be deemed in a certain sense its most final form,
because, in that rest from the labour of baffled and disappointed
endeavour which a perfectly ordered society might be supposed
to bring, it would still not be superseded. Its value is an intrinsic value, not derived from any result beyond itself to which
it contributes. In this respect, indeed, it does not differ from
any other expression of the good will. If it differs apparently

from the more obviously practical expressions of such a will, the reason is that these, while sharing its intrinsic value, have also a further value, as means, which it does not seem to possess. They issue in sensible ameliorations of human society. But these very ameliorations are relative to that intrinsic good, the perfection of the human soul, of which the heart at once self-abased and aspiring is itself a lasting mode. Whether such a heart, in this person or that, itself issues in outward 'transient' action of a noticeably beneficent kind, will depend mainly on the social surroundings, and on the intellectual and other qualifications of the particular person. If these in any case are such as to call for and to favour a large amount of useful social activity, we are apt under the impression of the outward effect to overlook the spiritual principle which yields it, and which may be the same in another person otherwise circumstanced and gifted, by whom no such apparent effect is produced. We praise the successful reformer, and forget that he is but what the man of unnoticed conscientious goodness might be in another situation and with other opportunities.

If the end by reference to which moral values are to be judged were anything but the perfect life itself, as resting on a devoted will, it would be right to depreciate the obscure saint by the side of the man to whose work we can point in the redress of wrongs and the purging of social vices. But if the supreme value for man is what we take it to be—man himself in his perfection—then it is idle to contrast the more observably practical type of goodness with the more self-questioning or consciously God-seeking type. The value of each is intrinsic and identical; for each rests on a heart or character or will which, however differently it may come to be exhibited as human capacities come to be more fulfilled, must still be that of the perfect man. The distinction between them, as looked at from the point of view from which moral values are properly estimated, is mainly accidental. It is a distinction of the circumstances under which the same principle of action is exercised. Under certain conditions of society, of individual temperament and ability, it takes the one form, under other conditions the other. In neither form is it barren of effects; but in one form its effects are more overt and 'transient,' in the other more impalpable and 'immanent.'

But the one order of effects no less than the other has its value as a means to that perfect life, to which the obscure saint and the true social reformer alike are not merely related as a means, but which each in his own person, under whatever limitations, represents.

304. From these considerations we return to the enquiry out of which they have arisen. Having distinguished the question, What ought to be done?—a question to be answered in detail by examination of the probable effects of contemplated action—from the question, What should I be ?—a question of motives and character—we pointed out that the latter question might properly be raised by a man with reference to his own actions, past or prospective. In regard to others he cannot fully know what the motives and character represented by any particular action have been or will be, and in the absence of such knowledge he certainly cannot be blamable for declining to guess. But as to himself any one may ask, Was I what I should have been in doing so and so ? or, Shall I in doing so and so be what I should be ? He may ask such a question reasonably, because it does not depend on the amount of his information, or on his skill in analysis, but on his honesty with himself, whether the answer shall be virtually a true one. But will he for raising such questions, and raising them with such an ideal of virtue before him as has been above indicated, be any the wiser as to what he ought to do, or any the more disposed to do it ?

305. Now it is obvious that, though he put such questions to himself with all possible earnestness, he will not for doing so, directly at any rate, be the better judge of what he should do, so far as the judgment depends on correct information or inference as to matters of facts, or on a correct analysis of circumstances. But a man's doubts as to his own conduct may be of a kind which such information and analysis are principally needed to resolve. He may be asking himself such questions as these : Was I right in relieving that beggar yesterday ? Was I right in making the declaration required on taking orders ? Was I right in voting against the Coercion Act last session ? And he *may* be asking these questions about himself in the same sense in which he might ask them about the actions of any one else, or in which they might be discussed by a debating society, with-

out any reference to the motives or character represented by the acts in question. The supposition that any one should ask such questions about his own conduct solely in this sense, is no doubt an extreme one. He could not really detach himself from the consideration of the state of mind, better or worse, which led him to act as he did. In relieving the beggar was he not merely compounding with his conscience for his self-indulgence in shirking the trouble which a more judicious exercise of benevolence would have cost him; or merely giving himself the pleasure of momentarily pleasing another, or of being applauded for generosity, at the cost of encouraging a mischievous practice? In making the declaration referred to, was his motive a pure desire to do good and teach the truth, or was he affected by any desire to lead a comfortable life, combining a maximum of reputation for usefulness with a minimum of wear and tear? In voting against the Coercion Act was he at all influenced by the wish to please an important fraction of his constituents, or by a pique against ministers? It is scarcely possible that any one, at all honest with himself, should consider his own conduct in the cases supposed without testing it by some such questions of motive as these.

But when the fullest and most honest consideration has been given them, they do not supersede the questions of fact and circumstance which the supposed cases necessarily involve. The man could not measure the value of his conduct in almsgiving, in taking orders, in voting against Coercion, without taking account of the effect of almsgiving in general and in the particular case; of the circumstances on which the usefulness of the Church, and the relative truth of the declarations required by it, depend; of those conditions of social life in general, and in Ireland specially, which make Coercion a necessity or a political evil. For though he may do what is good in result without being good, he cannot have been good unless he has done what is good in result. The question whether he has done what he ought in any particular case may be answered in the affirmative without its following that he has been what he ought to be in doing it; but unless it can be so answered he may not assume that he has been what he ought to be. And in order to answer it in such cases as we have been supposing, with due reference to circumstances and effects, that sort of knowledge and penetration is required which the most anxious self-interrogation, the most genuine self-abasement, will not directly supply.

306. But, it will be objected, this admission is inconsistent with the statement just now made, that a true answer to the question, Was I what I should have been in doing so and so? depends not on the amount of a man's information, but on his honesty with himself. It now appears that a man cannot have been what he should have been in doing any action, unless the action was of a kind to yield good results, and that the correctness of a man's judgment in certain cases on this latter point depends not on his honesty with himself, but on his knowledge and powers of analysis. How are the two statements to be reconciled? An explanation of this point will bring out the true function and value of the self-questioning conscience.

If the function of the conscience in challenging me with the question, Was I what I should have been in doing this or that? were to arrive at a precise estimate of the worth of my conduct in the particular case, the consideration of the effects of the action could be as little dispensed with as that of its motives. To make my conduct perfectly good, it would be necessary that the effects of the act should be purely for good, according to the true standard of good, as well as that my interest in doing it should be purely an interest in that good. It is obvious, however, that the exact measure in which my conduct has fallen short of this unattainable perfection, till we can see all moral effects in their causes, cannot be speculatively ascertained; nor is it of practical importance to attempt its ascertainment. What is of importance is that I should keep alive that kind of sense of shortcoming in my motives and character, which is the condition of aspiration and progress towards higher goodness. And to this end, while the question whether I have been duly patient and considerate and unbiassed by passion or self-interest in taking account of the probable consequences of my act, is an essential question—a question which it only needs that I should be honest with myself, not clever or well-informed, to answer—the question how the action has turned out in respect of consequences which I had not the requisite knowledge or ability to foresee, may be left aside without practical harm. If indeed the question as to motives and character, honestly dealt with, could leave me under the impression that in doing so and so I was all that I should have been, it would be important for me to be reminded that the action may have had evil consequences which I did not foresee—perhaps in my dulness and ignorance could not foresee—but which yet are part of my act. But just because the question of motives and character, honestly dealt with, is incompatible with self-complacency in the contemplation of any piece of past conduct, its moral function is fully served without supplementary enquiry into unforeseen consequences of the conduct. It is a sufficient spring for the endeavour after a higher goodness that I should be ashamed of my selfishness, indolence, or impatience, without being ashamed also of my ignorance and want of foresight. Without the former sort of shame, the latter, if it could be engendered, would be morally barren; while, given that personal endeavour after the highest which is the other side of self-abasement, this will turn the products of intellectual enlightenment and scientific discovery, as they come, to account in the way of contribution to human perfection. It will do this, and nothing else will.

307. If we are called on to say, then, whether a man will be any the wiser as to what he ought to do, or any the more disposed to do it, for applying an ideal of virtue to his own conduct in the form of the question, Was I in this or that piece of conduct what I should be? we must point out that this question itself expresses the source of all wisdom as to what we ought to do. It expresses the aspiration, the effort, in man to be the best that he has it in him to be, from which is ultimately derived the thought that there is something which ought to be done, and the enquiry what in particular it is. It represents the quest for right conduct, as carried on by the individual under that sense of personal responsibility for doing the best, for attaining the highest, which can alone make him a reformer of his own practice or of the practice of others. It is true indeed that no recognition of an ideal of virtue, however pure and high, no such incitement to the reform of oneself and one's neighbour as a comparison of the ideal with current practice can afford, will enlighten us as to the effect of different kinds of action upon the welfare of society, whether that welfare be estimated with

reference to a maximum of possible pleasure, or to an end which the realisation of a good will itself constitutes. As it stands before the mind of any particular person, the ideal will not directly yield an injunction to do anything in particular which is not in his mind already associated with good results, nor to abstain from anything which is not already associated with evil results. But while it will not immediately instruct him as to the physical or social consequences of action, and through such instruction yield new commands, it will keep him on the look-out for it, will open his mind to it, will make him ready, as soon as it comes, to interpret the instruction into a personal duty. The agents in imparting the instruction may be analysts and experimenters, to whom the ideal of virtue is of little apparent concern—who seldom trouble themselves with the question whether they are what they should be—though, unless in their intellectual employment they were controlled by an ideal of perfect work, they would not prove the instructors of mankind. But when the instruction has been conveyed, the self-imposed imperative to turn it to account for the bettering of life remains to be given; and it is only from a conscience responsive to an ideal of virtue that it can proceed. The lesson, for instance, of the mischief done by indiscriminate almsgiving, or by the sale of spirits, may have been most plainly taught by social or physical analysis, but it would be practically barren unless certain persons, each under a consciousness of responsibility for making the best of himself as a social being, charged themselves with the task of getting the lesson put into practice by society.

308. The notion that an ideal of virtue must be barren in the suggestion of particular duties previously unrecognised, has probably arisen from the necessity of expressing it verbally in the form of a definition or of a general proposition. From such a proposition as ' the true good for man is the realisation of his capabilities, or the perfecting of human life,' or ' the good will is a will which has such perfection for its object,'—or, again, from a definition of any particular form of the good will, of any specific virtue—we may be fairly challenged to deduce any particular obligation but such as is already included in the notions represented by the terms which stand as the subjects of these several propositions. From a knowledge that the true good, the good

will, the specific virtues, are as defined, no one will come to be aware of any particular duties of which he was not aware before he arrived at the definitions. The most that can be said (of which more below) will be that such definitions may put him on his guard against self-sophistications, which might otherwise obscure to him the clearness of admitted duties. If the practical consciousness, which we name an ideal of virtue, were no more than the speculative judgment embodied in a definition of the ideal, or than speculative reflection upon the ideal, the same admission would have to be made in regard to it. But it is much more than this; or, rather, it does not primarily involve any such speculative judgment at all, but only comes to involve such a judgment as a secondary result of that aspiration in men after a possible best of life and character, which primarily consti- tutes the consciousness of the ideal. Before a definition of the ideal can be possible, this aspiration must have taken effect in the ordering of life; and it is reflection on the product which it has thus yielded that suggests general statements as to the various virtues, and as to some supreme virtue; ultimately, as intellectual needs increase, formal definitions of virtue and the virtues.

But the acquaintance of educated men with such definitions, the employment of the analytical intellect upon them, is very different from what we mean by the practical consciousness of the moral ideal. This implies the continued action in the individual of the same spiritual principle that has yielded those forms of life and character which form the subject of our moral definitions; its continued action as at once compelling dissatis- faction with the imperfection of those forms, and creating a sensibility to the suggestions of a further perfecting of life which they contain. A definition of virtue, a theory of the good, is quite a different thing, in presence of such a living inward interpreter, from what it would be as an abstract propo- sition. A proposition of geometry, from which by mere analysis no truth could be derived which was not already contained in it, becomes fertile of new truth when applied by the geometer to a new construction. A rule of law, barren to mere analysis, yields new rules when interpreted by the judge in application to new cases. And thus a general ethical proposition, which by itself is merely a record of past moral judgments, and from which by mere analysis no rules of conduct could be derived but such as have been already accepted and embodied in it, becomes a source of new practical direction when applied by a conscience, working under a felt necessity of seeking the best, to circumstances previously not existent or not considered, or to some new lesson of experience.

309. Our conclusion, then, is that the state of mind which is now most naturally expressed by the unspoken questions, Have I been what I should be, shall I be what I should be, in doing so and so ? is that in which all moral progress originates. It must have preceded the formation of definite ideals of character, as well as any articulation of the distinction between outward action and its motives. It is no other than the sense of personal responsibility for making the best of themselves in the family, the tribe, or the state, which must have actuated certain persons, many or few, in order to the establishment and recognition of any moral standards whatever. Given such standards, it is the spirit which at once demands from the individual a loyal conformity to them, and disposes him, upon their suggestion, to construct for himself an ideal of virtue, of personal goodness, higher than they explicitly contain. The action of such an ideal, in those stages of moral development with which we are now familiar, is the essential condition of all further bettering of human life. Its action is of course partial in various degrees of partiality. It may appear as a zeal for public service on the part of some one not careful enough about the correctness of his own life, or on the other hand in the absorbed religious devotion of the saintly recluse. In the average citizen it may appear only as the influence which makes him conscientious in the discharge of work which he would not suffer except in conscience for neglecting, or as the voice, fitfully heard within, which gives meaning to the announcement of a perfect life lived for him and somehow to be made his own. Taking human society together, its action in one mode supplements its action in another, and the whole sum of its action forms the motive power of true moral development ; which means the apprehension on our part, ever widening and ever filling and ever more fully responded to in practice, of our possibilities as men and of the reciprocal claims and duties which those possibilities imply.

CHAPTER II.

310. SUPPOSING the considerations with which the last chapter ended to be admitted, we have still only convinced ourselves of the supreme value which belongs to an ideal of personal goodness, as a principle of action. The value of a certain *theory* of the ideal, of such a doctrine of the good and of goodness as has been previously sketched in this treatise, is a different question. It was this that we undertook to consider, and this we have so far not directly touched. Having taken the ideal to be a devotion of character and life in some form or other to the perfecting of man; having insisted that this perfection is to be understood as itself consisting in a life of such self-devoted activity on the part of all persons; we undertook to enquire what available criterion of right and wrong such a theory could afford; how, applied to the circumstances of life, it could be construed into particular duties, so as to give us some general guide to the line of conduct we should adopt where conventional morality fails us. This enquiry, it may be fairly said, is not met by dwelling on the effect of a moral ideal, which need not be, and generally is not, accompanied by any clear theory of itself, in awakening the individual to a recognition of new duties, as new situations arise and new experience is acquired. The most genuine devotion to the highest ideal of goodness will not save a man from occasional perplexity as to the right line of action for him to take. If it seems to do so, it will only be because, not being the highest kind of devotion, it makes him confident in merely traditional or inconsiderate judgments. If the perplexity were one which admitted of being put in the form, Shall I be acting according to my ideal of virtue, or as a good man should, in doing so and

so? a true devotion to the ideal might guide him through it. But in that case, it may be argued, the practical action of the ideal itself is enough. A theory about it, a philosophy of the true good, is superfluous. But if, on the other hand, the conscientious man's perplexity arises either from a conflict between two authorities which seem to have equal claims on his obedience, or from doubt as to the effect of different courses of contemplated action, while mere devotion to the ideal will not clear his path before him, of what avail will be any instruction that we could give him in accordance with our theory of the good and of goodness?

311. The discussion of this question has been advisedly postponed till we had considered the practical effect of an ideal of goodness, as possessing a man who may as yet be unacquainted with any philosophical theories about it. Any value which a true moral theory may have for the direction of conduct depends on its being applied and interpreted by a mind which the ideal, as a practical principle, already actuates. And it will be as well at once to admit that the value must in any case be rather negative than positive; rather in the way of deliverance from the moral anarchy which an apparent conflict between duties equally imperative may bring about, or of providing a safeguard against the pretext which in a speculative age some inadequate and misapplied theory may afford to our selfishness, than in the way of pointing out duties previously ignored. This latter service must always be rendered by the application of a mind, which the ideal possesses, to new situations, to experience newly acquired or newly analysed, rather than by reflection on any theory of the ideal. Whether a mind so possessed and applied is philosophically instructed or no, is in most circumstances matter of indifference. One is sometimes, indeed, tempted to think that Moral Philosophy is only needed to remedy the evils which it has itself caused; that if men were not constrained by a necessity of their intellectual nature to give abstract expression to their ideals, the particular misleading suggestions, against which a true philosophy is needed to guard, would not be forthcoming.

For these suggestions chiefly arise from the inadequacy of the formulae in which requirements imposed by a really valuable ideal have found intellectual expression. Under influence of such an ideal institutions and rules of life are formed, essential for their time and turn, but not fitted to serve as the foundation of a universally binding prescription. The generalising intellect, however, requires their embodiment in universal rules; and when these are found to conflict with each other, or with some demand of the self-realising spirit which has not yet found expression in a recognised rule, the result is an intellectual perplexity, of which our lower nature is quite ready to take advantage. Blind passion is enlisted in the cause of the several rules. Egoistic interests are ready to turn any of them to account, or to find an excuse for indulgence in what seems to be their neutralisation of each other. Meanwhile perhaps some nobler soul takes up that position of self-outlawry which Wordsworth expresses in the words put into Rob Roy's mouth :—

> 'We have a passion—make a law,
> Too false to guide us or control !
> And for the law itself we fight
> In bitterness of soul.
>
> And, puzzled, blinded thus, we lose
> Distinctions that are plain and few ;
> These find I graven on my heart ;
> *That* tells me what to do.'

For deliverance from this state of moral anarchy, which in various forms recurs whenever a sufficient liberation of the intellectual faculties has been attained, there is needed a further pursuit of the same speculative processes which have brought it about. As has just been said, no good will come of this, unless under the direction of a genuine interest in the perfecting of man ; but, given this interest, it is only through philosophy that it can be made independent of the conflicting, because inadequate, formulae in which duties are presented to it, and saved from distraction between rival authorities, of which the injunctions seem at once absolute and irreconcilable, because their origin is not understood.

312. But philosophy itself in its results may yield opportunity to a self-excusing egoism. The formulae in which it expresses conceptions of moral ends and virtues must always be liable to prove misleading, in the absence of that living interest in a practically true ideal which can alone elicit their higher signi-

ficance. They are generated in intellectual antagonism and must always probably retain the marks of their origin. Those which have served the purpose of enabling men to see behind and beyond their own moral prejudices or some absolute authoritative assertion of a merely relative duty, have not themselves conveyed complete and final truth. If they had done so, it would still have been a truth that could only be made instructive for men's guidance in their moral vocation, if applied to the particulars of life by a mind bent on the highest. But in fact the best practical philosophy of any age has never been more than an assertion of partial truths, which had some special present function to fulfil in the deliverance or defence of the human soul. When they have done their work, these truths become insufficient for the expression of the highest practical convictions operating in man, while the speculative intellect, if enlisted in the service of the pleasure-seeking nature, can easily extract excuses from them for evading the cogency of those convictions. But the remedy for this evil is still not to be found in the abandonment of philosophy, but in its further pursuit. The spring of all moral progress, indeed, can still lie nowhere else than in the attraction of heart and will by the ideal of human perfection, and in the practical convictions which arise from it ; but philosophy will still be needed as the interpreter of practical conviction, and it can itself alone provide for the adequacy of the interpretation.

313. This general account of the practical function which a philosophy of conduct has to serve will probably carry more conviction, if we consider some particular forms of perplexity as to right conduct in which philosophy might be of service, and again some instances of the opportunity which an inadequate philosophy may offer to egoistic tendencies. A previous reminder, however, may be needed that a case of perplexity as to right conduct, if it is to be one in which philosophy can serve a useful purpose, must be one of *bona fide* perplexity of conscience. Now the margin within which such perplexities can arise in a Christian society is not really very large. The effort after an ideal of conduct has so far taken effect in the establishment of a recognised standard of what is due from man to man, that the articulation of the general imperative, ' Do what is best for man-

kind [1],' into particular duties is sufficiently clear and full for the ordinary occasions of life. In fulfilling the duties which would be recognised as belonging to his station in life by any one who considered the matter dispassionately, without bias by personal inclination—in fulfilling them loyally, without shirking, ' not with eye-service as men-pleasers,'—we can seldom go wrong; and when we have done this fully, there will seldom be much more that we can do. The function of bringing home these duties to the consciences of men—of helping them to be honest with themselves in their recognition and interpretation of them—is rather that of the preacher than of the philosopher. *Speculatively* there is much for the philosopher to do in examining how that ordering of life has arisen, to which these duties are relative; what is the history of their recognition; what is the rationale of them; what is the most correct expression for the practical ideas which underlie them. And, as we shall see, there may be circumstances which give this speculative enquiry a practical value. These circumstances, however, must always be exceptional. Ordinarily it will be an impertinence for the philosopher to pretend either to supplement or to supersede those practical directions of conduct, which are supplied by the duties of his station to any one who is free from any selfish interest in ignoring them.

314. Perplexity of conscience, properly so called, seems always to arise from conflict between different formulae for expressing the ideal of good in human conduct, or between different institutions for furthering its realisation, which have alike obtained authority over men's minds without being intrinsically entitled to more than a partial and relative obedience; or from the incompatibility of some such formula or institution, on the one side, with some moral impulse of the individual on the other, which is really an impulse towards the attainment of human perfection, but cannot adjust itself to recognised rules and established institutions. From the perplexities thus occasioned we must distinguish those that arise from difficulty in the analysis of circumstances or in the forecast of the effects of

---

[1] I use this as a fair popular equivalent of Kant's formula—'Treat humanity, whether in your person or in that of another, never merely as a means, always at the same time as an end.'

actions. These are to be met, no doubt, by an exercise of the intellect, but by its exercise rather in the investigation of matters of fact than by that reflection upon ideas which is properly called philosophy.

From both kinds of practical perplexity again are to be distinguished those self-sophistications which arise from a desire to find excuses for gratifying unworthy inclinations. Such self-sophistications, we know, will often dignify themselves with the title of cases of conscience ; and the disrepute which has fallen upon 'casuistry' has been partly due to its having often been employed in their service. A man will pretend to be perplexed with a case of conscience, when really he is wishing to make out that some general rule of conduct does not apply to him, because its fulfilment would cause him trouble, or because it conflicts with some passion which he wishes to indulge. Most cases in which we argue that circumstances modify for us the obligation to veracity are of this kind. When such is the source of the 'perplexity,' it is not the most perfect philosophy, the completest possible theory of the moral ideal, that will be of avail for deliverance from it. Just so far as the character is formed to disinterested loyalty to the moral law, however imperfectly the law may be conceived, it will brush aside the fictitious embarrassment. As Kant puts it, that emotion which on one side is 'Achtung' for the moral law, on the other is 'Verachtung' for one's selfish inclinations. Such an emotion may not save a man from many concessions to his own weakness, but it will make him refuse with contempt to resort to casuistry for their justification. He may be enlightened enough to appreciate the relativity of most general rules of conduct, to understand that they admit of exceptions according to circumstances, but he will despise the suggestion of an exception to them in his own favour —an exception in order to save himself pain or gain himself pleasure. This sort of self-contempt affords a short method of settling questions to which the speculative intellect, if once it so far enlists itself in the service of passion as to treat them seriously, will 'find no end, in wandering mazes lost.'

315. There may be cases, however, in which the difficulty felt in adhering to a general rule, such as that of veracity, arises from an impulse entitled in itself to as much respect as the

conscientious injunction to adhere to the rule. A famous example is the temptation of Jeannie Deans to give false evidence on a single point for the sake of saving her sister, of whose substantial innocence she is assured. In such a case would Moral Philosophy, if it could gain a hearing, have any direction to give to the perplexed person? He is asking himself, Shall I in this case be acting as I ought, as a good man should, in adhering to the strict rule of veracity, or in departing from it to save the beloved person from a punishment which I know to be undeserved? Whatever the principle of our Moral Philosophy, can it help in answering the question? The Utilitarian theory, which is apt to take credit to itself for special practical availability, can here have no counsel to give. For by what possible calculus could the excess, on the whole, of pleasure over pain or of pain over pleasure, to be expected from adherence to the rule of veracity, be balanced against the excess of pleasure over pain or of pain over pleasure, to be expected in the particular case from its violation? But if we suppose the question to be dealt with according to the principles advocated in this treatise, we do not escape embarrassment. How shall the perplexed person say whether the motive which suggests adherence to the rule of veracity, or that which suggests departure from it, is the worthier of the two? A true Moral Philosophy does not recognise any value in conformity to a universal rule, simply as such, but only in that which *ordinarily* issues in such conformity, *viz.* the readiness to sacrifice every lower inclination in the desire to do right for the sake of doing it. But in the case supposed, may not the desire to save the beloved person, known to be substantially innocent, claim to be a disinterested desire to do right equally with a determination to adhere to the strict rule of veracity?

316. If the moral philosopher were called on to answer this question as a matter of general speculation, not for the guidance of a particular person in a particular case, he would have to say that it did not admit of being answered with a simple 'yes' or 'no.' For purposes of moral valuation neither the desire to save the life of the beloved person, nor the determination at any cost to adhere to the rule of strict veracity, can be detached from the relation which it bears to the whole history of a life, to the universe of a character; and this relation is not in any case ascertain-

able by us. Of two men, placed in precisely similar perplexities, one might adhere to the rule of veracity at the cost of sacrificing the life of a beloved and innocent person, the other might save the person at the cost of violating the rule of veracity, and it would be impossible for the moral philosopher to say which action were the better or the worse of the two ; because he would not know in regard to either that spiritual history upon which its moral value depends.

If on the other hand (an unlikely supposition) he had to assist the perplexed conscience[1] in deciding between the alternative actions in such a case as that supposed, he would have to press the question whether it is not at bottom some personal weakness which suggests the departure from the ordinary moral rule; whether it is really a greater devotion to the beloved person that suggests a falsehood for her sake, and not perhaps a backwardness to serve her in some more difficult and dangerous way, in which she might still be served though she had to bear the consequence of the truth being told. If that consequence should prove to be her painful and undeserved death, ' What are you,' the doubter must be asked, ' what is the victim whom your untruth might save, that the suffering of either should be set against the duty of adherence to a rule, of which the universal observance is a prime condition of the perfect ordering of social life, and therefore morally necessary ? Each of you, no doubt, has an absolute value which no rule, as such, can have. Rules are made for man, not man for rules. But the question is not really between the value of either of you and the value of a rule, but between the importance to be attached on the one hand to your pain or deliverance from pain, and that to be attached on the other to the moral life of society which every lie must injure, and to the integrity of your character as a person self-subordinated to the requirements of social good. Let the worst come from your truth-speaking; still it is not that which is of absolute value, either in you or in the victim of the law, which will suffer loss. Your devotion to the beloved person is indeed truly a good; but that devotion is not set aside by, but carried on into, the larger devotion which includes it, and which forbids your departure

---

[1] [The expression 'perplexed *conscience*' would probably have been modified on revision, in accordance with the distinctions laid down in § 321.]

from the rule of veracity. As to the beloved person herself, the question is more dark, for she is passive in the matter; it is not any action to be done by her that is under consideration, and no one can gain directly in intrinsic worth by the action of another. But it is certain that her deliverance from suffering through your wrong-doing could not be really for her good; it would not make her heart purer, or direct her will to higher objects; and you may trust on the other hand (though unable to foresee how such a result should come about) that in taking that consequence of her conduct, which only your wrong-doing could avert, she will gain in that spiritual capability which is alone to her a source of abiding good.'

317. The suggestion of such counsel being offered to any one under such trial as we have supposed, inevitably strikes us as inappropriate. We know that in fact under such circumstances the soul would not be at leisure for philosophical reflection. Its conduct must be determined by influences that act more swiftly and decisively; if in the severe path for which we have supposed the philosopher to be arguing, by an inbred horror of falsehood, which does not wait to give an account of itself, or by sense of the presence of a divine onlooker, whose disapproval, not for fear of penal consequences but for very shame, cannot be faced. According to the distinction previously drawn, it is the action of an ideal of virtue itself, not any theory about the ideal, that can alone be efficient in such a case. Though not in the emergency itself, however, yet in preparing the soul for it, a true philosophy may have an important service to render. It will be a service, indeed, rather of the defensive and negative than of the actively inciting kind—a service which in a speculative and dialectical age needs to be rendered, lest the hold of the highest moral ideas on the mind should be weakened from apparent lack of intellectual justification.

Those ideas, as we have often pointed out, are not abstract conceptions. They actuate men independently of the operations of the discursive intellect. They rather direct those operations than are their result. The idea, in its various forms, of something that human life should be, of a perfect being for whom this 'should be' already 'is,' cannot proceed from observation of matters of fact or from inference founded on such observation,

though in various ways (on which we cannot here dwell) it
regulates that observation and inference. Such ideas or principles
of action, at work before they are understood, not only give rise
to institutions and modes of life, but also express themselves in
forms of the imagination. In complication with effects of passion
and force, they produce the laws, whether enforced by opinion
or by the magistrate, which form the essential and permanent
element in the fabric of social obligation; and they also yield
the imagination of a supreme invisible but all-seeing ruler, to
whom service is due, from whom commands proceed as from an
earthly superior—the head of a family or the sovereign of a
state—and who punishes the violation of those commands. It is
in the form of this imagination that, in the case at least of all
ordinary good people, the idea of an absolute duty is so brought
to bear on the soul as to yield an awe superior to any personal
inclination. In sudden calls upon the will, when the sustaining
force of habit is of no avail, when no rewards or penalties, either
under the law of the state or the law of opinion, are to be looked
for, whatever the course of action adopted, can any of us be sure
that, except under the impression of the 'great task-master's
eye' upon him, he would do the work which upon reflection he
would admit should be done?

318. It is a necessity, however, of our rational nature that
these forms of imagination, in which our highest practical ideas
have found expression, should be subject to criticism. Is there
really a divine ruler, who issues commands which we can obey or
disobey; who somehow sees and hears us, though not through
eye or ear; whom it is possible for us to please or offend? Now
there is undoubtedly a sense in which these questions, once
asked, can only be answered in the negative. The most convinced Theist must admit that God is as unimaginable as He is
unperceivable,—unimaginable because unperceivable, for that
which we imagine (in the proper sense of the term) has the
necessary finiteness of that which we perceive; that statements, therefore, which in any strict sense could only be applied to an imaginable finite agent, cannot in any such sense
be applied to God. As applied to Him, they must at any
rate not be reasoned from as we reason from statements about
matters of fact. The practice of treating them as if they were

such statements, with the confusions and contradictions to which it inevitably leads, only enhances doubt as to the reality of the divine Spirit; of which we must confess that it is inexpressible in its nature by us, though operative in us through those practical ideas of a possible perfect life, of a being for whom this perfect life is already actual, which, acting upon imagination, yield the language of ordinary religion.

319. Now when criticism comes to do its inevitable work upon the language of imagination in which our fundamental moral ideas have found expression, a counter-work is called for from philosophy, which has an important bearing upon conduct. It has to disentangle the operative ideas from their necessarily imperfect expression, and to explain that the validity of the ideas themselves, as principles of action, is not affected by the discovery that the language, in which men under their influence naturally express themselves, has not the sort of truth which belongs to a correct statement of matters of fact. It has to show when and how—these ideas not being matters of fact or obtained by abstraction from matters of fact—the figures of speech employed in expressing the aspirations and endeavours to which they give rise, being derived by metaphor from sensible matters of fact, are liable to mislead us if we argue from them as though they conveyed literal truth. It has to point out what is the sense in which alone the question as to the truth of such language can be properly asked or answered. If the question is asked, for instance, whether there is truth in the language, habitual to the religious conscience, in which God is represented as giving us certain commands and seeing whether we perform them or no, the philosopher will remind us that to enquire whether such language is true, in the same sense in which it might be true that I ordered my servant to do certain things this morning and took notice whether he did them, is as inappropriate as it would be to enquire (according to an example employed by Locke in another connection) whether sleep is swift or virtue square. It can only be reasonably asked whether it is true in the sense that it naturally expresses, in terms of imagination, an emotion arising from consciousness of a relation which really subsists between the human soul and God. If the infinite Spirit so communicates itself to the soul of man as to

yield the idea of a possible perfect life, and that consequent
sense of personal responsibility on the part of the individual for
making the best of himself as a social being from which the
recognition of particular duties arises, then it is a legitimate expression by means of metaphor—the only possible means, except
action, by which the consciousness of spiritual realities can
express itself—to say that our essential duties are commands of
God. If again the self-communication of the infinite Spirit to
the soul of man is such that man is conscious of his relation to
a conscious being, who is in eternal perfection all that man has
it in him to come to be, then it is a legitimate expression of that
conscious relation by means of metaphor to say that God sees
whether His commands are fulfilled by us or no, and an appropriate emotion to feel shame as in His presence for omissions
or violations of duty incognisable by other men.

320. The above must not be taken to mean that it is to be
considered the business of philosophy to justify the language of
religious imagination universally and unconditionally. Even as
that language is current in Christendom, there may be much in
it that a true moral philosophy will have to condemn as inconsistent with the highest kind of moral conviction. Objection
may properly be taken, for instance, to the ordinary representa-
tion of God as a source of rewards and penalties ; as rewarding
goodness with certain pleasures bestowed from without, as
punishing wickedness with pains inflicted from without. The
objection to it, however, is not that it represents God under a
figure which is not a statement of fact (for the same objection
would apply equally to all the language of religion), but that the
figure is one which interferes with the true idea of goodness as
its own reward, of vice as its own punishment. It is an important function of philosophy to examine the current language
of religious imagination, not with the unreasonable view of
testing its speculative truth, as we might test the truth of
some doctrine about natural phenomena, but in order to satisfy
ourselves whether it worthily expresses the emotions of a soul in
which the highest moral ideas have done their perfect work.

With such an application of philosophy, however, we are not
at present concerned. Our present purpose is merely to point
out the service which philosophy may render to practical

morality in counteracting the advantage which scepticism may otherwise give to passion against duty. It is true, of course, that when the soul is suddenly called upon to face some awful moment, to which are joined great issues for good or evil in its moral history, it is not by ' going over the theory of virtue in one's mind,' not by any philosophical consideration of the origin and validity of moral ideas, that the right determination can be given. A judgment of the sort we call intuitive—a judgment which in fact represents long courses of habit and imagination founded on ideas—is all that the occasion admits of. But even in such cases it may make a great difference to the issue, whether the inclination to the weaker or less worthy course is or is not assisted by a suggestion from the intellect that the counter-injunction of conscience is illusory. And in such an age as ours this suggestion is likely to be forthcoming, if scepticism has been allowed to pull to pieces the imaginative vesture in which our formative practical ideas have clothed themselves, without a vindication by philosophy of the ultimate authority of the ideas themselves, and of so much in the language of religious imagination as is their pure and (to us) necessary expression.

321. We have still, however, to consider the service which philosophy may render in what we distinguished above as *bona fide* perplexities *of conscience; bona fide* perplexities, as distinct from those self-sophistications, born of the pleasure-seeking impulse, in dealing with which philosophy would be misapplied; perplexities *of conscience,* as distinct from cases like that of Jeannie Deans, where conscience speaks without ambiguity but is opposed by an impulse in itself noble and disinterested. In cases of this latter kind philosophy may, as we have seen, under special conditions of intellectual culture, have an important service to render; but it will not be in the way of setting aside apparent contradictions in the deliverance of conscience. It will rather be in the way of vindicating the real authority of that deliverance against a scepticism which might otherwise take advantage of the discovery that the forms of imagination, in which the deliverance is clothed, are not the same as statements of speculative truth. The kind of practical perplexity which we have now to consider arises not from any doubt as to the authority of conscience, nor from any attempt of selfish inclina-

tion to 'dodge' conscience by assuming its disguise, but from the fact that the requirements of conscience seem to be in conflict with each other. However disposed to do what his conscience enjoins, the man finds it difficult to decide what its injunction is.

In the crisis, for instance, through which several European states have recently passed, such a difficulty might naturally occur to a good Catholic who was also a loyal subject. His conscience would seem to enjoin equally obedience to the law of the State, and obedience to the law of the Church. But these laws were in conflict. Which then was he to obey? It is a form of the same difficulty which in earlier days must have occurred to Quakers and Anabaptists, to whom the law derived from Scripture seemed contradictory to that of the State, and to those early Christians for whom the law which they disobeyed in refusing to sacrifice retained any authority. In still earlier times it may have arisen in the form of that conflict between the law of the family and the law of the State, presented in the 'Antigone.' Nor is the case really different when the modern citizen, in his capacity as an official or as a soldier, is called upon to help in putting down some revolutionary movement which yet presents itself to his inmost conviction as the cause of 'God and the People.' This case may indeed appear different from those previously noticed, because, while those were cases of conflict between acknowledged authorities, this may seem rather to be one of conflict between private opinion and authority. But if the private opinion is more than a conceit which it is pleasant to air; if it is a source of really conscientious opposition to an authority which equally appeals to the conscience; if, in other words, it is an expression which the ideal of human good gives to itself in the mind of the man who entertains it; then it too rests on a basis of social authority. No individual can make a conscience for himself. He always needs a society to make it for him. A conscientious 'heresy,' religious or political, always represents some gradually maturing conviction as to social good, already implicitly involved in the ideas on which the accepted rules of conduct rest, though it may conflict with the formulae in which those ideas have been hitherto authoritatively expressed, and may lead to the overthrow of institutions which have previously contributed to their realisation.

322. In preparation for the times when conscience is thus liable to be divided against itself, much practical service may be rendered by a philosophy which, without depreciating the authority of conscience as such, can explain the origin of its conflicting deliverances, and, without pronouncing unconditionally for either, can direct the soul to the true end to which each in some qualified way is relative. In order to illustrate this in more detail, we will suppose a philosopher, holding the doctrines previously stated in this treatise, to be called upon for counsel in difficulties of the kind just noticed. It will of course occur to every one that the counsel given goes too far back in its reasons, and in its conclusions is of too neutral a kind, to command attention in times of social or religious conflict and revolution. But, though this is so, it might have its effect upon the few who lead the many, in preparing the mind through years of meditation for the days when prompt practical decision is required.

The philosopher, then, will begin by considering how the seeming contradiction in the deliverances of conscience comes about. He will point out that, though there would be no such thing as conscience at all but for the consciousness on the part of the individual that there is an unconditional good which, while independent of his likes and dislikes, is yet *his* good —though this consciousness is as irremovable as morality— yet it does not follow that all the judgments which arise out of this consciousness are unconditionally valid. The several dicta of conscience have had their history. Passing beyond the stage of mere conformity to custom, of mere obedience to persons and powers that be—a conformity and obedience which themselves arise out of an operative, though inarticulate, idea of common good—men have formed more or less general notions of the customs and powers, as entitled to their conformity and obedience. Certain formulae, expressing the nature of the authorities to which obedience is due, and their most familiar requirements, have become part of 'the *a priori* furniture' of men's minds, in the sense that they are accepted as valid independently of those lessons of experience which men are conscious of acquiring for themselves. Such are what are commonly called the 'dicta of conscience.' Certain injunctions of family duty, of obedience to the law of the State, of conformity to a law of honour or opinion, have assumed this character. So too in Christendom have certain ordinances of the Church, notwithstanding much variety of opinion as to what constitutes the Church.

323. Now in all such deliverances of conscience the content of the obligation is blended with some conception or imagination of an authority imposing the obligation, in a combination which only the trained analytical intellect can disentangle. Just as to children the duty of speaking the truth seems inseparable from the parental command to do so, so to many a simple Catholic, for instance, the fact that the Church commands him to live cleanly and honestly seems the source of the obligation so to live. To give just measure and to go to Mass are to him homogeneous duties; just as to unenlightened persons in a differently ordered religious community to give just measure and to observe the Sabbath may be so. An abrogation of the authority which imposes the ceremonial obligation would seem to imply a disappearance of the moral obligation as well; because this too in the mind of the individual has become associated with the imagination of an imponent authority, the same as that which enjoins the ceremonial observance. This does not arise from the existence of a Church as a co-ordinate institution with the State. Were there no Church, the difference would only be that, as in the Græco-Roman world, the State would gather to itself the sentiments of which, as it is, the Church seems the more natural object. Moral duties would still be associated with the imagination of an imponent authority, whose injunctions they would be supposed to be, though the authority might be single instead of twofold.

Nor would any considerate member of modern society, even the most enlightened, venture to say that his sense of moral duty was independent of some such imagination of an imponent, however resolutely he might refuse to recognise either the Church or any particular personage as the imponent. If he has ceased to describe himself naturally as a good Catholic or good Churchman, he may still attach significance to the description of himself as a good Christian; and this probably implies

to him the recognition of an imponent of obligation in the
founder of the Christian society or the author of a Christian
revelation. Or if he has ceased to recognise such an imponent,
he probably still calls himself a loyal subject; and in so doing
expresses the fact that he presents to himself some personal
external source—some source other than a spirit working in him
—of the law which he obeys; and that he obeys the law, not
from fear of pains and penalties, but from reverence for the
authority from which he believes it to proceed—as much, therefore, when he might evade it with impunity as when he runs
the risk of punishment. Perhaps there may be no ostensible
person, no emperor or king, whom he regards as the author of
the law which he obeys, and he may accordingly prefer to describe himself as a loyal citizen rather than as a loyal subject,
but he is very exceptional if he does not still think of some
association of persons, a 'sovereign people,' as the authority
from which law proceeds. If he ceased to present such an
authority to himself, having previously discarded the imagination of Church or King or Divine Lawgiver as imponents of
duty, he would be apt to find the obligation, not only of what
is local and temporary in positive law, but of what is essential
in the moral law, slipping away from him.

324. This imagination of an external imponent, however, is
not intrinsically necessary to the consciousness of what we call
metaphorically[1] moral law, while it is the source of apparent
conflict between different injunctions of conscience. It is the
very essence of moral duty to be imposed by a man on himself.
The moral duty to obey a positive law, whether a law of the
State or of the Church, is imposed not by the author or enforcer
of the positive law, but by that spirit of man—not less divine
because the spirit of man—which sets before him the ideal of
a perfect life, and pronounces obedience to the positive law to
be necessary to its realisation. This actual imposition, however,
of duties by man upon himself precedes and is independent of a

---

[1] I say 'metaphorically,' because what we primarily understand by 'law' is
some sort of command, given by a superior in power to one whom he is able to
punish for disobedience; whereas it is the essence of moral 'law' that it is a rule
which a man imposes on himself, and from another motive than the fear of punishment.

true conception of what duty is. Men who are really a law to
themselves, in the sense that it is their idea of an absolute
'should be,' of some perfection to be realised in and by them,
that is the source of the general rule of life which they observe,
are yet unable to present that rule to themselves as anything
else than the injunction of some external authority. It is this
state of mind that renders them liable to the perplexities of conscience described, in which duties appear to conflict with each
other.

There is no such thing really as a conflict of duties. A man's
duty under any particular set of circumstances is always one,
though the conditions of the case may be so complicated and
obscure as to make it difficult to decide what the duty really is.
That which we are apt to call a conflict of duties is really a competition of reverences for imagined imponents of duty, whose
injunctions, actual or supposed, do not agree. A woman perhaps
finds herself directed to act in one way by her father, in another
by her confessor. A citizen may find himself similarly distracted between the law of the State and that of the Church;
or between the ordinance of an ostensible sovereign and that of
a revolutionary committee, claiming to act in the name of God
and the People. In such cases, if the conscience were clear of
prepossession in favour of this authority or that, and were simply
prepared to recognise as duty the course which contributes most
to the perfect life, it might yet be difficult enough to ascertain
what this course of action would be, though there would be no
doubt that the one duty was to pursue that course of action
when ascertained. But the actual perplexity of conscience in
such cases commonly arises not from this difficulty, but from
the habit of identifying duty with injunctions given by external
authorities, and from the fact that in the supposed case the injunctions so given are inconsistent with each other.

325. Now the task of the moral philosopher in regard to such
cases would be a comparatively easy one, if it simply consisted
in trying to rid a man of his illusions of conscience; if he had
merely to point out the work of imagination in ascribing the
essential duties which conscience enjoins to an external imponent, and to show that the apparent conflict of duties is in fact
merely a conflict between certain external authorities which are

wrongly supposed to impose duties, whereas all that a purely external authority can impose is a command enforced by fear. If the philosopher aims at no more than this, he may succeed in his work, but its value will be doubtful. It may prove easier to convince men that duties, in the moral sense, cannot be imposed from without than, when this has been shown, to maintain the conviction that they exist at all. If the result of the philosopher's work is to popularise the notion that the authorities to which men have chiefly looked as imponents of duties, are merely powers able to induce obedience to their commands by threat of punishment for disobedience, without substitution of any new reverence for that which must be withdrawn from the authorities so regarded, we shall have nothing to thank him for. In truth the phrase ' external authority,' as applied to the imagined imponents of duty, involves something of a contradiction. If they were merely external, they would not be authorities, for an authority implies, on the part of the man to whom it is an authority, a conception of its having a claim upon his obedience ; and this again implies that his obedience to it is a self-imposed obedience—an obedience which commends itself to his reason as good, irrespectively of penalties attached to disobedience. The authority, in being recognised as an authority, has ceased to be a mere source of commands, enforced by fear of punishment for their violation, and in that sense to be merely external. Its injunctions now commend themselves to the subject of them, not indeed as proceeding from a spirit which is his own or himself, but as directed to the attainment of an end in which the subject is interested on his own account; which is, and is known by him to be, his true good. How the several injunctions in detail contribute to such an end he does not see; but he trusts the authority from which they proceed to have it more completely in view than he can himself. It is thus that the Church is an authority to the good Catholic, the State to the good citizen, the Bible to the orthodox Protestant. In each case the acknowledgment of the authority has become one and the same thing with the individual's presentation to himself of a true good, at once his own and the good of others, which it is his business to pursue.

326. Now it would be a blundering and reckless procedure on

the part of the moral philosopher, if he were first to construe too literally the language in which these authorities are described, so to speak, from without for rhetorical or logical purposes,— to take it as if it represented their true spiritual import for those who acknowledge them—and then, in his hurry to assert the truth that a moral obligation cannot be imposed from without, were to seek to dethrone them from their place in the moral imagination, and to substitute for them an improvised conscience that should make its own laws *de novo* from within.   It must rather be his object, without setting aside any of the established authorities which have acquired a hold on the conscience, to awaken such an understanding of the impulse after an ideal of conduct which, without being understood, has expressed itself in these authorities, as may gradually render men independent of the mode of its authoritative expression.   One who has learnt this lesson will have a rationale of the various duties presented to him in the name of Cæsar or of God, which will help him to distinguish what is essential in the duties from the form of their imposition, and to guide himself by looking to the common end to which they are alike relative.   Should an occasion arise when the duties seem to conflict, he will be prepared for the discovery that the conflict is not really between duties, but between powers invested by the imagination with the character of imponents of duty.   He will be able to stand this discovery without moral deterioration, because he has learnt to fix his eye on the moral end or function—the function in the way of furthering perfection of conduct—served by the authorities which he has been bred to acknowledge.   He can thus find in that end, or in the Spirit whose self-communication renders him capable of seeking it, a fit object for all the reverences claimed by those authorities, and which he now discovers to be due to them only by a derived and limited title.

327. It may thus fall to the moral philosopher, under certain conditions of society and of intellectual movement, to render an important practical service.   But he will render it simply by fulfilling with the utmost possible completeness his proper work of analysis.   As a *moral* philosopher he analyses human conduct; the motives which it expresses, the spiritual endowments implied in it, the history of thought, habits and institutions through

which it has come to be what it is. He does not understand his business as a philosopher, if he claims to do more than this. He will not take it for a reproach to be reminded that no philosopher can supply a 'moral dynamic.' The pretension to do so he would regard as a great impertinence. He finds moral dynamic enough in the actual spiritual nature of man, when that nature is regarded, as it is his business to regard it, not merely in its hitherto performance, but in its intrinsic possibilities. If he cannot help wishing for more, that is an incident of the very aspiration after perfection of conduct which constitutes the dynamic. His immediate business as a philosopher is not to strengthen or heighten this aspiration, much less to bring it into existence, but to understand it. As a man and a citizen, indeed, it is his function to serve as its organ; to give effect to it in his own conduct, to assist in communicating it to others. And since in being a philosopher he does not cease to be a man and a citizen, he will rejoice that the analysis, which alone forms his employment as a philosopher, should incidentally serve a purpose subordinate to the 'moral dynamic'—that it should help to remove any obstacle to the effort of the human soul after a perfect life.

The distraction of conscience caused, as we have seen, by competition of reverences for authorities whose injunctions come into conflict with each other, may form such an obstacle. Its outward effect may sometimes be a paralysis of action; sometimes, on the other hand, hasty and embittered action in opposition to one of the causes or authorities between the claims of which conscience is perplexed—action hasty and embittered for the very reason that the agent is afraid to face the consequence of dispassionate enquiry into the validity of the claims to which he blindly submits. So far as the impediment to the highest living, to the free development of human capabilities, is of this kind, the philosopher by mere thoroughness and completeness of ethical analysis may help to remove it. By giving the most adequate account possible of the moral ideal; by considering the process through which the institutions and rules of life, of which we acknowledge the authority, have arisen out of the effort, however blindly directed, after such an ideal, and have in their several measures contributed to its realisation; by showing that conscience in the individual, while owing its education to those institutions and rules, is not properly the mere organ of any or all of them, but may freely and in its own right apprehend the ideal of which they are more or less inadequate expressions; by thus doing his proper work as a philosopher of morals, he may help the soul to rise above the region of distraction between competing authorities, or between authorities and an inner law, to a region in which it can harmonise all the authorities by looking to the end to which they, or whatever is really authoritative in them, no less than the inner law, are alike relative.

328. That the soul, however, should derive any such benefit from philosophy implies a previous discipline, which cannot be derived from philosophy, but only from conduct regulated by the authorities which philosophy teaches it to understand. It is a complaint as old as the time of Plato that, in learning to seek for the rationale of the rules which they are trained to obey—to enquire what is the ideal of human good, which these rules serve and are justified by serving—men come to find excuses for disregarding them. And, no doubt, as Plato saw, till the character is set in the direction of the ideal, a theory of the ideal can be of no value for the improvement of conduct in any sense. It may be doubted, indeed, whether the apparent mischief, which arises in a speculative age from the habit of asking a reason why for the rules of respectability, does more than affect the excuses made for acts of self-indulgence of which men, innocent of criticism or speculation, would equally be guilty. But, however this may be, it remains true that the value of the Dialectic which asks and gives such an account of ideal good as at once justifies and limits obedience to practical authorities, is conditional upon its finding in the individual a well-formed habitual morality.

When it does so, it may influence life for good, by enlisting in the real service of mankind the zeal which would otherwise become a mis-directed loyalty or a spirit of unprofitable rebellion. It will teach a man to question the absoluteness of the authorities which speak in the name of Cæsar and of God— not with a view to shirking the precepts of either in the interest of his own pleasures, but in order that he may not be led by either into a 'conscientious' opposition to the other, obstructive to the work of which the promotion in different ways is the true function of each. When he finds that the requirements of Church or State, the observances of conventional morality or conventional religion, are in conflict with what some plead as their conscientious convictions, it will make him watchful to ascertain whether these new convictions may not represent a truer effort after the highest ideal than that embodied in the authorities which seek to suppress them. On the other hand, when he finds some conviction of his own in conflict with authority, it will teach him not indeed to conceal it for fear of inconvenient consequences, but to suppress all pride in it as if it were an achievement of his own; to regard it as proceeding, so far as it is good for anything, from the operation of the same practical reason in society which has given rise to the authorities with which his conviction brings him into collision. So regarding it, he will be respectful of the prejudices which he offends by expressing it; careful to eschew support which might be due not to an appreciation of what is good in the new conviction, but to mere aversion from the check put upon self-will by the authorities impugned; patient of opposition, and, in case of failure, ready to admit that there is more wisdom than he understood in the conventions which have been too strong for him.

CHAPTER III.

329. The chief theory of conduct which in Modern Europe has afforded the conscientious citizen a vantage-ground for judging of the competing claims on his obedience, and enabled him to substitute a critical and intelligent for a blind and un-questioning conformity, has no doubt been the Utilitarian. What we are now considering, it must be borne in mind, is the practical value of theories in regard to the moral ideal, as distinct from the possession of the character by the ideal itself. It is not to the purpose, therefore, to notice the work of religious reformers. It is probable indeed that every movement of religious reform has originated in some clearer conception of the ideal of human conduct, arrived at by some person or persons; a conception, perhaps, towards which many men have been silently working, but which finally finds in some one individual the character which can give decisive practical expression to it. But in the initiation of religious reforms the new theory of the ideal, as a theory, always holds a secondary place. It is not absent, but it is, so to speak, absorbed in a character—a character to which the speculative completeness of the theory is of little interest— and it is this character which gives the new conception of the ideal its power in the world. The influence exercised by Utili-tarianism, on the other hand, has been specially the influence of a theory. Whatever the errors arising from its Hedonistic psychology, no other theory has been available for the social or political reformer, combining so much truth with such ready applicability. No other has offered so commanding a point of view from which to criticise the precepts and institutions pre-sented as authoritative. When laws of the Church, or of the

State, or of ' opinion,' have become antagonistic to each other ; when any of them, again, has been found to conflict with one of those convictions of tender consciences, or of enthusiasts for humanity, which are a ' law of opinion ' in the making, Utilitarianism furnishes a test by which the competing claims of the different laws, or those of law on one side and individual conviction on the other, may be put to the test.

330. All persons having a private interest in the maintenance of the law or custom which the Utilitarian theory calls in question ; all who shrink from the trouble of having to examine established rules of conduct ; others who are rightly persuaded that the service rendered to mankind by rules that have become sacred is not to be measured by any account of their usefulness which the most enlightened observer can make out—these withstand Utilitarian criticism in the name of principle against expediency. Generally, however—at any rate when the question is one, not of conduct in private relations, but of laws or institutions, or of political conduct—that view of the right course to take which pleads ' principle,' as against suggestions said to be founded on ' expediency,' really only differs from the latter in respect of the more limited range of consequences which it takes into account. The ' principle ' alleged has originally derived its authority from reference to some social good which it has been found to serve. The ' expediency,' for the sake of which a departure from the established rule is pressed for, is equally founded on a conception of social good, but on the conception of a good in which a wider range of persons is contemplated as partaking.

The ill-repute which attaches to considerations of expediency, so far as it is well founded, is chiefly due to the fact that, when the question of conduct at issue is one which the person debating it has a private interest in deciding one way or the other—when he himself will gain pleasure or avoid pain by either decision— the admission of expediency as the ground of decision is apt to give him an excuse for deciding in his own favour. And, even when this personal bias is not operative, the man who looks to ' expediency ' may be apt to trust to some limited view of consequences, which is all that his own vision can command, while if he had ' stuck to principle ' he would really have been guided by a more complete view, gathered from the wisdom of ages. Neither of these mischiefs, however, arises from the Utilitarian principle of practical judgment, as fairly applied, but from that mis-application of it by interested or hasty individuals to which all principles are liable. Nor must it be forgotten that, when private interest affords a motive for deciding a practical ques-tion in a particular way, 'principle' will sometimes furnish a more convenient excuse than 'expediency.' Slaveholders, for instance, have never found any difficulty in justifying slavery 'on principle.'

331. On the whole there is no doubt that the theory of an ideal good, consisting in the greatest happiness of the greatest number, as the end by reference to which the claim of all laws and powers and rules of action on our obedience is to be tested, has tended to improve human conduct and character. This admission may be made quite as readily by those who consider such conduct and character an end in itself, as by those who hold that its improvement can only be measured by reference to an extraneous end, consisting in the quantity of pleasure pro-duced by it; perhaps, when due account has been taken of the difficulty of deciding whether quantity of pleasure is really increased by 'social progress,' *more* readily by the former than by the latter. It is not indeed to be supposed that the Utili-tarian theory, any more than any other theory of morals, has brought about the recognition or practice of any virtues that were not recognised and practised independently of it; or that any one, for being a theoretic Utilitarian, has been a better man —*i.e.* one more habitually governed by desire for human per-fection in some of its forms—than he otherwise would have been. But it has helped men, acting under the influence of ideals of conduct and rules of virtuous living, to fill up those ideals and apply those rules in a manner beneficial to a wider range of persons—beneficial to them in the sense of tending to remove certain obstacles to good living in their favour. It has not given men a more lively sense of their duty to others—no theory can do that—but it has led those in whom that sense has al-ready been awakened to be less partial in judging who the 'others' are, to consider all men as the 'others,' and, on the ground of the claim of all men to an equal chance of 'happiness,'

to secure their political and promote their social equality. To do this is not indeed directly to advance the highest living among men, but it is to remove obstacles to such living, which in the name of principle and authority have often been maintained.

332. The practical service, however, thus rendered by Utilitarianism has been independent of its analysis of well-being or good. It has been by insisting that it is 'the greatest number' whose highest good is to be taken into account, not by identifying that highest good with a greatest nett quantity of pleasure, that it has improved the organisation of human life. It is thus that it has given a wider and more impartial range to public spirit, to the desire to do good. It is thus that it has made men watchful of customary morality, lest its rules should be conceived in the interest of some particular class of persons, who—probably without being fully aware of it—have been concerned in establishing and maintaining them. It is thus that it has afforded men ground for enquiring, when laws, alike pleading the highest authority, were found to make conflicting claims on their obedience, whether either claim represented the real good of society, and which represented the good of the largest body of persons.

Very often this question may be sufficiently answered without any thorough analysis of what the good of society consists in, and thus the truth of the answer is independent of the truth of the theory which measures good by the quantity of pleasure experienced on the whole. In none of the great struggles between privileged and unprivileged classes, through which modern society has passed, would a man have been helped to a sounder judgment as to the part which he should take by a more correct definition of the good. The essential thing for his right guidance has been that, whatever might be the definition of good which he would accept, he should admit the equal title of all men to it in the same sense; that account should be taken of the widest possible range of society that can be brought into view, and that whatever is deemed good for any class or individuals in the society should be deemed good for all its members. In the struggle, for instance, through which the United States of America lately passed, a conscientious Virginian, divided in his mind between allegiance to his State and allegiance to the

Union, could have found no useful direction in the truest possible analysis of the nature of ultimate good. The kind of well-being ostensibly served by the laws of his State for those who had the benefit of the laws, was not a different kind from that served by the maintenance of the Union. The question was whether secession or maintenance of the Union would promote that well-being most impartially, and for the widest range of society.

Again, in most cases where a man has to decide how he may best promote the greatest good of others, it makes little practical difference in regard to the line of action to be taken, whether he considers their greatest good to lie in the possession of a certain character, as an end not a means, or in the enjoyment of the most pleasure of which they are capable. No one can convey a good character to another. Every one must make his character for himself. All that one man can do to make another better is to remove obstacles, and supply conditions favourable to the formation of a good character. Now, in a general way and up to a certain point, the line of action directed to this removal of obstacles and supply of conditions favourable to goodness, will also tend to make existence more pleasant for those whose good is being sought. For instance, healthy houses and food, sound elementary education, the removal of temptations to drink, which are needed in order to supply conditions favourable to good character, tend also to make life more pleasant on the whole. The question at issue between Hedonistic Utilitarians and their opponents as to the nature of ultimate good cannot affect their importance.

333. So far we have seen how a philosophy of morals may prevent the perplexity of conscience, and consequent paralysis or misdirection of spiritual energy, arising from a conflict between authorities which have alike some sacredness for the imagination, or between such an authority and some unauthorised conviction of the individual; how it may do this by directing the devotion, hitherto supposed to be due to certain imponents of duty, explicitly to the end from reference to which all true authority, without distinction, must be derived; how the form of philosophy which in the modern world has most conspicuously rendered this service has been the Utilitarian, because it has most definitely announced the interest of humanity, without distinction

of persons or classes, as the end by reference to which all claims upon obedience are ultimately to be measured. We may pay this homage to Utilitarianism without admitting that Hedonistic interpretation of the interest of humanity which has in fact generally been adopted by Utilitarians, especially by those who count themselves scientific. Impartiality of reference to human well-being has been the great lesson which the Utilitarian has had to teach. That 'unscientific' interpretation of well-being which the men most receptive of the lesson, on the strength of their own unselfish wishes and aspirations, have been ready to supply, has made them practically independent of any further analysis of it, when once the equality of claim to it had been thoroughly recognised. We may give Utilitarianism, therefore, full credit for the work it has done in rationalising the order of social and political life, while holding at the same time that its Hedonistic interpretation of well-being, if logically carried out, would deprive it of any practical influence for good; and that, as this interpretation in a speculative age comes to be more dwelt upon by the individual, it may itself induce practical evils, from which deliverance must be sought in a truer analysis of the ultimate good for man. It remains for us then to consider, whether there is any practical service—any service in the way of a direction of conduct—to be rendered in particular by such a theory of the good, of the moral ideal, as has been set forth above in opposition to the Hedonistic view. Are there any questions in regard to the right line to be taken in life, upon which men are liable to *bona fide* perplexity[1], and upon which this theory might offer a guidance that Utilitarianism, as a theory, could not supply? And, again, can it claim any useful office, simply in virtue of its being a philosophy of morals more adequate to the moral capability of man, as a counteracting influence to that weakening of conduct and lowering of aims, which in a speculative age a less adequate, and therefore misleading, philosophy may bring about?

334. Hitherto the practical effects of Utilitarianism, as a generally accepted theory, have been chiefly seen in its application to public policy rather than to private conduct. It has

---

[1] '*Bona fide* perplexity,' as having its origin really in intellectual difficulties, not in any selfish interest.

been the question, Ought such and such laws or institutions to
be maintained or altered? rather than the question, Ought I to
do this or that? which it has in fact generally been employed to
settle. Philosophic Utilitarians, of course, have always held
that the ultimate criterion of right and wrong in the actions
of individuals, as much as in laws and institutions, is to be
sought in the balance of resulting pleasure or pain, but they
have not generally been forward to press the application of this
criterion by individuals to their own actions. They have seldom,
indeed, taken the same line as Mr. Henry Sidgwick, who, while
he holds that no other scientific test of right conduct is possible
than that derived from calculating the quantity of pleasure produced by any course of action to all sentient beings capable of
being affected by it, yet explicitly rejects the doctrine that
pleasure is the sole object of desire; and who, even when he
has thus cleared the Utilitarian motive from the liability to be
identified with the pleasure of the person moved by it, still admits that the moral sentiments are in fact independent of it, and
expressly guards himself against being supposed to mean that
the desire of producing the utmost possible pleasure is the only
right or best motive of action[1]. Such Utilitarianism has more
of Butler and Hutcheson in it than of Bentham and Mill. But
there are probably few even among the more strictly Hedonistic
Utilitarians who hold that our ordinary judgments of actions,
as right or wrong, are formed upon any estimate by the individual of the effects of the actions in the way of producing
pleasure or pain, or who would wish them to be so formed.
Even when, as is commonly the case, they retain the psychological doctrine that pleasure—which must mean pleasure to
oneself—is the sole object of desire, pain the sole object of aversion, they would deny that in his best actions the individual was
actually influenced by what we naturally describe as interested
motives, or by a calculation of pleasure-yielding consequences.
They would admit that such actions are done from interest in
others, or from a feeling that they ought to be done; and they
would reconcile this admission with their doctrine as to pleasure
being the sole object of desire, by supposing that it is aversion
from some specific pain of shame, desire for some specific pleasure

[1] Methods of Ethics, Bk. I. Chap. iv, and Bk. IV. Chap. i.

in doing nobly or in contemplating the pleasure of others—by whatever process of evolution these sensibilities may have arisen —that form the motives to such actions. And, just as they would thus qualify their view of the kind of desire for pleasure which is the motive to an admirable action, so they would admit that in most cases the question, whether an action was right or wrong, was most likely to be correctly decided by the individual on the strength of judgments which we call intuitive, which may perhaps represent prolonged observation by his ancestors of the pleasure-giving and pain-giving effects of actions, but are independent of any such observation on his own part.

335. It is not to be expected, however, in an age of intellectual emancipation, when a scientific test of right action has been announced which is in itself easily intelligible (whatever upon thorough enquiry may turn out to be the difficulties of its application), that educated men will fail to employ it in their judgments of what they individually should do and should not do. Having got to the water, the ducklings will swim. The habit of calling authorities in question cannot be limited to philosophers; and, having once learned to call them in question, men will not stop short with the authorities that have regulated their civil and political relations. They will seek a rationale of their most intimate moral obligations; and when the Utilitarian philosopher offers them a scientific test of right and wrong, they will not be slow to apply it to the question which interests them most—the question how they may best conduct their own lives. In the European nations a constantly increasing number of persons find themselves in circumstances, in which a large option is allowed them as to the plan on which they will conduct their lives. The necessities of providing for a family, or of fulfilling the requirements of some employment without which they could not live, no longer determine the whole course of their existence. They can 'please themselves' in regard to a large part of their action; and they are naturally interested in finding a theory which, though it will probably have much less influence than they ascribe to it in really directing even their more optional conduct, will always give them a basis for arguing with themselves and others, whether that conduct is justifiable or otherwise.

How prevalent such argument has become, at least in ' cultivated circles,' need not be said.   Hedonism has become not only
a serious topic in the study, but often the babble of the drawing-
room.   Good people, of the sort who fifty years ago would have
found in the law of their neighbours' opinion, or in the requirements of their church or sect, or in the precepts of Scripture as
interpreted by church or sect, sufficient direction for so much of
their walk and conduct as it would have occurred to them to
think in need of any direction, may now be heard arguing
whether this occupation or that, this or that habit of action,
this or that way of spending their time, conveys the greater
amount of pleasure and is therefore the more to be approved.
That they attach serious importance to the question, that they
suppose its decision to go for a great deal in the actual guidance
of their lives, may be inferred from the surprise and displeasure
with which they would receive a suggestion that, after all, their
action is pretty much independent of it.   They may not be very
clear whether it is pleasure to themselves or to others that they
have in view ;   they may not have appreciated the distinction
between ' egoistic' and 'universalistic' Hedonism ; but there can
be no doubt of two things : (1) that to an extent unknown in
previous generations they are seeking a theoretical direction for
individual conduct, and seeking it in a consideration of the
natural consequences of conduct, as causing pleasure or pain ;
and (2) that they seem to themselves to be largely influenced in
conduct by this theoretical direction.

336. Those who are glad of a topic for denunciation may, if
they like, treat the prevalence of such opinions among educated
men as encouraging the tendency to vicious self-indulgence in
practice.   No such unfairness will here be committed.   There is
no good reason to apprehend that there is relatively more—we
may even hope that there is less—of such self-indulgence than
in previous generations ; though, for reasons just indicated, it
has a wider scope for itself, talks more of itself and is more
talked about, than at times when men were more tied down by
the necessities of their position.   We are no more justified in
treating what we take to be untrue theories of morals as positive
promoters of vice, than in treating what we deem truer theories as
positive promoters of virtue.   Only those in whom the tendencies

to vicious self-indulgence have been so far overcome as to allow
the aspiration after perfection of life to take effect, are in a
state to be affected either for better or for worse by theories of
the good. The worst that can truly be objected against the
prevalence of Hedonistic theory, just noticed, is that it may
retard and mislead those who are already good, according to the
ordinary sense of goodness as equivalent to immunity from vice,
in their effort to be better ; and the most that can be claimed
for the theory which we deem truer, is that it keeps the way
clearer of speculative impediments to the operation of motives,
which it seeks to interpret but does not pretend to supply. The
grounds for this objection and this claim are what we have now
to consider.

337. We have already explained the reasons to which we
ascribe the general acceptance of Hedonistic theory by persons
who are themselves by no means habitual pleasure-seekers.
They seem to be chiefly two. One is the confused notion that
the pleasure incidental to the satisfaction of desire, or to the
consciousness of work done, is itself the object of the desire, or
the end to which the work is directed. Simply for want of
thorough reflective analysis, men whose main interest is in the
achievement of objects quite different from any enjoyment of
pleasure, are ready to admit that their object is always some
pleasure or other, because they are conscious of always anticipating pleasure in the achievement of their objects. The other
reason is the impossibility of adequately defining an end that
consists in the realisation of human capabilities, until the realisation is accomplished. When we say that the 'summum
bonum,' by reference to which the value of men's actions is to
be measured, is the perfection of human life, as consisting in the
full realisation of human capabilities, some more detailed account
of this realisation, and of the perfection which it constitutes, is
naturally asked for. But such an account cannot be given in a
way that is likely at first to satisfy the questioner. We can
point indeed to a great realisation of human capabilities, which
has actually been achieved. Men have been in large measure
civilised and moralised ; nature has been largely subdued to their
use ; they have learnt to express themselves in the fine arts.
The ordinary activity of men, regulated by law and custom, has

its value as contributing to this realisation. But it is not for this ordinary activity, so regulated, that those who are seeking practical direction in a theory of the good need any guidance. It does not occur to them that they have any option in regard to it. They play their part in it as a matter of course. It is an aspiration after some further perfection than that already attained in those actual arrangements of life, which they have no choice but to accept and help to maintain, that makes them enquire into the ends of living. If the philosopher can only tell them to try to be better and to make others better; to seek a more complete fulfilment of the capabilities of human nature in themselves and in others; to make this the object of their lives and the end by reference to which they measure the value of actions; if he cannot at the same time tell them what this greater perfection will positively mean for themselves and others; they will be apt to think that he has told them nothing, and to contrast the emptiness of the end to which he professes to direct them, with the definite intelligibility of that which is explained to consist in a greatest possible quantity of pleasure for all sentient beings. For does not every one know what pleasure is and desire it, and cannot every one compare a greater with a less quantity of it?

338. For the moment we will suppose this contrast between the two ways of conceiving the chief good—between the definiteness of the one and the vagueness of the other—to be valid, as it is, no doubt, generally accepted. We will suppose the view that the ' summum bonum ' is the greatest possible nett quantity of pleasure to be adopted by some one, who has no inducement to find in it excuses for self-indulgence of that kind which, as we have seen, though it may find excuses for itself in theoretical Hedonism, is never really occasioned by it. We will suppose it to be disinterestedly applied by such an one to the direction of his life, in those respects in which he is likely to feel the need of direction. We have previously explained the grounds on which, as a matter of speculation, we reject this view, and need not here repeat them. The question now to be discussed is whether it is likely to have any effects which may make a reconsideration of it, and a more thorough insight into the truth of the view opposed to it, practically desirable. Is not its intrinsic unavail-

ability for supplying motive or guidance to a man who wishes to make his life better, likely to induce a practical scepticism in reflecting persons who have adopted it, which tends to paralyse the effort after a better life?

To speak of it as thus intrinsically unavailable is a statement which will probably be thought to need prompt vindication. It will be remembered that we are supposing a man to be in search of some guidance of conduct which mere conformity to established usage, and the fulfilment of the duties of his station according to what is expected of him, will not afford. As regards duties recognised by the law of opinion—those of common veracity and fair dealing, and of beneficence in its more obvious forms, family duties and those imposed by State or Church—it is easy to show that an overbalance of pain would on the whole result from their neglect to those capable of being affected by it, whether or no we consider this to constitute the reason why they should be fulfilled. We cannot doubt that a general desire to avoid pain has had much to do with the establishment of such duties, though we may think that alone it could not suffice for their establishment. And it is certain that any disturbance of the established order, simply as disturbance, must cause much pain. On the other hand, there is no considerable balance of pleasure to one who violates such duties, or to other exceptional persons to whom his act may be an occasion of pleasure, to be set against the general pain caused by it. From the nature of the case the pangs of fear and shame must go far to neutralise any access of pleasure to such persons. In such cases, therefore, if the test of felicific consequences is to be applied, there is no doubt as to the result that it will yield. But then these are not the cases in which the application of such a test is ever likely to be called for. It is for direction in cases where the rules of conventional morality fail them, or in the attempt to remedy the defects of that morality, that enlightened and conscientious persons look to their theory of the good. A man wishes to satisfy himself, for instance, whether he is justified in spending so much of his time, without neglect of any recognised duty, in the gratification of his taste for music, or of his curiosity in literature; in conforming to the expectation of his class by accepting a challenge to a duel, or by running race-horses, or by being a party to the purchase of votes at an election; whether he ought not, in consideration of the state of society, to give up his habit of moderate drinking, or apply less of his wealth to private enjoyments and more to public purposes. Or perhaps he finds himself in some situation, such as that which we illustrated from the ' Heart of Midlothian,' in which, for the sake of others as well as himself, there seems to be strong reason for departing from some ordinary rule of morality, and in which, having emancipated himself from those influences of imagination which might govern the conduct of less enlightened persons, he requires some rule of reason to direct him. When the problem is of this kind, how far will the Hedonistic theory really help to its solution?

339. In the first order of instances just suggested, the question before the individual, speaking generally, is whether he should depart from the course of action to which custom or inclination, or the sense of what the opinion of his class requires of him, would naturally lead him, with a view to some higher good; and this, on the principles of Hedonistic Utilitarianism, must mean, with a view to the production of a quantity of pleasure greater on the whole than that to be expected from the course of action which, but for the sake of this higher good, he would naturally follow. We will suppose the Hedonistic calculation, then, to be undertaken by an enlightened and dispassionate person in order to the settlement of this question. How is he to assure himself that the proposed immediate and undoubted sacrifice on his own part will be compensated by an addition to the sum of human enjoyments on the whole? We say *human* enjoyments, in order not to complicate the question at the outset by recognising the necessity of taking the pleasures of all sentient beings into account, though it is difficult to see how upon Hedonistic principles that necessity can be ignored; for if it is pleasure, as such, and not the person enjoying it, that has intrinsic value, all pleasures alike, by whatever beings enjoyed, must be considered in making up the main account. Though confining his view, however, to the pains and pleasures of men, our enquirer, if he refuses to be put off with answers which really imply non-Hedonistic suppositions, will find it difficult to assure himself that, by any interference with usage or resistance

to his own inclination, he can make the balance of human pleasures as against human pains greater than it is.

340. And in the process of dealing with this difficulty he is likely to find himself in the presence of one still more formidable, because more closely affecting the springs of his own conduct. He will have to face the question whether, upon the principles which have generally been taken as the foundation of philosophic Utilitarianism, the supposition that it is possible for him to do anything else than follow his pleasure-seeking impulses can be other than an illusion. In the first place he will be likely to call in question the common assumption that the aggregate of pleasures at any time enjoyed might, *under the circumstances*, be greater than it is. He will see that this assumption conflicts with the principles on which 'the proof of Utilitarianism' has been generally founded. These principles are that every one acts from what is for the time his strongest desire or aversion, and that the object of a man's strongest desire is always that which for the time he imagines as his greatest pleasure, the object of his strongest aversion that which for the time he imagines as his greatest pain. Now we have clearly no title to say that any one is mistaken in such imagination; that anything else would be a greater pleasure or pain *to him at the time* than that which, being what he is and under the given circumstances, he looks forward to as a greatest pleasure or pain. Of his present capacity for pleasure we have, on the hypothesis, no test but his desire, and of his desire no test but his action.

It will be objected, perhaps, that a man is really capable of other pleasure than that which at any time he imagines as his greatest and consequently desires, since his imagination of plea-sure is founded on past experience of pleasure, and this is not the measure of what he is capable of receiving. Now of course the pleasure which has been is not exactly that which shall be. A more intense pleasure may from time to time come in a man's way than any he has before experienced; and this may affect his imagination, and consequent desire, of pleasure for the future. But it does not follow from this that any one at any given time, possessed by imagination of a particular pleasure and by desire for it, is capable of any other pleasure than that. He may come to be so capable, but for the present he is not. The pleasure may turn out to be much less in enjoyment than in imagination; it may in the sequel lead to the most intense pain; but it remains true that for the time, if it is the pleasure which the man imagines as then for him the greatest, and which by inevitable consequence (on the given hypothesis) he most strongly desires, it is in fact the greatest pleasure of which he is capable. And, *mutatis mutandis*, the same will be true of pain. Our enquirer then will conclude that, supposing his principles to be true, the aggregate balance of pleasures at any time enjoyed by mankind is as great as it is possible for it to be, the persons and the circumstances being what they are; and that, since in each of his actions a man obtains the greatest pleasure or avoids the greatest pain which is at the time possible for him, there is no ground for saying that in the total result he obtains a less sum of pleasure than any which it was really possible for him to obtain, except through some good fortune independent of his own action.

341. This conclusion must at least suggest a reconsideration of the sense in which it is commonly said that such or such an action ought or ought not to be done. The Utilitarian who does not probe his Hedonistic principles to the bottom, has no difficulty in saying of any one that he ought to do what he does not, because, while he takes for granted that the largest balance of possible pleasure is the chief good, he does not question that it is open to the man who 'does what he ought not' to obtain a larger quantity of pleasure for himself and for others than he in fact obtains by acting as he does. But upon Hedonistic principles, as we have just seen, it is clearly not possible for a man, as his desires and aversions at any time stand, to obtain at the time by his own act more pleasure, or avoid more pain, than he in fact does. We cannot therefore, consistently with these principles, tell the man whom we count vicious that, according to the common Utilitarian language, he wilfully disregards his own true interest and throws away his own greatest happiness. At the most we can only tell him that more pleasure on the whole would have resulted from another course of action than that to which an inevitable strongest desire for pleasures, from time to time imagined as the greatest, has in fact led him. But even this, when the matter is looked into, will not seem so certain. It is not to be denied, of course, that if some instrument could

be invented, by which the degrees of intensity of successive pleasures and pains could be registered, and then the sum added up, in many cases where a man had led an immoral life the balance would be found much less on the side of pleasure, or much more on the side of pain, than would have resulted had the man led a different life; though on each occasion, according to the Hedonistic hypothesis, he must have obtained the most pleasure of which for the time he was capable. This is plainly the case where the man's actions have made his life much shorter, or much more painful in its later period, than it would have been had he acted differently. But here everything must depend on the nature of the individual case. For a man with a very strong constitution a certain course of action will have a different bearing on his future capacity for enjoyment from that which it has for a weaker man. On the other hand, if a man has some germ of disease in his system which must kill him before he is old, the method of seeking a rapid succession of intense pleasures, without reference to the effects they may have in later life, will be the right one for him to adopt with a view to enjoying the largest sum possible for him on the whole, while it would be the wrong one for a man who, with care, was sure to live to old age.

342. Even in regard to modes of living, then, which at first sight seem certain to yield a man more pain and less pleasure on the whole than he might have had, if he could have lived differently, we shall find that we have to make an indefinite number of exceptions. Even in regard to them, so far as the goodness or badness of a particular course of action is to depend on its relation to the nett sum of pleasure possible for the individual so acting, we shall have to say that it may be good for one and bad for another, according to physical conditions which we are not competent to ascertain. In other cases where, looking on from the outside, we are apt to think that the enjoyment of certain pleasures, the most intense of which the individual is for the time capable, diminishes the whole sum possible for him, we are arguing from our own conditions and susceptibilities. We argue that the enjoyment of certain pleasures brings a preponderance of pain in the long run, because it brings poverty or dishonour or the pangs of conscience, or deprives a man of the pleasures of friendship or family affection or a cultivated taste.

But, as to these pleasures which we suppose to be forgone, we have no means of measuring their intensity, as enjoyed by one man, against the intensity of pleasures which we count vicious, as enjoyed by another man. We cannot tell to what degree they would have been pleasures to the man whom we suppose to have deprived himself of them. As to the pains, again, which we suppose the immoral man to incur, their incidence depends largely on his position, the length of his purse, and a multitude of circumstances which vary with the individual case. We are not entitled to hold that, if incurred at all, they are to him what they would be to a man who had lived differently. The very pursuit of pleasures of sense may so dull the moral sensibilities that the pain, which an onlooker associates with those pleasures as their natural consequence, does not really follow for the person who has enjoyed them. It would thus seem that, though there are doubtless many men who by their manner of life make the balance of pleasures and pains, number and duration being duly set against intensity, less favourable to themselves than it might have been if they could have lived differently, yet we cannot with certainty tell any particular person that he is living such a life, and are not entitled to identify those in whose case the balance will turn out favourable with those whom we in fact count virtuous, nor those in whose case it will turn out unfavourable with those whom we count vicious.

343. It may be objected here perhaps that, although we cannot say with certainty of any particular course of action, as pursued by a particular person, that it diminishes the sum of pleasures open to him, we may be quite sure that action of that kind has a general tendency to diminish pleasure for the persons pursuing it. Does this mean, however, that the supposed course of action would diminish the sum of pleasures if generally pursued, or that it does so for the majority of those who pursue it? The former meaning is not to the purpose, when we are considering the question whether the lives actually lived by men bring them less pleasure on the whole than the same men would experience if they lived differently. Supposing a moral obligation upon the individual to act according to general rules, it will of course be his duty to consider whether any course of action which, as adopted by himself, is productive of a preponderance of

pleasure, would have a like result if generally adopted. But no such consideration can affect the question whether the line of action, actually pursued by this man or that, is consistent with the attainment by those persons of the maximum of pleasure possible for them. On this question the fact that the same line of action, if pursued by other people than those who do in fact pursue it, would diminish the balance of pleasure possible for those other people, has simply no bearing at all. In this regard each particular action or course of action must stand upon its own merits. If the morality of the action—the question whether it is morally good or bad—depends on the balance of pleasure or pain that will result from it—not from apparently similar actions done by other men, but from that particular action as done by the person who does it, and under the circumstances under which it is done; and if we cannot be sure that the particular action diminishes the balance of pleasures which, given the circumstances of the case and the desires and aversions of the agent, was really possible, as little can we be sure whether that particular action is morally good or bad, whether it should be done or should not be done.

344. It may be objected, however, that this uncertainty can only continue, so long as we confine our consideration to the consequences of the particular action to the agent himself; that it must disappear when we take into account its consequences to society in general, as on Utilitarian principles we are bound to do. But is this so? It must be remembered that we are supposing the principles of Hedonistic Utilitarianism to be strictly carried out. According to them ultimate value lies in pleasures as such, not in the persons enjoying them. A pleasure of a certain intensity, enjoyed by three persons, is of no more value than a pleasure of threefold intensity enjoyed by one. It must be remembered also that the question relates to the pleasure-giving effects of particular actions, not of kinds of action. Now actions are no doubt sometimes done, in regard to which it would be idle to doubt that the pain, or loss of pleasure, which they cause to others far outweighs any pleasure, or relief from pain, which they bring to those concerned in doing them. But is this the case with the every-day actions which men of a high moral standard would condemn, and to which the moral reformer

would seek to put an end? Is it really possible to measure the
addition to the pleasure of others, or diminution of their pains,
that would be caused by the agent's abstaining from any such
an act—which, on the hypothesis, yields him the most intense
pleasure of which for the time he is capable, or it would not be
done—against the loss of pleasure which he would thereby
undergo? The loss of pleasure would vary indefinitely with
different persons; it would be different in the same person at
different times, according to the degree of that susceptibility
upon which the intensity of the pleasure which is for the time
most intense for the individual depends. How can we be sure
that, in all or in most cases where such actions are done, the
certain loss of pleasure or increase of pain to each individual,
which, taking him as he is on occasion of each action, would be
implied in his acting otherwise than he does, would be so overbalanced by increase of pleasure or decrease of pain to others,
that the total sum of pleasure enjoyed by the aggregate of men,
taking them as they are, would be greater than it is?

345. If our supposed Hedonistic enquirer follows out these
considerations to their legitimate conclusion, they are likely at
least to have a modifying influence on any zeal which may have
possessed him for reforming current morality in himself and
others. They will at least make him less confident in judging
that men, as they are, should act otherwise than they do, less
confident in any methods of increasing the enjoyments of mankind, and in consequence more ready to let things take their
course. 'But after all,' it may be said, 'this may mean no more
than that they will make him less censorious, more patient of
the failings of mankind, more alive to the slowness of the
process by which alone any amelioration of the human lot can be
achieved. The conclusion supposed to be arrived at amounts to
no more than this, that, if we would increase the sum of enjoyments at any time open to men, we must first change their
desires and their surroundings. The enquirer who is in doubt
whether or no he should interfere with some custom, or resist
some inclination of his own, with a view to increasing human
enjoyments, may admit that by so doing he cannot make the
balance of pleasure greater than it at any time happens to be,
so long as men and circumstances remain what at the time they

are; but he may hope that his personal sacrifice, his disturbance (necessarily painful in itself) of mischievous class conventions, will so alter men and circumstances as to make the balance of enjoyments greater in the future than it at present is. This hope should be enough to induce any one, who does not need to be attracted by the glory of present recognised success, "to spurn delights and live laborious days." '

Now it is quite true that there is nothing in his acceptance of the supposed principles, however logically he applies them, to prevent our enquirer, if he is of sanguine temper, from hoping for an increase in the nett sum of human enjoyments. The question is whether they warrant him in believing that by any self-denial or reforming energy on his part the result can be affected. The 'vulgar' Utilitarian notion, of course, is that it is men's own fault that they are not happier on the whole than they are; that it is open to them by their own action to increase the sum of their enjoyments; that they ought to do so; that every one is responsible for contributing as much as he can, according to his lights and powers, to the stock of human happiness. But our enquirer, following out the principles of philosophical Utilitarianism, will be apt to doubt the justification of this belief, whatever he may think of its origin and service-ableness. 'The course of a man's action,' he will say, 'depends on the pleasures and pains that have happened to come in his way, through a chain of events over which he has had no control. These determine his desires and aversions, which in turn deter-mine his actions and through them to some extent the pleasures and pains of his future. No *initiative* by the individual any-where occurs. Desires indeed may arise in a man which he has not felt before, and may lead to action which increases the stock of human enjoyment; but they can only arise because some pleasures have fallen to his lot that he had not experienced before. Clearly then there is no alternative but to let the world have its way, and my own inclinations have their way. I may indulge the hope that the result will be some diminution of the misery of mankind. There may be observable tendencies which encourage this hope. New pleasures may arise for men in the natural course of events, which will so modify their action as in the future to yield more pleasure on the whole than they have had in the past. The inclinations which I find in myself, and which arise from pleasures that I have experienced, may contribute to this result. It may turn out that I have a taste which renders me a medium of increased pleasure to mankind. But, whether it prove so or no, that I should follow my tastes and inclinations is the only possibility.'

346. There is no ground for surmising that any so distinct conclusion is consciously arrived at even by the most thorough-going speculative Hedonists, except under the influence of self-indulgent habits which are quite independent of their theories, and may be common to them with men who in theory are 'Ascetics.' But if it is the logical issue of their theory, though a real consciousness of duty, which the theory fails to interpret, may prevent its distinct avowal even in the most secret dialogue of the soul with itself, it can scarcely fail to weaken their actual initiative in good works. In a man of strong speculative interest a suspicion that his theory does not justify his practice cannot go for nothing. Now that the above conclusion is the logical issue of the Hedonistic theory is what no one, aware of the extent to which that theory is adopted, and superior to the temptation of scoring a dialectical victory, would wish to make out if he could help it. But how is the conclusion to be avoided? If men at any given time are getting as much pleasure as under the conditions is possible for them—and that this is the case seems the necessary inference from the Hedonistic principles stated—the only way of increasing the sum will be by altering their possibilities of pleasure; by changing the conditions in the way of imagination and desire, which determine the greatest sum of pleasure possible for men as they are, in such a way that a larger sum shall be possible for them in the future. The Hedonist may hope that such an alteration will come about, either through some beneficence of nature, or through the effort of every man to compass means of attaining the pleasures which he most desires and avoiding the pains which he most dislikes. But how, according to his doctrine, should any one try to change the course of life to which habit and inclination lead him, in order to produce such an alteration? Such an attempt would imply that an alteration of what pleases or pains him most can be an object to a man, to whom yet, upon the hypothesis, desire for the

pleasure which most attracts him, aversion from the pain which
most repels him in imagination, is the only possible motive;
and is not this a contradiction?

347. If the speculative Hedonist, then, anxious about his duty
in the world, once comes to put to himself the question, why he
should trouble himself about a duty in the world at all, it would
seem that he can logically answer the question in only one way;
however inconsistent the answer may be with the fact that he
cannot help asking the question. He must conclude that he has
no duty in the world, according to the sense in which he naturally uses the word—no duty other than a necessity of following
the inclination for that which from time to time presents itself
to him as his greatest pleasure, or the aversion from what presents itself as his greatest pain. He must explain the seeming
consciousness of duty as best he can, by supposition of its arising
from antagonism between aversion from some apprehended pain
of punishment or shame, and inclination to some anticipated
pleasure. As the vulgar understand the phrases ' should do ' or
' ought to do '—as he himself understands them in his unphilosophical moments—he must count it absurd to say that anything
ought to be done by himself or any one else, which is not done;
absurd, that is, if it is taken to imply that any one has any real
option of acting otherwise than as, under imagination of a
greatest pleasure or greatest pain, he in fact does act, or that
there is a happiness actually open to men as they are, which by
their own fault they throw away. The whole phraseology of
obligation, in short, upon Hedonistic principles can best be
explained by a theory which is essentially the same as that of
Hobbes, and which in Plato's time was represented by the dictum
of certain Sophists that ' Justice is the interest of the stronger.'
A few words will explain the form in which such a theory would
naturally present itself to one who made the legitimate deduc-
tions from the principles in question.

348. The contemplation of certain actions by the individual, as
actions which he ought to do, implies at once that they can be
done, and that they are such as the individual, if left to his
natural desire for pleasure and aversion from pain, would not do.
But, upon Hedonistic principles, except through *some* desire for
pleasure or aversion from pain they could not be done. The

distinction of them, then, must lie in the kind of pleasure or pain which the individual contemplates as his inducement to do them. It must be a pleasure or pain which he looks for from the agency of others, who have power to reward or punish him— to reward or punish him, if with nothing else, yet with an approval or disapproval to which he is so sensitive that the approval may in his imagination outweigh every other pleasure, the disapproval every other pain Thus the consciousness 'I ought to do this or that' must be interpreted as equivalent to the consciousness that it is expected of me by others, who are 'stronger' than I am in the sense that they have power to reward or punish me—whether these 'others' are represented by the civil magistrate or by some public opinion, whether the rewards and punishments proceeding from them are in the nature of what we call physical, or what we call mental, pleasure and pain. It is their interest which is the ultimate foundation of the judgment, on the part of the individual, that he ought or ought not. This judgment only represents the interest of the individual, in so far as that which he presents to himself as his greatest pleasure or pain has come to depend upon his forecast of the will or sentiment of the others, who are stronger than he. The better and worse ἁπλῶς, or simply, being equivalent to the greater pleasure and greater pain simply, the *morally* better and worse are the greater pleasure and pain of those who have power to reward and punish, and who through that power are able so to affect the imagination of individuals as to make it seem a greatest pleasure to please them, a greatest pain to displease them. So far as in any society this power rests, directly or indirectly, with the majority, the morally better for any member of that society will be the greater pleasure of the greater number; not however because that greater number is the greater number, but because it possesses the power described. The action of the individual will be morally good, according as the greater pleasure of the individual—which is his only possible motive—corresponds with the greater pleasure of the stronger, in the sense explained, and thus leads him to do what is expected of him by the stronger. He is counted a good man when this is habitually the case with him. His conscience is that sympathy with the feeling of the stronger, in virtue of which an action that would displease the stronger, and therefore be morally bad, becomes painful to him on the contemplation. An action which a man does 'from sense of duty,' irrespectively, as it seems, of anticipated pleasure or pain, really represents a sympathetic sense of what is expected of him, which makes the contemplated pain of not doing it outweigh any pleasure to be gained by a contrary course. Perhaps he has no definite notion of any particular persons who expect it of him; perhaps there are no such persons; but his feeling about it is the result of a like feeling on the part of his ancestors, which, as felt by them, was directed to some definite source of hope or fear. Between fear of the sword or stick, and the sort of conscience which is said neither to fear punishment nor hope for reward, the gap seems wide, but it may not perhaps be too wide for evolution and hereditary transmission to fill.

349. Some such account of the 'phenomena of morality' seems the most logical which, upon Hedonistic principles, can be arrived at. If we admit that the only possible motive to action is desire for some pleasure or aversion from some pain, it offers the most consistent method of explaining that which all must admit to be the distinguishing thing in morality—the appearance, namely, of there being another standard of value than pleasure, of there being actions that proceed from another motive than desire for pleasure. If the question is asked, how that which is said to be the moral good and criterion, *viz.* the greatest nett sum of pleasures for the greatest number, can be a good or object of desire to the individual, who on the hypothesis can only desire his own pleasure, it may be replied that we are not called upon to consider it such an object of desire to him at all. On the contrary, in calling an action *morally* good we imply some element of repugnance to the desire of the person for whom it is *morally* good. It is not good as satisfying any *natural* desire for pleasure on his part, *i. e.* any such desire as he would have if left to himself. It is as causing pleasure to others, not to him, that it has come to be reckoned good. His interest in doing it is merely the result of the relation in which the action stands to others, as a source of pleasure to them and therefore approved by them. He does it as a means of gaining the pleasure of their approval, or of avoiding the pain of punishment or shame—the pleasure and pain to which for the time he happens to be most sensitive.

Again, upon this theory, we are saved the embarrassment of having to explain how, if the individual always chooses what pleases him best, he can miss a moral good which consists in or implies the greatest sum of pleasure possible for him. According to it, that which is morally best for the individual is not *his* greatest pleasure, but the greatest pleasure for those who can reward and punish him; who can make their approval and disapproval objects of his desire and aversion. Thus, though he always chooses the greatest imagined pleasure, the individual's acts may conflict with the morally best, unless desire for reward or approval, aversion from punishment or disapproval, keep his action in constant correspondence with the interest of those who make morality. There is no need then to attempt any impossible 'moral arithmetic,' any balance of the extent and durability of certain pleasures against the intensity of others, with a view to showing that the immoral man misses the greatest sum of pleasure possible to him. It is not *his* greatest pleasure, but the greatest pleasure of 'the stronger,' which forms the issue in all questions of morality. No question need be raised between what 'seems' good and what 'is' good. That which in the long run seems to those who wield the forces of society most conducive to their pleasure, is really so, and the strongest force in society tends to become equivalent, directly or indirectly, to that of the majority : so that a man's duty—that which he 'ought to do,' or which he feels is expected of him—tends to be that sort of action which conduces to the greatest happiness of the greatest number. But as there is no fixedness or finality either in the ruling influence of society, or in the modes of action which those who exercise this influence find most for their pleasure, no final or absolute judgment can be given as to the morally better or worse. Within certain limits the standard of morality fluctuates.

350. So much for the course of speculation which a logical mind, starting from the principles on which Utilitarianism has generally been founded, is likely to follow. In order to illustrate more definitely the weakening of moral initiative likely to result from it, we will suppose our enquirer, having been touched by a scruple as to his continuance in some practice in which, like others of his class, he has indulged, and which is not condemned

either by law or public opinion, to be examining this scruple in the light of his Hedonistic philosophy. Let the enquirer be some one so circumstanced as was C. J. Fox, and let gambling be the practice in question. Let us suppose a dialogue within the soul, excited by the suggestion that the practice is *morally* bad and ought to be given up.

'How can it be morally bad? I have come to the conclusion that the morally bad means that which conflicts with the will of the stronger, or, as the Utilitarians say, with a law enforced by some sanction, either the legal sanction or the popular sanction; but no such law is broken by the practice in question.'

'You forget the other sanctions, the religious and the natural.'

'If I forget the religious sanction, this shows that to me it is not a sanction. It is a purely subjective sanction, consisting in fear of the pains of another world. As a matter of fact, I do not find any ostensibly divine prohibition of gambling, sanctioned by the threat of such pains; but, if I did, it would not affect me, for it cannot be proved that such pains will ever be endured, and I do not happen to be afraid of them.'

'But the natural sanction? In gambling you are violating a law enforced by a natural sanction, as you will find when the painful consequences of your gambling propensities in due course of nature come to be felt.'

'Here at any rate we are shifting our ground. The first suggestion was that the practice was *morally* bad, and it would not be so if it were contrary to a law enforced by *natural* sanctions; if, in the natural course of things and without the intervention of any social force, it led to an overbalance of pain. But how can it be shown that in gambling I violate a law enforced by a natural sanction? There is no doubt about the intense pleasure I find in gambling, as measured, according to our principles, by my intense desire to gamble. The pleasures that I am supposed to forgo by gambling might not be pleasures to me; and, as for any future pains likely to result from the practice, they will scarcely be so intense, when my skin is hardened against many pangs which would be formidable if inflicted now, as to be compared with the pleasure I now find in following my bent.'

'Ah, but think of the long succession of them; how much they will amount to, when all put together.'

'But they never will be put together. I may fairly hope that one will be over, and relieved by some interval of pleasure, before another begins. Unbroken continuance of even slight pain is, no doubt, awful to anticipate. But there is no reason to think that the pain consequent on this indulgence will be unbroken, or that, if there were nothing to relieve it, I need live to endure it. If I found it becoming unbearable, I should have the remedy in my own hands.'

' Perhaps we have been arguing the question upon wrong grounds. The practice of gambling may not be demonstrably productive of more pain than pleasure to you individually, but there can be no doubt that it is so to society generally. It is true that, in the present state of law and of opinion, it does not violate any rule enforced by the political or by the popular sanction, and thus, in the restricted sense of the word, is not morally bad. But this state of law and opinion is itself in violation of a law having a *natural* sanction—the sanction consisting in the excess of pain above pleasure produced by gambling to society in general. It is thus bad in the sense of being pernicious, just as Hobbes admitted that a law, though it could not be unjust, might be pernicious. It ought to be changed, and you ought to refuse to conform to it, in deference to a higher law than that enforced by the state or public opinion, a law having the natural sanction which belongs to any rule necessary to the greatest happiness of the greatest number.'

'Here are three propositions, each more doubtful than the other. It is not very easy to show that the practice is pernicious in that sense of the word which alone, as Hedonists, we can admit; *viz.* that more pleasure, after deduction for counter-balancing pain, would at any time be felt by more persons if the practice were changed. You cannot dictate to people what their pleasures shall be. If the practice is so predominantly un-pleasant in its consequences to the majority as you say, why have they not found that out and stopped it? But granting that it is so, what do you mean by saying that it ought to be changed? This apparently is an obligation on the part of society, but to whom is it an obligation? An obligation on the part of the several members of the society to each other and to the whole society is intelligible. But in the absence of any law either of the state or of opinion against the practice, it cannot be said that any such obligation is violated by the practice. An obligation of society to itself is unintelligible. You say indeed that society ought to change the practice, because it violates a law enforced by a natural sanction. But here you are the victim of a figure of speech. You are personifying 'nature' as an imponent of obligation. Stripped of figures of speech, this proposition is merely a repetition of that already shown to be doubtful, that the practice is pernicious—productive of more pain than pleasure. If it is so, that is a reason for expecting that society with increasing experience will see fit to refuse to tolerate it, but none for saying that it ought to do so. Even less is it a ground for saying that, while the practice continues to be sanctioned by society, I ought not to indulge in it. My taste for gambling does not conflict either with positive law or with what is expected of me by society. To whom then am I under any obligation to renounce it? It cannot be held that it is a duty which I owe to myself; for, if there is any meaning in that phrase, it can only mean, according to our principles, that the practice tends more to my pain than to my pleasure, and this we have seen there is no reason for holding. If society with further experience changes its mind on the matter, it may then make it more painful for me to indulge my taste than to abstain; but there is no reason why I should anticipate the result of social conflict in this or in any other case. Indeed, according to Hedonistic principles, I could not if I would. For the present from time to time a strongest desire—strongest because excited by imagination of what is for the time my most intense pleasure —moves me to gamble, and I act accordingly. If society will furnish me with a stronger motive for abstaining, let it do so. I can only await the change of law or social opinion that will bring such a deterrent to bear on me.'

351. This sort of Hedonistic fatalism seems to be logically inherent in all Utilitarian philosophy which founds itself on the principle that pleasure is the sole object of desire. That this principle may be rejected by one who yet accepts the Utilitarian doctrine of ultimate good, we know from the example of Mr.

Henry Sidgwick. Whether his rejection of it is not really inconsistent with his view of the 'Summum Bonum' is a point to be considered later. What concerns us here is the fact that the principle stated is taken as the foundation of their Ethical doctrine alike by Bentham, J. S. Mill and Mr. H. Spencer, and that, the more the Utilitarian philosophy is applied to the direction of private conduct, the more practically important this principle is likely to become, and the more likely are speculative men to draw from it those legitimate inferences which we have been considering, to the embarrassment of their own higher impulses. That in the most illustrious spokesmen of Utilitarianism no such tendency has really appeared, is explained by their pre-occupation with great projects of political and social amelioration, which made their theoretical reduction of the good to pleasure of quite secondary importance. They had the great lesson to teach, that the value of all laws and institutions, the rectitude of all conduct, was to be estimated by reference to the well-being of all men, and that in the estimate of that well-being no nation or class or individual was to count above another. It mattered little for practical purposes that they held the well-being of society to consist simply of the nett aggregate of pleasures enjoyed by its members, and that they founded this view on the principle that some pleasure or other is the sole object of every desire. The mischief latent in this principle could only appear if it occurred to them to ask the question, which their reforming zeal was too strong to allow them to ask, why they should trouble themselves to alter their tastes and habits, or those of other people. It is only when this question has come to be commonly asked by men at once sufficiently free from the mastery either of the lower or of the higher passions, and with sufficient command over the circumstances of their lives, for the answer to have real influence over their conduct, that the theoretical consequences which we have seen to be involved in the Hedonistic principle become of serious practical import.

We have then to consider, not so much whether the principle that pleasure is the sole object of desire is itself tenable—on that enough has been already said in this treatise—as whether the doctrine which, having rejected this view of desire, professes to find the absolutely desirable or 'Summum Bonum' for man in some perfection of human life, some realisation of human capacities, is of a kind, not only to save speculative men from that suspicion of there being an illusion in their impulses after a higher life which Hedonism naturally yields, but also to guide those impulses in cases of honest doubt as to the right line of action to adopt.

CHAPTER IV.

THE PRACTICAL VALUE OF UTILITARIANISM COMPARED WITH THAT
OF THE THEORY OF THE GOOD AS HUMAN PERFECTION.

352. ACCORDING to the doctrine of this treatise, as we have
previously endeavoured to state it, there is a principle of self-
development in man, independent of the excitement of new
desires by those new imaginations, which presuppose new experiences, of pleasure. In virtue of this principle he anticipates
experience. In a certain sense he makes it, instead of merely
waiting to be made by it. He is capable of being moved by an
idea of himself, as becoming that which he has it in him to be
—an idea which does not represent previous experience, but
gradually brings an experience into being, gradually creates a
filling for itself, in the shape of arts, laws, institutions and habits
of living, which, so far as they go, exhibit the capabilities of
man, define the idea of his end, afford a positive answer to the
otherwise unanswerable question, what in particular it is that
man has it in him to become. The action of such an idea in the
individual accounts for two things which, upon the Hedonistic
supposition, are equally unaccountable. It accounts for the possibility of the question, Why should I trouble about making
myself or my neighbours other than we are? and, given the
question, it accounts for an answer being rendered to it, in the
shape of a real initiation of effort for the improvement of human
life.

The supposition, therefore, of a free or self-objectifying spiritual agency in human history is one to which a fair analysis of
human history inevitably leads us. But it remains to be asked
by what rule the effort is to be guided, which we suppose the

idea of a possible human perfection thus to initiate. That idea, according to our view, is primarily in man unfilled and un-realised; and within the experience of men it is never fully realised, never acquires a content adequate to its capacity. There are arts and institutions and rules of life, in which the human spirit has so far incompletely realised its idea of a possible Best; and the individual in whom the idea is at work will derive from it a general injunction to further these arts, to maintain and, so far as he can, improve these institutions. It is when this general injunction has to be translated into particulars that the difficulty arises. How is the essential to be dis-tinguished from the unessential and obstructive, in the processes through which an effort after the perfection of man may be traced? How are the arts to become a more thorough realisa-tion of the ideal which has imperfectly expressed itself in them? How are the institutions of social life, and the rules of conven-tional morality, to be cleared of the alien growths which they owe to the constant co-operation of selfish passions with interest in common good, and which render them so imperfectly organic to the development of the human spirit? Above all, how is this or that individual—circumstanced as he is, and endowed, physically and mentally, as he is—to take part in the work? When he is called upon to decide between adherence to some established rule of morality and service to a particular person, or to face some new combination of circumstances to which recog-nised rules of conduct do not seem to apply, how is he to find guidance in an idea which merely moves him to aim at the best and highest in conduct? In short, as we put the difficulty after first stating the doctrine which finds the basis of morality in such an idea (§ 198)—' So far as it can be translated into practice at all, must not its effect be either a dead conformity to the code of customary morality, anywhere and at any time es-tablished, without effort to reform or expand it, or else unlimited licence in departing from it at the prompting of any impulse which the individual may be pleased to consider a higher law?'

Unless these questions can be satisfactorily answered, it would seem that our theory of the basis of morality, though its adop-tion might save some speculative persons from that distrust of their own conscience to which Hedonism would naturally lead them, can be of no further practical value. It may still serve to dispel the notion that the inclination to take one's ease and let the world have its way is justified by philosophy. It may still have an important bearing on that examination by the individual of his own walk and conduct, in which the question of motive should hold the first place; for it recognises, as the one motive which should be supreme, a desire which the Hedonist must ignore. But it will have no guidance to offer to the impulse which it explains, and of which it asserts the importance. In those cases in which, as we have previously pointed out, the question, Ought this or that to be done? has to be answered irrespectively of motive and with reference merely to the effects of actions, it will be of no avail. For that purpose we need some conception of a 'Summum Bonum' or ultimate good, definite enough to enable us to enquire whether the effects of a particular action contribute to that end or no. But if the idea of a possible perfection of life cannot be translated into any definite conceptions of what contributes to the attainment of that life, except such as are derived from existing usage and law, it cannot afford such a criterion as we want of the value of possible actions, when we are in doubt which of them should be done; for we want a criterion that shall be independent of law and usage, while at the same time it shall be other than the casual conviction of the individual.

353. Now, as we have more than once admitted, we can form no positive conception of what the ultimate perfection of the human spirit would be; what its life would be when all its capabilities were fully realised. We can no more do this than we can form a positive conception of what the nature of God in itself is. All the notions that we can form of human excellences or virtues are in some way relative to present imperfections. We may say perhaps, with the Apostle, that Faith, Hope and Charity ' *abide* ; ' that they are not merely passing phases of a life which may come to enter on conditions in which they would cease to be possible; and there may be a sense in which this is true. But when we come to speak of the functions in which those virtues manifest themselves, we find that we are speaking of functions essentially relative to a state of society in which it is impossible to suppose that the human

spirit has reached its full development. 'Charity beareth all things, believeth all things, hopeth all things;' but if all men had come to be what they should be, what would there be for Charity to bear, to hope, and to believe?

Though the idea of an absolutely perfect life, however, cannot be more to us than the idea that there must be such a life, as distinct from an idea of what it is—and we may admit this while holding that this idea is in a supreme sense formative and influential—it does not follow that there is any difficulty in conceiving very definitely a life of the individual and of society more perfect, because more completely fulfilling the vocation of individual and society, than any which is being lived. There may have been a period in the history of our race when the idea of a possible perfection was a blindly moving influence; when it had not yet taken sufficient effect in the ordering of life and the formation of virtues for reflection on these to enable men to say what it would be to be more perfect. But we are certainly not in that state now. We all recognise, and perhaps in some fragmentary way practise, virtues which both carry in themselves unfulfilled possibilities, and at the same time plainly point out the direction in which their own further development is to be sought for. It has already been sought in this treatise to trace the ideal of the cardinal virtues, as recognised by the conscience of Christendom. In none of these would the man who came nearest the ideal 'count himself to have attained,' nor would he have any difficulty in defining the path of his further attainment. No one is eager *enough* to know what is true or make what is beautiful; no one ready *enough* to endure pain and forgo pleasure in the service of his fellows; no one impartial *enough* in treating the claims of another exactly as his own. Thus to have more 'intellectual excellence;' to be more brave, temperate and just, in the sense in which any one capable of enquiring what it is to be more perfect would now understand these virtues, is a sufficient object for him to set before himself by way of answer to the question, so far as it concerns him individually; while a state of society in which these virtues shall be more generally attainable and attained, is a sufficient account of the more perfect life considered as a social good.

354. It would seem then that, though statements at once

positive and instructive as to the absolutely Best life may be beyond our reach, yet, by help of mere honest reflection on the evidence of its true vocation which the human spirit has so far yielded in arts and sciences, in moral and political achievement, we can know enough of a better life than our own, of a better social order than any that now is, to have an available criterion of what is good or bad in law and usage, and in the tendencies of men's actions. The working theory of the end, which we derive from the doctrine that the ultimate good for man must be some full development of the human spirit in character and conduct, may be represented by some such question as the following : Does this or that law or usage, this or that course of action— directly or indirectly, positively or as a preventive of the oppo- site—contribute to the better-being of society, as measured by the more general establishment of conditions favourable to the attainment of the recognised excellences and virtues, by the more general attainment of those excellences in some degree, or by their attainment on the part of some persons in higher de- gree without detraction from the opportunities of others ? In order to put this question we must, no doubt, have a definite notion of the direction in which the ' Summum Bonum ' is to be sought, but not of what its full attainment would actually be ; and this, it will be found, is all that we need or can obtain for our guidance in estimating the value of laws and institutions, actions and usages, by their effects. It will do nothing indeed to help us in ascertaining what the effects of any institution or action really are. No theory whatever of the ' Summum Bonum,' Hedonistic or other, can avail for the settlement of this ques- tion, which requires analysis of facts and circumstances, not con- sideration of ends. But it will sufficiently direct us in regard to the kind of effects we should look out for in our analysis, and to the value we should put upon them when ascertained.

In all cases then in which, according to the distinction pre- viously explained, the question at issue is not, What ought I to be ? but, What ought to be done ? the criterion just stated should be our guide in answering it. As we have seen, the question, What ought I to be ? includes the question, What ought to be done ? for I am not what I ought to be—my character and motives are not what they should be—unless my actions, in virtue of their effects, are such as ought to be done. But, as we have also seen, for that purpose which the question, Am I what I ought to be? mainly serves in ethical develop- ment—the purpose, namely, of self-reproval and consequent in- citement of the effort to be better—no elaborate enquiry into the effects of actions done is commonly needed. So far, however, as such an enquiry is involved in the process of self-examination, the criterion to be employed in the valuation of effects will be such as we have described. It will have to be employed, again, in all cases where we are judging the actions of others, whose state of character is incognisable by us, or considering whether outward action of a certain kind, irrespectively of motives, is good or bad, whether certain institutions or practices of society should be maintained or given up—these being all questions solely of effect. It is a criterion, indeed, which will seldom come to the front, even in the minds of those who are most clearly aware that it is their criterion, because in all ordinary cases of disinterested doubt as to the value of institutions and usages, and of actions in which we are not ourselves concerned, the question which occupies us is, What under all the conditions of the case are the effects actually produced? not, What is the value of the effects? But it should be, and (as we hold) with all men who have assimilated the higher moral culture of Christendom really is, the measure of value which is kept in view in the effort to ascertain the effects of action, and which is tacitly applied in the estimate of all ascertained effects that are susceptible of moral valuation.

355. The Utilitarian, if he can bring himself to attend to what is here advanced, will probably say that in ordinary cases and for practical purposes he can accept our criterion, but that he cannot regard it as ultimate or scientific, and that it fails us just in those cases where an ultimate or scientific criterion is needed, because in them the rules of established morality are insufficient or inapplicable. He will not object to measure the better-being of society in an ordinary way 'by the more general establishment of conditions favourable to the attainment of the recognised excellences and virtues, by the more general attain- ment of those excellences in some degree, or by their attainment on the part of some persons in higher degree without detraction

from the opportunities of others,' because he will hold that these recognised virtues and excellences represent an incalculable accumulation of experience as to the modes in which the largest balance of pleasure may be obtained. Their exercise according to him does not constitute the 'Summum Bonum,' but under ordinary conditions it is an ascertained means to it. 'Is there then,' the reader may ask us, 'any practical difference between the Utilitarian criterion and yours? You say that the effects of actions, institutions, etc., are to be valued according to their relation to the production of personal excellence, moral and intellectual. The Utilitarian does not deny this; but whereas, according to you, the excellence is itself the ultimate end, according to the Utilitarian it has its value only as a means—speaking generally, a necessary and unfailing means—to the production of the largest possible sum of pleasure. Since you are both agreed, then, that the effects to be looked at in all ordinary moral valuation are effects that have a bearing on meritorious character, whether there be a further end beyond that character or no, the several criteria come to pretty much the same thing. It will only be in exceptional cases that any difference between the two views of the criterion need appear; in the estimation, for instance, of some practice (such as vivisection may perhaps be reckoned) which stands in no ascertained relation, direct or indirect, to the maintenance, advancement, or diffusion of meritorious conduct; or in the estimation of some exceptional act to which the general rule, that the nett maximum of possible pleasure is only to be reached by following the paths of recognised virtue, is rendered inapplicable by some peculiarity in the circumstances of the case or in the position of the agent. Here the Utilitarian must apply his ultimate criterion directly. He must seek to ascertain the balance of pleasure or pain resulting from the particular practice or action, without the help of those records of prolonged observation upon pleasure-giving and pain-giving consequences which the established rules of morality in effect supply. This is no doubt a difficult task; but, upon the theory which rejects the Hedonistic calculus as criterion on the ground that virtuous character and conduct is an end in itself, is any criterion in such cases available at all?'

356. Now it is satisfactory to acknowledge that the theory of the criterion for which we are arguing does not for practical purposes differ much from the Utilitarian, so long as the Utilitarian view of the criterion is not founded—as it generally has been, and perhaps logically should be—on the Hedonistic theory of motives. The doctrine that pleasure is the only possible object of desire logically excludes the possibility of aspiration for personal holiness, of effort after goodness for its own sake. According to it the state of will and character which we have previously used the phrase 'purity of heart' to describe, is not only an unrealisable ideal, but an ideal which cannot excite desire for its attainment at all. This theory of motives, therefore, is incompatible in principle with the whole view of the nature of virtue, as issuing from a character in which the interest in being good is dominant, already set forth in this treatise. But if the Utilitarian is committed to no more than a certain doctrine of the criterion of morality—the doctrine that the value of actions and institutions is to be measured in the last resort by their effect on the nett sum of pleasures enjoyable by all human, or perhaps by all sentient, beings, the difference between him and one who would substitute for this 'nett sum, etc.' ' the fulfilment of human capacities' may be practically small. A desire for the enjoyment of pleasure by others—whether in the largest quantity possible, or in some more positively conceivable form—is so entirely different from desire for a pleasure that, if the Utilitarian considers his 'Summum Bonum,' or any limited form of it, to be a possible object of desire to the individual, he clears himself practically, even though it be at the sacrifice of consistency, from chargeability with any such theory of motives as would exclude the possibility of a 'pure heart.'

We are brought, then, to this point. The Utilitarian theory of ultimate good, if founded upon the Hedonistic theory of motives, we have found to be 'intrinsically unavailable for supplying motive or guidance to a man who wishes to make his life better,' because that theory of motives, when argued out, appears to exclude, not indeed the hope on the part of the individual that his own life and that of mankind may become better, *i. e.* more pleasant, but the belief that it can rest with him to exercise any initiative, whether in the way of resistance to inclination or of painful interference with usage, which may affect the result. We saw reason to think that this logical consequence of the theory tended to have at least a weakening influence upon life and conduct, and that there was accordingly a practical reason for seeking a substitute in another theory of ultimate good. But the question now arises whether this substitute shall be sought, according to the previous argument of this treatise, in a theory which would place the 'Summum Bonum' in a perfection of human life, not indeed positively definable by us, but having an identity with the virtuous life actually achieved by the best men, as having for its principle the same will to be perfect; or rather in a revision of the Utilitarian theory, which shall make it independent of the Hedonistic theory of motives, while retaining the account of the 'Summum Bonum' as a maximum of possible pleasure. We will endeavour to consider candidly what the latter alternative has to recommend it.

357. It is noticeable in the first place that, if the Utilitarian doctrine of the chief good as criterion—the doctrine that the greatest possible sum of pleasures is the end by reference to which the value of actions is to be tested—is dissociated from the Hedonistic doctrine of motives, though it may be cleared from liability to bad practical effects, it has also lost what has been in fact its chief claim to the acceptance of ordinary men. The process of its acceptance has been commonly this. Because there is pleasure in all satisfaction of desire, men have come to think that the object of desire is always some pleasure; that every good is a pleasure. From this the inference is natural enough that a greatest possible sum of pleasures is a greatest possible good— at any rate till it is pointed out that the possibility of desiring a sum of pleasures, which never can be enjoyed as a sum, would not follow from the fact that the object of desire was always some imagined pleasure. But once drop the notion that pleasure is the sole thing desired, and the question arises why it should be deemed that which 'in our calm moments' is to be counted the sole thing desirable, so that the value of all which men do or which concerns them is to be measured simply by its tendency to produce pleasure. We suppose ourselves now to be arguing with men who admit the possibility of disinterested motives, who

value character according as it is habitually actuated by them; who neither understand by such motives desires for that kind of pleasure of which the contemplation of another's pleasure is the condition, nor allow themselves to suppose that, granting benevolence to be always a desire to produce pleasure, it is therefore a desire for (*i. e.* to enjoy) pleasure. Why, we ask such persons, do you take that to be the one thing ultimately desirable, which you not only admit to be not the sole thing desired, but which you admit is not desired in those actions which you esteem the most?

358. It may be surmised that the chief attraction which the Hedonistic criterion has had for such persons has lain in its apparent definiteness. The conception of the 'Summum Bonum,' as consisting in a greatest possible nett sum of pleasures, has seemed to afford a much more positive and intelligible criterion than the conception of a full realisation of human capacities, which we admit to be only definable by reflection on the partial realisation of those capacities in recognised excellences of character and conduct. It promises an escape, too, from the circle in which, as already observed, we seem to move, when we say that we ought to do so and so because it is virtuous or noble to do it, and then have to explain what is virtuous or noble as what we ought to do. A 'Summum Bonum' consisting of a greatest possible sum of pleasures is supposed to be definite and intelligible, because every one knows what pleasure is. But in what sense does every one know it? If only in the sense that every one can imagine the renewal of some pleasure which he has enjoyed, it may be pointed out that pleasures, not being enjoyable in a sum—to say nothing of a greatest possible sum—cannot be imagined in a sum either. Though this remark, however, might be to the purpose against a Hedonist who held that desire could only be excited by imagined pleasure, and yet that a greatest sum of pleasure was an object of desire, it is not to the purpose against those who merely look on the greatest sum of pleasures as the true criterion, without holding that desire is only excited by imagination of pleasure. They will reply that, though we may not be able, strictly speaking, to imagine a sum of pleasures, every one knows what it is. Every one knows the difference between enjoying a longer succession of pleasures and a shorter

one, a succession of more intense and a succession of less intense pleasures, a succession of pleasures less interrupted by pain and one more interrupted. In this sense every one knows the difference between enjoying a larger sum of pleasures and enjoying a smaller sum. He knows the difference also between a larger number of persons or sentient beings and a smaller one. He attaches therefore a definite meaning to the enjoyment of a greater nett amount of pleasure by a greater number of beings, and has a definite criterion for distinguishing a better action from a worse, in the tendency of the one, as compared with the other, to produce a greater amount of pleasure to a greater number of persons.

359. The ability, however, to compare a larger sum of pleasure with a smaller in the sense explained—as we might compare a longer time with a shorter—is quite a different thing from ability to conceive a greatest possible sum of pleasures, or to attach any meaning to that phrase. It seems, indeed, to be intrinsically as unmeaning as it would be to speak of a greatest possible quantity of time or space. The sum of pleasures plainly admits of indefinite increase, with the continued existence of sentient beings capable of pleasure. It is greater to-day than it was yesterday, and, unless it has suddenly come to pass that experiences of pain outnumber experiences of pleasure, it will be greater to-morrow than it is to-day; but it will never be complete while sentient beings exist. To say that ultimate good is a greatest possible sum of pleasures, strictly taken, is to say that it is an end which for ever recedes; which is not only unattainable but from the nature of the case can never be more nearly approached; and such an end clearly cannot serve the purpose of a criterion, by enabling us to distinguish actions which bring men nearer to it from those that do not. Are we then, since the notion of a greatest possible sum of pleasures is thus unavailable, to understand that in applying the Utilitarian criterion we merely approve one action in comparison with another, as tending to yield more pleasure to more beings capable of pleasure, without reference to a 'Summum Bonum' or ideal of a perfect state of existence at all? But without such reference is there any meaning in approval or disapproval at all? It is intelligible that without such reference the larger sum of pleasures should be desired as against

the less; on supposition of benevolent impulses, it is intelligible that the larger sum should be desired by a man for others as well as for himself. But the desire is one thing, the approval of it—the judgment 'in a calm hour' that the desire of the action moved by it is reasonable—is quite another thing. Without some ideal—however indeterminate—of a best state of existence, with the attainment of which the approved motive or action may be deemed compatible, the approval of it would seem impossible. Utilitarians have therefore to consider whether they can employ a criterion of action, as they do employ it, without some idea of ultimate good; and, since a greatest possible sum of pleasures is a phrase to which no idea really corresponds, what is the idea which really actuates them in the employment of their criterion.

360. When, having duly reflected on these points, we try (if the expression may be pardoned) to make sense of the Utilitarian theory—bearing in mind at once its implication of the conception of a 'Summum Bonum,' and the impossibility that of pleasures, so long as sentient beings continue to enjoy themselves, there should be any such greatest sum as can satisfy the conception— we cannot avoid the conclusion that the 'Summum Bonum' which the Utilitarian contemplates is not a sum of pleasures, but a certain state of existence; a state in which all human beings, or all beings of whose consciousness he supposes himself able to take account, shall live as pleasantly as is possible for them, without one gaining pleasure at the expense of another. The reason why he approves an action is not that he judges it likely to make an addition to a sum of pleasures which never comes nearer completion, but that he judges it likely to contribute to this state of general enjoyable existence. If he says that the right object for a man is to increase the stock of human enjoyments, it is presumable that he is not really thinking of an addition to a sum of pleasant experiences, however large, which might be made and yet leave those who had had the experiences with no more of the good in possession than they had before. He does not mean that a thousand experiences of pleasure constitute more of a good than nine hundred experiences of the same intensity, or less of a good than six hundred of a double intensity. He is thinking of a good consisting in a certain sort of social life, of which he does not particularise the nature to himself further than by conceiving

it as a pleasant life to all who share in it, and as one of which all have the enjoyment, if not equally, yet none at the cost of others. By increasing the stock of enjoyments he means enabling more persons to live pleasantly, or with less interruption from pain. The good which he has before him is not an aggregate of pleasures but a pleasant life—a life at all times and for all persons as pleasant, as little marred by pain, as possible; but good, *qua* a life in which the persons living are happy or enjoy themselves, not *qua* a life into which so many enjoyments are crowded.

361. Now the objection to this conception of a chief good is not that, so far as it goes, it is otherwise than true. According to our view, since there is pleasure in all realisation of capacity, the life in which human capacities should be fully realised would necessarily be a pleasant life [1]. The objection is that, instead of having that definiteness which, because all know what pleasure is, it seemed at first to promise, it turns out on consideration to be so abstract and indefinite. It tells us nothing of that life, to the attainment of which our actions must contribute if they are to be what they should be, but merely that it would be as pleasant as possible for all persons, or for all beings of whose consciousness we can take account. The question is whether in thinking of an absolutely desirable life, as the end by reference to which the effects of our actions are to be valued, our view must be confined to the mere quality of its universal pleasantness, and whether in consequence productivity of pleasure is the ultimate ground on which actions are to be approved. The view for which we plead is that the quality of the absolutely desirable life, which renders it such in man's thoughts, is that it shall be the full realisation of his capacities; that, although pleasure must be incidental to such realisation, it is in no way distinctive of it, being equally incidental to any unimpeded activity, to the exercise of merely animal functions no less than to those that are properly human; that, although we know not in detail what the final realisation of man's capacities would be, we know well enough, from the evidence they have so far given of themselves, what a fuller development of them would be; and that thus, in the injunction to make life as full a realisation as possible of human capacities,

[1] [Cf. however § 276.]

we have a definiteness of direction, which the injunction to make life as pleasant as possible does not supply.

362. Such definiteness of direction as is derivable from the latter injunction really depends on the assumption that, with a view to the general enjoyment of life, conduct should follow the paths of recognised virtue. On supposition that the requirements of conventional morality represent a great mass of experience as to the social behaviour by which life is rendered more generally pleasant, we may be sure that as a rule their violation is not the way to help men on the whole to live more pleasantly. The supposition need not be disputed. But how did these requirements, or what is really beneficent in them, come to be formed? There was a time when they did not yet amount to the requirements of a conventional morality—when a large part of them were as yet only the convictions of a few peculiar people as to what was needed in the interest of a better social being. Whence then did these few derive direction for those efforts to make social life what it should be, which our present conventional morality was not there to guide, and which any conventional morality then current would have discountenanced? Would not the mere injunction to make human life as pleasant as possible, failing the interpretation which our present conventional morality may supply, but which it was not then there to supply, have had either no significance for them or a misleading one—a misleading significance if taken to be interpreted by the then recognised standards of meritorious conduct, and otherwise none? Has not the spirit in which the better being of society has in fact been promoted been generally that which Mr. Browning puts into the mouth of his Rabbi Ben Ezra?—

> 'Then, welcome each rebuff
> That turns earth's smoothness rough,
> Each sting that bids nor sit nor stand but go!
> Be our joys three-parts pain!
> Strive, and hold cheap the strain;
> Learn, nor account the pang; dare, never grudge the throe!'[1]

[1] [The following passage from the Epilogue to 'Romola,' which the author intended to quote at some point in this chapter, may be added here: 'We can only have the highest happiness, such as goes along with being a great man, by having wide thoughts, and much feeling for the rest of the world as well as ourselves; and this sort of happiness often brings so much pain with it, that we can only tell it from pain by its being what we would choose before everything else, because our souls see it is good.']

And would this spirit ever have found its inward law in an injunction to produce as much pleasure as possible—to seek as its supreme object to obtain that for others which it would reject for itself? Does not the same spirit still find such an injunction unmeaning or repellent, in those cases where it needs, owing to the felt insufficiency of the rules of conventional morality, to resort for direction to some conception of ultimate good?

363. It may be retorted, however, that by our own confession the injunction to realise the capacities, to make the most and best, of the human soul, derives its definite content from reference to the recognised virtues and excellences of life. It is an injunction to attain these more fully, to render them more generally attainable, to give further realisation to the spirit which has expressed itself in them. If it on the one hand, and the injunction to make life as pleasant as possible on the other, have alike need of this reference in order to acquire definite meaning, what advantage has the former over the latter? Its advantage we take to be this. The former injunction does, while the latter does not, correspond to the inward law by which men have been governed in the effort and aspiration that have yielded the various excellences in the way of art and knowledge, no less than of conduct, which now determine our ideal of further perfection. Accordingly in those cases—very exceptional, as we have all along pointed out—where the difference between the two injunctions would make itself practically apparent, the one would, while the other would not, suggest a manner of life, a standard of achievement in knowledge and art, higher than that which current expectations call for. A man who interprets the recognised virtues and excellences as having been arrived at with a view to the increase of pleasure, who holds them to be valuable only as means to that end, has not the clue to guide him in cases where it is no longer enough to follow the 'law of opinion' or social expectation, but where it behoves him to act in the higher spirit of those virtues and excellences—a spirit which he must interpret for himself. The question whether it would conduce more to general pleasure that he should set up for being better than his neighbours, instead of swimming with the stream; that he should follow the severer

path of duty, where his departure from it would be unknown or uncondemned, and where it would save himself and those whom he loves from much suffering; that he should seek the highest beauty in art, the completest truth in knowledge, rather than conform to popular taste and opinion—this is a question which he will find for ever unanswerable; and, in presence of its unanswerability, the fact that his own pleasure will undoubtedly be served by deciding it in the easier way is likely to have considerable weight. If, on the other hand, he were governed by the conviction that the recognised virtues and excellences are ends in themselves, because in them the human spirit in some measure fulfils its divine vocation, attains something of the perfection which it lies in it to attain, he would find in reflection on them an indication of the ends to be kept in view, where the rule of being virtuous according to some established type of virtue is insufficient, as well as a constant direction to estimate at its highest the claim on his personal devotion to the further perfecting of man.

364. Before we attempt finally to illustrate the manner in which these different conceptions of ultimate good, and the different injunctions founded on them, would be likely under certain conditions to affect the practical judgment, it will be well to remove one more possible misapprehension as to the distinction between them. They are not to be distinguished as if according to one the 'Summum Bonum' were a state of desirable consciousness, while according to the other it was not. It is agreed that in presenting a 'Summum Bonum' to ourselves we present it as a state of desirable consciousness. Except as some sort of conscious life it can be to us nothing; and to say that we think of it as desirable is the same thing as to say that we think of it as good. The question is whether we think of it as good or desirable because we anticipate pleasure in it, or because and so far as we already desire it, knowing that there must be pleasure in the satisfaction of a desire, though pleasure be not the object of the desire. Utilitarians, however—even such Utilitarians as Mr. Henry Sidgwick [1]—are apt to argue as if to hold that the ultimate standard of moral valuation is some-

[1] *Methods of Ethics,* Book III. chap. xiv. § 2. pp. 368–370 (2nd Edition).

thing else than the productivity of pleasure, was to hold that it is something else than productivity of desirable consciousness. So to argue is quite consistent in those who take pleasure to be the sole object of desire; for with them, if any kind of conscious life admits of being desired—and unless it admits of being desired, it cannot be desirable—it must be on the ground of the pleasure anticipated in it. But if this view is rejected, as it is rejected by Mr. Sidgwick, it does not appear why a state of consciousness should not be desired for another reason than for the sake of the pleasure anticipated in it, or why it should not be for another reason that 'when we sit down in a calm hour' we deem it desirable.

The present writer holds as strongly as Mr. Sidgwick could do that it is only in some form of conscious life—more definitely, of self-conscious life—that we can look for the realisation of our capacities or the perfection of our being; in other words, for ultimate good. While regarding Truth, Freedom, Beauty, etc., as constituent elements of the highest good, not as means to a good beyond them, he would understand by them, in Mr. Sidgwick's words [1], the 'relations of conscious minds which we call cognition of Truth, contemplation of Beauty, Independence of action, etc.' He admits further that desire for perfection of being—the desire of which the operation in us gives meaning to the statement that the attainment of such perfection is supremely desirable—carries with it some anticipation of the pleasure there would be in satisfaction of the desire, an anticipation which renders the description of the highest state as one of happiness or bliss natural to us. His contention is that to suppose pleasure on that account to be the object of our desire for supreme or ultimate good, is to repeat the mistake, to which Mr. Sidgwick is so thoroughly alive, of confusing the pleasure which attends the satisfaction of a desire with the object of the desire, and the anticipation of that pleasure with the desire itself. It is not because looked forward to as pleasant, that the

---

[1] Methods of Ethics, p. 368. Mr. Sidgwick writes, 'the objective relations of conscious minds.' I have omitted 'objective' from not being quite sure of its significance in this connection. Nor am I sure that I could accept 'Independence of action' as an equivalent for 'Freedom,' in that sense in which I look upon 'Freedom' as a constituent of the highest good.

form of conscious life in which our capacities shall be fully
realised is an object of desire to us; it is because, in such self-
conscious beings as we are, a desire for their realisation goes
along with the presence of the capacities, that the form of
conscious life in which this desire shall be satisfied is looked
forward to as pleasant. And it is because the object of this
desire, when reflected on, from the nature of the case presents
itself to us as absolutely final, not because we anticipate pleasure
in its attainment as we do in that of any and every desired
object, that 'in a calm hour' we pronounce it supremely desirable.

365. Now it would be unfair to convey the impression that
Mr. Sidgwick, in identifying that 'desirable consciousness,' which
he holds that ultimate good must be, simply with pleasure, is
chargeable with confusion between the object of a desire and the
pleasure anticipated in its satisfaction. The result of such a
confusion, unless avoided by a further one, would be 'Egoistic'
Hedonism, not the 'Universalistic' Hedonism which he himself
adopts. In the common Hedonistic ratiocination—we always anticipate pleasure in the satisfaction of desire, therefore pleasure is
the sole thing desired, therefore the sole thing desirable—pleasure
must throughout mean pleasure for the person supposed to desire it.
Since it is not pretended that it means anything else in the two
former steps of the ratiocination, it must mean it also in the last.
It can be taken to mean the pleasure of others, or of all men,
only through a confusion between desire to enjoy pleasure and
desire to produce it, from which Mr. Sidgwick keeps quite free.
It is not upon any such ratiocination that he founds his own
conclusion that 'desirable feeling' (by which he understands
pleasure) 'for the innumerable multitude of living beings, present
and to come [1],' is the one end 'ultimately and intrinsically desirable;' but on an appeal to what he calls 'common sense.'
'As rational beings we are manifestly bound to aim at good
generally, not merely at this or that part of it [2],' and in the last
resort we can give no meaning to good but happiness, which =
desirable consciousness, which = pleasure. Reason therefore bids
us aim at a supreme good, made up of the goods (or happinesses)
of all sentient beings; at the good of one sentient being equally

[1] *Methods of Ethics*, p. 371. [2] Ibid. p. 355.

with another, 'except in so far as it is less, or less certainly knowable or attainable.'

Now in this theory it is clear that an office is ascribed to Reason which in ordinary Utilitarian doctrine, as in the philosophy of Locke and Hume on which that doctrine is founded, is explicitly denied to it. To say that as *rational* beings we are bound to aim at anything whatever *in the nature of an ultimate end*, would have seemed absurd to Hume and to the original Utilitarians. To them reason was a faculty not of ends but of means. As a matter of fact, they held, we all do aim at pleasure as our ultimate end; all that could properly be said to be reasonable or unreasonable was our selection of means to that end. They would no more have thought of asking why pleasure ought to be pursued than of asking why any fact ought to be a fact. Mr. Sidgwick, however, does ask the question, and answers that pleasure ought to be pursued because reason pronounces it desirable ; but that, since reason pronounces pleasure, if equal in amount, to be equally desirable by whatever being enjoyed, it is universal pleasure—the pleasure of all sentient beings—that ought to be pursued. It is not indeed an object that every one ought at all times to have consciously before him [1], but it is the ultimate good by reference to which, 'when we sit down in a calm hour,' the desirability of every other good is to be tested.

366. In this procedure Mr. Sidgwick is quite consistent with himself. His rejection of 'Egoistic' in favour of 'Universalistic' Hedonism rests upon a ground which in Mr. Mill's doctrine it is impossible to discover. His appeal to reason may be made to justify the recognition of an obligation to regard the happiness of all men or all animals equally, which, upon the doctrine that pleasure is the one thing desirable because the one thing desired, can only be logically justified by the untenable assumption that the only way to obtain a maximum of pleasure for oneself is to have an equal regard for the pleasure of everyone else. But Mr. Sidgwick's way of justifying his Altruism constrains us to ask him some further questions. What does he understand by the 'reason' to which he ascribes the office of deciding what the one 'ultimately and intrinsically desirable end' is; not on

[1] Methods of Ethics, p. 381.

the means to it, but on the nature of the end itself? In saying that it is reasonable to pursue desirable consciousness, is he not open to the same charge of moving in a circle which he brings against those who say that it is reasonable to live according to nature, or virtuous to seek perfection, while after all they have no other account to give of the life according to nature but that it is reasonable, or of perfection but that it is the highest virtue[1]? What does he mean by desirable consciousness but the sort of consciousness which it is reasonable to seek?

He apparently avoids the circle, no doubt, by describing the desirable consciousness as pleasure; but the escape is only apparent. A statement that it is reasonable to seek pleasure would not itself be chargeable with tautology, but, unless it meant that it was reasonable to seek pleasure for the sake of some chief good other than pleasure (in which sense the statement is not likely to be made), it would be absurd. If we hold pleasure to be itself the good, because the object of all desire, and if we are careful about our words, we may call it reasonable to seek certain means to it, but not to seek pleasure itself. Mr. Sidgwick himself, as we have seen, is not guilty of this absurdity, because he carefully distinguishes the desired from the desirable. His doctrine is not that it is reasonable to seek pleasure in that sense in which Hedonistic writers take it to be the one thing desired, *i. e.* as the pleasure of the person seeking it, but that it is reasonable to seek to convey pleasure to all sentient beings, because this universal enjoyment, though it is only in certain exceptional 'calm hours' *desired*, is intrinsically and ultimately *desirable* or good. Now does he mean anything else by 'desirable' in this connection than 'reasonably to be desired'? If not, does not his doctrine come to this, that it is reasonable to seek as ultimate good that form of conscious life which is reasonably to be desired?

367. It will be understood that, in thus criticising Mr. Sidgwick's account of ultimate good, our object is not to depreciate it, but to show how much more truth there is in it, from our point of view, than in the common statement of Utilitarianism. We have previously explained how it comes about that any true theory of the good will present an appearance of moving

[1] Methods of Ethics, p. 352.

in a circle. The rational or self-conscious soul, we have seen, constitutes its own end; is an end at once to and in itself. Its end
is the perfection of itself, the fulfilment of the law of its being.
The consciousness of there being such an end expresses itself in
the judgment that something absolutely should be, that there is
something intrinsically and ultimately desirable. This judgment
is, in this sense, the expression of reason; and all those who, like
Mr. Sidgwick, recognise the distinction between the absolutely
desirable and the *de facto* desired, have in effect admitted that
reason gives—is the source of there being—a supreme practical
good. If we ask for a reason why we should pursue this end,
there is none to be given but that it is rational to do so, that
reason bids it, that the pursuit is the effort of the self-conscious
or rational soul after its own perfection. It is reasonable to
desire it because it is reasonably to be desired. Those who like
to do so may make merry over the tautology. Those who
understand how it arises—from the fact, namely, that reason
gives its own end, that the self-conscious spirit of man presents
its own perfection to itself as the intrinsically desirable—will not
be moved by the mirth. They will not try to escape the charge
of tautology by taking the desirableness of ultimate good to
consist in anything else than in the thought of it as that which
would satisfy reason—satisfy the demand of the self-conscious
soul for its own perfection. They will not appeal to pleasure, as
being that which in fact we all desire, in order to determine our
notion of what reason bids us desire. They will be aware that
this notion cannot be determined by reference to anything but
what reason has itself done; by anything but reflection on the
excellences of character and conduct to which the rational effort
after perfection of life has given rise. They will appeal to the
virtues to tell them what is virtuous, to goodness to tell them
what is truly good, to the work of reason in human life to tell
them what is reasonably to be desired; knowing well what they
are about in so doing, and that it is the only appropriate procedure, because only in the full attainment of its end could reason
learn fully what that end is, and only in what it has so far
attained of the end can it learn what its further attainment
would be.

368. It is perhaps unjustifiable to ascribe to any one a course

of thought which he would himself disavow; but we naturally ask for a reason why Mr. Sidgwick, having accepted principles, as it would seem, so antagonistic to those of the philosophic Utilitarians, should end by accepting their conclusion. When we consider on the one hand his implied admission that it is reason which presents us with the idea of ultimate good, and on the other his profession of inability to look for that good in anything but the pleasure of all sentient beings, the conjecture suggests itself that, while really thinking of the ultimately desirable as consisting in the satisfaction of reason, he shrank from a statement seemingly so tautological and uninstructive as that the end which reason bids us seek is the satisfaction or perfection of the rational nature itself. He was thus led to cast about for an account of the supreme good in terms which should not imply its essential relation to reason. 'Pleasure of all sentient beings' does not imply any such relation, for there is nothing in the enjoyment of pleasure which reason is needed to constitute; and no one, except under constraint of some extravagant theory, denies that pleasure is good. Thus the statement that universal pleasure is the ultimate good which reason bids us seek, seems on the one hand to avoid the admitted absurdity of saying that reason bids us seek our own pleasure, and, on the other, the tautology of saying that reason bids us seek the satisfaction of reason.

But why does no one deny that pleasure is good? Because every one is conscious of desiring pleasure for himself. That is to say, pleasure is good, not as = the desirable, but as = the desired; and the pleasure which is *thus* good is not universal pleasure but the pleasure of the subject desiring it, as related to his desire. Thus between the proposition that pleasure is good as = the desired, and the proposition that universal pleasure is good as = the rationally desirable, the connection (as Mr. Sidgwick is too acute not to perceive) is merely verbal. The latter can only be derived from the former on supposition that reason presents to itself as the *desirable*—as good in *this* sense—the enjoyment by every sentient being of the pleasure which he in fact desires, and which is good for him in *that* sense. Even if this supposition be granted, it will still be the satisfaction of reason that constitutes the good in the sense of the ultimately desirable, though reason will be supposed to satisfy itself in the contemplation of the enjoyment by every being of that which is good in the sense of being desired, viz. pleasure. The question will then be whether reason can thus satisfy itself. Is it in contemplation of the enjoyment of unbroken pleasure by all sentient beings that we are to think of the rational soul as saying to itself that at length its quest for ultimate good has found its goal?

369. To this question—which, it will of course be understood, is not put by Mr. Sidgwick himself, but to which, in our view, his doctrine leads—his answer seems ambiguous. He holds indeed that a maximum of possible pleasure for all sentient beings is the ultimate good at which reason bids us aim, but he explains that by pleasure he means 'desirable consciousness.' Now unless we are to forget the distinction between the desired and the desirable which we might learn from Mr. Sidgwick himself[1], we cannot suppose that the rational soul, in presenting a *desirable* consciousness on its own part as involved in ultimate good, presents it simply as so much pleasure. The very fact that it asks for a consciousness which is desirable or *should be* desired, shows that it cannot satisfy itself with that which every one naturally desires, but of which for that reason no one can think as what he should desire. The presentation of an object as one that *should be* desired implies that it is not desired *as a pleasure* by the person to whom it so presents itself. A man may speak significantly of another person's pleasure as desirable, but not of his own. The desirableness *of a pleasure* must always express its relation to some one else than the person desiring the enjoyment of the pleasure. Thus to suppose a consciousness to be at once desired as a pleasure, and contemplated as desirable by the same person, is a contradiction. To the man who 'in a calm hour' sets before himself a certain form of conscious life as the object which reason bids him aim at, though it is not impossible that pleasure should be the desirable quality in that life as he seeks to bring it about for other people, it cannot be the desirable quality in it as he seeks to obtain it for himself. When we are told, therefore, that ultimate good is desirable consciousness or pleasure for all sentient beings, we reply that, though it may be sought as pleasure for all sentient beings, it cannot be sought as his own pleasure

[1] Methods of Ethics, p. 361.

by one who also contemplates it as the consciousness desirable for himself. The description of ultimate good as pleasure, and the description of it as desirable (not desired) consciousness, are incompatible descriptions, so far as they are descriptions of a state of being which the rational soul seeks as its own.

370. Now, according to the view already stated in this treatise, the rational soul in seeking an ultimate good necessarily seeks it as a state of its own being. An ultimate, intrinsic, absolute good has no meaning for us, except that which it derives from the effort of the rational soul in us to become all that it is conscious of a capacity for becoming. As the rational soul is essentially the principle of self-consciousness, so the idea of ultimate good on the part of every one capable of it is necessarily the idea of a perfect self-conscious life for himself. The desirableness of that life is its desirableness as his own life. But to any one actuated by it the idea of a perfection, of a state in which he shall be satisfied, for himself will involve the idea of a perfection of all other beings, so far as he finds the thought of their being perfect necessary to his own satisfaction. Moral development, as has been previously explained more at large, is a progress in which the individual's conception of the kind of life that would be implied in his perfection gradually becomes fuller and more determinate; fuller and more determinate both in regard to the range of persons whose participation in the perfect life is thought of as necessary to its attainment by any one, and in regard to the qualities on the part of the individual which it is thought must be exercised in it. In the most complete determination within our reach, the conception still does not suffice to enable any one to say positively what the perfection of his life would be; but the determination has reached that stage in which the educated citizen of Christendom is able to think of the perfect life as essentially conditioned by the exercise of virtues, resting on a self-sacrificing will, in which it is open to all men to participate, and as fully attainable by one man, only in so far as through those virtues it is attained by all. In thinking of ultimate good he thinks of it indeed necessarily as perfection for himself; as a life in which he shall be fully satisfied through having become all that the spirit within him enables him to become. But he cannot think of himself as satisfied in any life other than

a social life, exhibiting the exercise of self-denying will, and in which 'the multitude of the redeemed,' which is all men, shall participate. He has other faculties indeed than those which are directly exhibited in the specifically moral virtues—faculties which find their expression not in his dealings with other men, but in the arts and sciences—and the development of these must be a necessary constituent in any life which he presents to himself as one in which he can find satisfaction. But 'when he sits down in a calm hour' it will not be in isolation that the development of any of these faculties will assume the character for him of ultimate good. Intrinsic desirableness, sufficiency to satisfy the rational soul, will be seen to belong to their realisation only in so far as it is a constituent in a whole of social life, of which the distinction, as a social life, shall be universality of disinterested goodness.

371. We should accept the view, then, that to think of ultimate good is to think of an intrinsically desirable form of conscious life; but we should seek further to define it. We should take it in the sense that to think of such good is to think of a state of self-conscious life as intrinsically desirable for oneself, and for that reason is to think of it as something else than pleasure—the thought of an object as pleasure for oneself, and the thought of it as intrinsically desirable for oneself, being thoughts which exclude each other. The pleasure anticipated in the life is not that which renders it desirable; but so far as desire is excited by the thought of it as desirable, and so far as that desire is reflected on, pleasure comes to be anticipated in the satisfaction of that desire. The thought of the intrinsically desirable life, then, is the thought of something else than pleasure, but the thought of what? The thought, we answer, of the full realisation of the capacities of the human soul, of the fulfilment of man's vocation, as of that in which alone he can satisfy himself—a thought of which the content is never final and complete, which is always by its creative energy further determining its own content, but which for practical purposes, as the mover and guide of our highest moral effort, may be taken to be the thought of such a social life as that described in the previous paragraph. The thought of such a life, again, when applied as a criterion for the valuation of the probable effects of action, may be taken

to be represented by the question stated in § 354 :—' Does this or that law or usage, this or that course of action—directly or indirectly, positively or as preventive of the opposite—contribute to the better being of society, as measured by the more general establishment of conditions favourable to the attainment of the recognised virtues and excellences, by the more general attainment of those excellences in some degree, or by their attainment on the part of some persons in higher degree without detraction from the opportunities of others?' It remains for us now finally to consider the availability of the injunctions and criteria founded on such a theory of ultimate good, as compared with those derivable from the identification of ultimate good with a universal enjoyment of pleasure, in those exceptional cases in which their comparative availability is likely to be put to the test.

372. As has been already remarked, these cases will be exceptional owing to the efficiency of the direction for outward conduct which conventional morality now commonly affords. The origin of that morality is not here in question. If there is reason to hold, as it has been previously sought to show, that the progressive principle in morality, through which the recognised standard of virtuous living among us has come to be what it is, has not been an interest either in the enjoyment or in the production of pleasure, there is so far a presumption against general pleasure being the ultimate good to which we should look for direction when conventional morality fails us. But the reader naturally asks for a conclusion more definite than this presumption. He will wish to satisfy himself whether, in the settlement of real questions of conduct, our theory of ultimate good has any advantage over that which Mr. Sidgwick describes as Universalistic Hedonism—whether under any conditions it might afford other and better guidance. In discussing this point we must suppose the person who resorts to either theory for guidance to have accepted the direction of conventional morality, so far as it goes —the one on the ground that it represents a decisive amount of transmitted experience as to the pleasure-giving or pain-giving effects, on the whole, of different kinds of action; the other on the ground that its observance, unless the contrary can be shown,

must be taken as at least a condition of the social well-being which he would measure by the prevalence of a virtuous will.

We must also keep out of sight difficulties that do not relate to the *valuation* of the anticipated effects of actions, but to the question what effects are to be anticipated from them. In many cases the whole practical difficulty of deciding whether a contemplated action ought or ought not to be done, is the difficulty of deciding what effects are likely to follow from it; not of valuing the effects if once they could be ascertained, but of ascertaining what they will be. No theory of ultimate good has an advantage over another in dealing with this difficulty, since none rather than another can claim to give us knowledge of facts, or to make us clear-sighted and patient in the analysis of circumstances. Any difference in respect of influence upon the practical judgment between the two theories in question must arise from the different value which they severally lead us to put upon effects ascertained or expected, not from any different methods which they suggest of ascertaining the effects of action, nor from any difference in the importance which they lead us to attach to doing so.

373. In a previous paragraph (§ 338) examples have been given of the kind of question in regard to personal conduct, in his answer to which a speculative person might be affected for the worse by a logical application of the Utilitarian theory of good, so far as that theory is founded on the principle that pleasure is the only possible object of desire. We are now supposing this principle to be dropped, but the Utilitarian doctrine of the chief good to be retained. We are dealing with a theory in which the action of disinterested motives, in the natural sense of the words (as desires which have not pleasure directly or indirectly for their object), is fully recognised, and the identification of ultimate good with a maximum of universal pleasure is accepted on the ground of its supposed intrinsic reasonableness. The question is whether, in cases of the kind supposed, a logical application of this conception of ultimate good, as a criterion of what should be done, will be of any avail. The cases are of a kind in which it has to be decided whether, in words already used (§ 363), a man 'should set up for being better than his neighbours or should swim with the stream ; whether he should

follow the severer path of duty where his departure from it would be unknown or uncondemned, and where it would save himself and those whom he loves from much suffering; whether he should seek the highest beauty in art, the completest truth in knowledge, rather than conform to popular taste and opinion.' For the purposes of such a decision our contention is not that of itself the theory of Universalistic Hedonism would yield a wrong answer, but that it would yield none at all, and would thus in effect leave the decision to be made by the enquirer's inclination to the course of action which is most pleasant or least painful to him individually.

374. We have already seen how, when the question before the individual is whether for the sake of some higher good he should depart from the course of action to which custom or inclination, or the sense of what the opinion of his class requires of him, would naturally lead him, the logical tendency of the doctrine that pleasure is the sole object of desire must be to entangle him in a Hedonistic fatalism, which would mean paralysis of the moral initiative. Universalistic Hedonism, as Mr. Sidgwick conceives it, is not chargeable with this tendency. It justifies the question, What should I do for the bettering of life? for it recognises the possibility of an initiative not determined by imagination of pleasure or pain. But for doubts of the kind we are considering, where conventional morality cannot be appealed to as representing accumulated experience of consequences in the way of pleasure and pain, it seems to afford no solution. We have supposed a man in doubt whether, in consideration of the claims of society, he is justified in spending so much of his time in the gratification of his taste for music or of his curiosity in literature, or in continuing a habit of 'moderate drinking.' Let such an one translate 'in consideration of the claims of society' into 'with a view to producing as much pleasure as possible to all beings capable of it.' Must it not be apparent to him, just so far as he really apprehends the nature of the problem which he professes to set before himself, that it is wholly insoluble? What knowledge has he, or from the nature of the case can he obtain, either of the conditions on which the pleasures of all other beings, present and to come, depend or will depend, or of the various degrees to which other men—to say nothing of the

animals—are susceptible of pleasure, that he should be able to judge whether the suggested breach of custom, the suggested resistance to personal inclination, is likely to contribute to the ' Summum Bonum' which he adopts as his criterion ? Unless he has really some other conception of ultimate good to fall back upon, will he not inevitably take refuge in the justification which the theory of Universalistic Hedonism affords him for attaching most importance to the most certainly known pleasures, and let custom and inclination decide him ?

375. In fact, the man who is challenged by doubts of the kind described, who asks himself whether he is duly responding to claims which conventional morality does not recognise, always has another standard of ultimate good to fall back upon, however much his Hedonistic philosophy may obscure it to him. That standard is an ideal of a perfect life for himself and other men, as attainable for him only through them, for them only through him; a life that shall be perfect, in the sense of being the fulfilment of all that the human spirit in him and them has the real capacity or vocation of becoming, and which (as is implied in its being such fulfilment) shall rest on the will to be perfect. However unable he may be to give an account of such an ideal, it yet has so much hold on him as to make the promotion of goodness for its own sake in himself and others an intelligible end to him. The reader, however, will be weary of hearing of this ideal, and will be waiting to know in what particular way it can afford guidance in cases of the kind supposed, where conventional morality and Utilitarian theory alike fail to do so. We have argued that no man could tell whether, by denying himself according to the examples given, he would in the whole result increase the amount of pleasant living in the world, present and to come. Can he tell any better whether he will further that realisation of the ideal just described, in regard to which we admit the impossibility of saying positively what in its completeness it would be ?

376. We answer as follows. The whole question of sacrificing one's own pleasure assumes a different aspect, when the end for which it is to be sacrificed is not an addition to a general aggregate of pleasures, but the harmonious exercise of man's proper activities in some life resting on a self-sacrificing will. According

to the latter view, the individual's sacrifice of pleasure does not—as so much loss of pleasure—come into the reckoning at all; nor has any balance to be attempted of unascertainable pains and pleasures spreading over an indefinite range of sentient life. The good to be sought is not made up of pleasures, nor the evil to be avoided made up of pains. The end for which the sacrifice is demanded is one which in the sacrifice itself is in some measure attained—in some measure only, not fully, yet so that the sacrifice is related to the complete end, not as a means in itself valueless, but as a constituent to a whole which it helps to form. That realisation of the powers of the human spirit, which we deem the true end, is not to be thought of merely as something in a remote distance, towards which we may take steps now, but in which there is no present participation. It is continuously going on, though in varying and progressive degrees of completeness; and the individual's sacrifice of an inclination, harmless or even in its way laudable, for the sake of a higher good, is itself already in some measure an attainment of the higher good.

Thus, whereas according to any Hedonistic doctrine of true good, though it be 'Universalistic' Hedonism not 'Egoistic,' the certain present loss of pleasure to the individual himself and to his intimates, involved in sacrifices of the kind we are considering, is so much deduction from true good, only to be justified by a larger accession of pleasure in other quarters or at other times —an accession from the nature of the case less certain to the man meditating the sacrifice than the loss—upon the other view, while the loss of pleasure implied in the sacrifice to the person who makes it, and to any others whom he can induce willingly to accept any like loss that arises out of it for them, is morally, or relatively to the true good, matter of indifference, the exercise of a devoted will in the sacrifice, on the part of all concerned in it, is an actual and undoubted contribution to true good. The degree of its value will only be doubtful, so far as there may be uncertainty in regard to its tendency to yield more or less further good of the same kind in the sequel. We say 'more or less,' for that it tends to yield some further good of the same kind can never be really doubtful. Self-sacrifice, devotion to worthy objects, is always self-propagatory. If the question is asked,—

> ' Of love that never found his earthly close,
>   What sequel ? '

there is at least the answer,

> ' But am I not the nobler through thy love ?
>   O, three times less unworthy [1] ! '

In like manner, upon the view that of the life which forms the true and full good the self-devoted will must be the principle, if the question is asked, What comes of any particular act of self-sacrifice ? there is at least the answer that the act does not need anything further to come of it, in order to be in itself in little the good. But it is only if we falter in that view of the good, on the strength of which we give this answer, that we can doubt the beneficent result, in whatever manner or degree, of the act in itself good. The good will in one man has never failed to elicit or strengthen such a will in another.

377. But it will be said that we are so far dealing only in generalities. It may be admitted that an act or habit of self-sacrifice is a good in itself, but there are many ways in which a man may sacrifice himself, and he is responsible for choosing the most useful. It is of little profit to tell him of the intrinsic nobility of self-sacrifice, unless we can give him some means of judging for what sort of objects he in particular should be prepared to give up his tastes and inclinations, or to run the gauntlet of established custom. To revert to one of the examples employed, no one would think of saying absolutely that there was merit in sacrificing a taste for music. On the contrary, there may be a duty to cultivate it. The question whether it should be sacrificed or cultivated must depend on the position and general capabilities of the individual, on the circumstances of his time, on the claims of surrounding society. Some direction therefore is needed for the individual in making his sacrifices; some criterion of the ends which he should keep before him in deciding for this sacrifice rather than for that. How can the view of the good for which we have been pleading afford such direction or criterion ?

The answer lies in a consideration of that unity of the human spirit throughout its individual manifestations, in virtue of which

---

[1] Tennyson's ' Love and Duty.'

the realisation of its possibilities, though a personal object to each man, is at the same time an object fully attainable by one only in so far as it is attained by the whole human society. The statement that the act of self-sacrifice has its value in itself is not to be understood as denying that it has its value in its consequences, but as implying that those consequences, to be of intrinsic value, must be of a kind with the act itself, as an exercise of a character having its dominant interest in some form of human perfection. The injunction that would be founded on the view of that perfection as the end would never be 'Sacrifice inclination' simply, but 'Sacrifice inclination in so far as by so doing you may make men better;' but the bettering of men would mean their advance in a goodness the same in principle as that which appears in the sacrifice enjoined, and this sacrifice itself would be regarded as already an instalment of the good to be more largely attained in its consequences. The direction to the individual, in doubt whether he should deny himself some attractive pursuit or some harmless indulgence, would be, not that he should make the sacrifice for the sake of making it, but that he should be ready to make it, if upon honest consideration it appear that men would be the better for his doing so.

378. Universalistic Hedonism might give the same direction; but in the interpretation of the direction there would be a great difference—a difference which might very well amount to that between demanding the sacrifice and allowing the indulgence. The Hedonist, understanding by the bettering of men an addition to the pleasures enjoyed by them, present and to come, has at any rate an obscure computation before him. In such cases as we are now considering he would not have the presumption, afforded by a call of conventionally recognised duty, that obedience to it, however painful to the individual, would be felicific in the general result. The presumption from his point of view must always be against the 'reasonableness' of making the sacrifice, till the probability of an excess of pleasure from its ulterior consequences over the pain more immediately produced by it could be clearly made out. Such a probability must generally be very difficult to arrive at. It does not at all follow, as is apt to be assumed, because an observance of conventional morality may be required in the interest of general

pleasure, that an advance upon conventional morality is so. Upon the view that the exercise of a virtuous will is an end in itself, the question about a possible 'too much' of virtue cannot arise. But it is otherwise if an opposite view is taken. If virtue is of value only as a means to general pleasure, it becomes necessary to enquire what is the degree of it which so contributes—to what extent an increase in the number of self-devoted persons, and a more intense and constant self-devotion on their part, is desirable, in order to an increase in the sum of pleasures for all human, or all sentient, beings. Thus in his forecast of the 'felicific' results to be looked for from any advance upon the 'law of opinion' in the way of self-denying virtue, the Hedonistic Utilitarian may not avail himself of the short method that would be represented by the maxim, 'The more virtue, the more pleasure.' He may not assume that, because the suggested self-denial would tend to increase virtue among men, it would tend to increase pleasure. The pleasure-increasing tendency must be made out on its own account; and, unless the self-denial in question is one that upon physiological evidence can be proved likely in its consequences to cause some decisive reduction in physical suffering, it is not easy to see how this should be done. When it had been done, the balance between the remoter and less certain gain and the proximate loss would have still to be struck. Upon such principles the case against making the 'uncalled for' sacrifice, even though dispassionately conducted, would generally be invincibly strong.

379. From the other point of view, even though the precise nature and strength of the call for the sacrifice could not clearly be made out, the presumption would still be in favour of its being made, on the ground of the intrinsic value attaching alike to the exercise of the self-denying character, and to those results, of a kind with itself, which through the influence of example it is sure to produce among men. It is true that this general presumption will not help a man to decide which of many particular courses of self-denying action, which it is open to him to pursue but which he would not be thought the worse of for not pursuing, is the one which it is best for him to pursue. It is his duty not to waste himself among various efforts, each of which might be well-intentioned and involve real self-denial, but none

of them in the direction in which he in particular under the circumstances of the case might do most good. For deciding, however, whether any particular sacrifice is one that he ought to make, he has much more available guidance, according to our view, than a computation of the total range of pleasures and pains to be looked for as a consequence of the sacrifice. He has to ask, according to the terms in which the question has been above put, whether the suggested sacrifice on his part is one by which he may best contribute to the well-being of society, ' as measured by the more general establishment of conditions favourable to the attainment of the recognised virtues and excellences, by the more general attainment of those excellences in some degree, or by their attainment on the part of some persons in higher degree without detraction from the opportunities of others.' It is not to be disguised, of course, that with such an end before him as this question represents, he may find it difficult to ascertain, by analysis of circumstances and enquiry into facts, in what degree the various forms of self-denying activity open to him are likely to contribute to the end. As has already been pointed out, such analysis and enquiry are not to be dispensed with upon one theory of the end any more than upon another. The question is of the object with reference to which the analysis and enquiry are to be conducted; whether in order to ascertain tendencies to produce a maximum of pleasure over all time to all beings capable of it, or in order to ascertain tendencies to produce a perfection of human society, resting on the universal prevalence of the will to be perfect. When the point at issue is whether some sacrifice should be made which is uncalled for by social convention, while its tendency in the former direction will generally be found unascertainable, its tendency in the latter will be within the ken of any dispassionate and considerate man.

380. A man asks himself—to revert once more to that instance—whether he is justified in giving so much of his time to the gratification of his taste for music; which must mean, whether there are not claims upon him for the service of mankind which cannot be satisfied while he does so. Now it may really be a difficult question for him to settle whether he cannot serve mankind more effectually by giving more of his time to music

rather than less. It is a question for the settlement of which there may be needed careful analysis of his own faculties, of the needs of society about him, of his particular opportunities and powers of meeting those needs; and in settling it the truest conception of ultimate good will not prevent the mistakes to which hastiness, prejudice, and self-conceit naturally lead. Still there is all the difference between approaching the question with some definite conception of the claims of mankind, of the good to be sought for them, and without any such conception. The Hedonistic theory, as we have tried to show, affords no such conception. It insists indeed on the claim of every man to have as much pleasure as is compatible with the attainment of the greatest possible amount on the whole, but this claim cannot be translated into a claim to be or to do, or to have the chance of being or doing, anything in particular. We cannot found upon it even a claim of every man to be free; for who can be sure that the freedom of all men, when the whole range of the possibilities of pleasure is taken into account, tends to an excess of pleasure over pain? Still less can we found upon it a claim of every one to be helped to be good, according to our present standard of goodness. Hedonistic theory can only bid us promote the received virtues and excellences among men with an *if* which makes the injunction of no avail in such a case as we are considering. They are to be promoted up to the limit at which their promotion still certainly yields more pleasure than pain to the universe of human or sentient beings; and it is impossible to say what this limit is.

It is otherwise when the exercise of the recognised virtues and excellences, as resting upon a self-devoted will or will to be perfect, is considered to be an end in itself—to be itself, if not in completeness yet in principle and essence, the ultimate good for man. The general nature of the claim of other men upon him is plain to every one who contemplates it with reference to such an end. It is a claim for service in the direction of making the attainment of those virtues and excellences, by some persons and in some form, more possible. The question for the individual will still remain, how he in particular may best render this service, and it may be one of much difficulty. He may easily deceive himself in answering it, but he will not have the excuse for answering it in favour of his own inclination, which is afforded by reference to a 'Summum Bonum' of which the most readily ascertainable constituent must always be his own pleasure.

381. As to the particular instance we have been considering, while intrinsic value will not be denied to excellence in music as having a place in the fulfilment of man's vocation, it is a question, so to speak, of spiritual proportion, whether the attainment of such excellence is of importance in any society of men under the given conditions of that society. For, like all excellence in art, it has its value as an element in a whole of spiritual life, to which the moral virtues are essential; which without them would be no realisation of the capacities of the human soul. In some Italian principality of the last century, for instance, with its civil life crushed out and its moral energies debased, excellence in music could hardly be accounted of actual and present value at all. Its value would be potential, in so far as the artist's work might survive to become an element in a nobler life elsewhere or at a later time. Under such conditions much occupation with music might imply indifference to claims of the human soul which must be satisfied in order to the attainment of a life in which the value of music could be actualised. And under better social conditions there may be claims, arising from the particular position of an individual, which render the pursuit of excellence in music, though it would be the right pursuit for others qualified as he is, a wrong one for him. In the absence of such claims the main question will be of his particular talent. Has he talent to serve mankind—to contribute to the perfection of the human soul—more as a musician than in any other way? Only if he has will he be justified in making music his main pursuit. If he is not to make it his main pursuit, the question will remain, to what extent he may be justified in indulging his taste for it, either as a refreshment of faculties which are to be mainly used in other pursuits—to be so used, because in them he may best serve mankind in the sense explained—or as enabling him to share in that intrinsically valuable lifting up of the soul which music may afford.

382. Such questions are not to be answered by 'intuition,' nor do they arise under conditions under which our guidance in duty

needs to be intuitive—needs to be derived from convictions which afford immediate direction independently of any complicated consideration of circumstances. They only arise for persons who have exceptional opportunity of directing their own pursuits, and who do not need to be in a hurry in their decisions. To most people sufficient direction for their pursuits is afforded by claims so well established in conventional morality that they are intuitively recognised, and that a conscience merely responsive to social disapprobation would reproach us for neglecting them. For all of us it is so in regard to a great part of our lives. But the cases we have been considering are those in which some 'counsel of perfection' is needed, which reference to such claims does not supply, and which has to be derived from reference to a theory of ultimate good. In such cases many questions have to be answered, which intuition cannot answer, before the issue is arrived at to which the theory of ultimate good becomes applicable; but then the cases only occur for persons who have leisure and faculty for dealing with such questions. For them the essential thing is that their theory of the good should afford a really available criterion for estimating those further claims upon them which are not enforced by the sanction of conventional morality, and a criterion which affords no plea to the self-indulgent impulse. Our point has been to show, in the instance given, that such a criterion is afforded by the theory of ultimate good as a perfection of the human spirit resting on the will to be perfect (which may be called in short the theory of virtue as an end in itself), but not by the theory of good as consisting in a maximum of possible pleasure.